A SCHOLASTIC MISCELLANY:
ANSELM TO OCKHAM

THE LIBRARY OF CHRISTIAN CLASSICS

ICHTHUS EDITION

A SCHOLASTIC MISCELLANY: ANSELM TO OCKHAM

Edited and Translated
by
EUGENE R. FAIRWEATHER, M.A., B.D., Th.D.

Philadelphia
THE WESTMINSTER PRESS

Published simultaneously in Great Britain and the United States of America
by the S.C.M. Press Ltd., London, and The Westminster Press, Philadelphia

First Published MCMLVI

Library of Congress Catalog Card Number: 56–5104
9 8 7 6 5 4 3 2 1

GENERAL EDITORS' PREFACE

The Christian Church possesses in its literature an abundant and incomparable treasure. But it is an inheritance that must be reclaimed by each generation. THE LIBRARY OF CHRISTIAN CLASSICS is designed to present in the English language, and in twenty-six volumes of convenient size, a selection of the most indispensable Christian treatises written prior to the end of the sixteenth century.

The practice of giving circulation to writings selected for superior worth or special interest was adopted at the beginning of Christian history. The canonical Scriptures were themselves a selection from a much wider literature. In the Patristic era there began to appear a class of works of compilation (often designed for ready reference in controversy) of the opinions of well-reputed predecessors, and in the Middle Ages many such works were produced. These medieval anthologies actually preserve some noteworthy materials from works otherwise lost.

In modern times, with the increasing inability even of those trained in universities and theological colleges to read Latin and Greek texts with ease and familiarity, the translation of selected portions of earlier Christian literature into modern languages has become more necessary than ever; while the wide range of distinguished books written in vernaculars such as English makes selection there also needful. The efforts that have been made to meet this need are too numerous to be noted here, but none of these collections serves the purpose of the reader who desires a library of representative treatises spanning the Christian centuries as a whole. Most of them embrace only the age of the Church Fathers, and some of them have long been out of print. A fresh translation of a work already translated may shed much new light upon its meaning. This is true even of Bible translations despite the work of many experts through the centuries. In some instances old translations have been adopted in this series, but wherever necessary or desirable, new ones have been made. Notes have been supplied where these were needed to explain the author's meaning. The introductions provided for the several treatises and extracts will, we believe, furnish welcome guidance.

John Baillie
John T. McNeill
Henry P. Van Dusen

CONTENTS

                                                          page
PREFACE 13
LIST OF ABBREVIATIONS 15
GENERAL INTRODUCTION: The Intellectual
  Achievement of Medieval Christendom . . . 17
  GENERAL BIBLIOGRAPHY 33
ANSELM OF CANTERBURY 47
  BIBLIOGRAPHY 63
ANSELM:
  AN ADDRESS (PROSLOGION) 69
  AN EXCERPT FROM THE AUTHOR'S REPLY TO THE
    CRITICISMS OF GAUNILO 94
  LETTER TO POPE URBAN II ON THE INCARNATION OF
    THE WORD (EXCERPT) 97
  WHY GOD BECAME MAN 100
  THE VIRGIN CONCEPTION AND ORIGINAL SIN (SELEC-
    TIONS) 184
  A PRAYER TO SAINT MARY TO OBTAIN LOVE FOR HER
    AND FOR CHRIST 201
  THE QUESTION OF INVESTITURES: TWO LETTERS TO
    POPE PASCHAL II (EXCERPTS) 208
EADMER:
  HISTORY OF RECENT EVENTS IN ENGLAND (EXCERPT) . 211
  THE LIFE AND CONVERSATION OF SAINT ANSELM
    (EXCERPT) 213
THEOLOGIANS OF THE TWELFTH CENTURY
  BIBLIOGRAPHY 232
  IVO OF CHARTRES: DECRETUM, THE PROLOGUE (EXCERPT) 238
  GRATIAN: THE CONCORD OF DISCORDANT CANONS
    (EXCERPT) 243

12 CONTENTS

page

JOHN OF SALISBURY: THE POLICRATICUS (EXCERPT) . 247
ANSELM OF LAON: A FRAGMENT ON ORIGINAL SIN . 261
THE SCHOOL OF ANSELM OF LAON:
A QUESTION ON ORIGINAL SIN 263
THE GLOSS ON I CORINTHIANS, CHAPTER 15 . . 267
PETER ABAILARD:
EXPOSITION OF THE EPISTLE TO THE ROMANS (EXCERPT
FROM THE SECOND BOOK)—*Translation by Gerald E.
Moffatt* 276
ETHICS OR THE BOOK CALLED "KNOW THYSELF"
(EXCERPT) 288
HYMN FOR SATURDAY VESPERS—*Translation by John
Mason Neale* 298
HUGH OF SAINT VICTOR: ON THE SACRAMENTS OF THE
CHRISTIAN FAITH (EXCERPT)—*Translation by Car-
mino J. de Catanzaro* 300
RICHARD OF SAINT VICTOR:
MYSTICAL COMMENTS ON THE PSALMS (EXCERPT) . 319
ON EZEKIEL'S VISION, PROLOGUE (EXCERPT) . 321
ON THE TRINITY (SELECTIONS) 324
ADAM OF SAINT VICTOR: SEQUENCE FOR A SAINT'S DAY
—*Translation by Robert Bridges* 332
PETER LOMBARD: THE FOUR BOOKS OF SENTENCES
(SELECTIONS)—*Translation and Notes by Owen R. Orr* . 334
STEPHEN LANGTON:
A QUESTION ON ORIGINAL SIN 352
FRAGMENTS ON THE MORALITY OF HUMAN ACTS . 355
THE GOLDEN SEQUENCE, A HYMN ATTRIBUTED TO
STEPHEN LANGTON—*Translation by John Mason Neale* 359

THE THIRTEENTH CENTURY AND AFTER
BIBLIOGRAPHY 375
BONAVENTURE: DISPUTED QUESTIONS CONCERNING
CHRIST'S KNOWLEDGE (EXCERPT) . . . 379
MATTHEW OF AQUASPARTA:
DISPUTED QUESTIONS ON FAITH (EXCERPT)—*Trans-
lation and Notes by Robert D. Crouse* 402
JOHN DUNS SCOTUS: COMMENTARY ON THE SENTENCES
(EXCERPT) 428
WILLIAM OCKHAM: AN EXCERPT FROM EIGHT
QUESTIONS ON THE POWER OF THE POPE . . . 437
INDEXES 443

PREFACE

The plan of this volume is determined by its place in the series, and in particular by its relation to Volume XI, which is devoted to the greatest theologian of the thirteenth century. For the sake of a balanced presentation of scholastic theology, the bulk of this volume is occupied by works of Anselm of Canterbury and theologians of the twelfth century, while the later authors represented come from outside the Thomist tradition. Within these limits, I have attempted to illustrate the principal interests of the great scholastic theologians.

The translations aim at reproducing the authors' thought as accurately as possible, but no attempt is made at a word-for-word rendering at the expense of intelligibility. At points where unambiguous translation seemed impossible, the original words have been supplied in footnotes.

A partial list of abbreviations is provided; others are conventional and/or obvious. Scripture references follow the chapter and verse divisions of the Vulgate; the Authorized Version of 1611 and the Psalter of *The Book of Common Prayer* (1662) are cited when necessary for clarity. The Douai Version, as the classical version closest to the Bible used by our authors, is followed whenever possible in Biblical quotations.

An editor who is not a professional medievalist cannot produce such a comprehensive volume without considerable risk! I have tried to reduce this risk, however, by the use of careful documentation and expert advice. My debt to the writings of Professor Etienne Gilson, of the Pontifical Institute of Mediaeval Studies, Toronto, is obvious enough, but I am also indebted to him for much sound advice. Rev. J. T. Muckle, C.S.B., of the same Institute, has generously helped me with one text, while

Rev. G. B. Phelan, of St. Michael's College, Toronto, and Rev. W. Lyndon Smith, of Trinity College, have readily advised me on several points. The general editors, notably Dr. John T. McNeill, and the staff of The Westminster Press have been most co-operative and considerate.

I have relied heavily on the Library of the Pontifical Institute, and must record my thanks to Rev. J. F. Stapleton, C.S.B., Librarian, as well as to the Rectors of the Canadian College, Rome, and the Institut Catholique, Paris, and to Canon A. O. Standen, Librarian of Canterbury Cathedral, for the hospitality of their respective libraries.

The help of my contributors has been invaluable. Rev. C. J. de Catanzaro, Assistant Professor at Trinity College, and Canon G. E. Moffatt, of St. Peter's Cathedral, Charlottetown, P.E.I., are responsible for translations only (except for one note initialed by the latter), while Rev. R. D. Crouse, of Trinity College, and Rev. O. R. Orr, formerly of Trinity College, are responsible for the notes accompanying their translations, unless otherwise indicated. I am especially grateful to Mr. Crouse for some additional notes, initialed by him, and for his competent help in other ways.

E.R.F.

Trinity College, Toronto.

LIST OF ABBREVIATIONS

A.V.   Authorized Version of 1611.

Beiträge   *Beiträge zur Geschichte der Philosophie und Theologie des Mittelalters* (Aschendorff, Münster i. W., various dates).

CE   *The Catholic Encyclopaedia.*

CMH   *Cambridge Medieval History.*

CSEL   *Corpus scriptorum ecclesiasticorum latinorum* (the "Vienna *corpus*").

DECH   *A Dictionary of English Church History* (ed., S. L. Ollard and G. Crosse, 2d ed., London, 1919).

DNB   *Dictionary of National Biography.*

DTC   *Dictionnaire de théologie catholique.*

Fliche and   A. Fliche and V. Martin (eds.), *Histoire de l'église*
Martin   *depuis les origines jusqu'à nos jours* (Bloud et Gay, Paris, 1937–   ).

G.E.M.   Indicates note by Gerald E. Moffatt.

Gilson,   E. Gilson, *History of Christian Philosophy in the Middle*
History   *Ages* (Random House, New York, 1954).

Gilson,   E. Gilson, *The Spirit of Mediaeval Philosophy*
Spirit   (Scribners, New York, 1936).

Grabmann,   M. Grabmann, *Die Geschichte der scholastischen*
Geschichte   *Methode*, 2 vols. (Freiburg i. Br., 1909).

Landgraf,   A. M. Landgraf, *Einführung in die Geschichte der*
Einführung   *theologischen Literatur der Frühscholastik* (Gregorius-Verlag, Regensburg, 1948).

15

MGH	*Monumenta Germaniae historica.*
P.B.V.	Prayer Book version of the Psalter.
PG	Migne, *Patrologia graeca.*
PL	J. P. Migne, *Patrologiae cursus completus, series latina (Patrologia latina).*
R.D.C.	Indicates note by Robert D. Crouse.
Schmitt	F. S. Schmitt (ed.), *S. Anselmi opera omnia.*

General Introduction

The Intellectual Achievement of Medieval Christendom

I

THE GREAT TEACHERS OF MEDIEVAL SCHOLASTI-cism are among the most significant intellectual ancestors of the modern West, and their theological and philosophical ideas have played a large part in the doctrinal formation of every Christian communion which stems from western Europe. This does not mean, however, that they do not need a formal introduction to their descendants, or that such an introduction can altogether lack an apologetic flavor. At best, the very word "scholasticism" tends to suggest the unfamiliar; at worst, the repugnant. It brings before our minds a world apparently very different from our own in its culture, its forms of intellectual expression, its politics, its whole orientation toward reality. It reminds us of a religious system which precipitated a radical reaction on the part of the forefathers of many modern Christians. It suggests ponderous theological tomes, written in spare, technical Latin, very different from the vigorous German of Luther's polemical tracts or from the graceful French of Calvin's epoch-making work, from the rich English of Hooker, or, for that matter, from the literary grandeur of Bossuet. We look back from an age of scientific positivism and religious pluralism to an era of metaphysical speculation and sacral unity, from a time when the tensions of a divided world and the desperate urgency of faith and antifaith fill men's hearts with fear to the far-off centuries when, as every schoolboy knows, theologians were free to devote their attention to the problems of angelic choreography on the points of needles![1] It all seems strange and unreal and uncongenial.

[1] The origin and history of this *canard* would make an interesting study for some diligent researcher.

If it seems strange, however, that can only be because we have not taken the trouble to find out what the scholastics were trying to say. "Scholasticism," if the term has any definable meaning,[2] simply stands for the theology and philosophy and the subsidiary disciplines of the schools of western Europe in the great period of medieval culture. The "schoolmen" are the men who lived and studied and taught and prayed in the intellectual centres of a rapidly developing society, in the monastic and cathedral schools of the eleventh and twelfth centuries—Bec,[3] Laon,[4] Chartres,[5] Saint Victor,[6] Notre Dame de Paris[7]—and the universities of the thirteenth and fourteenth centuries—Paris[8] and Oxford[9] and the long line of their younger sisters.[10] But that means that we should not feel strange in their company. For, however rebellious some of their spiritual and intellectual children may have become, it is true of Luther and Calvin,[11] Gerhard and Turretinus,[12] Descartes and Spinoza,[13] Leibniz and Kant,[14] as it is true of Hooker and

[2] A list of abusive definitions of "scholastic" and "scholasticism" may be found in M. de Wulf, *Histoire de la philosophie médiévale*, 6th ed. (Institut supérieur de philosophie, Louvain, 1934–1937), I, 15 n. (Eng. tr., Nelson, Edinburgh, 1952, p. 7 n.) For judicious statements, see the text of this edition of de Wulf, as well as M. D. Chenu, *Introduction à l'étude de saint Thomas* (Institut d'études médiévales, Montreal, 1950), 51–60.

[3] Represented in this volume by the texts of Anselm of Canterbury.

[4] See the examples of the work of Anselm of Laon and his school in this volume.

[5] See the selections from Ivo of Chartres and John of Salisbury in this volume.

[6] Represented in this volume by Hugh, Richard and Adam of St. Victor.

[7] See the selections from Peter Abailard and Peter Lombard.

[8] See, for example, the texts of Stephen Langton, Bonaventure, Matthew of Aquasparta, in this volume.

[9] See, for example, the selections from Scotus in this volume.

[10] While the older universities in southern Europe must not be overlooked, they did not make the same direct and conspicuous contribution to the development of scholasticism. Cf. H. Rashdall, *The Universities of Europe in the Middle Ages*, 2d ed. rev. by F. M. Powicke and A. B. Emden (Oxford University Press, London, 1936), I, 75–268.

[11] Note the influence of medieval (particularly "nominalist") ideas on the Reformation formulation of the doctrines of (a) justification and (b) the divine sovereignty.

[12] Cited as outstanding examples of the revival of "scholastic" techniques in Lutheran and Reformed theology respectively.

[13] Cf. E. Gilson (ed.), R. Descartes, *Discours de la méthode: texte et commentaire* (2d ed., Vrin, Paris, 1930); H. A. Wolfson, *The Philosophy of Spinoza* (Harvard University Press, Cambridge, 2 vols. 1934), Chs. IV–VII, and *passim*.

[14] Note, for instance, the discussion of the "ontological argument," derived from the proof of God's existence in Anselm's *Proslogion*, by these and other modern philosophers.

Pearson,[15] Cajetan and Suarez,[16] that the forms of thought they spontaneously used, the questions they raised, the solutions they offered, are in no small degree conditioned by the work of the thinkers and saints of the age that burst into flower in Anselm of Canterbury and had already begun to fade by the time of William Ockham. If, then, we really get inside the medieval mind, we shall find much that is familiar, and much that will help us to understand the important elements of "fragmented scholasticism" in our own outlook.

As for the unreality of scholastic theology, that too is something of an illusion. The work of the schoolmen was an indispensable part of the life and activity of the formative age of European civilization. To begin with, the theology and philosophy that sometimes seem remote from real, concrete problems represent the response of disciplined but fresh minds to the intellectual challenge of the day—a response that at its best was both more creative and more Christian than much that has replaced it. Like the Renaissance and the Reformation in their turn, the Middle Ages were confronted with a massive world-view which embodied the perennial challenge of naturalism to Christian thought. The fact that for them the crisis took a metaphysical rather than an aesthetic or a scientific form should not obscure the deep continuity of the debate through medieval and modern times. But whereas the heirs of the Reformation, devoted to the principles of *sola fides, sola scriptura, sola gratia,* too often lost contact with the secular challenge, and so tended to be less creative, while the children of the Renaissance, hypnotized by the literature and science of classical antiquity and repelled by the aridities of a declining scholasticism, absorbed the naturalistic attitudes of Greece, and so tended to be less Christian, the teachers of medieval Christendom boldly and deliberately undertook the Herculean labor of rethinking Hellenism into a Christian philosophy, allied with a vigorous theology.[17] Only a very parochial mentality could confront the vast syntheses of medieval scholasticism and still assert with

---

15 Two great Anglican theologians of a strongly Thomistic orientation. Cf. R. Hooker, *Laws of Ecclesiastical Polity,* Book I, *passim;* J. Pearson, *Minor Theological Works* (ed. E. Churton, Oxford, 1844), I, 8 f.

16 The Dominican, Thomas de Vio Caietanus (1469–1534), was perhaps the most influential commentator on the *Summa theologiae* of Aquinas. The Jesuit, Francis Suarez (1548–1617), was one of the most brilliant of later scholastic theologians.

17 Cf. E. Gilson, *God and Philosophy* (Yale University Press, New Haven, 1941), Chs. I, II; Gilson, *Spirit,* Chs. III, IV.

a clear conscience that the great divorce between an anti-Hellenic supernaturalism and a naturalistic Hellenism, typical of postmedieval thought, has been pure gain. Recognizing as we must the imperfections and the unfinished business of the medieval achievement, we should also acknowledge that it was the most daring constructive attempt in the Church's history to think of grace and nature, faith and reason, Christianity and culture, God and his creation, in terms that would neither separate nor confuse them, neither strip God of his sovereignty nor do violence to the integrity of his creatures. In other words, scholastic theology and philosophy are, at the very least, a noble effort to face the abiding problems raised by the correlation of Christian faith in God, Creator and Redeemer, with man's knowledge of himself and his world.

Moreover, medieval thought faced these problems in the very concrete and actual setting of the contemporary Church and of the society which the Church was endeavoring to shape. Scholasticism was the instrument of the Church's understanding of itself and of the world in which it was inescapably involved, and throughout its development it was concerned with the education of those who were to play important roles in the establishment of a Christian society. The great scholastic masters were the teachers, not only of monks and friars, of parish priests and ecclesiastical administrators, but also of bishops and popes, of princes and kings. Moreover, their work was intimately connected with the activities of political thinkers, lawyers, and canonists, with whom they shared both methods and problems. Indeed, the intellectual movement went on in a cultural and academic milieu whose very existence was conditioned by the needs of society as a whole.[18] The scholastic theologians and philosophers, then, were inevitably concerned with the synthesis of grace and nature in life as well as in thought or, as they would have preferred to say, in action as well as in contemplation. If the sacral synthesis of the Middle Ages seems to us to be oversimplified—so that, perhaps, we identify "medievalism" with "clericalism," or even, more superficially still, confuse both with the "feudalism" of immature medieval society[19]—it was, nonetheless, a clearsighted attempt

[18] Cf. R. W. Southern, *The Making of the Middle Ages* (Hutchinson's University Library, London, 1953), Ch. II.
[19] On the character of "feudalism," cf. M. L. B. Bloch, *La Société féodale*, 2 vols. (Michel, Paris, 1939–1940); F. L. Ganshof, *Feudalism* (Longmans, London, 1952); C. Stephenson, *Medieval Feudalism* (Cornell University

to hold together aspects of life which God, in creation and redemption, had joined together, and which modern man, to his cost, has put asunder.

If we appreciate all this, our indifference or antagonism will readily turn to sympathetic interest. The "Middle Ages"[20] will cease to be an obscure period of transition between classical antiquity and its rebirth, and will appear in their own right as the scene of a brilliant attempt, illuminated by Christian faith and motivated by fundamental exigencies of the mind and heart of man, to deal with the weighty issues presented by one of those successive renewals of Hellenism that have marked Western cultural history. This mysterious period was neither a golden age of unquestioning faith and social stability nor a mere interlude between one great civilization and another; contrary to both these popular pictures, it was a historical epoch which witnessed a dynamic attempt to deal with serious intellectual questions, and to approach the problems of culture and society in the light of carefully formulated answers. The men we called "medievals" were, in their own eyes, *moderni*[21]— human beings giving present answers to present problems in the light of past experience. If it is unfair and unrealistic to romanticize them, as if their work contained all the answers in a form untouched by time, it is unjust and self-stultifying to accept the estimate of them offered by the intellectually tired men of the literary Renaissance, or to judge them by the incapacity of so many of their descendants to cope with the problems of the scientific revolution. For our own enlightenment, we should try to see them as living men and women like

Press, Ithaca, New York, 1942); J. T. McNeill, "The Feudalization of the Church," in J. T. McNeill, M. Spinka, H. R. Willoughby (eds.), *Environmental Factors in Christian History* (University of Chicago Press, Chicago, 1939), 187–205.

20 On the term "Middle Ages," cf. G. Gordon, *Medium Aevum and the Middle Age* (Oxford, 1925); O. Halecki, *The Limits and Divisions of European History* (Sheed and Ward, London, 1950), 145–161. The earliest forms appear to be: *media tempestas* (1469), *media aetas* (1518), *medium aevum* (1604); cf. Gilson, *History*, 552.

21 Cf. Richard of St. Victor, *In visionem Ezechielis, prologus* (PL, 196, 527). For an expression of the medieval attitude toward antiquity, see the famous statement of Bernard of Chartres, quoted by John of Salisbury, *Metalog.*, III, 4 (PL, 199, 900): "We are like dwarfs sitting on the shoulders of giants; we see more things, and things that are further off, than they did—not because our sight is better, or because we are taller than they were, but because they raise us up and add to our stature by their gigantic height."

ourselves, confronted with vital questions, different often in form, but in essence akin to the problems of our own age and of all time, and offering answers to those questions with a freshness and a confidence that we may well envy, even if sometimes we smile at the evidence of a certain naïvety. To use the language of our own culture, if the history of thought is the laboratory of the thinker, then the medieval experiment has its own indisputable claim to be an essential subject of investigation for the Christian thinker.[22]

II

We must now turn to a survey of the terms of the medieval intellectual experiment, and try to illustrate some of the propositions just advanced. To begin with, the historical context of medieval thought is the story of the "making of Europe."[23] We start from the chaos of a disrupted world, the aftermath of the fall of Rome and the triumph of barbarism, and with the limited order which feudal society managed to impose on that chaos. Out of this society we see emerging, little by little, the cosmopolitan civilization of twelfth century Europe, centered in the resurgence of urban life, marked by the emergence at least of the French and English nations, and held together by the cultural unity of the Latin Church.[24] As the story goes on, we learn of powerful aspirations toward unity, expressed in the papalism and the imperialism of the thirteenth and fourteenth centuries,[25] and witness the rebellion of maturing nationality against papal tutelage in the age of conciliarism and laicism, of Protestantism and Gallicanism.[26] However we may assess the relative utility of the various institutions which formed and were formed by medieval society, and whether we see medieval history as a steady progress toward modern times or (more

---

[22] Cf. E. Gilson, *The Unity of Philosophical Experience* (Sheed and Ward, London, 1938), Ch. XII, "The Nature and Unity of Philosophical Experience."

[23] Cf. C. Dawson, *The Making of Europe* (Sheed and Ward, London, 1939).

[24] Cf. C. H. Haskins, *The Renaissance of the Twelfth Century* (Cambridge, Massachusetts, 1927).

[25] Cf. W. Ullmann, *Medieval Papalism: The Political Theories of the Medieval Canonists* (Methuen, London, 1949); *The Growth of Papal Government in the Middle Ages* (Methuen, London, 1955).

[26] Cf. G. de Lagarde, *La Naissance de l'esprit laïque au déclin du moyen âge*, 6 vols. (Editions Béatrice, Saint-Paul-Trois-Châteaux, 1934–1946); *Recherches sur l'esprit politique de la Réforme* (Paris, 1926); V. Martin, *Les Origines du Gallicanisme*, 2 vols. (Bloud et Gay, Paris, 1939).

correctly, I think) as a dialectic of achievement and defeat, we cannot withhold recognition from a stupendous development of civilization. For when we watch the transition from the fragmentary society of the early Middle Ages, completely at the mercy of wind and weather, of arbitrary force and undisciplined power, to an organized international community, bound together not only by common interests, economic and military, but also by a common allegiance to certain recognized principles, embodied in a great institution, what we are witnessing is nothing less than the rise of Europe—that is, in some sense, of Christendom[27]—from its precarious infancy to its long primacy.

In the writings to which this volume is devoted we shall find a variety of expressions of the spiritual element in medieval civilization. In concentrating our attention on this aspect of medieval life, we shall be considering the deepest roots of the thought and action of the period. If we owe the possibility of the medieval experiment to the urban culture of western Europe and to the ordered society which protected it, we owe the character of the achievement to the ideals of the institution which, through long centuries, fostered the culture and taught the fundamentals of law and order to the society. It is time, then, for us to consider the character and aims of that institution.

III

The Latin Church of the Middle Ages stood, first and foremost, for the Latin patristic tradition, with its own tentative synthesis of Christianity and *romanitas*.[28] The Church came to the new peoples of the West both as the repository of saving truth and as the legatee of Roman prestige and culture. For the fulfillment of the Church's historical vocation in the Middle Ages, this taking of cultural form by Christianity was a fact of primary importance, whose effects can be seen in the steady effort to maintain the cultural and educational minimum necessary for the Church's organized life and worship. Of equal importance, however, was the embodiment of the authority of the Church in a particular institution, the papacy,

---

[27] Not, of course, in the sense of the simple and essential identification of Christendom with Europe, favored by some.
[28] Cf. C. N. Cochrane, *Christianity and Classical Culture* (Oxford University Press, New York, 1944); E. M. Pickman, *The Mind of Latin Christendom* (Oxford University Press, New York, 1937).

whose position rested, not simply on the prestige of the Eternal City, but in some sense on the historical foundations of Christianity itself.[29] It was thanks to the papacy, above all, that the principles of order and discipline by which the Church sought to mold the new world were not only contemplated in theology but also realized in the structured life of the Church. Given the confusion out of which medieval society had to emerge, it is hard to see how the community of Western Christendom, with its culture and intellectual life, could ever have come into being apart from the renewal of the papacy in the eleventh century, under such great popes as Leo IX and Gregory VII.[30]

It is true that the medieval popes and their most intransigent supporters did not exercise a wholly beneficent influence on the development of Christian life and thought, even in the great age of medieval culture. Then as now, the caution of the ecclesiastical statesman could and did lead to an obscurantism which threatened theological and philosophical advance,[31] while the political interests of the papacy contributed to certain more or less conspicuous distortions in the pattern of the Church's life.[32] Nevertheless, the papacy did protect and foster the intellectual activity of some of the greatest of medieval teachers, and any estimate of its contribution to the maturing of the medieval mind has to take into account the close parallel between the course of intellectual development and the fortunes of the Roman see. It is noteworthy, for example, that the first great theologian of medieval Europe, Anselm of Canterbury, appeared in the midst of the papal struggle for *libertas ecclesiae*, that the greatest century of scholasticism, which saw the intellectual achievement of the brilliant Dominican and Franciscan theologians and their "secular" colleagues in the

[29] Cf. H. E. Symonds, *The Church Universal and the See of Rome* (S.P.C.K., London, 1939); T. G. Jalland, *The Church and the Papacy* (S.P.C.K., London, 1944), Chs. II–VI; O. Cullmann, *Peter: Disciple, Apostle, Martyr* (The Westminster Press, Philadelphia, 1953).

[30] Cf. Z. N. Brooke, "Gregory VII and the First Contest Between Empire and Papacy," in *CMH*, 5, 51–111; J. P. Whitney, "The Reform of the Church," *ibid.*, 1–50; A. Fliche, *La Réforme grégorienne*, 3 vols. (Spicilegium Sacrum Lovaniense, Louvain, 1924–1937).

[31] Cf. E. Gilson, "La Servante de la théologie," in *Etudes de philosophie médiévale* (Strasbourg, 1921), 30–50.

[32] The depression of the episcopate in the interests of papal authority is an obvious example; cf. T. G. Jalland, "The Parity of Ministers," in K. E. Kirk (ed.), *The Apostolic Ministry* (Hodder and Stoughton, London, 1946), 305–349; E. R. Fairweather, *Episcopacy Re-asserted* (Mowbrays, London, 1955), 48 f.

universities, was the triumphal period ushered in by the pontificate of Innocent III, and that the decline of medieval thought coincided with the aftermath of the suicidal reign of Boniface VIII. It is significant also that canon law—bound up as it was, in our period at least, with the enforcement of papal order in the Church—was both one of the formative influences of theological method and a genuine intellectual stimulus by way of the problems of law and Church order which it raised for theology.[33] In the light of all this, even when we question the ultimate claims made for Rome as "mother and mistress of all churches," or recognize the destructive as well as constructive role which the popes played in the life of the Church and Christian society, we can hardly ignore the contribution providentially made by the papacy to medieval civilization. If the incompatibility of its social futility and religious and moral degradation with its inherited claims led to the sixteenth century revolt against the Renaissance papacy, the loyalty which the medieval popes were able to command from the keenest minds and the most devoted souls of their time, despite innumerable criticisms of the policies of the papal *curia*, compels us to acknowledge their role in the accomplishments of medieval society.

IV

On the intellectual side, the great work of the medieval Church was done through its schools—*the* schools of the Middle Ages—and notably through the universities of northwestern Europe, so that in fact the history of the schools provides a convenient outline of the development of medieval thought. The story begins with the schools associated with monastic communities and cathedral towns, where, apart from anything else, an indispensable work was done in the preservation of the cultural heritage of the Roman past.[34] Their contribution to later thought, however, was not merely that of conservation. If at first these schools concentrated on the narrower problems of an ecclesiastical education, and devoted themselves to transmitting the essential skills of the cleric, they came, under pressure both of expanding intellectual interests and of new social needs, to embrace in their curriculum the whole range

[33] Cf. J. de Ghellinck, "Theological Literature During the Investiture Struggle," *Irish Theol. Quart.*, 7 (1912), 313–341.
[34] Cf. R. W. Southern, *op. cit.*, 185–203; L. Maitre, *Les Ecoles épiscopales et monastiques en Occident avant les universités (768–1180)* (Paris, 1924).

of the "liberal arts." The transition is marked by the rise to pre-eminence of the cathedral schools—such as Chartres, Orléans, and Paris—over against the monastic schools, and coincides with the rise of urban society, notably in France.[35] In scholarly method itself, the great feature of the transition is the advance from the reduced repetitions of earlier commentaries[36] and the *florilegia* of patristic excerpts,[37] which constituted such a large part of the intellectual diet of the early Middle Ages, to the fresh thinking, the dialectical techniques, the *quaestiones*[38] and the *sententiae*,[39] of the twelfth century. In this development, the *artes*, notably "grammar" and "dialectic," came into their own.[40] The earlier period had been marked almost exclusively by the former, indispensable as it was to the very existence of a learned literature; in the twelfth century, however, dialectic came to the fore. Although the one-sided triumph of dialectic was later to contribute to the deplorable schism between metaphysics and letters in the later Renaissance, careful training in dialectic was unquestionably an essential condition of the growth of theology to maturity.

The next stage in the organization of intellectual activity was marked by the appearance of the universities.[41] These institutions indicate the new social importance of intellectual life, as well as the great stimulus to intellectual effort provided by the contacts of medieval society with the world beyond Christendom—notably, with the Moslem world.[42] The result of these contacts was the confrontation of Christian thought with a

35 Cf. R. W. Southern, *op. cit.*, 203–218; M. Deanesly, "Medieval Schools to c.1300," in *CMH*, 5, 765–779; P. Delhaye, "L'Organisation scolaire au XIIᵉ siècle," *Traditio*, 5 (1947), 211–268.
36 Cf. C. Spicq, *Esquisse d'une histoire de l'exégèse latine au moyen âge* (Vrin, Paris, 1944), 9–25.
37 Cf. R. W. Southern, *op. cit.*, 191; C. H. Haskins, *op. cit.*, 113; M. J. Congar, art. "Théologie," *DTC*, 15, 361.
38 In this connection, a "question" means an investigation, discussion, problem for debate. "The *quaestio* was the characteristic method of thought and exposition for scholasticism, especially in theology and philosophy" (F. Pelster, art. "Quaestio," *Lexikon für Theologie und Kirche*, 8 [Herder, Freiburg i. Br., 1936], 579). Cf. M. J. Congar, *art. cit.*, 370–373.
39 Here, a "sentence" means an opinion, thesis, etc. Cf. M. Grabmann, art. "Sentenz," *Lexikon für Theologie und Kirche*, 9 (1937), 477 f.
40 Cf. P. Abelson, *The Seven Liberal Arts: A Study in Mediaeval Culture* (New York, 1906); C. H. Haskins, *op. cit.*, *passim*.
41 Cf. H. Rashdall, *op. cit.*, I, 269–584 (Paris); III, 1–273 (Oxford), and *passim*.
42 Cf. R. W. Southern, *op. cit.*, 29–31, 36–41, 65–68, 71–73; C. H. Haskins, *op. cit.*, Ch. IX.

comprehensive philosophical and scientific *Weltanschauung*, and the consequent reworking of the materials of the latter in the *Summae*,[43] the *Commentaria* on Peter Lombard's *Sententiae*,[44] the Aristotelian commentaries,[45] the *Quaestiones disputatae*,[46] and the *Quodlibeta*,[47] of the thirteenth and fourteenth centuries. While the history of the university as an institution begins before this period, the intellectual supremacy of the universities coincides with the full emergence of the "natural" element of the medieval syntheses—namely, the classical metaphysics and science—and it was in the fully grown universities that scholasticism performed its greatest feats.

V

"The classical metaphysics and science" means, above all else, the doctrine of Aristotle. Indeed, the whole history of medieval thought can be organized in terms of the progressive rediscovery of Aristotle,[48] since that rediscovery provided the essential stimulus for the formulation of "Christian philosophy." For the early Middle Ages, of course, Aristotle was essentially the grammarian, or logician of the *logica vetus*[49]—almost exclusively the teacher of method—and with few exceptions theology was little more than warmed-over patristic exegesis. In the second major period of medieval thought (that of

[43] Cf. M. Grabmann, *art. cit.*; Robert of Melun, *Sententiae* (Cod. Brug. 229, fol. 1 recto): *Quid enim summa est, nonnisi singulorum brevis comprehensio?*
[44] Cf. F. Stegmüller, *Repertorium commentariorum in Sententias Petri Lombardi*, 2 vols. (Schöningh, Würzburg, 1947).
[45] Those of Thomas Aquinas' are the best; cf. refs. in W. D. Ross, *Aristotle* (3d ed., Methuen, London, 1937).
[46] Cf. A. M. Landgraf, "Zur Technik und Überlieferung der Disputation," *Collectanea franciscana*, 20 (1950), 173–188; Gilson, *History*, 247. A *quaestio disputata* is "a formal exercise which occupied an important place in the regular teaching of the universities."
[47] Public disputations, commonly held about the second week of Advent and the third and fourth weeks of Lent, at which anyone could raise any question. Cf. P. Glorieux, *La Littérature quodlibétique*, 2 vols. (Le Saulchoir, Kain, 1925–1935).
[48] Cf. M. J. Congar, *art. cit.*, 359 f.
[49] The "old logic" included Boethius' versions of Aristotle's *Categoriae* and *De interpretatione* and his commentaries on these works, together with his commentaries on the *Isagoge* of Porphyry, and certain treatises of his own. The "new logic" adds to these the rest of Aristotle's *Organon*, along with the *Liber sex principiorum* ascribed to Gilbert of La Porrée. Cf. Gilson, *History*, 627; M. Grabmann, "Aristoteles im zwölften Jahrhundert," *Mediaeval Studies*, 12 (1950), 123–162.

Anselm of Canterbury and the twelfth century), Aristotle is still essentially the teacher of method, but this time as dialectician, or logician of the *logica nova*. It is at this point that the real effort of dialectical organization and exposition begins, and, incidentally, that *theologia* first comes to be used in our sense, to describe the systematic statement of the content of Christian faith.[50] The development of theology, however, is still incomplete, since this period suffers from one important limitation. Except for Anselm of Canterbury, in whom, though his philosophical interests were relatively limited, Augustine the metaphysician seems to have come to life again, the thinkers of the age of dialectic tend to lack any metaphysical basis or content for their dialectical development of theology. The natural consequence of this situation was the profound distrust of the *dialectici* and *philosophi*, characteristic of so many of the wisest and greatest men of the age.[51]

The whole picture changed with the discovery of Aristotle as "the philosopher" in the full sense, when the complete canon of his writings appeared in the West. Because of the circumstances of the transmission of Aristotle's works, scholars in this third period of medieval thought were faced with at least two problems when they undertook to make use of Aristotelian material. In the first place, the authentic system of Aristotle, which constituted the fundamental common factor of "Arabian" philosophy as a whole, had to be isolated from the dubious conclusions drawn and the alien ideas introduced under Neoplatonic influence.[52] Only then could the second problem—that of the assimilation of Aristotelian thought—be faced. While the Christian world owed a good deal of its knowledge of Aristotle to Islamic translators and commentators, and Moslem interpretations of Aristotle played a large part both in the exegesis of his writings and in the debates connected with the assimilation of his teaching, the most adequate solutions of both problems were worked out, naturally enough, only when Christian thinkers added an independent knowledge of Aristotelianism as a whole to their earlier knowledge of his logical doctrines.

The question at issue was that of the philosophical formulation of Christian thought and the extent to which the new

50 Cf. J. Rivière, "Theologia," *Revue des sciences religieuses*, 16 (1936), 47–57.
51 Cf. Gilson, *History*, 164 (on Bernard of Clairvaux).
52 On Arabian Aristotelianism, cf. Gilson, *History*, 181–183; 235–246.

influences were to predominate, and on these points there were sharp disagreements within the medieval schools. We must, of course, recognize the paramount influence of Aristotle, whose all-embracing system both stimulated fresh philosophical thinking and provided a large proportion of the terms and concepts required for that enterprise. We should not, however, exaggerate his importance. While no schoolman after the beginning of the thirteenth century could avoid taking up a position in relation to Aristotle, it is not true that every good schoolman tried hard (though with varied success) to be an Aristotelian. The nearest approach in this respect to the school-book image of a scholastic philosopher must have been Siger of Brabant and the "Averroists," who are not the most convincing representatives of medieval thought.[53] On the other side, however, at least three less hidebound treatments of Aristotle must be considered, and the existence of a number of eclectic doctrines recognized. The most positive of these treatments is that of Thomas Aquinas, who sought with considerable success to understand Aristotle's ideas, as his commentaries on Aristotle's text indicate, but who also undertook to place the whole system in the new metaphysical context of his own philosophy of being, and drew some rather novel conclusions in this fresh perspective.[54] A more negative approach to the problem is represented by Bonaventure's reformulation of Franciscan "Augustinianism" in the light of the doctrinal debates of the mid-thirteenth century, as a result of which he accepted Aristotelian *scientia* (though with certain Augustinian modifications), but looked for *sapientia* to Augustine's Neoplatonism.[55] The approach of the later Franciscan masters also took a good deal of the Aristotelian material very seriously, but tended (less radically in Duns Scotus, more radically in Ockham) to challenge Aristotelian interpretations of "nature" in the interests of a strong affirmation of the freedom of the divine will.[56] It is impossible, then, to sustain the thesis that scholastic thought, on its philosophical side, was either in intention or in fact a resuscitation of original Aristotelianism.

[53] Cf. Gilson, *History*, 389–399; 718f.; P. Mandonnet, *Siger de Brabant et l'averroïsme latin au XIIIe siècle*, 2 vols. (2d ed., Louvain, 1908–1911); F. Van Steenberghen, *Siger de Brabant d'après ses oeuvres inédites* (Institut supérieur de philosophie, Louvain, 1931).

[54] Cf. E. Gilson, *Le Thomisme* (5th ed., Vrin, Paris, 1948).

[55] Cf. E. Gilson, *La Philosophie de saint Bonaventure* (2d. ed., Vrin, Paris, 1943).

[56] Cf. Gilson, *History*, 460 f.; 498 f.

VI

In so far as the facts lend themselves at all to such simple assertions, it can be said that the one figure who above all others dominates medieval Christian thought is Augustine.[57] Even for Aquinas, with his careful discrimination of the claims of faith and reason, Augustine's influence counts for more than is often recognized, and it is rash to assume that, when Augustine and Aristotle meet in his mind, the former has no effect on the fate of the latter. On the contrary, the primacy of Augustinian theology is assured by the central place occupied by theology in the medieval syntheses, including the Thomist.

This is not intended to justify the gibe that scholastic philosophy was the distortion and misinterpretation of Aristotle in the interests of Christian apologetics. We must, however, recognize that the choice of problems to be tackled, as well as some weighty suggestions for their solution, came from the association of philosophy with theology in the same minds, and from the understanding of the vocation of philosophy as, in some sense, that of *ancilla theologiae*.[58] This is true of all the schools of any importance, with the probable exception of the still rather mysterious Averroists. It is well known that the theological authority of Augustine led to the introduction of Augustinian metaphysical ideas into a wide range of systems in the name of Christian truth, sometimes to the considerable confusion of philosophy.[59] As for thinkers like Aquinas and Scotus, if they obviated this kind of confusion by a clearer analysis of the respective functions of revelation and reason, and in so doing freed philosophy from the menace of "theol-

---

[57] Cf. essays by H. X. Arquillière and others in *Augustinus Magister* (Etudes Augustiniennes, Paris, 1954), II, 991–1153; J. de Ghellinck, "Une Edition ou une collection médiévale des Opera omnia de saint Augustin," in *Liber floridus: mittellateinische Studien* (Eos Verlag der Erzabtei St. Ottilien, 1950), 63–82; A. H. Thompson in *CMH*, 6, 647: "The course which medieval dogma was to take was determined by the overpowering influence of Saint Augustine upon religious thought."

[58] On the background and use of the expression, *philosophia ancilla theologiae*, cf. H. A. Wolfson, *Philo* (Harvard University Press, Cambridge, 1947), I, 145 ff. (Philo); 156 (Clement of Alexandria); 157 (Peter Damian); Gilson, *History*, 616 (Peter Damian); E. Gilson, *Introduction à l'étude de saint Augustin* (2d. ed., Vrin, Paris, 1943), 318 (R.D.C.).

[59] Cf. E. Gilson, "Pourquoi saint Thomas a critiqué saint Augustin," *Archives d'hist. doctrinale et littéraire du moyen âge*, 1 (1926), 5–127.

ogism,"[60] their philosophies were nonetheless consciously left open to the influence of faith and theology, and their philosophical analyses were put at the service of theological exposition. *A fortiori*, this statement can be applied to the conservative Augustinianism of Bonaventure and others. But it still does not follow that medieval philosophy can simply be dismissed as veiled apologetics. The point, rather, is this, that the medieval mind had such a strong sense both of the unity of truth and of the hierarchy of truths that it believed that the truth of faith could illuminate reason and guide it to its ultimate end.

Deum et animam scire cupio[61]: here, then, is the center of reference for scholastic thought. The theological problems of the nature of God, the condition of man, the union of man with God, are accepted as the basic questions of human life. Whatever qualifications may be required in view of his early date, Anselm, the first of the great schoolmen, is the prototype of scholastic thought, in his attempt to prove God's existence as a way of understanding his faith, in his analysis of man's sinful state, or in his explanation of the mystery of his redemption for eternal life with God. Again and again we meet the same themes: God, his nature and his triune life; man, his creation, his sinfulness, his need of grace; Christ and his sacraments—all of them interpreted under the guidance of Augustine, even by those who rebel against Augustinian influences or advance far beyond Augustinian positions. We see the same characteristic concern in the efforts to define the nature of theology or to discover the true principles of Biblical exegesis—the concern, that is, to adapt the techniques of art and science to the service of faith. Or when we turn to philosophy, again and again it is impossible to resist the impression that here we have another kind of quest for understanding on the part of faith (or better, perhaps, on the part of the believer). God as Being, God as Creator, man as creature, man as capable of eternal fellowship with God—here are the focal points. If a question like the "problem of universals" plays a large part in the formation of scholasticism, it does so ultimately because the solution affects the philosophical approach to God, the interpretation of the divine law for man's moral life, or the theological treatment of the Trinity, of man's sin, of redemption, of the sacraments. In concentrating on these points, then, we are not simply selecting texts that will serve to illustrate

---

60 Cf. E. Gilson, *The Unity of Philosophical Experience*, Ch. II.
61 Augustine, *Soliloq.*, I, 2:7 (*PL*, 32, 872).

certain "Christian" interests of the schoolmen, when equally
significant "neutral" texts might just as well have been chosen.
Rather, in reading the material contained in this volume, we
shall be investigating some of the deepest concerns of the
medieval mind.

All this does not mean that medieval scholasticism is of
interest only to the student of Christian theology or of the
history of religions. The philosophical work of the schoolmen,
both in metaphysics and anthropology—to say nothing of the
work of the later Middle Ages in logic and scientific theory—
is of immense importance for our understanding of the continuity of Greco-Roman-Western culture and thought. Moreover, it is often of great value in its own right; Aquinas' metaphysic of existence, for example, is a crucially important
contribution to the philosophy of being.[62] At the same time,
the medieval syntheses will obviously have a fuller interest for
those who are concerned with the confrontation of the gospel
and the world. To these, indeed, they should have a unique
interest, in so far as they are products of a culture which, with
all its imperfections and crudities, still looked to God, Creator
and Redeemer, for the ultimate meaning of all life. In that
sense, at least, medieval scholasticism embodies the ideal of all
Christian thought, and is rich in wisdom for us who have to
live in the disoriented world of today.

[62] Cf. E. Gilson, *Being and Some Philosophers* (2d. ed., Pontifical Institute of
Mediaeval Studies, Toronto, 1952).

GENERAL BIBLIOGRAPHY

GENERAL STUDIES OF THE MIDDLE AGES

The classical study of the medieval world, still of immense value despite the great advance of medieval studies since its publication, is H. O. Taylor, *The Mediaeval Mind: A History of the Development of Thought and Emotion in the Middle Ages*, 2 vols. (4th ed., 5th printing, Harvard University Press, Cambridge, 1949). A slighter but useful book is F. B. Artz, *The Mind of the Middle Ages*, *A.D. 200-1500* (Knopf, New York, 1953). Excellent essays on many aspects of medieval culture will be found in C. G. Crump and E. F. Jacob (eds.), *The Legacy of the Middle Ages* (Clarendon Press, Oxford, 1938). E. R. Curtius, *European Literature and the Latin Middle Ages* (Pantheon Books, New York, 1953), is a mine of information. Two volumes by C. Dawson should also be consulted: *Religion and the Rise of Western Culture* (Sheed and Ward, London, 1950); *Medieval Essays* (Sheed and Ward, London, 1953), an enlarged edition of his *Medieval Religion* (Sheed and Ward, London, 1934). R. W. Southern, *The Making of the Middle Ages* (Hutchinson's University Library, London, 1953), is a fine study of the formation of European civilization and thought from the late tenth to the early thirteenth century.

Extensive bibliographies will be found in the following: L. J. Paetow, *A Guide to the Study of Medieval History* (2d ed. by D. C. Munro and G. C. Boyce, Crofts, New York, 1931); J. W. Thompson, *Reference Studies in Medieval History*, 3 vols. (2d ed., Chicago, 1925–1926); C. P. Farrar and A. P. Evans, *Bibliography of English Translations from Medieval Sources* (Columbia University Press, New York, 1946).

MEDIEVAL HISTORY

The outstanding comprehensive treatment of the period covered by this volume will be found in *The Cambridge Medieval History*, Vols. V–VII (Cambridge University Press, Cambridge, 1926–1932). C. W. Previté-Orton, *The Shorter Cambridge Medieval History*, 2 vols. (Cambridge University Press, 1952), is a skillful reduction of the entire work to a continuous narrative; material bearing on this volume is contained in Vol I, 471–643, and Vol. II, 645–951. H. W. C. Davis, *Medieval Europe* (London, 1911, frequently reprinted), is a handy outline of medieval history. C. Stephenson, *Mediaeval History: Europe from the Second to the Sixteenth Century* (3d ed., Harper, New York, 1951), is one of the best and most up-to-date short histories. P. Boissonnade, *Life and Work in Medieval Europe* (London, 1927), is a good account of social and economic life. O. J. Thatcher and E. H. McNeal, *A Source Book for Mediaeval History* (New York, 1905), is valuable for reference.

The following should also be consulted: Z. N. Brooke, *A History of Europe, from 911 to 1198* (Methuen, London, 1938); J. Bryce, *The Holy Roman Empire* (rev. ed., New York, 1904), Chs. VII–XVI; J. F. O'Sullivan, *Medieval Europe* (Crofts, New York, 1943); H. Pirenne, *A History of Europe from the Invasions to the XVI Century* (Allen and Unwin, London, 1939); H. Pirenne, *Histoire économique de l'Occident médiéval* (Desclée, Bruges, 1951); F. M. Powicke, *Ways of Medieval Life and Thought* (Odhams Press, London, 1950); J. W. Thompson and E. N. Johnson, *An Introduction to Medieval Europe, 300–1500* (Norton, New York, 1937).

THE MEDIEVAL CHURCH

The most adequate survey of the history of the medieval Church will be found in the relevant volumes of A. Fliche, V. Martin, and E. Jarry (eds.), *Histoire de l'église depuis les origines jusqu'à nos jours*, planned for 26 vols. (Bloud et Gay, Paris, 1937-   ). Vols. VIII–XIII (most of which have now appeared) cover our period. M. Deanesly, *A History of the Medieval Church* (3d ed., Methuen, London, 1934), and F. J. Foakes Jackson, *An Introduction to the History of Christianity*, A.D. 590–1314 (New York, 1921), are standard outlines. An interesting survey of the period will be found in K. S. Latourette, *A History of Christianity* (Harper, New York, 1953), Chs. XIII–XXV. G. G. Coulton, *Five Centuries of Religion*, 4 vols. (Cambridge University Press, Cambridge, 1923–1950), is a substantial and carefully documented work by a determined critic of medieval Christianity. His collection of translations from primary sources, *Life in the Middle Ages*, 4 vols. (Cambridge University Press, 1928–1930), should also be consulted.

For a general survey of the relations of Church and State, with emphasis on our period, F. Gavin, *Seven Centuries of the Problem of Church and State* (Princeton University Press, Princeton, 1938), is excellent. G. Tellenbach, *Church, State and Christian Society at the Time of the Investiture Contest* (tr. and ed. R. F. Bennett, Blackwell, Oxford, 1940), is most valuable. Some illuminating essays will be found in *Sacerdozio e Regno da Gregorio VII a Bonifacio VIII* (*Miscellanea historiae pontificiae*, Vol. XVIII, nn. 50–57, Rome, 1954). Other material on this subject is cited in the special bibliographies and in various notes.

On the religious orders and their place in the life and action of the medieval Church, H. B. Workman, *The Evolution of the Monastic Ideal from the Earliest Times down to the Coming of the Friars* (London, 1927), is useful, though not profound. Two works by M. D. Knowles, *The Monastic Order in England: A History of Its Development from the Times of St. Dunstan to the Fourth Lateran Council* (University Press, Cambridge, 1940), and *The Religious Orders in England* (University Press, Cambridge, 1948), are most valuable, and are more comprehensive than their titles suggest. The Benedictines and their offshoots may be studied in C. Butler, *Benedictine Monachism* (2d ed., London, 1924); J. McCann, *Saint Benedict* (Sheed and Ward, London, 1937); J. Evans, *Monastic Life at Cluny, 910–1157* (Oxford University Press, London, 1931); W. W. Williams, *Studies in St. Bernard of Clairvaux* (London, 1927). For the Franciscans, see R. M. Huber, *A Documented History of the Franciscan Order (1182–1517)* (Nowiny Publishing Apostolate, Milwaukee, 1944); A. G. Little, *Guide to Franciscan Studies* (London, 1920). For the Dominicans, see R. F. Bennett, *The Early Dominicans: Studies in Thirteenth-Century Dominican History* (University Press, Cambridge, 1937); P. Mandonnet, *St. Dominic and His Work* (Herder, St. Louis, 1945).

P. Pourrat, *Christian Spirituality*, Vol. II (London, 1924), is a good introduction to the spiritual life of medieval Christendom. A. Wilmart, *Auteurs spirituels et textes dévots du moyen âge* (Bloud et Gay, Paris, 1932), contains a number of important texts. C. Butler, *Western Mysticism: The Teaching of SS. Augustine, Gregory and Bernard on Contemplation and the Contemplative Life*

(New York, 1923), is a stimulating introduction to the background of our period. On the later German mystics, see W. Preger, *Geschichte der deutschen Mystik im Mittelalter* (Leipzig, 1881); J. Zahn, *Einführung in die deutsche Mystik* (Paderborn, 1918).

On the controversial question of the medieval Church's struggle with heresy, the following may be consulted: G. G. Coulton, *Inquisition and Liberty* (Heinemann, London, 1938); H. C. Lea, *A History of the Inquisition of the Middle Ages*, 3 vols. (New York, 1888); A. L. Maycock, *The Inquisition from Its Establishment to the Great Schism* (London, 1927); E. Vacandard, *The Inquisition: A Critical and Historical Study of the Coercive Power of the Church* (New York, 1926).

T. G. Jalland, *The Church and the Papacy* (S.P.C.K., London, 1944), Ch. VI, is a judicious estimate of the role of the medieval popes in Christian history. Full accounts of "papalist" theory and policy will be found in W. Ullmann, *Medieval Papalism: The Political Theories of the Medieval Canonists* (Methuen, London, 1949), and the same author's *The Growth of Papal Government in the Middle Ages* (Methuen, London, 1955). J. Haller, *Das Papsttum: Idee und Wirklichkeit*, 5 vols. (Erschienen im Port Verlag, Stuttgart [1–2], and Schwabe, Basel [3–5], 1951–1953), may also be consulted.

A convenient survey of the history of canon law will be found in R. C. Mortimer, *Western Canon Law* (Black, London, 1953). Extensive treatments will be found in P. Fournier and G. Le Bras, *Histoire des collections canoniques en Occident depuis les fausses décrétales jusqu' au Décret de Gratien*, 2 vols. (Sirey, Paris, 1931–1932), and J. F. von Schulte, *Die Geschichte der Quellen und Literatur des canonischen Rechts von Gratian bis auf die Gegenwart*, 3 vols. in 4 (Stuttgart, 1875–1880).

The following are also useful for the study of medieval Church history in its different aspects: A. C. Flick, *The Rise of the Mediaeval Church and Its Influence on the Civilization of Western Europe from the First to the Thirteenth Century* (New York, 1909); A. Hauck, *Kirchengeschichte Deutschlands*, 5 vols. (Hinrichs, Leipzig, 1922–1929); P. Hughes, *A History of the Church*, Vols. II–III (Sheed and Ward, London, 1939, 1947); A. Lagarde, *The Latin Church of the Middle Ages* (New York, 1915); G. Schnürer, *Kirche und Kultur im Mittelalter*, 3 vols. (2d ed., Schöningh, Paderborn, 1927–1930); K. S. Latourette, *A History of the Expansion of Christianity*, Vol. II: *The Thousand Years of Uncertainty* (Harper, New York, 1938); H. von Schubert,

Geschichte der christlicher Kirche im Frühmittelalter (Tübingen, 1921); W. R. W. Stephens and W. Hunt (eds.), *A History of the English Church*, 9 vols. (London, 1906–1916).

H. X. Arquillière, *L'Augustinisme politique: essai sur la formation des théories politiques au moyen âge* (Vrin, Paris, 1934); A. Dempf, *Sacrum Imperium* (Oldenbourg, Munich, 1929); A. Luchaire, *Innocent III, la papauté et l'empire* (Paris, 1906); M. Maccarone, *Chiesa e stato nella dottrina di papa Innocenzo III* (Lateranum, Rome, 1940); J. Rivière, *Le Problème de l'église et l'état au temps de Philippe le Bel* (Louvain, 1926); J. B. Sägmüller, "Die Idee von der Kirche als Imperium Romanum im kanonischen Recht," *Theol. Quartalschrift*, 80 (1898), 50–80; A. L. Smith, *Church and State in the Middle Ages* (Oxford, 1913); T. F. Tout, *The Empire and the Papacy, 918–1273* (London, 1914).

L. E. Binns, *The History of the Decline and Fall of the Medieval Papacy* (Methuen, London, 1934); Z. N. Brooke, *The English Church and the Papacy from the Conquest to the Reign of John* (University Press, Cambridge, 1931); F. Cimitier, *Les Sources du droit ecclésiastique* (Bloud et Gay, Paris, 1930); H. E. Feine, *Kirchliche Rechtsgeschichte*, Vol. I: *Die katholische Kirche* (Böhlaus, Weimar, 1950); J. T. McNeill and H. M. Gamer, *Medieval Handbooks of Penance* (Columbia University Press, New York, 1938).

Medieval Culture

A valuable introduction to medieval literature and other aspects of culture will be found in K. Vossler, *Mediaeval Culture: An Introduction to Dante and His Times*, 2 vols. (Harcourt, Brace, New York, 1929). For the history of the various vernacular literatures of the Middle Ages, the following may be consulted: W. A. Nitze and E. P. Dargan, *A History of French Literature* (New York, 1922); F. de Sanctis, *History of Italian Literature*, 2 vols. (Oxford University Press, London, n.d.), Vol. I; A. Biese, *Deutsche Literaturgeschichte*, Vol. I (25th ed., Beck, Munich, 1930); W. L. Renwick and H. Orton, *The Beginnings of English Literature* (Cresset Press, London, 1939).

The Latin literature of the Middle Ages, which occupied a central place in medieval culture, is usefully surveyed in F. A. Wright and T. A. Sinclair, *A History of Later Latin Literature from the Middle of the Fourth to the End of the Seventeenth Century* (Routledge, London, 1931). The most learned account of Latin literature to the end of the twelfth century is contained in M. Manitius, *Geschichte der lateinischen Literatur des Mittelalters*,

3 vols. (Beck, Munich, 1911–1931). Medieval Latin poetry is studied intensively in two works by F. J. E. Raby, *A History of Secular Latin Poetry in the Middle Ages*, 2 vols. (Clarendon Press, Oxford, 1934), and *A History of Christian Latin Poetry from the Beginnings to the Close of the Middle Ages* (2d ed., Clarendon Press, Oxford, 1953).

A comprehensive account of the literature of the Middle Ages down to the beginning of our period will be found in A. Ebert, *Allgemeine Geschichte der Literatur des Mittelalters bis zum Beginne des XI. Jahrhunderts*, 3 vols. (I, 2d ed., Leipzig, 1889; II–III, 1st ed., 1880, 1887). J. E. Sandys, *A History of Classical Scholarship* (3d ed., Cambridge, 1921,) I, 517–678, gives a good summary of medieval knowledge of classical literature. H. Waddell, *The Wandering Scholars* (6th ed., Constable, London, 1932), contains a picturesque account of some of the earlier medieval humanists.

An interesting selection of texts in translation will be found in J. B. Ross and M. M. McLaughlin (eds.), *The Portable Medieval Reader* (Viking Press, New York, 1949). A representative anthology of Latin poetry is given in S. Gaselee, *The Oxford Book of Medieval Latin Verse* (Clarendon Press, Oxford, 1937). Good verse translations, as well as texts, will be found in H. Waddell, *Medieval Latin Lyrics* (4th ed., Penguin Books, Harmondsworth, 1952).

Good summary accounts of medieval art are provided by C. R. Morey, *Mediaeval Art* (Norton, New York, 1942), and W. R. Lethaby, *Medieval Art, from the Peace of the Church to the Eve of the Renaissance, 312–1350* (3d ed., rev. D. Talbot Rice, Nelson, Edinburgh, 1949). French religious art is studied in detail by E. Mâle, *L'Art religieux du XIIᵉ siècle en France* (3d ed., Colin, Paris, 1928), *L'Art religieux du XIIIᵉ siècle en France* (7th ed., Colin, Paris, 1931), *L'Art religieux de la fin du moyen âge en France* (3d ed., Paris, 1925).

See also: T. S. R. Boase, *English Art, 1100–1216* (Clarendon Press, Oxford, 1953); J. Evans, *English Art, 1307–1461* (Clarendon Press, Oxford, 1949); J. Evans, *Art In Medieval France* (Oxford University Press, London, 1948); W. Molsdorf, *Christliche Symbolik der mittelalterlichen Kunst* (2d ed., Leipzig, 1926).

P. H. Lang, *Music in Western Civilization* (Norton, New York, 1941), Chs. V–VIII, contains an excellent summary of the history of medieval music. Several more technical essays on the subject will be found in M. F. Bukofzer, *Studies in Medieval and Renaissance Music* (Norton, New York, 1950).

For an account of formal "higher" education in western Europe before the rise of the universities, see L. Maitre, *Les Ecoles épiscopales et monastiques en Occident avant les universités (768–1180)* (2d ed., Paris, 1924). The classical treatment of the medieval universities is H. Rashdall, *The Universities of Europe in the Middle Ages*, 3 vols. (2d ed., rev. F. M. Powicke and A. B. Emden, Oxford University Press, London, 1936). H. Denifle, *Die Universitäten des Mittelalters bis 1400* (Berlin, 1885), may usefully be consulted. For a collection of important documents, see H. Denifle and E. Chatelain, *Chartularium Universitatis Parisiensis*, 4 vols. (Paris, 1889–1897), supplemented by *Auctarium Chartularii Universitatis Parisiensis* (Paris, 1933–   ). C. H. Haskins, *The Renaissance of the Twelfth Century* (Cambridge, Massachusetts, 1927), is a famous and readable account of intellectual life and scholastic activity in the decades immediately preceding the beginnings of the universities.

MEDIEVAL THEOLOGY

The theology of the Middle Ages, although it has been the object of countless monographic studies, has not been well served as far as the production of comprehensive treatments is concerned. While A. Forest, F. Van Steenberghen, and M. de Gandillac, *Le Mouvement doctrinale du XIᵉ au XIVᵉ siècle* (Fliche and Martin, *Histoire de l'église*, XIII, Bloud et Gay, Paris, 1951), is a useful introduction (save, as it seems to me, for certain errors of perspective in the interpretation of thirteenth century thought), it concentrates almost exclusively on philosophical or closely related issues. F. Cayré, *Patrologie et histoire de la théologie*, Vol II (4th ed., Desclée, Paris, 1947) and B. J. Otten, *A Manual of the History of Dogmas*, Vol. II (2d ed., St. Louis, 1925), are perhaps the best manuals available. The relevant sections of M. Grabmann, *Die Geschichte der katholischen Theologie seit dem Ausgang der Väterzeit* (Herder, Freiburg i. Br., 1933), are reliable but too sketchy. A. M. Landgraf, *Dogmengeschichte der Frühscholastik*, 7 vols. (of 10) now published (Pustet, Regensburg, 1952–1955), is a magnificent study of the period from the eleventh to the early thirteenth century, but stops short of the great debates of the later period.

Two of the older histories of dogma should be mentioned, although with a caveat. R. Seeberg, *Lehrbuch der Dogmengeschichte*, 4 vols. (Vol. III, 4th ed., Deichert, Leipzig, 1930), is the more satisfactory; unfortunately, the English translation

(1904), recently reprinted (Baker Book House, Grand Rapids, 1952), was made from the first edition (1895–1898), and is now badly dated. A. Harnack, *Lehrbuch der Dogmengeschichte*, 3 vols. (4th ed., Tübingen, 1910)—English translation from the third German edition, 7 vols., London, 1897–1899—suffers from the same disadvantage, and is marred at some points by a rather doctrinaire approach to historical questions; at the same time, it is informative and at some points brilliant and stimulating. J. Schwane, *Histoire des dogmas*, Vols. IV–V (2d ed., French tr., Paris, 1903), is also old, but is still useful for reference. A. C. McGiffert, *A History of Christian Thought*, Vol. II: *The West from Tertullian to Erasmus* (Scribner, New York, 1948), is too brief and selective to provide more than an elementary introduction. S. H. Mellone, *Western Christian Thought in the Middle Ages: An Essay in Interpretation* (Blackwood, Edinburgh, 1935), deals more adequately with our period, but does not profess to be a comprehensive treatment.

A number of volumes dealing with themes discussed by our authors are listed in their proper places; certain works, however, concerning matters of general interest, may usefully be listed here. Thus attention should be drawn to two studies of medieval Biblical exegesis: B. Smalley, *The Study of the Bible in the Middle Ages* (2d ed., Blackwell, Oxford, 1952), a pioneer work in English, and C. Spicq, *Esquisse d'une histoire de l'exégèse latine au moyen âge* (Vrin, Paris, 1944), which occupies very much the same place in French scholarship. Both these works underline the strongly Biblical element in medieval theology. On the more strictly "scholastic" side, we should note several studies of medieval theological method. The problem of the relations of faith, reason, and knowledge is dealt with by W. Betzendörfer, *Glauben und Wissen bei den grossen Denkern des Mittelalters: ein Beitrag zur Geschichte des Zentralproblems der Scholastik* (Klotz, Gotha, 1931); T. Heitz, *Essai historique sur les rapports entre la philosophie et la foi de Bérenger de Tours à saint Thomas d'Aquin* (Paris, 1909); J. M. Verweyen, *Philosophie und Theologie im Mittelalter* (Bonn, 1911). Brief but illuminating discussions of the same problems will be found in E. Gilson, *Christianity and Philosophy* (Sheed and Ward, New York, 1939), and *Reason and Revelation in the Middle Ages* (Scribner, New York, 1938). Two useful studies of the nature of technical theology are: B. Geyer, "Der Begriff der scholastischen Theologie," in *Synthesen in der Philosophie der Gegenwart: Festgabe A. Dyroff* (Bonn, 1926), 112–125; J. Kraus, *Theologie und Wissenschaft nach der Lehre der Hochscholastik*, in *Beiträge*, XI/3–4 (Münster i.W., 1912).

The principal collection of medieval theological texts is, of course, to be found in approximately the latter half of J. P. Migne's great *Patrologiae cursus completus, series latina*; while many of these texts do not meet modern critical standards, the bulk of them are still inaccessible in any more satisfactory form. Critical editions of individual authors (where available) and texts of later writers are listed in the special bibliographies, when necessary. As guides to the use of Migne, and indications of collateral material, the following are indispensable: P. Glorieux, *Pour revaloriser Migne, tables rectificatives* (*Mélanges de science religieuse*, 9 [1952], cahier supplémentaire); A. M. Landgraf, *Einführung in die Geschichte der theologischen Literatur der Frühscholastik* (Gregorius-Verlag, Regensburg, 1948).

MEDIEVAL PHILOSOPHY

A general knowledge of scholastic philosophy is easier to acquire than familiarity with scholastic theology, thanks to the labors of several distinguished philosophers. Of these, the most noteworthy is E. Gilson, a number of whose works are milestones in the progress of medieval studies. *The Spirit of Mediaeval Philosophy* (Scribner, New York, 1936) is perhaps the best single introduction to the mind of medieval Christendom. The *History of Christian Philosophy in the Middle Ages* (Random House, New York, 1955) is the best general introduction to the history of medieval philosophy, and its approximately 250 pages of notes are encyclopedic in their range. This volume does not, however, entirely supersede *La Philosophie au moyen âge* (2d ed., Payot, Paris, 1944), with its important comments on the general cultural setting of medieval philosophy.

Among other histories of medieval philosophy, the following should be noted. A. Forest *et al.*, *Le Mouvement doctrinale* (listed in the previous section), is a comprehensive account of the thought of our period. B. Geyer, *Die patristische und scholastische Philosophie* (Mittler, Berlin, 1928), is the eleventh edition of Vol. II of F. Ueberweg's famous *Grundriss der Geschichte der Philosophie*, and contains bibliographical material of great importance. M. de Wulf, *Histoire de la philosophie médiévale*, 3 vols. (6th ed., Institut supérieur de philosophie, Louvain, 1934–1937), is the last and much improved edition of a classic in the field; one volume of a revised English translation has appeared (Nelson, Edinburgh, 1952). F. C. Copleston, *A History of Philosophy*, Vol. II: *Mediaeval Philosophy—Augustine to Scotus*, and Vol. III: *Ockham to Suarez* (Burns Oates and Washbourne, London, 1950, 1953), is especially valuable for its exposition of the later scholasticism. Two useful summaries are P. Vignaux, *La Pensée au moyen âge* (Colin, Paris, 1938), and (less profound) D. J. B. Hawkins *A Sketch of Mediaeval Philosophy* (Sheed and Ward, London, 1946). Reference should also be made to two pioneer works: B. Hauréau, *Histoire de la philosophie scolastique*, 2 vols. in 3 (Paris, 1872–1880); F. Picavet, *Esquisse d'une histoire générale et comparée des philosophies médiévales* (2d ed., Paris, 1907). K. Werner, *Die Scholastik des späteren Mittelalters*, 4 vols. (Vienna, 1881–1887), is a classical treatment of later medieval thought. For the history of scholastic techniques in philosophy and theology, M. Grabmann, *Die Geschichte der scholastischen Methode*, 2 vols. (Freiburg i. Br. 1909–1910), should be consulted.

Other serviceable works include: E. Bréhier, *La Philosophie au moyen âge* (2d ed., Michel, Paris, 1949); M. H. Carré, *Realists and Nominalists* (Oxford University Press, London, 1946); S. J. Curtis, *A Short History of Western Philosophy in the Middle Ages* (Macdonald, London, 1950).

On Islamic thought and its influence on the medieval West, the following may be consulted: T. J. de Boer, *The History of Philosophy in Islam* (Luzac, London, 1933); L. Gardet and M. M. Anawati, *Introduction à la théologie musulmane* (Vrin, Paris, 1948); L. Gauthier, *Introduction à l'étude de la philosophie musulmane* (Paris, 1923); M. Horten, *Die philosophische Systeme der spekulativen Theologen im Islam* (Bonn, 1912); G. Quadri, *La Philosophie arabe dans l'Europe médiévale, des origines à Averroès* (Payot, Paris, 1947).

On medieval Jewish thought, consult I. Husik, *A History of Medieval Jewish Philosophy* (Jewish Publication Society of America, Philadelphia, 1946), and G. Vajda, *Introduction à la pensée juive du moyen âge* (Vrin, Paris, 1947).

The following are of interest in connection with certain problems covered in the present volume: R. Klibansky, *The Continuity of the Platonic Tradition During the Middle Ages*, I: *Outlines of a Corpus Platonicum Medii Aevi* (Warburg Institute, London, 1950); O. Lottin, *Psychologie et morale au XIIe et XIIIe siècles*, 4 vols. (Abbaye du Mont César, Louvain, 1942–1954); K. Michalski, *Le Problème de la volonté à Oxford et à Paris au XIVe siècle* (reprinted from *Studia philosophica*, Vol. II, Lvov,

1937); J. Rohmer, *La Finalité morale chez les théologiens de saint Augustin à Duns Scot* (Vrin, Paris, 1939).

A useful collection of translations of important philosophical texts, with introductions, will be found in R. McKeon, *Selections from Medieval Philosophers*, 2 vols. (Scribner, New York, 1929–1930).

OTHER ASPECTS OF MEDIEVAL THOUGHT

In the field of political theory, in addition to works already cited in connection with the problem of Church and State or the principles of canon law, the following should be mentioned: R. W. and A. J. Carlyle, *A History of Mediaeval Political Theory in the West*, 6 vols. (Blackwood, Edinburgh, 1903–1938); W. A. Dunning, *A History of Political Theories, Ancient and Mediaeval* (New York, 1927); O. Gierke, *Political Theories of the Middle Age* (Eng. tr. F. W. Maitland, University Press, Cambridge, 1951); B. Jarrett, *Social Theories of the Middle Ages* (Newman Book Shop, Westminster, Maryland, 1942); P. Vinogradoff, *Roman Law in Medieval Europe* (2d ed., Clarendon Press, Oxford, 1929).

On the role of medieval thinkers in the development of scientific theory, see P. Duhem, *Le Système du monde: histoire des doctrines cosmologiques de Platon à Copernic*, 5 vols. (Paris, 1913–1917), and C. H. Haskins, *Studies in the History of Mediaeval Science* (Cambridge, Massachusetts, 1924), as well as the histories of philosophy.

ANSELM OF CANTERBURY

Introduction to Anselm of Canterbury

I

ANSELM OF CANTERBURY HAS, NOT UNREASON-
ably, been named the "Father of Scholasticism."[1] His
work opened the second and decisive period in the
history of medieval thought, when the analysis of philosophical
ideas and their systematic theological use acquired a new
importance. In the eleventh century, more than a few theologians would have stopped short at Biblical exegesis, as
traditionally conceived; Anselm, however, spoke for the future
when he vindicated the rights of the Christian reason. Since he
wrote before the *logica nova* came into use,[2] he was restricted
in his application of dialectic to the problems of Christian
thought, but he did raise and answer the fundamental question.
In this way he prepared the ground for the advances of the
twelfth and thirteenth centuries, in which, thanks to the recovery and assimilation, first, of the Aristotelian logic and then
of the Aristotelian metaphysics and anthropology, medieval
philosophy and theology reached the peak of their development.

In 1076, when Anselm composed his *Monologion*, or *Example
of Meditation on the Grounds of Faith*, it was far from clear that
Christian thought was about to move in this direction. The
irresponsibility of the most fully committed "dialecticians,"
who often seemed to repudiate everything that lay beyond the
simplest rational explanation, constituted a real challenge to
the doctrinal tradition of the Church. The names of Berengar
of Tours and Roscellinus of Compiègne indicate the problem.
The former was condemned, not so much for criticizing the
dominant eucharistic theology, based on the doctrine of

[1] Cf. Gilson, *History*, 139; Grabmann, *Geschichte*, I, 58.
[2] On the *logica vetus* and *logica nova*, see the "General Introduction."

Paschasius Radbertus and Ambrose, in the interests of an interpretation that looked for its precedents to Ratramnus and Augustine, as for seeming to reduce the eucharistic mystery to a dialectical puzzle.[3] As for Roscellinus, his difficulties seem to have arisen, not from the deliberate intention of undermining dogmatic principles, but from the sheer impossibility of stating the doctrine of the Trinity in terms of the nominalism deduced by the dialecticians from the *logica vetus*.[4] It is not surprising, therefore, that many of the leaders of the revival of Church life in the eleventh century and later should have shown such reserve respecting the application of reason to the truths of faith. Deeply aware as they were of manifold threats to the integrity of the Church, the Gregorian reformers were hostile both to the political claims of feudal society and to the intellectual claims of dialectic. Thus, to men like Peter Damiani, Bruno of Segni or Manegold of Lautenbach, dialectic was at best the bondservant of faith—*ancilla theologiae* in the most radically subordinate sense.[5]

Anselm's response to the problem was more judicious. Though he was a loyal supporter of the movement for reform, and of the papal authority in which that movement had found its center, his whole temper of mind led him to seek a more excellent way than simple authoritarianism. Despite his hostility to the simple-minded rationalism of the dialectical extremists, he carefully kept to the path pointed out by his teacher and predecessor, Lanfranc, during the Berengarian controversy.[6] He attempted, in other words, to deal with the misuse of dialectic by exemplifying, even more wholeheartedly than Lanfranc, its proper Christian use, which he took so seriously as to consider it part of the responsibility of the mature believer.[7] Severely critical though he was of the superficialities of nominalism and the extravagances of rationalism, he was insistent on the real function of reason in the life of faith. Ironically enough, this deliberate two-sidedness of his thought has led some of his interpreters to label him as an extreme rationalist, tending to

3 Cf. J. Geiselmann, *Die Eucharistielehre der Vorscholastik* (Paderborn, 1926), 290–406.
4 Cf. F. Picavet, *Roscelin philosophe et théologien d'après la légende et d'après l'histoire* (Paris, 1911).
5 Cf. E. Gilson, "La Servante de la théologie," in his *Etudes de philosophie médiévale* (Strasbourg, 1921), 30–50.
6 Lanfranc's *De corpore et sanguine domini* will be found in *PL*, 150. Cf. A. J. Macdonald, *Lanfranc: A Study of his Life, Work and Writing* (enlarged ed., S.P.C.K., London, 1944), 41–55.   7 Cf. *Cur deus homo*, I, 1.

replace faith by reason, while others have tried to turn his use of reason into a pure exposition of faith, or even a kind of mysticism. We must, however, attempt a more balanced assessment of his position if we are to make any progress in the understanding of one of the greatest of Christian teachers.

Anselm's attitude is indicated fairly enough in the alternative title of the *Proslogion—Faith in Search of Understanding*. Dialectic is the instrument and not the source of faith. Nevertheless, faith cannot rest in itself, but must seek to understand through the work of reason. It is true that understanding has to do with the content of faith and begins with the assurance of faith. Anselm's purpose is to attain to an intermediate point between faith and vision, between the fundamental conviction of the Christian here below and the consummation of faith in unveiled communion with God hereafter.[8] At the same time, he sees in reason, guided by the principles of dialectic, the essential instrument of his purpose. The problem is to see how he relates these two factors, faith and reason, in his attempts to achieve understanding. We shall discover that, in relating them rather differently in different areas of his intellectual work, he becomes the parent at once of Christian philosophy and of scholastic theology.

II

The great charter of medieval Christian philosophy is to be found in the *Proslogion*, written about 1077–1078 to perfect the rational approach to God begun in the *Monologion*.[9] While Anselm's entire intellectual effort could be described as "faith seeking understanding," the formula was initially applied to the kind of argument used in these works. To describe this method as "philosophical" is, of course, to disagree with some of the most distinguished contemporary interpreters of Anselm's thought, and perhaps to court misunderstanding as well. Nevertheless, I think that it can only be made intelligible as a philosophical method. We must, indeed, reckon with the conclusions often drawn from Anselm's general formulation of the relation of reason to faith. For him, reason functions within the context of faith; we believe with a view to understanding,

---

8 Cf. *De fide trinitatis* [*Epist. de incarn. verbi*], *praef.*: "I understand the *intellectus*, which we receive in this life, to be a kind of mean between faith and vision" (*PL*, 158, 261; Schmitt does not include the *praefatio* in his text of the work but prefixes it to *Cur deus homo* [II, 39–41]).
9 For the dates of Anselm's writings, cf. Landgraf, *Einführung*, 52 f.

and do not seek understanding in order to believe. We can, however, question the impossibility of a genuine "philosophy" in this context and under these conditions. If there were no other reason for raising this question, we should be compelled to do so by the failure of alternative explanations of the argument of the *Proslogion*.

The alternative most sharply opposed to a philosophical interpretation is presented by Anselm Stolz, for whom the *Proslogion* is a piece of mystical theology. "Nothing," he writes, "is more preposterous than to see a philosopher in the author of the *Proslogion*."[10] Anselm is looking for an understanding that lies between faith and vision, and this can only be a union with God in contemplation, parallel to the union with God in the joy of charity sought by Cistercian mysticism. Anselm's effort of intelligence is analogous to Bernard's mystical *askesis*.

This interpretation is not easy to reconcile with the dialectical character of Anselm's argument. It is true that the latter at least once links understanding and "experience" in such a way as to suggest an intimate connection of his intellectual enterprise with contemplation of and experienced communion with God.[11] The point at issue, however, is the nature of this contemplation, and it is clear that, motivated though the argument of the *Proslogion* is by love for God, it is essentially intellectual, concerned with rational apprehension rather than affective experience.[12] To call this effort "mysticism" is to broaden that term beyond any definite meaning.

Karl Barth offers a more plausible interpretation, when he asserts that all Anselm's work is essentially theological.[13] By this he means that it is an attempt to use reason to draw out the content of the Biblical affirmations. On this assumption, Barth presents the *Proslogion* as a study of the implications of the "divine Name," and not as a proof of the existence of God.[14] Like everything else that Anselm wrote, it begins with faith in the God of revelation, and looks forward with eschatological longing to complete vision.[15]

This exegesis has the merit of accounting for the starting point and the declared motive of the *Proslogion*. It makes sense both of the repeated emphasis on the priority of faith and of the

---

[10] A. Stolz, "Zur Theologie Anselms im Proslogion," *Catholica*, 2 (1933), 1–21.
[11] Cf. *Epist. de incarn. verbi*, 1 (tr. below).   [12] Cf. *ibid.* (Schmitt, II, 17).
[13] Cf. K. Barth, *Fides quaerens intellectum* (Kaiser, Munich, 1931).
[14] Cf. *ibid.*, 76.   [15] Cf. *ibid.*, 11–13.

contemplative form of the argument. Too rational for mysticism, the little book does seem too devotional for philosophy. Moreover, Barth's argument makes a strong appeal to at least two widely divergent outlooks. From the standpoint of "neo-Orthodoxy," it may make Anselm a witness to an "ultra-Augustinian" repudiation of natural theology. From the viewpoint of at least one type of "neo-Scholasticism," it may spare us from having to explain how Anselm can be a real philosopher when he is so dependent on faith. Nonetheless, there are insuperable difficulties in Barth's presentation. To begin with, Anselm does not claim to be elucidating the "divine Name," given in revelation, but insists that he is "proving" God's existence. Moreover, while he begins his argument within the framework of faith, and takes its premise (namely, the notion of God as "that than which a greater cannot be thought") from the revealed truth of God's nature, he supposes that the notion of God, once stated, is evident to unbelievers, and that his argument from that notion, once carried through, is independent of faith.[16] If this is theology, it looks very much like "natural theology"!

Both these interpretations are criticized by Etienne Gilson, who shows how neither can account for more than certain aspects of Anselm's argument.[17] His own alternative, however, is inconclusive. In support of his thesis that the *Proslogion* is not philosophy, any more than it is theology or mysticism, Gilson observes that Anselm never describes his work as "philosophy"—a term that he associated with paganism and its radical limitations.[18] He notes also that, even if the methodology of the *Proslogion* is not necessarily determinative for Anselm's thought as a whole, it is applied in the *Monologion* to the ultimate Christian mystery, the doctrine of the Trinity, which it would seem rather perverse to identify as an object of "philosophy."[19] Having dismissed three proposed interpretations, Gilson inquires why we should not ask history to tell us what doctrinal pigeonholes we must provide, instead of looking for doctrines to fit into our accepted pigeonholes, and suggests that a compartment marked "Christian Gnosticism" is needed to accommodate Anselm's argument.[20]

It is difficult, all the same, to avoid the suspicion that

16 Cf. *Proslogion*, 4.
17 Cf. E. Gilson, "Sens et nature de l'argument de saint Anselme," *Archives d'histoire doctrinale et littéraire du moyen âge*, 9 (1934), 5–51.
18 Cf. *ibid.*, 43.   19 Cf. *ibid.*, 23, 47.   20 Cf. *ibid.*, 43, 49 ff.

"Christian Gnosticism" stands for a whole set of pigeonholes, in which mysticism, theology, and philosophy each have a place. I call the third element in this complex "philosophy," because I do not see what else it can be and still remain a coherent procedure. At any rate, it will be wise to investigate the philosophical interpretation of the *Proslogion* before even seeming to attribute vagueness or confusion to such a tidy and precise thinker as Anselm.[21]

Certainly, the fact that Anselm did not think of himself as a "philosopher" does not prove that he was not thinking philosophically. Nor, unless we assume that genuine philosophy must be, at the very least, indifferent to faith, need Anselm's emphasis on the latter disturb us. For even though the idea of God is presented to us by revelation, once it is grasped by the mind its intrinsic necessity ensures its objectivity, according to Anselm's own metaphysic of truth. Once the idea takes shape in our minds, it falls under a general theory of truth, which asserts that every necessary proposition is true, and that every true thought implies the reality of its object. As Gilson points out, this is not a deduction of God's existence from the idea of his existence, but a statement of the necessary implications of the idea of God, given Anselm's epistemology. It is not a vicious circle, because it discovers and does not assume the existence of God. It discovers this in clarifying the necessity of affirming it.[22] If an idea is necessary, and therefore true and right, its *rectitudo* presupposes its objectivity, just as the rectitude of the will when man acts presupposes an objective standard to which the will conforms. What the argument of the *Proslogion* is essentially concerned to do is to show the necessary existence of the supreme truth and goodness on which the ultimate rectitude of mind and will depends, and to show this by way of the unique necessity implicit in the very notion of the divine Being.

Inasmuch as the idea from which the proof is developed is intelligible to the "fool" as well as to the believer, it is hard to see how this can be interpreted except as a philosophical proof, open to philosophical criticism and distortion. It can be criticized by questioning the implied doctrine of truth—that is, since Anselm's philosophy has an Augustinian basis, by questioning the Augustinian doctrine of the illumination of our minds by the divine truth in all certain judgments.[23] On the

---

21 Cf. *ibid.*, 49.   22 Cf. *ibid.*, 15.
23 Cf. A. Koyré, *L'Idée de Dieu dans la philosophie de saint Anselme* (Paris, 1923), Chapter 7.

other hand, it will be distorted if we try to make sense of it out of this context. This, of course, is what happened when it found itself, as the "ontological argument," in the philosophies of Descartes, Leibniz, and Hegel, dominated as these were by the principle of autonomous reason.[24] But this was a risk it had to run as a genuinely philosophical doctrine.

We must not, then, overstate the dependence of Anselm's argument on faith. Anselm intends to avoid subjecting the assurance of faith to the judgment of dialectic, rather than to assert any simple dependence of reason on faith.[25] As for the objection that he concedes more to reason, as he uses it, than later theology would allow to philosophy, this is probably nothing more than a matter of dialectical exuberance, under the influence of the temper of the times.[26] Certainly, we are not entitled to conclude from it that his rational speculation was not intended to be what we should call philosophical.

In the light of the foregoing, it does not seem unreasonable to claim Anselm as the parent of a mode of thought which, while it finds its center in the issues where philosophy and faith overlap—supremely, then, in the questions of being and God, and of human nature and destiny—and recognizes in faith the ultimate key to reality, is genuinely philosophical, working from principles accessible to reason. In its original sense, the formula *fides quaerens intellectum* does provide a program for just such a "Christian philosophy" and, whatever else it may mean, *intellectus* does include the quest for philosophical demonstration.[27]

III

It is, however, from the same impulse toward *intellectus* that scholastic theology emerges and begins to raise dialectical questions about the mysteries of faith. The great example of this kind of investigation, which moves more definitely within the framework of Christian dogma, and bases its deductions on the assumed coherence of revealed truth, is *Cur deus homo*, although other treatises (notably *Epistola de incarnatione verbi* and *De conceptu virginali*) must be taken into account.

24 For the later history of the argument, cf. G. Runze, *Die ontologische Gottesbeweis* (Halle, 1882), or any standard history of philosophy.
25 Cf. *Proslogion*, 1; *Epist. de incarn. verbi*, 1; *Cur deus homo*, I, 25.
26 Cf. Gilson, *art. cit.*, 20, n. 1; M. Cappuyns, "L'argument de saint Anselme," *Recherches de théologie ancienne et médiévale*, 6 (1934), 320.
27 Cf. Gilson, *Spirit.* 34–41; but note modification in Gilson, *art. cit.*, 48, n. 2.

Since Anselm speaks in *Cur deus homo*, just as in his more philosophical moods, of "understanding" and "necessary reasoning," and formulates the "necessary reasons" for the incarnation in deliberate abstraction from the fact of Christ's existence,[28] it may seem perverse to distinguish his technique here from that of the *Proslogion*. Is not his whole theology a rationalism which, far from losing philosophy in faith, reduces the understanding of faith to philosophy? He does, indeed, rely heavily on close-knit reasoning, so that arguments which others might use to clarify the inherent intelligibility of the nature and acts of God are presented by him as "necessary reasons," quite explicitly distinguished from arguments from "congruity."[29] But this theological rationalism must not be construed in a naturalistic sense. When he offers necessary reasons, in contrast to mere probabilities, his essential claim is that his arguments are based on objective and unchanging truth, and demand certain assent, and he does not intend to stress the aspect of reason in opposition to faith. Thus the argument of *Cur deus homo*, for all its abstraction from faith in Christ, starts from the dogmatic principles of creation, eternal life, and original sin.[30] It may be that here, as in his whole attitude towards reason and truth, he assumes too simple a correspondence between the necessities of human reasoning and objective reality, and that in particular he sometimes overlooks the mystery of God's freedom.[31] In this respect, his theology is at the opposite pole to the voluntarism of Ockham, at the close of the great age of medieval thought.[32] But if it is rationalism, it is a genuinely theological rationalism, and in this expression of *fides quaerens intellectum* Anselm reveals himself as the parent of scholastic theology.

IV

Cur deus homo, Anselm's theological masterpiece, has given rise to a good deal of controversy and misrepresentation respecting the substance of its argument. Thus, while the text can speak for itself, it will be useful to indicate what it is and is not

[28] Cf. *Cur deus homo*, I, 10; 20.
[29] Cf. A. Jacquin, "Les 'rationes necessariae' de saint Anselme," *Mélanges Mandonnet*, II, 71 f.
[30] Cf. *Cur deus homo*, II, 1–4.
[31] But cf. *ibid.*, II, 5.
[32] On the voluntarist and libertarian motives of Ockham's teaching, cf. Gilson, *History*, 498 f.

intended to prove. This can best be done against a brief statement of the background of Anselm's work.[33]

The treatise is, at least in part, a response to the apologetic need for an intelligible formulation of the doctrine of redemption.[34] It tries to show how the atonement is related to the nature of God and man, and to the exigencies of the human situation—all in terms of the deepest meaning of the sacrifice of the God-Man, rather than with the help of the images to which the great Biblical and patristic symbol of man's redemption from bondage had been reduced by lesser writers. It is not that this great symbol—Gustaf Aulén's "classical" theory[35]—is ignored by Anselm; on the contrary, what he is really trying to do is to show how man's release from slavery to sin and death was accomplished. But it must be admitted that his picture of the process is rather different from that of some of his critics!

Despite the absence of sacrificial terminology, the core of Anselm's soteriology is an explanation of the work of redemption along the lines of the most profound and authentically "classical" presentation offered by Hebrews. In the latter, man's deliverance from sin and death is rooted in the taking of human nature by the divine Son, so that in that nature he might be the true priest, offering the acceptable sacrifice for human sin, and so opening the way to eternal life with God.[36] In this doctrine[37] there are two inseparable elements: the initiative of divine love and power and the Godward action of human nature. Contrary to the widespread impression that the patristic doctrine was almost exclusively concerned with the manward (or "devilward") action of God—described variously as "deification," "rescue," or "ransom," or expressed in more bizarre symbols of a transaction with Satan—in which human nature played only a passive role,[38] these two elements are consistently present in the Fathers, both Greek and Latin, although in varying proportions. What Anselm does is to

---

[33] Cf. J. Rivière, various works listed below.
[34] Cf. *Cur deus homo*, I, 1–4; Gilbert Crispin, *Disp. Iudaei cum Christiano* (PL, 159, 1005–1036); R. W. Southern, *The Making of the Middle Ages*, 234–237.
[35] Cf. G. Aulén, *Christus Victor* (S.P.C.K., London, 1931), 20–23.
[36] Cf. Heb. 2:9–18; 4:14 to 5:10; 10:10, 19–22.
[37] Note the parallels in the Pauline presentation of our salvation through the obedience of Christ (Rom., ch. 5), in Ephesians (chs. 4:31 to 5:2), and elsewhere.
[38] This merely ornamental function of human nature seems to be what Aulén means by "continuity" (cf. *op. cit.*, 21 f.).

grasp both elements, with a clearsightedness unknown at least
to his immediate predecessors, and express them in terms of the
"satisfaction" made to the divine honor, or reparation paid to
the divine glory—a concept which not only appears verbally in
the Latin Fathers, but also expresses an essential idea of their
theology.[39] Even if we regret the concentration on one formula,
to the exclusion of others more deeply rooted in Scripture and
in the Church's eucharistic worship, we should not dismiss
Anselm's view that he is at least trying to express a Biblical
idea in patristic language.[40]

As for the main points of his argument, we must recognize
in the first place that he is attempting to explain the divine
humility in the incarnation, and that he achieves this with
matchless clarity by expounding the essence of man's redemption
as a divine-human work. From start to finish the argument is
dominated by the action of God—of God who made man,[41] of
God who was made man to offer, in manhood, an acceptable
satisfaction to the divine nature.[42] There is duality, of course,
in the sense that the satisfaction required and made is a human
act, but there is an underlying unity in the fact that it is God's

---

[39] Cf. Hilary of Poitiers, *In Ps.*, 53, 12 (*PL*, 9, 344): "That passion was freely
undertaken, itself truly to make satisfaction for penal obligation";
Fulgentius of Ruspe, *Epist.* 14:37 (*PL*, 65, 425): "And yet a victim could
not have been offered by us, if Christ had not been made a victim for us
—Christ in whom the very nature of our race is a true saving victim";
Gregory, *Moralia*, XVII, 30:46 (*PL*, 76, 32): "A man was to be sought
who should be offered for men, so that for the rational sinner a rational
victim might be immolated."

[40] To suggest that this formulation is dependent on (of all things) feudal
notions of honor is quite gratuitous, even though his social environment may have contributed to the form of expression he adopts. It is,
I think, correct to relate Anselm's soteriology to the developed penitential
system, where secular influences (such as the Teutonic *Wergeld*) may have
exercised considerable influence; cf. J. T. McNeill and H. M. Gamer,
Medieval Handbooks of Penance (Columbia University Press, New York,
1938), 35 ff. It should be noted, however, that the penitential system has
a very long history, and that the connection of this system with the
theology of the atonement began quite early (cf. n. 39, above), so that
the background of Anselm's doctrine is much more complex than the
exponents of a simple "feudalist" interpretation recognize. McIntyre's
comment is relevant to the whole problem: "The Church had a long
tradition of theology about penitence, and this tradition determined
the kind of use its exponents made of contemporary ideas. So long as that
tradition and the theological concepts associated with it remained
dominant, the secular influence could only be secondary" (J. McIntyre,
St. Anselm and His Critics, Oliver and Boyd, Edinburgh, 1954, p. 86).

[41] Cf. *Cur deus homo*, II, 1; 4.   [42] Cf. *ibid.*, II, 6–7.

omnipotent love that makes an acceptable human act possible. Anselm is concerned at once to stress the truth that God alone can be man's Redeemer, and to show the real significance of his taking human nature and dying a human death.

Secondly, Anselm avoids the slightest suggestion that the atonement is the placating of an angry God, the satisfaction of an offended Father by the punishment of a loving Son. Satisfaction means the reconciliation of man to God, the restoration of man to his true relation to God, the renewal of the moral order of God's world.[43] When Anselm argues that the honor of God must be satisfied, he clearly asserts that it is God who has undertaken the satisfaction of his own honor.[44] Furthermore, God has done this, not because man's sin affects him in his transcendent being or rouses him to wrath,[45] but because his love will not leave man in bondage to sin and death, while man can be restored in a way compatible with his own nature and dignity as a spiritual creature only if God makes it possible for man's blasphemy to be rectified on man's side.[46] If Anselm asserts that it is unfitting for God to leave his own honor unsatisfied, his whole line of argument makes it clear that this assertion assumes God's purpose in creating man for eternal blessedness. In other words, he presupposes the delicate balance of the Christian doctrine of creation, which states that God created man out of sheer *agape*, but that man can find his true good, and so realize God's purpose, only by living to God's glory.

Thirdly, the Anselmian doctrine is not a doctrine of "substitution," if this signifies a kind of transaction between Father and Son, to which mankind is juridically related. It is true that the argument ends with the suggestion that it is equitable for the satisfaction, which Christ made but did not need for himself, to be applied to man's salvation.[47] We must note, however, that, according to Anselm's own fundamental theory, the possibility of this application rests on the community, not only of nature but also of race, between Christ and mankind.[48] Moreover, in his devotional writings in particular, he gives eloquent expression to his sense of the communion of Christians with the Son of God in his incarnation and Passion. Thus, if Anselm insists that only the God-Man can make acceptable satisfaction for sin, we cannot leap to the conclusion that this

---

43 Cf. *ibid.*, I, 12–13; 21–23; S. H. Mellone, *Western Christian Thought in the Middle Ages*, 99 f.
44 Cf. *Cur deus homo*, II, 6–8.
45 Cf. *ibid.*, I, 15.
46 Cf. *ibid.*, I, 19; 24.
47 Cf. *ibid.*, II, 19.
48 Cf. *ibid.*, II, 8.

satisfaction is efficacious for others simply by way of forensic imputation. It is true that the later theology of the atonement in the West (including the theology of Protestant Scholasticism) was dominated by Anselm's formulation of the issues, but that does not mean that he was responsible for all the vagaries of later speculation.

V

While the influence of Anselm's soteriology is generally known, it is not always recognized that, at least from the end of the twelfth century, his doctrine of original sin was more influential still, even to the point of overcoming the prestige of Augustine. The latter was commonly interpreted as identifying the essence of original sin with "concupiscence," the innate tendency to evil that affects man's sense-life.[49] To this line of thought Anselm opposed the thesis that original sin is the deprivation of the original justice enjoyed by our first parents. Since the latter, according to Anselm's doctrine of justice, consisted of the rectitude of the will (i.e., of its conformity to the divine will), original sin is essentially the privation of this rectitude. Thus the "inordinate affection" of concupiscence— the rebellion of the senses against the reason—is reduced to a mere effect of the rebellion of the rational will against God.

In the twelfth century, while Anselm's doctrine was main-tained by Odo of Tournai[50] and received partial support from other writers, and while it opened the way to other departures from Augustinianism, such as the theories of Abailard and Stephen Langton, the Augustinian position still held the field, supported as it was by the school of Anselm of Laon, by Peter Lombard, Robert of Melun, and other important writers. Anselm of Canterbury's doctrine, however, won over the greatest theologians of the later Middle Ages—though at first, at least, in a modified form—thanks to the mediating formula of Albert the Great, who taught that there are two essential factors in original sin: privation of justice as the "formal" and concupiscence as the "material" element. This means that man's sinful condition lies primarily in the loss of the gratuitous gifts which maintained and ordered his nature in a right

---

[49] On divergent medieval and modern treatments of Augustine's doctrine, cf. J. de Blic, "Le Péché originel selon saint Augustin," *Recherches de science religieuse*, 16 (1926), 97–119.
[50] Cf. his work, *De peccato originali* (PL, 160, 1071–1102).

relation to God, and only secondly in the expression of this loss in man's sensuous nature. Despite Bonaventure's attempt to use Albert's formula, while retaining an Augustinian emphasis on concupiscence, the development was bound to end in an Anselmian victory, particularly in the light of the more precise discrimination of nature and grace characteristic of Thomas Aquinas and his successors. In fact, as time went on, Anselm's doctrine itself was reinterpreted along the lines of an identification of original sin with the privation of sanctifying grace, while even the "preternatural" gifts of paradisal man, associated with older ideas of original justice and original sin, were pushed into the background.[51]

The importance of the whole discussion lies in the clarification of the typically "Catholic" idea of original sin as a twofold state or condition: the deprivation of grace, and the consequences of that loss for the stability and well-being of human nature. Because of Anselm's work, the line was sharply drawn between this doctrine and any attempts to turn the "Fall" into a metaphysical catastrophe or a symbol of an essential aspect of human nature. I suspect that for this he would have received Augustine's commendation against some, at least, of the "Augustinianisms" that later history has so freely produced.

VI

What the great Christian teachers of the Middle Ages said in their classrooms or wrote in their books cannot be isolated from their participation in the spiritual life of the Church and their contribution to the forms of that life. As far as Anselm is concerned, his special place in the history of Christian devotion rests on his encouragement and expression of "Marian" piety. Thus, for instance, in his prayers to Mary he provides one of the most graceful and moving examples of a tendency which, while rooted in the patristic age, took in the Middle Ages new forms which are still characteristic of Latin Christendom. Theological criticisms apart, the rather high-flown language of these prayers will not appeal to every taste. Such language is, however, the common idiom of Anselm's devotional writings, and it is applied here to a theme to which the medieval soul devoted some of its most intense poetic efforts.

51 For this outline, cf. O. Lottin, *Psychologie et morale aux XIIe et XIIIe siècles*, IV (Pt. 3:1 [Abbaye du Mont César, Louvain, 1954]), 9–280; A. Michel, art. "Justice originelle," *DTC*, 8, 2039–2041.

The earlier Middle Ages had already given a considerable impetus to Marian theology and piety, with a certain emphasis on the doctrine of the assumption. In the eleventh and twelfth centuries, however, theology and devotion moved further along two lines: speculation about Mary's immaculate conception, and a more human and warmly emotional piety, intimately related to the new types of devotion to the humanity of Christ. The fact that Anselm and Bernard, the two greatest exponents of the new types of Marian devotion, did not accept the idea of the immaculate conception shows that these two tendencies were not inseparably connected. That they were, nevertheless, closely associated, is indicated by the emergence of both, not only in the same geographical area—England and Normandy —but also in the same circles. Thus, if Anselm did not recognize the immaculate conception, it was among men closely connected with him that the feast of the conception of Mary was first introduced into the West, while it was his own companion and secretary, Eadmer, who, when he had simply reproduced Anselm's teaching in his *On the Excellency of the Virgin Mary*,[52] went on, in his *On the Conception of Saint Mary*,[53] to deduce an explicit affirmation of the immaculate conception from his teacher's own principles.

Anselm, then, contributed indirectly to the doctrinal development which culminated in Duns Scotus and was finally canonized for the Roman Church by Pius IX.[54] His direct contribution, however, to the exaltation of Mary, lay in the area of devotional expression. "Saint Anselm continues to exalt the greatness of Mary, as tradition did, and to insist on her eminent role in the work of grace; but he introduces into the relations of the soul with Mary a gentleness and tenderness that were rare up to that point."[55] In this way he played his part in the "humanizing" of piety toward the incarnation, so characteristic of the later Middle Ages.[56] It may be argued that in the long run devotion to Mary had a rather ambiguous effect on this process, since concentration on the "Mother of mercy" could (and often did) lead to an emphasis on Christ as the divine Judge rather than to a deeper awareness of Christ's

---

52 *PL*, 159, 557–580.
53 *PL*, 159, 301–318.
54 In the bull *Ineffabilis Deus*, of December 8, 1854.
55 J. Leclercq, in H. du Manoir (ed.), *Maria*, II (Beauchesne, Paris, 1952), 556.
56 Cf. G. L. Prestige, *Fathers and Heretics* (S.P.C.K., London, 1940), 383–403.

humanity. It is easy, however, to exaggerate this development, and to overlook the intimate association of Marian piety and "Christ-mysticism" in some of the most important expressions of the medieval spirit. Certainly Anselm's type of devotion to Mary reveals the same motives that underlay the emergence, under Franciscan influence, of the Christmas "Crib" and the "Stations of the Cross," and that contributed largely to the characteristic medieval development of eucharistic piety.

VII

Anselm was prevented by historical necessities from living as a simple monk and scholar. The reforming movement, with its concern for the freedom of the Church to perform its essential function in human life, had precipitated conflicts in which he found himself deeply involved. On the whole, his role in the controversies of his time, centered round the issue of "investitures," was a pacific one. While he was well aware of the necessity of reform in the Church's life and independence for the Church's action, he does not seem to have been an enthusiastic supporter of the advanced "Gregorian" policy. His loyalty to the papacy has a clear witness in his sufferings on its behalf, but he rested his case on the authority of the pope rather than on a theory of the ideal relations of the Church and the civil power. Thus the "anti-Gregorian" tendencies of Paschal II seem to have met with his somewhat relieved approval, and he took no action to make difficulties for those churchmen who had failed to follow him in the strenuous period between his breach with William II and his reconciliation with Henry I. Perhaps we should see here, as in his attitude toward dialectic, that judicious moderation which made him the type of the best in medieval thought, and enabled so much of his work to survive the upheavals of later history, both intellectual and ecclesiastical.[57]

[57] On Anselm's political activities, cf. H. W. C. Davis, art. "Anselm," *DECH*, 16–18. There is an extensive account of Anselm's conflict and reconciliation with Henry I in Eadmer's *Historia novorum*, from which an excerpt is printed below, after the texts of Anselm himself. The terms of the reconciliation anticipate those of the settlement of the German Investiture Controversy in the Worms Concordat of 1122. Text of the latter in C. Mirbt, *Quellen zur Geschichte des Papsttums und des römischen Katholizismus* (Mohr, Tübingen, 1934), 161 f.; translation in B. J. Kidd, *Documents Illustrative of the History of the Church*, III (S.P.C.K., London, 1941), 140–142.

VIII

Anselm was born at Aosta, now in the northwest corner of Piedmont, and then belonging to the Kingdom of Burgundy, in or about 1033. His father was a Lombard landowner, his mother a Burgundian of royal (or at least noble) descent. Accounts of his childhood and youth portray him as sensitive, studious, and devout; there is some doubt of the weight to be given to his self-accusations of later wild conduct. About 1056, after a quarrel with his father, he set out to see the world, arriving in 1059 at the Norman abbey of Bec, which had been founded in 1034 by the knight Herluin, and raised from obscurity by the brilliant teaching of the famous Lanfranc of Pavia. In 1060 he took monastic vows at Bec, and in 1063, on Lanfranc's departure to the new foundation of Saint-Etienne at Caen, he succeeded him as prior. In 1078 he became abbot of Bec, having already administered the abbey during Herluin's last years. In 1093, after a good deal of skirmishing with William II, he was named and consecrated archbishop of Canterbury. Because of his support of the papal position, he lived in exile, in Italy and elsewhere, from 1097 until William's death in 1100, and again from 1103 to 1106. Returning to Canterbury in that year, he died in the early morning of Wednesday in Holy Week, April 21, 1109.[58] In his own writings, as in his friends' narratives, Anselm appears as an acute thinker, a devout Christian, a loyal churchman, a conscientious ruler, a gentle teacher and guide.[59]

[58] See the list of biographical material below.
[59] This last characteristic is pleasantly illustrated by the second passage from Anselm's friend and biographer, Eadmer, "On the Upbringing of Boys," below.

BIBLIOGRAPHY

TEXTS

The standard edition of Gabriel Gerberon (Paris, 1675, reprinted in *PL*, 158–159) has now been replaced by the critical edition of F. S. Schmitt, *Sancti Anselmi Cantuariensis Archiepiscopi Opera Omnia*. The five volumes have a rather checkered history, thanks to wartime crises, but all have been published in Great Britain by Thomas Nelson (Edinburgh, 1946–1951). Attention should also be drawn to Schmitt's earlier editions of separate works (Hanstein, Bonn, various dates) and to his publication *Ein neues unvollendetes Werk des hl. Anselm von Canterbury* (*Beiträge*, 33/3 [1936]). Eadmer's biographical writings can be found in *PL*, 158, 49 ff., and 159, 341 ff., and in a more modern edition in M. Rule (ed.), *Eadmeri Historia novorum in Anglia et opuscula duo de vita sancti Anselmi et quibusdam miraculis eius* (Rolls Series, London, 1884).

TRANSLATIONS

The only satisfactory English translations of Anselm are the versions of the *De veritate*, by R. McKeon ("Saint Anselm, Dialogue on Truth," in *Selections*, I, 150–184), and *Proslogion*, by A. C. Pegis (*The Wisdom of Catholicism* [Random House, New York, 1949], 203–228). A clumsy and sometimes inaccurate rendering of certain texts will be found in S. N. Deane, *St. Anselm: Proslogium; Monologium; an Appendix on Behalf of the Fool by Gaunilon; and Cur Deus Homo* (Chicago, 1903). A rather better translation of *Cur deus homo*, with a selection of letters, was published anonymously in "The Ancient and Modern Library of Theological Literature" (London, n.d.). The version by E. S. Prout in an earlier "Christian Classics Series" (London, n.d.) may also be noted.

63

French translations include: A. Koyré, *Fides quaerens intellectum, i.e., Proslogion* (Vrin, Paris, 1930); text and translation; P. Rousseau, *Oeuvres philosophiques de saint Anselm* (Aubier, Paris, 1945); translations of *Monologian, Proslogion, De veritate*, etc.

German translations include: R. Allers, *Anselm von Canterbury: Leben, Lehre, Werke* (Thomas-Verlag, Vienna, 1936); good introductory material, translations of *Monologion, Proslogion*, and several other works (whole or part); A. Kemmer, *Mystiches Beten: Proslogion und ausgewählte Gebete* (Rex-Verlag, Lucerne, 1949); A. Stolz, *Anselm von Canterbury* (Kösel-Pustet, Munich, 1937); translations of *Proslogion, Monologion, Cur deus homo*, and some smaller pieces.

Spanish translations include: B. Maas (introduction by G. Blanco), *Proslogion* (Ministerio de Educación, Buenos Aires, 1950).

LIFE AND GENERAL INTRODUCTION

R. W. Church, *Saint Anselm* (London, 1905), is a classic, and very valuable as a brief introduction to Anselm's life and character. J. Clayton, *St. Anselm: A Critical Biography* (Bruce, Milwaukee, 1933), is accurate on the whole, but sometimes irrelevantly polemical. There is a useful and sympathetic account of Anselm's life, with a brief survey of his writings, in J. T. McNeill, *Makers of Christianity* (New York, 1935, pp. 106–114). M. Rule, *The Life and Times of St. Anselm*, 2 vols. (London, 1883), is very full and informative, but marred by too numerous digressions. C. de Rémusat, *Anselme de Cantorbéry, tableau de la vie monastique et de la lutte du pouvoir spirituel avec le pouvoir temporel au XIᵉ siècle* (2d ed., Paris, 1868), still merits attention.

See also: G. Ceriani, *S. Anselmo* ("La scuola," Brescia, 1946); E. Domet de Vorges, *Saint Anselme* (Paris, 1901); A. Levasti, *Sant' Anselmo, vita e pensiero* (Laterza, Bari, 1929); H. Ostlender, *Anselm von Canterbury, der Vater der Scholastik* (Düsseldorf, 1927); J. M. Rigg, *St. Anselm of Canterbury: A Chapter in the History of Religion* (London, 1896); A. C. Welch, *Anselm and His Work* (New York, 1901); *Revue de philosophie*, 15 (1909), devoted to studies of Anselm; J. Bainvel, art. "Anselme de Cantorbéry," *DTC*, 1, 1327–1360; H. W. C. Davis, art. "Anselm," *DECH*, 16–18; W. H. Kent, art. "Anselm, Saint," *CE*, 1, 546–550; W. R. W. Stephens, art. "Anselm," *DNB*, 2, 10–31; F. S. Schmitt, "Zur Chronologie der Werke des hl. Anselm von Canterbury," *Revue Bénédictine*, 44 (1932), 322–350.

PHILOSOPHICAL TEACHING

There is no definitive work on the philosophical elements in Anselm's thought comparable to the studies by E. Gilson of Augustine, Bonaventure, Aquinas, and Duns Scotus. The best work available is probably C. Filliatre, *La Philosophie de saint Anselme, ses principes, sa nature, son influence* (Paris, 1920).

See also: F. Baeumker, *Die Lehre Anselms von Canterbury über den Willen und seine Wahlfreiheit* (*Beiträge*, 10/6 [1912]); A. Cichetti, *L'agostinismo nel pensiero di Anselmo d'Aosta* (Rome, 1951); J. Fischer, *Die Erkenntnislehre Anselms von Canterbury* (*Beiträge*, 10/3 [1911]); E. Lohmeyer, *Die Lehre vom Willen bei Anselm von Canterbury* (Lucka, 1914); S. vanni Rovighi, *Sant' Anselmo e la filosofia del secolo XI* (Fratelli Bocca, Milan, 1949); N. Balthasar, "Idéalisme anselmien et réalisme thomiste," *Annales de l'Institut supérieur de philosophie*, 1 (1912), 431–467. M. Losacco, "La dialettica in Anselmo d'Aosta," *Sophia*, 1 (1933), 188–193.

PROSLOGION

One book and three articles are of particular importance as introductions to the method and argument of the *Proslogion*: K. Barth, *Fides quaerens intellectum: Anselms Beweis der Existenz Gottes in Zusammenhang seines theologischen Programms* (Kaiser, Munich, 1931); M. Cappuyns, "L'Argument de saint Anselme," *Recherches de théologie ancienne et médiévale*, 6 (1934), 313–330; E. Gilson, "Sens et nature de l'argument de saint Anselme," *Archives d'histoire doctrinale et littéraire du moyen âge*, 9 (1934), 5–51; A. Stolz, "Zur Theologie Anselms im Proslogion," *Catholica*, 2 (1933), 1–21.

See also: A. Daniels, *Quellenbeiträge und Untersuchungen zur Geschichte der Gottesbeweise in dreizehnten Jahrhundert mit besonderer Berücksichtigung des Arguments im Proslogion des hl. Anselm* (*Beiträge*, 8/1–2 [1909]); A. Koyré *L'Idée de Dieu dans la philosophie de saint Anselme* (Paris, 1923); J. Marias, *San Anselmo y el insensato, y otros estudios de filosofía* (2d ed., Revista de Occidente, Madrid, 1954); G. Runze, *Der ontologische Gottesbeweis, kritische Darstellung seiner Geschichte seit Anselm bis auf die Gegenwart* (Halle, 1882); J. L. Springer, *Argumentum ontologicum: proeve eener existentieele interpretatie van het speculatieve godsbewijs in het Proslogion van S. Anselmus, aartsbisschop van Canterbury* (Van Gorcum, Assen, 1946); A. Stöckl, *De argumento, ut vocant, ontologico* (Munich, 1862); A. Antweiler, "Anselmus von Canterbury, Monologion und

Proslogion," *Scholastik*, 8 (1933), 551–560; F. S. Schmitt, "Der ontologische Gottesbeweis Anselms," *Theologische Revue*, 32 (1933), 211–223; F. Spedalieri, "Anselmus an Gaunilo? seu de recta argumenti sancti doctoris interpretatione," *Gregorianum*, 28 (1947), 55–77; F. Spedalieri, "De intrinseca argumenti sancti Anselmi vi et natura," *Gregorianum*, 29 (1948), 204–212; A. Stolz, " 'Vere esse' im Proslogion des hl. Anselm," *Scholastik*, 9 (1934), 400–409; A. Stolz, "Das Proslogion des hl. Anselm," *Revue Bénédictine*, 47 (1935), 331–347.

THEOLOGY

Two articles on the significance of Anselm's "necessary reasons" should be consulted: A. Jacquin, "Les 'rationes necessariae' de saint Anselme," *Mélanges Mandonnet* (Vrin, Paris, 1930), II, 67–78; C. Ottaviano, "Le 'rationes necessariae' in San Anselmo," *Sophia*, 1 (1933), 91–97.

See also: J. S. de Aguirre, *Sancti Anselmi theologia*, 3 vols. (Salamanca, 1678–1681; 2d ed., Rome, 1688–1690); R. Perino, *La dottrina trinitaria di S. Anselmo nel quadro del suo metodo teologico e del suo concetto di Dio* (Herder, Rome, 1952); J. Porta, *Theologia scholastica secundum principia sancti Anselmi* (Rome, 1690).

CUR DEUS HOMO

The following studies of J. Rivière on the history of the doctrine of the atonement are fundamental for the understanding of Anselm's argument: *The Doctrine of the Atonement* (London, 1909), Vol. II; *Le Dogme de la rédemption chez saint Augustin* (3d ed., Gabalda, Paris, 1933), especially pp. 348–364; *Le Dogme de la rédemption après saint Augustin* (Paris, Gabalda, 1930); *Le Dogme de la rédemption au début du moyen âge* (Vrin, Paris, 1934).

For a full and competent defense of Anselm's teaching on the atonement, consult J. McIntyre, *St. Anselm and His Critics: A Re-interpretation of the Cur Deus Homo* (Oliver and Boyd, Edinburgh, 1954).

See also: G. Aulén, *Christus Victor: An Historical Study of the Three Main Types of the Idea of the Atonement* (S.P.C.K., London, 1931); G. C. Foley, *Anselm's Theory of the Atonement* (New York, 1909); B. Funke, *Grundlagen und Voraussetzungen der Satisfaktionstheorie des hl. Anselm von Canterbury* (Münster i.W., 1903); L. Heinrichs, *Die Genugtuungstheorie des hl. Anselmus von Canterbury* (Paderborn, 1909).

De Conceptu Virginali

Three standard surveys of the history of the medieval theology of original sin should be consulted: J. N. Espenberger, "Die Elemente der Erbsünde nach Augustin und der Frühscholastik," in *Forschungen zur christlichen Literatur-und Dogmengeschichte*, V, 1 (Mainz, 1905), 79–184; J. B. Kors, *La Justice primitive et le péché originel d'après saint Thomas* (Le Saulchoir, Kain, 1922); O. Lottin, *Psychologie et morale au XIIe et XIIIe siècles*, Vol. IV, Pt. 3:1 (Abbaye du Mont César, Louvain, 1954).

See also: A. Gaudel, art. "Péché originel," *DTC*, 12, 275–606 (for Anselm, cf. col. 435–441); R. M. Martin, "La Question du péché originel dans saint Anselme," *Revue des sciences philosophiques et théologiques*, 5 (1911), 735–749; A. Michel, art. "Justice originelle," *DTC*, 8, 2020–2042 (for Anselm, cf. col. 2033 f.).

Marian Devotion

The following are of particular importance: H. du Manoir (ed.), *Maria: études sur la sainte vierge*, II (Beauchesne, Paris, 1952), 95–121 (C. C. Martindale, "Notre Dame dans la littérature Anglaise; piété mariale en Angleterre"); 547–578 (J. Leclercq, "Dévotion et théologie mariales dans le monachisme bénédictin"); X. Le Bachelet and M. Jugie, art. "Immaculée conception," *DTC*, 7, 845–1218 (on the development of the feast, cf. col. 986–995; on Anselm, cf. col. 995–1001).

See also: E. Bishop, *On the Origins of the Feast of the Conception of the Blessed Virgin Mary* (London, 1904); A. W. Burridge, "L'Immaculée conception dans la théologie de l'Angleterre médiévale," *Revue des questions historiques*, 32 (1936), 585–591); R. T. Jones, *S. Anselmi Mariologia* (St. Mary of the Lake Seminary, Mundelein, Ill. 1937); E. Waterton, *Pietas Mariana Britannica* (London, 1879); A. Wilmart, *Auteurs spirituels et textes dévots du moyen âge latin* (Bloud et Gay, Paris, 1932).

Church and State

In addition to the general histories of medieval society and the medieval Church, the following should be consulted: H. Boehmer, *Kirche und Staat in England und in der Normandie im XI. und XII. Jahrhundert* (Leipzig, 1899); Z. N. Brooke, *The English Church and the Papacy from the Conquest to the Reign of*

John (Cambridge University Press, Cambridge, 1931); H. W. C. Davis, art. "Investitures Controversy," *DECH*, 296 f.; R. Schmitz, *Der englische Investiturstreit* (Innsbruck, 1884); W. R. W. Stephens, *The English Church from the Norman Conquest to the Accession of Edward I* (London, 1901); G. H. Williams, *The Norman Anonymous of 1100 A.D.*, Harvard Theological Studies, 18 (Harvard University Press, Cambridge, 1951).

ORIGINAL TEXTS

The following translations have all been made from Schmitt's edition. The original texts will be found in that edition, as indicated.

Proslogion, Schmitt, I, 93–122.

Excerpt from *Responsio editoris*, I, 133 f.

Excerpt from *Epistola de incarnatione verbi*, II, 8–10.

Cur deus homo, II, 42–133.

De conceptu virginali, II, 140–149; 161–170.

Oratio ad sanctam Mariam, III, 18–25.

Letters, IV, 111 f.; 118 f.

The translations of Eadmer are made from M. Rule's edition, pp. 186, 339–341.

An Address
(Proslogion)

THE TEXT

PREFACE

Some time ago, at the urgent request of some of my brethren, I published a brief work,[1] as an example of meditation on the grounds of faith. I wrote it in the role of one who seeks, by silent reasoning with himself, to learn what he does not know. But when I reflected on this little book, and saw that it was put together as a long chain of arguments, I began to ask myself whether *one* argument might possibly be found, resting on no other argument for its proof, but sufficient in itself to prove that God truly exists, and that he is the supreme good, needing nothing outside himself, but needful for the being and well-being of all things. I often turned my earnest attention to this problem, and at times I believed that I could put my finger on what I was looking for, but at other times it completely escaped my mind's eye, until finally, in despair, I decided to give up searching for something that seemed impossible to find. But when I tried to put the whole question out of my mind, so as to avoid crowding out other matters, with which I might make some progress, by this useless preoccupation, then, despite my unwillingness and resistance, it began to force itself on me more persistently than ever. Then, one day, when I was worn out by my vigorous resistance to the obsession, the solution I had ceased to hope for presented itself to me, in the very turmoil of my thoughts, so that I enthusiastically embraced the idea which, in my disquiet, I had spurned.

I thought that the proof I was so glad to find would please some readers if it were written down. Consequently, I have

[1] The *Monologion*, probably Anselm's first work, was written at Bec in the second half of 1076 (cf. Landgraf, *Einführung*, 53). Text in Schmitt, I, 7–87.

written the little work that follows, dealing with this and one or two other matters, in the role of one who strives to raise his mind to the contemplation of God and seeks to understand what he believes. Neither this essay nor the other one I have already mentioned really seemed to me to deserve to be called a book or to bear an author's name; at the same time, I felt that they could not be published without some title that might encourage anyone into whose hands they fell to read them, and so I gave each of them a title. The first I called *An Example of Meditation on the Grounds of Faith,* and the second *Faith Seeking Understanding.*

But when both of them had been copied under these titles by a number of people, I was urged by many people—and especially by Hugh,[2] the reverend archbishop of Lyons, apostolic legate in Gaul, who ordered this with apostolic authority—to attach my name to them. In order to do this more fittingly, I have named the first *Monologion* (or *Soliloquy*), and the second *Proslogion* (or *Address*).

CHAPTER I

The Awakening of the Mind to the Contemplation of God

Now then, little man, for a short while fly from your business; hide yourself for a moment from your turbulent thoughts. Break off now your troublesome cares, and think less of your laborious occupations. Make a little time for God, and rest for a while in him. Enter into the chamber of your mind, shut out everything but God and whatever helps you to seek him, and, when you have shut the door, seek him.[3] Speak now, O my whole heart, speak now to God: "I seek thy face; thy face, Lord, do I desire."[4]

And do thou, O Lord my God, teach my heart where and how to seek thee, where and how to find thee. Lord, if thou art not here, where shall I seek thee who art absent? But if thou art everywhere, why do I not see thee who art present? But surely

---

[2] On Archbishop Hugh of Lyons, see M. Rule, *The Life and Times of St. Anselm,* I, 363; II, 172, 327, 353, 400. A close friend of Anselm, and one of his hosts in exile, Hugh died in October 1107. The following letters addressed by Anselm to Hugh survive: 100 (Schmitt, III, 231 f.); 109 (241 f.); 176 (Schmitt, IV, 57–60); 261 (175); 389 (Schmitt, V, 333 f.).
[3] Cf. Matt. 6:6.
[4] Ps. 26:8 (P.B.V., 27:9); not an exact quotation.

thou dwellest in "light inaccessible."[5] And where is light inaccessible? Or how shall I approach light inaccessible? Or who will lead me and bring me into it, that I may see thee there? And then, by what signs, under what form, shall I seek thee? I have never seen thee, O Lord my God; I do not know thy face. What shall he do, O Lord most high, what shall this exile do so far from thee? What shall thy servant do, tormented by love of thee, and cast so far from thy face?[6] He pants for the sight of thee, and thy face is too far from him. He desires to approach thee, and thy dwelling is unapproachable. He longs to find thee, and does not know thy dwelling place. He strives to seek for thee, and does not know thy face. O Lord, thou art my God and thou art my Lord, and I have never seen thee. Thou hast made me and remade me, and thou hast bestowed on me all the good things I possess, and still I do not know thee. Finally, I was made in order to see thee, and I have not yet done that for which I was made.

O pitiful lot of man, who has lost that for which he was made! O hard and frightful Fall! Alas, what he has lost and what he has found! What has departed from him and what has remained! He has lost the blessedness for which he was made, and has found the misery for which he was not made. That without which nothing is happy has deserted him, and that which by itself is nothing but misery has remained. Then, "man ate the bread of angels,"[7] for which he hungers now; now, he eats the "bread of sorrow,"[8] of which he knew nothing then. Alas, the common mourning of mankind, the universal lamentation of the sons of Adam! He revelled in abundance, while we sigh with hunger. He was rich, while we are beggars. He was happy in his possessions, and wretched when he abandoned them, while we are unhappy in our poverty and wretched with longing—and alas, we remain empty! When he could have done it so easily, why did he not keep for us what we so grievously lack? Why did he bar us from the light and cover us with darkness? To what purpose did he take life away from us and inflict death upon us? Whence have we wretches been expelled, whither have we been driven! From what height have we been thrown down, to what depth struck down! We have been sent from our fatherland into exile, from the vision of God into our own blindness, from the delight of immortality into the bitterness and terror of death. O wretched change! From so great a

5 I Tim. 6:16.
7 Ps. 77:25 (P.B.V., 78:26).
6 Ps. 50:13 (P.B.V., 51:11).
8 Ps. 126:2 (A.V., 127:2).

good to so great an evil! Our loss is heavy, our sorrow heavy; everything is a burden.

But alas, wretched as I am, one of the wretched sons of Eve, driven far from God, what have I begun, what have I accomplished? Where was I going, where have I arrived? To what did I aspire, in the midst of what do I sigh? "I have sought good things,[9] and behold trouble!"[10] I have striven after God, and have fallen back upon myself. I sought rest in my solitude, and "met with trouble and sorrow"[11] in my inmost self. I wanted to laugh for the joy of my soul, and I was forced to roar "with the groaning of my heart."[12] I hoped for joyfulness, and see how my sighs are crowded together!

And "thou, O Lord, how long?"[13] "How long, O Lord, wilt thou forget" us; "how long dost thou turn away thy face from" us?[14] When wilt thou look upon us and hear us? When wilt thou enlighten our eyes[15] and "show us thy face"?[16] When wilt thou give us back thyself? Look upon us, O Lord, hear us, enlighten us, show us thy own self. Restore thyself to us, that it may be well with us, whose life is so evil without thee. Take pity on our efforts and strivings towards thee, for we have no strength apart from thee. Thou dost call us; "help us."[17] I beseech thee, O Lord, let me not despair while I sigh for thee, but let me find relief when I hope for thee. O Lord, my heart is bitter in its desolation; sweeten it, I beseech thee, with thy consolation. O Lord, in my hunger I began to seek thee; I beseech thee, let me not, still fasting, fall short of thee. Famished, I have approached thee; let me not draw back unfed. Poor as I am, I have come to the wealthy, miserable to the merciful; let me not go back empty and despised. And if "before I eat I sigh,"[18] after my sighs give me something to eat. O Lord, I am bent over and can only look downward; raise me up so that I can reach upward. "My iniquities," which "have gone over my head," cover me altogether, "and as a heavy burden" weigh me down.[19] Rescue me, take away my burden, lest their "pit shut her mouth upon me."[20] Let me receive thy light, even from afar, even from the depths. Teach me to seek thee, and when I seek thee show thyself to me, for I cannot seek thee unless thou

9 Ps. 121:9 (A.V., 122:9).
10 Jer. 14:19.
11 Ps. 114:3 (A.V., 116:3).
12 Ps. 37:9 (P.B.V., 38:8).
13 Ps. 6:4 (P.B.V., 6:3).
14 Ps. 12:1 (P.B.V., 13:1).
15 Cf. Ps. 12:4 (P.B.V., 13:3).
16 Ps. 79:4, 8 (P.B.V., 80:3, 7).
17 Ps. 78:9, (P.B.V., 79:9).
18 Job 3:24.
19 Ps. 37:5 (P.B.V., 38:4).
20 Ps. 68:16 (P.B.V., 69:16).

teach me, or find thee unless thou show me thyself. Let me seek thee in my desire, let me desire thee in my seeking. Let me find thee by loving thee, let me love thee when I find thee.

I acknowledge, O Lord, with thanksgiving, that thou hast created this thy image in me, so that, remembering thee, I may think of thee, may love thee.[21] But this image is so effaced and worn away by my faults, it is so obscured by the smoke of my sins, that it cannot do what it was made to do, unless thou renew and reform it. I am not trying, O Lord, to penetrate thy loftiness, for I cannot begin to match my understanding with it, but I desire in some measure to understand thy truth, which my heart believes and loves. For I do not seek to understand in order to believe, but I believe in order to understand. For this too I believe, that "unless I believe, I shall not understand."[22]

CHAPTER II

God Truly Is

And so, O Lord, since thou givest understanding to faith, give me to understand—as far as thou knowest it to be good for me—that thou dost exist, as we believe, and that thou art what we believe thee to be. Now we believe that thou art a being than which none greater can be thought. Or can it be that there is no such being, since "the fool hath said in his heart, 'There is no God' "?[23] But when this same fool hears what I am saying— "A being than which none greater can be thought"[24]—he understands what he hears, and what he understands is in his understanding, even if he does not understand that it exists. For it is one thing for an object to be in the understanding, and another thing to understand that it exists. When a painter

---

21 Cf. Gen. 1:27; *Monologion*, 67 (Schmitt, I, 77 f.). In the text, Anselm reflects Augustine's teaching in *De trin.*, XIV, 8 (*PL*, 42, 1044), where the image of God in man is defined in terms of the mind's *memoria, intelligentia* and *dilectio*, directed toward itself, and in *De trin.*, XIV, 12:15 (*PL*, 24, 1048), where the emphasis is on man's ability to turn these powers toward his Creator.

22 Cf. Isa. 7:9, as read by Augustine in the Old Latin version, and frequently quoted by him, e.g., *Epist.* 120:1 (*CSEL*, 34, 706); *Sermo* 89:4 (*PL*, 38, 556).

23 Ps. 13:1 (P.B.V., 14:1); 52:1 (P.B.V., 53:1).

24 On this formula, cf. Boethius, *De consol. philos.*, III, prosa 10 (*CSEL*, 67, 65): "Since nothing better than God can be thought"; Seneca, *Naturales quaestiones*, I, *prologus* (*L. Annaei Senecae opera*, ed. F. Haase [Leipzig, 1893], II, 159): "Greatness . . . than which nothing greater can be thought."

considers beforehand what he is going to paint, he has it in his understanding, but he does not suppose that what he has not yet painted already exists. But when he has painted it, he both has it in his understanding and understands that what he has now produced exists. Even the fool, then, must be convinced that a being than which none greater can be thought exists at least in his understanding, since when he hears this he understands it, and whatever is understood is in the understanding. But clearly that than which a greater cannot be thought cannot exist in the understanding alone. For if it is actually in the understanding alone, it can be thought of as existing also in reality, and this is greater. Therefore, if that than which a greater cannot be thought is in the understanding alone, this same thing than which a greater cannot be thought is that than which a greater can be thought. But obviously this is impossible. Without doubt, therefore, there exists, both in the understanding and in reality, something than which a greater cannot be thought.[25]

CHAPTER III

God Cannot Be Thought of as Nonexistent

And certainly it exists so truly that it cannot be thought of as nonexistent. For something can be thought of as existing, which cannot be thought of as not existing, and this is greater than that which *can* be thought of as not existing. Thus, if that than which a greater cannot be thought can be thought of as not existing, this very thing than which a greater cannot be thought is *not* that than which a greater cannot be thought. But this is contradictory. So, then, there truly is a being than which a greater cannot be thought—so truly that it cannot even be thought of as not existing.

And *thou* art this being, O Lord our God. Thou so truly art, then, O Lord my God, that thou canst not even be thought of as not existing. And this is right. For if some mind could think of something better than thou, the creature would rise above the Creator and judge its Creator; but this is altogether absurd. And indeed, whatever is, except thyself alone, can be thought of as not existing. Thou alone, therefore, of all beings, hast being in the truest and highest sense, since no other being so truly exists, and thus every other being has less being. Why, then, has

[25] On the "ontological argument," see the "Introduction" to Anselm.

"the fool said in his heart, 'There is no God,' "[26] when it is so obvious to the rational mind that, of all beings, thou dost exist supremely? Why indeed, unless it is that he is a stupid fool?

CHAPTER IV

How the Fool Has Said in His Heart What Cannot Be Thought

But how did he manage to say in his heart what he could not think? Or how is it that he was unable to think what he said in his heart? After all, to say in one's heart and to think are the same thing. Now if it is true—or, rather, since it is true—that he thought it, because he said it in his heart, but did not say it in his heart, since he could not think it, it is clear that something can be said in one's heart or thought in more than one way. For we think of a thing, in one sense, when we think of the word that signifies it, and in another sense, when we understand the very thing itself.[27] Thus, in the first sense God can be thought of as nonexistent, but in the second sense this is quite impossible. For no one who understands what God is can think that God does not exist, even though he says these words in his heart—perhaps without any meaning, perhaps with some quite extraneous meaning. For God is that than which a greater cannot be thought, and whoever understands this rightly must understand that he exists in such a way that he cannot be non-existent even in thought. He, therefore, who understands that God thus exists cannot think of him as nonexistent.

Thanks be to thee, good Lord, thanks be to thee, because I now understand by thy light what I formerly believed by thy gift, so that even if I were to refuse to believe in thy existence, I could not fail to understand its truth.

CHAPTER V

God Is Whatever It Is Better to Be than Not to Be, and He, the Only Self-existent Being, Makes All Other Things from Nothing

What, therefore, art thou, O Lord God, than whom nothing greater can be thought? What art thou, save the highest of all beings,[28] alone self-existent,[29] who hast made all other things

---

[26] Cf. note 23.
[27] Cf. *Monologion*, 10 (Schmitt, I, 25).
[28] Cf. *ibid.*, 1–2 (I, 13 ff.).
[29] Cf. *ibid.*, 3–4 (I, 15 ff.).

from nothing?[30] For whatever is not this highest being is less than can be thought. But we cannot think this of thee. What good, then, is lacking to the highest good, through which every good exists? Therefore thou art just, truthful, blessed, and whatever it is better to be than not to be. For it is better to be just than not just, blessed than not blessed.[31]

CHAPTER VI

How God Is Sensible, Even Though He Is Not a Body

But granted that it is better to be sensible, almighty, merciful, impassible, than otherwise, how canst thou be sensible if thou art not a body? Or how art thou almighty if thou canst not do all things? Or how art thou at once merciful and impassible? For only bodily things are sensible, since the senses have to do with the body and reside in the body; how, then, art thou sensible, when thou art not a body, but the supreme Spirit, better than a body?[32]

But sensation is the same thing as knowledge, or exists for the sake of knowledge, for he who senses knows in the way that is proper to the senses—knows colors, for instance, through sight, and flavors through taste. Thus it is not inappropriate to say that he who knows anything in some way senses in some way. And so, O Lord, even though thou art not a body, thou art truly sensible—not, as an animal, with bodily sense, but because thou hast the highest knowledge of all things.

CHAPTER VII

How He Is Almighty, Although There Are Many Things That He Cannot Do

But then, how art thou almighty if thou canst not do all things? Yet if thou canst not be corrupted, nor lie, nor make what is true false—for instance, by making what has been done not to have been done—and so on, how canst thou do all things?

Is it that to be able to do these things is not power but powerlessness? For he who can do these things can do what is not

---

[30] Cf. *ibid.*, 7–8 (I, 20 ff.).   [31] Cf. *ibid.*, 15 (I, 28 f.).
[32] Cf. *ibid.*, 15 (I, 29).

expedient for him, and what he ought not to do. The more capable he is of these things, the more power adversity and perversity have over him, and the less power he has against them. Thus he who can do these things is able to do them by powerlessness, and not by power. For he is said to be able to do something, not because he himself can do it, but because his powerlessness puts him in another's power. Or else the term is used in another sense, just as many other words are improperly used. For example, we say "to be" in the place of "not to be," and "to do" instead of "not to do" or "to do nothing." We often say to a man who denies that something exists, "It is as you say it is," although it would seem more correct to say, "It is not, as you say it is not." Again, we say, "This man is sitting as that one is doing," or "This man is resting as that one is doing," although to sit is not to do something, and to rest is to do nothing. So, then, when someone is said to have the power to do or suffer something which is not expedient for him or which he ought not to do, "power" really stands for "powerlessness." For the more power of this sort a man has, the more powerful adversity and perversity are against him, and the more powerless he is against them.[33] Therefore, O Lord God, thou art more truly almighty just because thou canst do nothing through lack of power, and nothing has power against thee.

CHAPTER VIII

How God Is Compassionate and Impassible

But again, how art thou at once compassionate and impassible? For if thou art impassible, thou canst not suffer with others, and if thou canst not suffer with others, thy heart is not wretched out of sympathy for the wretched—but this is what being compassionate means. Yet if thou art not compassionate, whence does such great consolation come to the wretched?[34]

How is it, then, O Lord, that thou both art and art not compassionate? Art thou compassionate with respect to us, but

[33] Cf. Augustine, *Sermo* 213:1 (*PL*, 38, 1061); 214:4 (1068).
[34] On the question of the "impassibility" of God, cf. J. K. Mozley, *The Impassibility of God: A Survey of Christian Thought*, Cambridge, 1926 (Anselm, Aquinas, and Duns Scotus are discussed, pp. 111–119); F. von Hügel, *Essays and Addresses on the Philosophy of Religion*, second series (Dent, London, 1939), 167–213.

not according to thy being? Yes, thou art compassionate according to our sense, but not according to thine. For when thou lookest upon us, wretched as we are, we feel the effect of thy compassion, but thou dost not feel emotion. So, then, thou art compassionate, because thou savest the wretched and sparest those who sin against thee, and yet thou art not compassionate, because thou art not affected by any share in our wretchedness.

CHAPTER IX

How the Wholly Just and Supremely Just Spares the Wicked, and How He Justly Shows Mercy on the Wicked

But how canst thou spare the wicked if thou art wholly just and supremely just? For how does the wholly and supremely just do something that is not just? But what justice is there in giving eternal life to one who deserves eternal death? O good God, good to the good and to the evil, on what ground dost thou save the evil, if this is not just, and thou doest nothing that is not just?

Can it be that thy goodness is incomprehensible, lying hidden in the inaccessible light where thou dwellest?[35] Surely in the deepest and most secret place of thy goodness there lies hidden the source from which the river of thy mercy flows. For though thou art wholly and supremely just, yet thou art kind even to the evil, just because thou art completely and supremely good. For thou wouldest be less good, if thou wert not kind to any evildoer. For he who is good both to the good and to the evil is better than he who is good only to the good, and he who is good to the wicked both by sparing them and by punishing them is better than he who is good only by punishing them. Thus thou art merciful, just because thou art wholly and supremely good. And though it might be apparent why thou dost reward the good with good things and the evil with evil things, it is altogether wonderful that thou, who art wholly just and lackest nothing, shouldest bestow good things on those who are evil and guilty in thy sight. O the height of thy goodness, O God! We see the ground of thy mercy, but we do not see it fully. We see whence the stream flows, but we do not observe the source whence it is born. Out of the fullness of thy

[35] Cf. I Tim. 6:16.

goodness thou art kind to those who sin against thee, and still the reason lies hidden in the height of that same goodness. It is, of course, of thy goodness that thou rewardest the good with good things and the evil with evil things, but this seems to be demanded by the very nature of justice. But when thou givest good things to the wicked, we know that the supremely good has willed to do this, and at the same time we marvel that the supremely just has been able to do it.

O mercy, from what abundant sweetness and sweet abundance dost thou flow forth to us! O measureless goodness of God, with what affection must thou be loved by sinners! For thou savest the just when justice is with them, but thou freest those whom justice condemns—the former, with the help of their merits, the latter, despite their demerits; the former, by acknowledging the good things which thou hast given, the latter, by overlooking the evil things which thou hatest. O measureless goodness, passing all understanding, let that mercy which proceeds from thy great wealth come upon me! It flows forth from thee; let it flow into me! Spare in mercy, lest thou punish me in justice! For though it is hard to understand how thy mercy is consistent with thy justice, yet we must believe that what flows forth from thy goodness—itself nothing without justice—is in no way opposed to justice, but agrees perfectly with justice. Indeed, if thou art merciful because thou art supremely good, and thou art supremely good only because thou art supremely just, then thou art merciful simply because thou art supremely just. Help me, O just and merciful God, whose light I seek, help me to understand what I say. I repeat: truly thou art merciful simply because thou art just.

Is thy mercy, then, born of thy justice? Dost thou, then, spare the wicked because of justice? If this is so, O Lord, if this is so, teach me how it is so. Is it because it is just for thee to be so good that thou canst not be thought of as better, and for thee to act with such power that thou canst not be thought of as more powerful? What, indeed, is more just than this? But this would not be true, if thou wert good only in punishment, and not in forbearance, and if thou only madest those who are not good, and not the wicked, into good men. In this way, then, it is just for thee to spare the wicked, and to make good men out of the wicked. Finally, what is unjustly done should not be done, and what should not be done is unjustly done. Therefore, if it is not just for thee to pity the wicked, thou shouldest not have

pity on them, and if thou shouldest not have pity, thou pitiest
unjustly. But if it is wrong to say this, then it is right to believe
that thou justly showest mercy to the wicked.[36]

CHAPTER X

How God Justly Punishes and Justly Spares the Wicked

But it is also just for thee to punish the wicked. For what is
more just than for the good to receive good things, and the
evil evil things? How, then, is it just for thee to punish the
wicked, but also just for thee to spare the wicked?

Perhaps it is just in one respect for thee to punish the wicked,
and just in another respect for thee to spare the wicked. For
when thou dost punish the wicked it is just, since it is in
accordance with their merits, and yet when thou dost spare the
wicked it is just, because it befits thy goodness, though not their
merits. For in sparing the wicked thou art just according to
thy nature and not to ours, just as thou art compassionate
according to our nature and not to thy own. For thou art

---

[36] This identification of the justice or righteousness of God (*iustitia dei*) with
mercy is especially interesting in view of Luther's famous summary
statement of the scholastic teaching, which has tended to encourage
exaggerated ideas of the place of legal justice and fear of judgment in
medieval thought as a whole. Cf. Luther, *Enarrationes in Genesim*, on
Gen. 27:38 (*Werke*, Weimarer Ausgabe, 43, 537): "The expression, 'the
justice of God,' ... was usually expounded in this way: The justice of
God is the virtue by which God himself is intrinsically just and condemns
sinners. All the doctors had interpreted this passage (Rom. 1:17) in this
way, with the exception of Augustine: The justice of God equals the
wrath of God." H. Denifle, *Luther und Luthertum*, Band 1/2 (2d ed., Mainz,
1905), "Die abendländischen Schriftausleger bis Luther über Justitia
Dei (Rom. 1:17) und Justificatio," collects over 300 pages of texts,
ranging from the fourth century to the sixteenth, and drawn from such
authors as Ambrosiaster (pp. 1–3), Augustine (pp. 3–8), Abailard (pp.
49–52), Hugh of St. Cher (pp. 108–111), John of La Rochelle (pp. 122–
130), Thomas Aquinas (pp. 136–144), Nicholas of Lyra (pp. 189–194),
Denys the Carthusian (pp. 253–259), and John Colet (pp. 297–300),
which go to show how representative Anselm is of the theology of the
medieval West. Cf. Lanfranc (Denifle, p. 29), on Rom. 3:21: "*The
justice of God*—that, namely, by which God justifies believers—*has been
manifested*"; Peter Lombard (p. 57), on Rom. 1:17: "*For the justice of God,
etc.* As if he were to say: Truly the gospel is unto salvation for everyone
who believes, because for him it is unto righteousness, which is the cause
of salvation."

compassionate, not because thou feelest an emotion, but because we feel the effect of thy compassion. Similarly, in saving us whom in justice thou mightest destroy, thou art just, not because thou rewardest us as we deserve but because thou doest what becomes thee, the highest good. So, then, without contradiction, thou dost justly punish and justly spare.[37]

CHAPTER XI

How All the Ways of the Lord Are Mercy and Truth, and Yet the Lord Is Just in All His Ways

But according to thy nature, O Lord, is it not also just to punish the wicked? It is certainly just for thee to be so just that thou canst not be thought of as more just. But this thou couldest not be, if thou wert only to reward the good with good things, and not the evil with evil things. For he who gives both the good and the evil what they deserve is more just than he who rewards the good alone. Thus, according to thy nature, O just and gracious God, it is just both to punish and to spare. It is true, then, that "all the ways of the Lord are mercy and truth,"[38] and at the same time that "the Lord is just in all his ways."[39] And this involves no contradiction, because it is not just either for those whom thou dost will to punish to be saved or for those whom thou dost will to spare to be condemned. For what thou willest is alone just, and what thou dost not will is not just. Accordingly, thy mercy is born of thy justice, because it is just for thee to be so good that thou art good in sparing (as well as in punishing). And perhaps this is why the supremely just can will good things for the wicked. At the same time, though we may be able to grasp why thou canst will to save the wicked, we can find no reason to explain why, among men who are equally evil, thou dost save some, and not others, through thy supreme goodness, and dost condemn the latter, and not the former, through thy supreme justice.[40]

So, then, thou art truly sensible, almighty, compassionate, and impassible, just as thou art living, wise, good, blessed, eternal, and whatever it is better to be than not to be.

[37] Cf. Augustine, *Enarr. in Ps.* 147:13 (*PL*, 37, 1922).
[38] Ps. 24:10 (P.B.V., 25:9).
[39] Ps. 144:17 (P.B.V., 145:17).
[40] Cf. Augustine, *Contra Faust. Man.*, 21:2–3 (*PL*, 42, 389 f.).

CHAPTER XII

God Is the Very Life by Which He Lives, and His Other Attributes Likewise

But certainly, whatever thou art, thou art through thyself, and not through another. Thus thou art the very life by which thou livest, and the wisdom by which thou art wise, and the very goodness by which thou art good to the good and to the wicked—and so with all thine attributes. [41]

CHAPTER XIII

How God Alone Is Uncircumscribed and Eternal, Although Other Spirits Are Uncircumscribed and Eternal

But everything that is in some way enclosed by place or time is less than that which no law of place or time confines. Therefore, since there is nothing greater than thou, no place or time holds thee, but thou art everywhere and always. And since this can be said of thee alone, thou alone art uncircumscribed and eternal. How is it, then, that other spirits are also said to be uncircumscribed and eternal?

Thou alone, it is true, art eternal, since of all beings thou alone dost not begin to be, just as thou dost not cease to be. [42] But how art thou alone uncircumscribed? Is it that a created spirit is circumscribed when compared with thee, but uncircumscribed in comparison with the body? Certainly anything that, when it is wholly in one place, cannot be elsewhere at the same time, is completely circumscribed; this is true of corporeal things alone. On the other hand, that which at once is wholly everywhere is uncircumscribed; and we know that this is true of thee alone. But if something when it is wholly in one place, can at the same time be wholly in *some* other place, but not in every place, it is at once circumscribed and uncircumscribed; we know that this is the case with created spirits. For if the soul were not wholly present in each member of its body, it would not sense as a whole in each one of them. Thou, therefore, O Lord, art uniquely uncircumscribed and eternal, and yet other spirits also are uncircumscribed and eternal. [43]

[41] Cf. *Monologion*, 16 (Schmitt, I, 30 f.).　　[42] Cf. *ibid.*, 18 (I, 32 f.).
[43] Cf. *ibid.*, 22 (I, 39 ff.).

CHAPTER XIV

How and Why God Is Seen and Yet Not Seen by Those Who Seek Him

Hast thou found, O my soul, what thou wast seeking? Thou wast seeking God, and thou hast found that he is a certain highest being of all, than whom nothing better can be thought. He is life itself, light, wisdom, goodness, eternal blessedness and blessed eternity; he is everywhere and always. Now if thou hast not found thy God, how is it that he is what thou hast found— that thou hast understood him with such certain truth and true certainty? But if thou hast found him, why dost thou not perceive what thou hast found? Why, O Lord God, does my soul not perceive thee, if it has found thee?

Can it be that it has not found him, whom it has found to be light and truth? But how could it understand this, save by seeing the light and the truth? Or could it understand anything at all about thee, save through "thy light and thy truth"?[44] If, then, it has seen light and truth, it has seen thee. If it has not seen thee, it has seen neither light nor truth. Can it perhaps have seen light and truth, and still not have seen thee, because it saw thee to some extent, but did not see thee as thou art?[45]

O Lord my God, who formed me and reformed me, tell my soul, which so desires thee, what thou art beyond what it has seen, that it may see clearly what it desires. It strains itself to see more, and sees nothing beyond what it has seen, save darkness. Or rather, it does not see darkness, since there is no darkness in thee,[46] but it sees that it can see nothing more, because of its own darkness. Why is this, O Lord, why is this? Is its eye darkened by its own weakness, or dazzled by thy glory? In fact, it is both darkened in itself and dazzled by thee. That is, it is both obscured by its own littleness and overpowered by thine immensity. In truth, it is both restricted by its own narrowness and overcome by thy fullness. For how great that light is, from which every truth that gives light to the rational mind shines forth! How full that truth is, in which is everything that is true, and beyond which there is only nothingness and falsehood! How boundless it is, when at one glance it sees everything that has been made, and knows by whom and through

44 Ps. 42:3 (P.B.V., 43:3).   45 Cf. I John 3:2.
46 Cf. I John 1:5.

whom and in what way all has been made from nothing! What purity is there, what simplicity, what certainty, what splendor! Certainly it is more than any creature can understand.

CHAPTER XV

God Is Greater than Can Be Thought

And so, O Lord, thou art not simply that than which a greater cannot be thought; rather, thou art something greater than can be thought. For since something like this can be thought, if thou art not this very being, something greater than thou can be thought—but this cannot be.

CHAPTER XVI

That This Is the Light Inaccessible, in Which He Dwells

In truth, Lord, this is the light inaccessible, in which thou dwellest.[47] For truly there is nothing else that can penetrate this light and behold thee there. Truly, then, I do not see this, since it is too bright for me, and yet I see through it whatever I see, just as the weak eye sees what it does see through the light of the sun, though it cannot bear that light in the sun itself. My understanding is not equal to it. It shines too brightly, and my mind cannot grasp it, nor can the eye of my soul bear to look toward it for long. It is blinded by its glory, it is overcome by its fullness, it is overwhelmed by its immensity, it is bewildered by its greatness. O supreme and inaccessible light, O full and blessed truth, how far thou art from me, who am so near to thee! How distant thou art from my sight, though I am so close to thine! Thou art wholly present everywhere, and I do not see thee. In thee I move and in thee I exist,[48] and I cannot come near to thee. Thou art within me and about me, and I do not perceive thee.

CHAPTER XVII

God Possesses, All Ineffably, Harmony, Fragrance, Sweet Savor, Softness, and Beauty

Still thou dost conceal thyself, O Lord, from my soul, in thy light and blessedness, and so it still dwells in darkness and in its own wretchedness. For it looks all around, and does not see thy

47 Cf. I Tim. 6:16.   48 Cf. Acts 17:28.

beauty. It listens, and does not hear thy harmony. It smells, and does not sense thy fragrance. It tastes, and does not recognize thy sweet savor. It touches, and does not feel thy softness. For thou dost possess all these qualities, O Lord God, in thy own ineffable way, while thou hast given them to things created by thee in their own perceptible way. But the senses of my soul have been frozen and stupefied and blocked up by the ancient enfeeblement of sin.[49]

CHAPTER XVIII

THERE ARE NO PARTS IN GOD OR IN THE ETERNITY WHICH HE IS

Once more, behold, disquiet! Behold, once more sorrow and mourning confront him who seeks joy and gladness! My soul had begun to hope for fulfillment, and behold, it is again overwhelmed by poverty! I sought for nourishment, and behold, I begin to hunger more than before! I was striving to rise up to the light of God, and I fell back into my own darkness. Indeed, I not only fell into it, but I feel myself enveloped in it. Before my mother conceived me,[50] I fell. In truth, I was conceived in that darkness, and I was born wrapped up in it. In truth, we all fell long ago in him, "in whom" we "all have sinned."[51] In him we all have lost what he easily held and wickedly lost for himself and for us. Now, when we wish to seek it, we do not know it, and when we seek we do not find it, and what we find is not what we are seeking. Do thou "help me for thy goodness' sake, O Lord."[52] "I have sought thy countenance, O Lord; thy countenance will I search for. Turn not thy face from me."[53] Lift me up from myself to thee. Cleanse, heal,

---

[49] On this chapter, cf. Augustine, *Conf.*, X, 6:8 (*CSEL*, 33, 231 f.).

[50] Cf. Ps. 50:7 (P.B.V., 51:5).

[51] Rom. 5:12. The Greek text, misinterpreted in this sense by Origen, was mistranslated in the Old Latin and the Vulgate, as "in whom" rather than "in that." This construction was followed by Ambrosiaster and Augustine, and was influential in "Augustinian" thought all through the Middle Ages. Cf. W. Sanday and A. C. Headlam, *The Epistle to the Romans* (International Critical Commentary), 5th ed. (Edinburgh, 1902), 133–134; H. Lietzmann, *An die Römer* (Handbuch zum Neuen Testament), 4th ed. (Mohr, Tübingen, 1933), 61–62; M. J. Lagrange, *Epître aux Romains* (Etudes Bibliques, Gabalda, Paris, 1950), 106–107.

[52] Ps. 24:7 (P.B.V., 25:6).

[53] Ps. 26:8, 9 (P.B.V., 27:9,10); not quoted according to the Vulgate.

sharpen, "enlighten"[54] the eye of my mind, that it may behold thee.[55] Let my soul gather up her powers, and with all her understanding reach out again to thee, O Lord.

What art thou, O Lord, what art thou? How shall my heart think of thee? Certainly thou art life, thou art wisdom, thou art truth, thou art goodness, thou art blessedness, thou art eternity, and thou art every true good. But these are many, and my narrow understanding cannot take in so much in a single glance, and take delight in all at once. How, then, O Lord, art thou all these things? Are they parts of thee, or, on the contrary, is each one of them the whole that thou art? For whatever is made up of parts is not absolutely one, but in a way is many and different from itself, and it can be divided either in reality or in thought. But all this is foreign to thee, than whom nothing better can be thought. Therefore, there are no parts in thee, O Lord, and thou art not many; rather, thou art so truly one being, and identical with thyself, that thou art unlike thyself in nothing, but art unity itself, divisible by no understanding. Thus life and wisdom and the rest are not parts of thee, but all are one, and each of them is the whole that thou art, and what all the rest are. Since, then, there are no parts in thee or in thy eternity which thou art, there is no part of thee or of thy eternity anywhere or ever, but thou art everywhere whole, and thy eternity is always whole.[56]

CHAPTER XIX

GOD IS NEITHER IN PLACE NOR IN TIME, BUT ALL THINGS ARE IN HIM

But if thou hast been, and art, and shalt be, through thy eternity, and to have been is not to be going to be, and to be is not to have been or to be going to be, how is thy eternity always whole?

Is it that nothing of thy eternity passes so that it no longer is, and that nothing of it is going to be in the future as though it were not already? Thus thou wast not yesterday, and thou shalt not be tomorrow, but yesterday and today and tomorrow thou art. Indeed, it is not even that thou art yesterday and today and tomorrow; rather, thou simply art, outside all time. For yesterday and today and tomorrow belong solely to time,

---

[54] Cf. Ps. 12:4 (P.B.V., 13:3).   [55] Cf. S. of Sol. 6:12 (A.V., 6:13).
[56] On this chapter, cf. *Monologion*, 17 (Schmitt, I, 31 f.).

but, though nothing exists without thee, thou art not in place or time, but all things are in thee. For nothing contains thee, but thou containest all things.[57]

CHAPTER XX

GOD IS BEFORE AND BEYOND ALL THINGS, EVEN ETERNAL THINGS

Thou, therefore, fillest and embracest all things; thou art before and beyond all things. And I can see how thou art before all things, for before they were made thou art.[58] But how art thou beyond all things? For in what way canst thou be beyond those things that have no end?

Is it because they simply cannot exist without thee, but thou art in no way diminished if they return to nothingness? For thus, in a way, thou art beyond them. Or is it also that they can be thought to have an end, whereas this cannot be thought of thee? For thus they do have an end in a certain way, while thou art without end. And undoubtedly that which can have no end is beyond that which in some way comes to an end. Or perhaps thou dost surpass all things, even eternal things, in so far as thy eternity and theirs is wholly present to thee, while they do not possess that part of their eternity which is still to come, any more than that which is already past. Thus, certainly, thou art always beyond them, since thou art always present where they have not yet arrived—or, rather, that point is always present to thee.[59]

CHAPTER XXI

WHETHER WE SHOULD SPEAK OF THE "AGE OF THE AGE" OR "AGES OF AGES"

Is this, then, the "age of the age"[60] or "ages of ages"[61]? For just as an age made up of times contains all temporal things, so thy eternity contains the ages of time themselves. This eternity is an age because of its indivisible unity, but it is ages because of its unbounded immensity. And though thou art so great, O

---

[57] Cf. *ibid.*, 21–22 (I, 36 ff.).   [58] Cf. Ps. 89:2 (P.B.V., 90:2).
[59] On this chapter, cf. *Monologion*, 19 (Schmitt, I, 33 ff.).
[60] *Saeculum saeculi*; cf. Ps. 111:9 (P.B.V., 112:9) and many other texts.
[61] *Saecula saeculorum*; cf. I Peter 4:11 and many other texts.

Lord, that all things are full of thee and are in thee,[62] nevertheless thou art so truly spaceless that there is neither middle
nor half nor any part in thee.

CHAPTER XXII

GOD ALONE IS WHAT HE IS AND HE WHO IS

Thou alone, therefore, O Lord, art what thou art and thou
art he who is. For when something is one thing in its totality
and another in its parts, and contains some changeable element,
it is not completely what it is.[63] And if something began from
nonbeing, and can be thought of as nonexistent, and returns
to nonbeing unless it subsists through something else—and if it
has a past reality which no longer is, and a future reality yet
to come—it cannot be said to exist, properly and absolutely.
But thou art what thou art, since whatever thou art, at any
time or in any way, this thou art wholly and always.

And thou art he who properly and simply is,[64] because thou
hast neither past existence nor future existence, but only present
existence,[65] nor canst thou be thought not to exist at any time.
And thou art life and light and wisdom and blessedness and
eternity and many such goods, and yet thou art only the one
and supreme good, wholly self-sufficient, in need of nothing—
while all things need thee for their being and their well-being.[66]

CHAPTER XXIII

THIS GOOD IS EQUALLY THE FATHER AND THE SON AND THE HOLY SPIRIT, AND THIS IS THE ONE THING NEEDFUL, COMPLETE AND WHOLE AND SOLE GOOD

This good is thyself, O God the Father; this good is thy Word,
that is, thy Son. For there can be nothing save what thou art,
or greater or less than thou art, in the Word by which thou

---

[62] Cf. *Monologion*, 14 (Schmitt, I, 27).

[63] Cf. *ibid.*, 25 (I, 43 f.); Boethius, *De hebdomadibus* (= the tractate, *Quomodo substantiae in eo quod sint bonae sint*, etc.), in *The Theological Tractates; The Consolation of Philosophy* (ed. H. F. Stewart and E. K. Rand, Loeb Classical Library, London, 1918), 38–51.

[64] Cf. Ex. 3:14; see also the famous discussion of the metaphysical conse-
quences of this text in Gilson, *Spirit*, Chapter III. Cf. E. Gilson, *God and Philosophy* (Yale University Press, New Haven, 1941), Chapter II.

[65] Cf. Augustine, *Enarr. in Ps.* 89:3 (*PL*, 37, 1142).

[66] On this chapter, cf. *Monologion*, 28 (Schmitt, I, 45 f.).

speakest thyself. For thy Word is as true as thou art truthful, and therefore it is truth itself, as thou art, and not another truth than thou; besides, thou art so simple that nothing which is not what thou art can be born of thee. This same good is the one Love which is common to thee and to thy Son, that is, the Holy Spirit, proceeding from both.[67] For this same Love is not unequal to thee or to thy Son, since thou lovest thyself and him, and he loves thee and himself, as fully as thou art and he is. Moreover, that which is not unequal to thee and to him is not another than thou art and he is, nor can there proceed from the supreme simplicity anything other than the being from which it proceeds. Moreover, what each person is singly, this the whole Trinity, Father, Son, and Holy Spirit, is together. For each person is nothing other than the unity which is supremely simple and the simplicity which is supremely one, and can be neither multiplied nor diversified.

"But one thing is necessary."[68] And this is that one thing needful, in which there is every good—or, rather, which is every good, and the one and complete and only good.[69]

CHAPTER XXIV

A CONJECTURE, RESPECTING THE NATURE AND GREATNESS OF THIS GOOD

Now, my soul, arouse and lift up thy whole understanding, and consider, as fully as thou canst, the nature and greatness of that good. For if particular goods are delightful, think seriously how delightful that good must be. It contains the pleasantness of all goods—and not the kind of pleasantness we have experienced in created things, but something as different as the Creator is from the creature. For if created life is good, how good creative life must be! If the salvation he brings about is delightful, how delightful the salvation that bestows all salvation must be! If the wisdom that consists in the knowledge of created things is lovable, how lovable is the wisdom that created all things from nothing! Finally, if there are many great delights in delightful things, what wonderful and great delight is to be found in him who made the delightful things themselves!

---

67 For Anselm's apologetic for the doctrine of the "double procession," against the Greek Church, cf. *De processione spiritus sancti* (Schmitt, II, 177–219).
68 Luke 10:42.
69 On this chapter, cf. *Monologion*, 29–63 (Schmitt, I, 47 ff.).

CHAPTER XXV

The Great Goods That Belong to Those Who Enjoy This Good

Think of him who enjoys this good; what will be his, and what will not be his! Beyond question, whatever he wishes will be his, and what he does not want will not be his. In fact, he will there have goods of body and soul, such as "eye hath not seen, nor ear heard," nor "the heart of man" conceived.[70] Then why dost thou wander through so many things, little man, seeking the goods of thy soul and of thy body? Love the one good, which includes every good, and it suffices. Desire the simple good, which is all good, and it is enough. For what dost thou love, my flesh? What dost thou desire, my soul? It is there; whatever thou lovest is there, whatever thou desirest.

Does beauty delight thee? "The just shall shine as the sun."[71] Does swiftness or strength or the free and irresistible movement of the body delight thee? "They shall be like the angels of God,"[72] for "it is sown a natural body, it shall rise a spiritual body"[73]—in power, that is, though not in nature. Does a long and vigorous life delight thee? There is a healthful eternity and eternal health, since "the just shall live for evermore,"[74] and "the salvation of the just is from the Lord."[75] If thou seekest satisfaction of hunger, they "shall be satisfied when" the "glory" of God "shall appear."[76] If thou seekest intoxication, "they shall be inebriated with the plenty of" God's "house."[77] If melody delights thee, there the choirs of angels sing together to God without ending.[78] If any pleasure which is pure, and not impure, delights thee, God shall "make them drink of the torrent" of his "pleasure."[79]

Or does wisdom delight thee? The very wisdom of God will show itself to them. Or friendship? They shall love God more

[70] I Cor. 2:9.
[71] Matt. 13:43.
[72] Matt. 22:30; not quite according to the Vulgate.
[73] I Cor. 15:44.
[74] Wisdom of Solomon 5:16 (A.V., 5:15).
[75] Ps. 36:39 (P.B.V., 37:40); a play on the word *salus* = health *or* salvation.
[76] Ps. 16:15 (P.B.V., 17:16).
[77] Ps. 35:9 (P.B.V., 36:8).
[78] Cf. *Missale Romanum*, "Preface" for the Feast of Pentecost.
[79] Ps. 35:9 (P.B.V., 36:8).

than themselves, and each other as themselves; and God shall love them more than they love themselves, for they love him and themselves and each other through him, while he loves himself and them through himself. Or dost thou seek harmony? They shall all have one will, since the will of God alone is to be their will. Or power? They shall be all-powerful to accomplish what they will, as God is to fulfill his own will. For as God will be able to do what he wills through himself, so they will be able to do what they will through him. Just as they shall will only what he wills, so he shall will whatever they will; and what he wills cannot fail to be. Or do honor and riches delight thee? God will set his good and faithful servants over many things;[80] more than that, they "shall be called" (and shall be) "the children of God,"[81] and "gods,"[82] and where his Son shall be, there they shall be also[83]—"heirs indeed of God, and joint-heirs with Christ."[84] Or dost thou seek true security? Certainly they shall be as sure that those goods—or rather, this good—will never fail them in any way, as they are sure that they will not lose it of their own accord, and that God who loves them will not take it away from those who love him against their will, and that nothing more powerful than God will separate them from God against their will.[85]

What joy there must be, what great joy, where there is such a good, and so great a good! Human heart, needy heart, heart acquainted with hardships—indeed, overwhelmed by hardships—how greatly wouldest thou rejoice if thou didst abound in all these things! Question thy inmost self; could it contain its joy if such great blessedness were its own? But certainly, if someone else, whom thou lovedst as thy own self, possessed the same blessedness, thy joy would be doubled, for thou wouldest rejoice no less for him than for thyself. And if two or three or many more possessed it, thou wouldest rejoice for each of them as much as for thyself, if thou didst love each one as thyself. Therefore, in that perfect charity of countless blessed angels and men, where no one will love another less than himself, everyone will rejoice for each of the others just as he does for himself. Therefore, if the heart of man can scarcely contain its own joy over its own great good, how will it hold so many great joys? And indeed, since each will rejoice in another's good in so far as he loves him, and in that perfect happiness

---

80 Cf. Matt. 25:21, 23.   81 Matt. 5:9; cf. I John 3:1 f.
82 Cf. John 10:34 f.   83 Cf. John 14:3.
84 Rom. 8:17.   85 Cf. Rom. 8:38 f.

each one will love God incomparably more than himself and all others put together, he will be inestimably more joyful over God's happiness than over his own and all others' with him. But if they love God with their whole heart, their whole mind, their whole soul,[86] and yet their whole heart, their whole mind, their whole soul is not equal to the dignity of this love, they will certainly so rejoice with their whole heart, their whole mind, their whole soul, that their whole heart, their whole mind, their whole soul will not be equal to the fullness of their joy.

CHAPTER XXVI

Is This the Full Joy Which the Lord Promises?

My God and my Lord, my hope and my heart's joy, tell my soul if this is the joy of which thou sayest to us through thy Son: "Ask and you shall receive, that your joy may be full."[87] For I have found a joy that is full and more than full. Indeed, when the heart is filled, the mind is filled, the soul and the whole man are filled with that joy, still joy will abound beyond measure. So, then, the whole of that joy will not enter into those who rejoice, but those who rejoice will enter wholly into joy. Speak, Lord, and tell thy servant within his heart, if this is the joy into which thy servants shall enter, when they enter "into the joy" of their "Lord."[88] But surely "eye hath not seen, nor ear heard" that joy in which thy chosen ones shall rejoice, "neither hath it entered into the heart of man."[89] Then I have not yet said or conceived, O Lord, how greatly these thy blessed ones shall rejoice. Assuredly, they shall rejoice as fully as they love, and they shall love as fully as they know. How fully will they know thee then, O Lord? How greatly will they love thee? In truth, "eye hath not seen, nor ear heard, neither hath it entered into the heart of man" in this life, how fully they shall know and love thee in that life.

I pray, O God, that I may know thee, that I may love thee, so that I may rejoice in thee. And if I cannot do this to the full in this life, at least let me go forward from day to day until that joy comes to fullness. Let the knowledge of thee go forward in me here, and there let it be made full. Let love for thee increase, and there let it be full, so that here my joy may be

86 Cf. Matt. 22:37. 87 John 16:24.
88 Matt. 25:21. 89 I Cor. 2:9.

great in hope, and there it may be full in reality.[90] O Lord, through thy Son thou dost command us—rather, thou dost counsel us—to ask, and dost promise that we shall receive, that our "joy may be full."[91] O Lord, I ask what thou dost counsel through our "wonderful Counselor"[92]; let me receive what thou dost promise through thy truth, that my "joy may be full." O God of truth, I ask that I may receive, that my "joy may be full." Meanwhile, let my mind meditate upon it, let my tongue speak of it. Let my heart love it, let my tongue discourse upon it. Let my soul hunger for it, let my flesh thirst for it,[93] let my whole substance desire it, until I enter "into the joy" of my "Lord,"[94] who is the triune and one God, "blessed forever. Amen."[95]

[90] Cf. Augustine, *Sermo* 21:1 (*PL*, 38, 142).
[91] John 16:24.
[92] Cf. Isa. 9:6.
[93] Cf. Ps. 62:2 (P.B.V., 63:2).
[94] Matt. 25:21.
[95] Rom. 1:25.

An Excerpt from the Author's Reply to the Criticisms of Gaunilo

THE TEXT

3. But, you say, suppose that someone imagined an island in the ocean, surpassing all lands in its fertility. Because of the difficulty, or rather the impossibility, of finding something that does not exist, it might well be called "Lost Island." By reasoning like yours, he might then say that we cannot doubt that it truly exists in reality, because anyone can easily conceive it from a verbal description.[1] I state confidently that if anyone discovers something for me, other than that "than which a greater cannot be thought," existing either in reality or in thought alone, to which the logic of my argument can be applied, I shall find his lost island and give it to him, never to be lost again. But it now seems obvious that this being than which a greater cannot be thought cannot be thought of as non-existent, because it exists by such a sure reason of truth. For otherwise it would not exist at all. In short, if anyone says that he thinks it does not exist, I say that when he thinks this, he either thinks of something than which a greater cannot be thought or he does not think. If he does not think, he does not think of what he is not thinking of as nonexistent. But if he does think, then he thinks of something which cannot be thought of as nonexistent. For if it could be thought of as nonexistent, it could be thought of as having a beginning and an end. But this is impossible. Therefore, if anyone thinks of it, he thinks of something that cannot even be thought of as nonexistent. But he who thinks of this does not think that it does not exist; if he did, he would think what cannot be thought. Therefore, that than which a greater cannot be thought cannot be thought of as non-existent.

[1] Cf. Gaunilo, *Pro insipiente*, 6 (Schmitt, I, 128).

4. You say, moreover, that when it is said that the highest reality cannot be *thought of* as nonexistent, it would perhaps be better to say that it cannot be *understood* as nonexistent, or even as possibly nonexistent.[2] But it is more correct to say, as I said, that it cannot be thought. For if I had said that the reality itself cannot be understood not to exist, perhaps you yourself, who say that according to the very definition of the term what is false cannot be understood,[3] would object that nothing that is can be understood as nonexistent. For it is false to say that what exists does not exist. Therefore it would not be peculiar to God to be unable to be understood as nonexistent.[4] But if some one of the things that most certainly are can be understood as nonexistent, other certain things can similarly be understood as nonexistent. But this objection cannot be applied to "thinking," if it is rightly considered. For although none of the things that exist can be understood not to exist, still they can all be thought of as nonexistent, except that which most fully is. For all those things—and only those—which have a beginning or end or are composed of parts can be thought of as nonexistent, along with anything that does not exist as a whole anywhere or at any time (as I have already said[5]). But the only being that cannot be thought of as nonexistent is that in which no thought finds beginning or end or composition of parts, but which any thought finds as a whole, always and everywhere.

You must realize, then, that you can think of yourself as nonexistent, even while you know most certainly that you exist. I am surprised that you said you did not know this.[6] For we think of many things as nonexistent when we know that they exist, and of many things as existent when we know that they do not exist—all this not by a real judgment, but by imagining that what we think is so. And indeed, we can think of something as nonexistent, even while we know that it exists, because we are able at the same time to think the one and know the other. And yet we cannot think of it as nonexistent, while we know that it exists, because we cannot think of something as at once existent and nonexistent. Therefore, if anyone distinguishes these two senses of the statement in this way, he will understand that nothing, as long as it is known to exist, can be thought of as nonexistent, and that whatever exists, except that than which a greater cannot be thought, can be thought

[2] *Ibid.*, 7 (I, 129).   [3] *Ibid.*
[4] *Ibid.*   [5] *Responsio*, 1 (I, 131 f.).
[6] Gaunilo, *loc. cit.*

of as nonexistent, even when it is known to exist. So, then, it is peculiar to God to be unable to be thought of as nonexistent, and nevertheless many things, as long as they exist, cannot be thought of as nonexistent. I think that the way in which it can still be said that God is thought of as nonexistent is stated adequately in the little book itself.[7]

[7] Cf. *Proslogion*, Chapter IV.

Letter of Anselm to Pope Urban II on the Incarnation of the Word

THE TEXT

AN EXCERPT FROM PART ONE

FAITH AND UNDERSTANDING

Fir*t*, then, the heart is to be purified by faith—for God is spoken of as "purifying their hearts by faith"[1]—and first the eyes are to be enlightened through keeping the Lord's commandments, because "the commandment of the Lord is lightsome, enlightening the eyes,"[2] and first we should become little children by humble obedience to the testimonies of God, in order to learn the wisdom given by the "testimony of the Lord," which "is faithful, giving wisdom to little ones."[3] (Thus the Lord says, "I confess to thee, O Father, Lord of heaven and earth, because thou hast hid these things from the wise and prudent, and hast revealed them to little ones."[4]) First, I say, let us disregard the things that belong to the flesh, and let us live according to the Spirit, instead of destroying the deep things of faith by our judgment. For he who lives according to the flesh is carnal or animal, and it is said of him that "the sensual man perceiveth not these things that are of the Spirit of God."[5] But he who "by the Spirit" mortifies "the deeds of the flesh"[6] is made spiritual, and it is said of him that "the spiritual man judgeth all things; and he himself is judged of no man."[7] For it is true that the more richly we are nourished in Holy Scripture by the things that feed us through obedience, the more accurately we are carried along to the things that satisfy through knowledge. For, indeed, it is vain for a man to undertake to say, "I have understood more than all my teachers,"[8] when he does not dare to add, "Because thy testimonies are my meditation."[9] And he is a liar when he recites, "I have had

---

[1] Acts 15:9.   [2] Ps. 18:9 (P.B.V., 19:8).   [3] Ps. 18:8 (P.B.V., 19:7).
[4] Matt. 11:25.   [5] I Cor. 2:14.   [6] Rom. 8:13.
[7] I Cor. 2:15.   [8] Ps. 118:99 (P.B.V., 119:99).   [9] *Ibid.*

understanding above ancients,"[10] if he is not familiar with what follows, "Because I have sought thy commandments."[11] Certainly this is just what I say: He who will not believe will not understand. For he who will not believe will not gain experience, and he who has not had experience will not know. For experience surpasses hearing about a thing, as greatly as knowledge by experience excels acquaintance by hearing.

And not only is the mind forbidden to rise to the understanding of the higher matters without faith and obedience to God's commandments, but sometimes even the understanding that has been given is withdrawn and faith itself is overthrown by disregard for a good conscience. For the apostle says of some: "When they knew God, they have not glorified him as God, or given thanks; but became vain in their thoughts, and their foolish heart was darkened."[12] And when he commanded Timothy to war "a good warfare,"[13] he said, "Having faith and a good conscience, which some rejecting have made shipwreck concerning the faith."[14] Let no one, then, heedlessly plunge into the obscure questions that concern divine things without first seeking earnestly, in soundness of faith, for gravity of conduct and of wisdom. Otherwise, running about with heedless frivolity through a multitude of sophistical distractions, he may be trapped by some stubborn falsehood.

Everyone is to be warned to approach the questions of the "sacred page"[15] most cautiously; but particularly those dialecticians of our own time (or, rather, the heretics of dialectic), who think that universal substances are only the

---

[10] Ps. 118:100 (P.B.V., 119:100).   [11] *Ibid.*
[12] Rom. 1:21.   [13] I Tim. 1:18.   [14] I Tim. 1:19.
[15] Anselm's phrase, *sacrae paginae quaestiones*, is a neat reminder of the pattern of development of theological method in the eleventh and twelfth centuries. (a) The term *sacra pagina* refers, of course, to Holy Scripture. The noun *pagina* appears in some classical authors, as well as early Christian writers, in the sense, sometimes of writing material (paper or papyrus), sometimes of the content written on paper, etc. Despite the fact that it only appears once in the Vulgate (Jer. 36:23), and in the diminutive form *pagella* at that, it became, qualified by some such term as *sancta, sacra, divina, caelestis,* or *evangelica,* a conventional description of the Bible in the writings of Jerome (*Epist.* 22:17, *CSEL*, 54, 165), Augustine (*De nupt. et concup.*, II, 27:47, *PL*, 44, 463), Leo (*Epist.* 28:1 [the "Tome"], *PL*, 54, 757), and Gregory (*Homil. in Evang.*, 34, 7, *PL*, 76, 1249). Though not widely used in the next few centuries, it became generally popular in the age of Anselm of Canterbury (to a great extent, it seems, under the influence of the school associated with his namesake, Anselm of Laon; cf. J. de Ghellinck, *L'Essor de la littérature latine au XIIe siècle* [Desclée, Paris, 1946], I, 41–43). In this period, however, under the

"breath of the voice," and who cannot understand that color is something different from body, or wisdom from the soul, are to be blown right out of the discussion of spiritual questions. For in their souls reason, which should be the chief and judge of everything in man, is so muffled up in corporeal imaginings that it cannot unroll itself from them, nor is it able to distinguish them from the things it ought to contemplate pure and unadulterated. For instance, how can someone who does not yet understand how several men are one man in species comprehend how in that most mysterious and lofty nature several persons, each one of whom is perfect God, are one God? Or how can someone whose mind is so dark that he cannot distinguish between his own horse and its color, distinguish between the one God and his several relations? Finally, he who cannot understand that anything except the individual is man will only be able to understand "man" as referring to a human person. For every individual man is a person.[16] How, then, will he be able to understand that manhood, but not a person, was taken by the Word—in other words, that another nature, not another person, was taken?

I have said these things so that no one will presume, before he is able, to discuss the loftiest questions of faith, and so that, if he does presume to do so, no difficulty or impossibility of understanding will be able to shake him from the truth to which he has adhered by faith.

impact of the new interest in systematic theology and theological methodology, its denotation comes to include theological commentary on Scripture as well as the text itself (cf. J. de Ghellinck, *Le Mouvement théologique du XIIᵉ siècle*, 2d ed. [Desclée, Paris, 1948], 109), until finally the term stands for theology or divinity, understood as emerging out of the investigation of Scripture (cf. *Sententiae divinitatis, prologus, Beiträge*, VII/2–3, p. 7*, lines 8–11). For a full account, cf. J. de Ghellinck, " 'Pagina' et 'Sacra Pagina,' " in *Mélanges Auguste Pelzer* (Institut supérieur de philosophie, Louvain, 1947), 23–59. (*b*) The addition of the word *quaestiones* points to the advance from simple exposition of the Biblical text to dialectical development of its themes. The "question," which became the typical form of scholastic theological and philosophical writing, grew quite naturally out of the application of dialectical techniques to problems of Biblical theology. For an example of a "question" *in situ* in a Biblical commentary, cf. the excerpt from Abailard's *Exposition of the Epistle to the Romans*, in this volume. For an example of a theological work on the lines suggested by Anselm's phrase, cf. Robert of Melun (d. 1167), *Quaestiones de divina pagina*, in *Oeuvres de Robert de Melun* (ed. R. Martin), I (Spicilegium sacrum Lovaniense, Louvain, 1932). The nature of *quaestiones* is more fully discussed below, in the introduction to "Theologians of the Twelfth Century."

16 Cf. *Monologion*, 79 (Schmitt, I, 86).

Why God Became Man

THE TEXT

Preface

I have been compelled to finish the following work as best I could, more hastily than I found convenient, and therefore more briefly than I wished, all because of certain persons who copied the first part of it for themselves without my knowledge, before it had been finished and revised. For I should have included and added a number of points to which I have not referred at all, if I had been allowed to publish it at leisure and at an appropriate time. For it was in great distress of mind —the source and reason of my suffering God knows—that I began it, by request, in England, and finished it as an exile in the province of Capua.[1] I have named it *Why God Became Man*, from the theme on which it was written, and I have divided it into two short books. The first of these contains the objections of unbelievers who reject the Christian faith because they regard it as contrary to reason, along with the answers of believers. It ends by proving by necessary reasons (Christ being put out of sight, as if nothing had ever been known of him) that it is impossible for any man to be saved without him. In the same way, as if nothing were known of Christ, it is shown in the second book, by equally clear reasoning and truth, that human nature was created in order that hereafter the whole man, body and soul, should enjoy a blessed immortality. It is proved that it is necessary for this purpose for which man was made to be achieved, but only through a Man-God, and so that all the things we believe concerning Christ must necessarily take place.

[1] Cf. Eadmer, *De vita et conversatione Anselmi*, II, 30 (ed. M. Rule, pp. 391 f.). Anselm began *Cur deus homo* in England in 1094, and completed it in Italy in 1098 (Cf. Landgraf, *Einführung*, 53).

I request all those who wish to copy this book to set at its beginning this little preface, along with the chapter headings of the whole work. In this way, anyone into whose hands it may fall will be able to see, as it were on its face, whether there is anything in the whole work that he should not neglect.

BOOK ONE

CHAPTER I

THE QUESTION ON WHICH THE WHOLE WORK DEPENDS

Both by word of mouth and by letter I have received many earnest requests that I should commit to writing the proofs of a particular doctrine of our faith, as I usually present them to inquirers. I am told that these proofs are thought to be both pleasing and adequate. Those who make this request do not expect to come to faith through reason, but they hope to be gladdened by the understanding and contemplation of the things they believe, and as far as possible to be "ready always to satisfy every one that asketh" them "a reason of that hope which is in" them.[2] The question at issue is habitually presented as an objection by unbelievers, who scoff at Christian simplicity as absurd, while it is pondered in their hearts by many of the faithful. The question is this: For what reason or necessity did God become man and, as we believe and confess, by his death restore life to the world, when he could have done this through another person (angelic or human), or even by a sheer act of will? Many of the unlearned, as well as the learned, ask this question and want an answer. Many, then, ask to have this dealt with; moreover, while the investigation seems difficult, the explanation is intelligible to all, and is appealing because of the usefulness and beauty of the reasoning. Thus, although the holy fathers have really said enough on the subject, I shall undertake to show to those who ask what God may deign to disclose to me concerning it. And since investigations that are carried on by means of question and answer are clearer to many (especially to slower) minds, and so are more acceptable, I shall take one of those who discuss this subject—the one who among

---

[2] I Peter 3:15. Cf. Augustine, *Epist.* 120:4 (*CSEL*, 34/2, 707).

the rest presses me more urgently—to debate with me, so that in this way Boso[3] may ask and Anselm answer.

Boso. While the right order requires that we should believe the deep things of the Christian faith before we undertake to discuss them by reason, it seems careless for us, once we are established in the faith, not to aim at understanding what we believe.[4] Therefore, since I think that by God's prevenient grace I hold the faith of our redemption so firmly that nothing can shake my constant allegiance, even if I can find no reason to help me grasp what I believe, I beg you to show me what many, as you know, seek with me. Tell me what necessity and reason led God, although he is almighty, to take upon him the lowliness and weakness of human nature in order to renew it.

Anselm. What you ask from me is above me, and I am afraid to handle "the things that are too high for me."[5] If someone thinks, or even sees, that I have not given him adequate proof, he may decide that there is no truth in what I have been saying, and not realize that in fact my understanding has been incapable of grasping it.

B. You should not fear this so much, but you should rather remember what often happens when we talk over some question. You know how God often makes clear what was concealed before. You should hope from the grace of God that, if you willingly share what you have freely received,[6] you may be worthy to receive the higher things to which you have yet to attain.

A. There is another reason for thinking that we can hardly (if at all) deal fully with this problem now. We should need to know about power and necessity and will and several other things which are so closely connected that no one of them can be fully considered without the others. Therefore, to discuss them involves a special undertaking which, though difficult enough, is not altogether useless, since the knowledge of them resolves certain difficulties created by ignorance.

B. Then you had better speak briefly about these questions, each in its proper place, so that we shall know enough to carry

---

[3] Boso, first a monk and then (1124–1136) abbot of Bec, spent several years with Anselm at Canterbury. The extant letters of Anselm to Boso are: 146 (Schmitt, III, 292 f.); 174 (IV, 55 f.); and possibly 209 (IV, 104 f.), which refers to the transcription of *Cur deus homo* for the use of Bec (or of Christ Church, the cathedral priory, at Canterbury?).

[4] Cf. *Epist. de incarn. verbi,* 1 (Schmitt, II, 6 f.).

[5] Cf. Ecclesiasticus. 3:22 (A.V., 3:21).

[6] Cf. Matt. 10:8.

out the present task, while what remains to be said can be put off to another time.[7]

A. I also hesitate to respond to your request for the serious reason that the subject matter is not only of great importance, but is fair with a reason above human understanding, just as it has to do with him who is "beautiful above the sons of men."[8] I am always indignant with poor artists when I see our Lord himself painted with an ugly form, and I am afraid that I may find myself in the same position if I dare to set out such a beautiful theme in rude and contemptible language.

B. Even this should not hold you back, because you allow anyone to speak better if he can, and you do not order anyone not to write more beautifully if your language does not please him. But, to stop all your excuses, I am not asking you to do anything for the learned. You will be doing it for me, and for those who make the same request with me.

CHAPTER II

How What Is to Be Said Should Be Taken

A. I see the persistence with which you and your fellows make this request, out of love and religious zeal, and I shall try, to the best of my ability, not so much to show you something as to search with you—with the help of God and of your prayers, which you who ask for this have often promised me when I asked for them with this very task in mind. But there is one condition. I want everything I say to be taken on these terms: that if I say anything that a greater authority does not support, even though I seem to prove it by reason, it is not to be treated as more certain than is warranted by the fact that, at present, I see the question in this way, until God somehow reveals something better to me.[9] If I can answer your questions to a certain extent, it ought to be regarded as certain that a wiser than I will be able to do this more fully. Indeed, we must recognize that, whatever a man can say on this subject, the deeper reasons for so great a thing remain hidden.

---

[7] Cf. F. S. Schmitt, "Ein neues, unvollendetes Werk des hl. Anselm von Canterbury" (*Beiträge*, 33/3, p. 23): "Disciple: There are many matters on which I have been hoping for your answer for a long time—including power and powerlessness, possibility and impossibility, necessity and liberty."

[8] Ps. 44:3 (P.B.V., 45:3).   [9] Cf. *Monologion*, 1 (Schmitt, I, 14).

CHAPTER III

THE OBJECTIONS OF UNBELIEVERS AND REPLIES OF THE FAITHFUL

B. Allow me, then, to use the words of unbelievers. When we eagerly seek out the grounds of our faith, it is fair to put forward the objections of those who will on no account assent to that faith without reason. It is true that they seek the reason because they do not believe, while we seek it because we believe; nevertheless, it is one and the same thing that we seek. And if in your answer you say anything that sacred authority seems to oppose, let me press the point until you make it clear that there is no real opposition.

A. Say whatever seems good to you.

B. The unbelievers, who laugh at our simplicity, charge that we do God injury and insult when we assert that he descended into the womb of a woman, that he was born of a woman, that he grew, nourished by milk and human foods, and—not to speak of many other things that seem inappropriate for God— that he bore weariness, hunger, thirst, blows, and a cross and death between the thieves.

A. We do no injury or insult to God, but with heartfelt thanks we praise and proclaim the ineffable height of his mercy. It is precisely in so far as he has restored us, marvelously and beyond expectation, from the great and merited evils under which we lay to the great and unmerited goods that we had lost, that he has shown greater love and mercy toward us. And if they would earnestly consider how fittingly the restoration of mankind was secured in this way, instead of laughing at our simplicity they would join us in praising the wise loving-kindness of God. For when death had entered into the human race through man's disobedience, it was fitting that life should be restored through the obedience of man.[10] When the sin which was the cause of our condemnation had its beginning from a woman, it was fitting for the author of our justice and salvation to be born of a woman.[11] Since the devil, when he

---

[10] Cf. Rom. 5:12, 19; Leo, *Sermo* 25, 5 (*PL*, 54, 211 f.).

[11] Cf. Justin, *Dial. cum Tryph.*, 100 (*PG*, 6, 710–711); Irenaeus, *Adv. haer.*, III, 22:4; V, 19:1 (*PG*, 7, 958–959; 1175–1176); Tertullian, *De carne Christi*, 17 (*PL*, 2, 827 f.); *Epist. ad Diognetum*, 12:8 (J. B. Lightfoot and J. R. Harmer, *The Apostolic Fathers* [London, 1893], 500); Ambrose, *Expos. in Luc.*, 2:28 (*CSEL*, 32/4, 56); Augustine, *Sermo* 232, 2:2 (*PL*, 38, 1108).

tempted man, conquered him by the tasting of a tree, it was fitting for him to be conquered by man's bearing of suffering on a tree.[12] And a good many other things, when we consider them carefully, show the inexpressible beauty of our redemption, thus accomplished.

CHAPTER IV

These Answers Seem to Unbelievers to Be Inconclusive, and like So Many Pictures

B. It must be admitted that all these things are beautiful, and like so many pictures. But if they do not rest on something solid, they are not enough to convince unbelievers that we ought to believe that God was willing to suffer the things of which we speak. For when a man wants to paint a picture, he selects something solid to paint on, so that his painting will endure. No one paints on water or in air, because no traces of the picture would remain. Now when we present unbelievers with these harmonies you speak of, as so many pictures of a real event, they think that this belief of ours is a fiction, and not a real happening, and so they judge that we are, as it were, painting on a cloud. Thus the rational soundness of the truth— that is, the necessity which proves that it was fitting and possible for God to condescend to the things which we proclaim—must first be shown. Then, so that what we may call the very body of the truth may shine more brightly, those harmonies are to be set forth as a kind of picture of the body.

A. Surely we argue conclusively enough that it was fitting for God to do the things we speak of, when we say that the human race, that very precious work of his, was altogether ruined; that it was not fitting for God's plan for man to be entirely wiped out; and that this same plan could not be put into effect unless the human race were delivered by its Creator himself.

CHAPTER V

The Redemption of Man Could Be Accomplished by No One Except God

B. If it were said that this deliverance was somehow accomplished by some other person (whether by an angel or by a man) rather than by God, the human mind would receive this much

---

12 Cf. *Missale Romanum*, "Preface" of the Passion; Venantius Fortunatus, hymn, *Pange lingua gloriosi*, st. 2–3 (original text in *MGH*, Auctores antiquissimi, IV, pt. 1, p. 28, lines 4–9).

more patiently. After all, God could have made some man without sin, not from the sinful mass[13] or from another man, but as he made Adam, and it seems to me that this work could have been carried out through him.

A. Do you not understand that if any other person redeemed man from eternal death, man would rightly be reckoned as his servant? But in that case man would in no sense have been restored to the dignity he would have had if he had not sinned. For he who was to be the servant of God alone, and equal in everything to the good angels,[14] would be the servant of a being who was not God, and whom the angels did not serve.[15]

CHAPTER VI

How Unbelievers Criticize Us When We Say that God Has Redeemed Us by His Death, that He Has Thus Shown His Love Toward Us, and that He Has Come to Conquer the Devil on Our Behalf

B. This is just what puzzles them most, when we call this deliverance "redemption." In what captivity, they ask us, in what prison or in whose power were you held, from which God could not deliver you, without redeeming you by so many labors and in the end by his own blood?[16] Perhaps we will reply: He redeemed us from sins and from his own wrath and from hell and from the power of the devil, whom he came himself to conquer for us, since we could not do it for ourselves. He also bought back the Kingdom of Heaven for us,[17] and in doing all these things in this way he showed how much he loved us. But then they will answer: If you say that God, who, according to you, created all things by his commandment, could not do all this by a simple command, you contradict yourselves by making him powerless. Or if you admit that he could have done this, but preferred to act as he did, how can you

---

13 On the *massa peccatrix*, cf. Ambrosiaster, *Comm. in ep. ad Rom.*, 5:12 (*PL*, 17, 97); Augustine, *Sermo* 26, 12:13 (*PL*, 38, 177).
14 Cf. Luke 20:36.
15 On this chapter, cf. Augustine, *De trin.*, XIII, 18:23 (*PL*, 42, 1032); Gilbert Crispin, *Disp. Iudaei cum Christiano* (*PL*, 159, 1022 f.).
16 On man's captivity to the devil, cf. Augustine, *Sermo* 27, 2:2 (*PL*, 38, 179).
17 On "redemption" from this captivity, cf. Origen, *Comm. in ep. ad Rom.*, 2:13 (*PG*, 14, 911); Ambrose, *Epist.* 72, 8 (*PL*, 16, 1299).

prove that he is wise, when you assert that he was willing to suffer such unseemly things without any reason?[18] For all the things that you allege depend on his will. For the wrath of God is nothing but his will to punish. If, then, he does not will to punish the sins of man, man is free from sins and from God's wrath and from hell and from the power of the devil, all of which he suffers on account of his sins, and he regains the things he was deprived of on account of those same sins. For in whose power is hell or the devil, or whose is the Kingdom of Heaven, save his who created all things? Thus, whatever you fear or desire is subject to his will, which nothing can withstand. Therefore, if he was willing to save the human race only in the way you describe, when he could have done it by sheer will, to put it mildly, you really disparage his wisdom. For surely, if for no reason a man did by hard labor what he could have done with ease, no one would regard him as wise. And you have no rational ground for saying that God showed in this way how much he loved us[19] unless you can show that it was quite impossible for him to save man in some other way. It is true that, if he could not have done it otherwise, it might have been necessary for him to show his love in this way. But now, when he could save man in another way, why should he do and endure the things you describe? Does he not show the good angels how much he loves them, without enduring such things for them? As for saying that he came to conquer the devil for you,[20] in what sense do you dare to assert that? Does not the omnipotence of God reign everywhere? How, then, did God need to come down from heaven to defeat the devil? Unbelievers seem to be able to bring objections of this sort against us.[21]

CHAPTER VII

THE DEVIL HAD NO JUSTICE ON HIS SIDE AGAINST MAN. WHY HE SEEMS TO HAVE HAD IT. WHY GOD DELIVERED MAN IN THIS WAY

We also commonly say that God was bound to strive with the devil by justice, rather than by force, in order to set man

---

[18] Cf. Augustine, *De trin.*, XIII, 10:13 (*PL*, 42, 1024); Leo, *Sermo* 63, 1 (*PL*, 54, 353).

[19] Cf. Rom. 5:8; Augustine, *loc. cit.*

[20] Cf. *Epist. de incarn. verbi*, 10 (Schmitt, II, 26).

[21] Cf. Augustine, *De agone Christiano*, 11 (*PL*, 40, 297).

free.[22] On this showing, when the devil killed Him in whom there was no reason for death, and who was God, he would justly lose his power over sinners. Otherwise God would have done unjust violence to him, since he was justly in possession of man; after all, he did not seize man by violence, but man handed himself over to him freely. But I cannot see what force this argument has. If the devil or man belonged to himself or to anyone but God, or remained in some power other than God's, perhaps it would be a sound argument. But the devil and man belong to God alone, and neither one stands outside God's power[23]; what case, then, did God have to plead with his own creature, concerning his own creature, in his own affair, unless it was in order to punish his servant, who had persuaded his fellow servant to desert their common master and go over to him, and as a traitor had received a fugitive, as a thief received another thief with what he had stolen from his master? For each was a thief, since one was persuaded by the other to steal himself from his master.[24] What, then, would be more just than for God to do this? Or how could it be unjust for God, the Judge of all, to rescue man, thus held, from the power of him who so unjustly held him—whether to punish him by some other means than the devil or to spare him? For even though it was just for man to be tormented by the devil, it was unjust for the devil to torment him. It is true that man deserved to be punished, and that it was most fitting for this to be done by him whose suggestion man accepted when he sinned. But the devil had earned no right to punish him; on the contrary, this was the height of injustice, since the devil was not moved to do it by love of justice, but was driven by malicious impulse. For he did not do it by God's orders, but only with the permission of God's incomprehensible wisdom, which orders even evil things for good.

I think that those who suppose that the devil has any right to keep man in his possession are led to this conclusion because they see that man is justly subject to ill-treatment by the devil, and that God justly allows this, and on this account they think that the devil justly inflicts it. For sometimes the same thing is both just and unjust, when looked at from different points of view, and for that reason is judged totally just or totally unjust

22 Cf. Irenaeus, *Adv. haer.*, V, 21:3 (*PG*, 7, 1182); Augustine, *De trin.*, XIII, 13 (*PL*, 42, 1027); Leo, *Sermo* 22, 3 (*PL*, 54, 196).
23 Cf. Augustine, *De trin.*, XIII, 12 (*PL*, 42, 1026).
24 Cf. Augustine, *Enarr. in Ps.* 68, 1:9, (*PL*, 36, 848).

by those who do not consider the question carefully. Perhaps someone will strike an innocent person unjustly, and thus will justly deserve to be struck himself. But if the man who is struck ought not to avenge himself, and yet does strike the person who struck him, he acts unjustly. In this case the blow is unjust on the side of him who gives it, since he should not avenge himself, but it is just on the side of him who receives it, because for striking an unjust blow he justly deserves to be struck. From different standpoints, therefore, the same action can be just and unjust, while it may happen that one person will judge it simply just, and another unjust. In this sense, then, the devil is said to torment man justly, because it is just for God to permit it, and just for man to suffer it. But if man is said to suffer justly, this is not because of its own inherent justice, but because he is punished by the just judgment of God.

But someone may bring forward "the handwriting of the decree" that the apostle says "was against us" and was effaced by the death of Christ,[25] and may assume that this means that the devil, by the handwriting of a kind of contract, justly exacted sin from man, before the Passion of Christ, as a sort of interest on the first sin to which he tempted man and as punishment for that sin. In this way he would seem to prove his just rights over man. I am certain, however, that it is not to be understood in this way.[26] For the handwriting is not the devil's, since it is called "the handwriting of the decree," and the decree was not the devil's, but God's. For by God's just judgment it had been decreed and, as it were, confirmed by handwriting that, since man had freely sinned, he should not be able by himself to avoid sin or the penalty of sin. For he is "a wind that goeth and returneth not,"[27] and "whosoever committeth sin is the servant of sin,"[28] nor should he who sins be discharged without punishment, unless mercy spares the sinner, and delivers and restores him. So, then, we should not believe that by means of this handwriting any justice can be found on the devil's side when he torments man. Finally, just as there is no injustice whatever in a good angel, in an evil angel there is

---

25 Col. 2:14.
26 Varied interpretations of the "handwriting" are offered by Hilary, *Tr. in Ps.*, 129:9 (*PL*, 9, 273); Ambrosiaster, *Comm. in ep. ad Rom.*, 5:12 (*PL*, 17, 97); Ambrose, *De virgin.*, 19:126 (*PL*, 16, 314); Augustine, *De pecc. mer.*, II, 30 (*CSEL*, 60, 120); Leo, *Sermo* 22, 4 (*PL*, 54, 197); Gregory, *Homil. in evang.*, 29, 10 (*PL*, 76, 1218).
27 Ps. 77:39 (P.B.V., 78:40).
28 John 8:34.

absolutely no justice. Therefore, there was no reason, as far as the devil was concerned, why God should not use his power against him to deliver man.

CHAPTER VIII

How, Although the Lowly Things We Ascribe to Christ Do Not Belong to His Divinity, Unbelievers Find It Unseemly for Them to Be Attributed Even to His Manhood, and Why They Do Not Think that This Man Died Willingly

A. The will of God should be a good enough reason for us when he does anything, even though we cannot see why he wills it. For the will of God is never irrational.

B. That is true, when it is certain that God does will what is being discussed. But many will never admit that God wills something that seems contrary to reason.

A. What seems to you to be contrary to reason in our statement that God willed the things we believe concerning his incarnation?

B. To put it briefly—for the Most High to stoop to such lowly things; for the Almighty to do anything with such great labor.

A. Those who speak this way do not understand what we believe. For we affirm without any doubt that the divine nature is impassible, and that it can in no sense be brought down from its loftiness or toil in what it wills to do. But we say that the Lord Jesus Christ is true God and true man, one person in two natures and two natures in one person. Thus, when we say that God bears humiliation or weakness, we do not apply this to the sublimity of the impassible nature, but to the weakness of the human substance which he bore, and so we know no reason that opposes our faith. For we do not ascribe any debasement to the divine substance, but we show that there is one person, God and man. Therefore, in the incarnation of God we do not suppose that he undergoes any debasement, but we believe that the nature of man is exalted.[29]

B. All right then; let nothing that is said about Christ with reference to human weakness be attributed to the divine nature. But still, can it ever be proved just or reasonable that God

[29] Cf. Leo, *Sermo*, 46, 1 (*PL*, 54, 292); *Quicumque vult* (*alias*, "The Athanasian Creed").

treated (or allowed to be treated) in this way that Man whom
the Father called his "beloved Son," in whom he was "well
pleased,"[30] and whom the Son made himself to be? For what
justice is there in giving up the most just man of all to death on
behalf of the sinner? What man would not be judged worthy of
condemnation if he condemned the innocent in order to free
the guilty? The whole thing seems to go back to the same incongruity that I mentioned before.[31] For if he could not save
sinners except by condemning the just, where is his omnipotence? But if he could, but would not, how are we to defend
his wisdom and justice?

A. God the Father did not treat that Man as you seem to
think, or give up the innocent to death for the guilty. For he
did not force him to die or allow him to be slain against his
will; on the contrary, he himself readily endured death in order
to save men.

B. Perhaps he was not unwilling, since he consented to the
will of the Father, and yet in a way the Father seems to have
compelled him by his command. For it is said that Christ
"humbled himself, becoming obedient" to the Father "unto
death, even to the death of the cross, for which cause God also
hath exalted him"[32]; and that "he learned obedience by the
things which he suffered"[33]; and that the Father "spared not
even his own Son, but delivered him up for us all."[34] Similarly
the Son says, "I came, not to do mine own will, but the will of
him that sent me."[35] And when he is about to go to his Passion,
he says, "As the Father hath given me commandment, so do
I."[36] And again, "The chalice which my Father hath given me,
shall I not drink it?"[37] And in another place: "Father, if it be
possible, let this chalice pass from me. Nevertheless, not as I
will, but as thou wilt."[38] And, "Father, if this chalice may not
pass away, but I must drink it, thy will be done."[39] According
to all these passages, Christ seems to have endured death more
by force of obedience than by the free decision of his own will.

30 Cf. Matt. 3:17.
31 Cf. Chapter VI, above.
32 Phil. 2:8 f.
33 Heb. 5:8.
34 Rom. 8:32.
35 John 6:38 (varies widely from Vulgate).
36 John 14:31.
37 John 18:11.
38 Matt. 26:39.
39 Matt. 26:42.

CHAPTER IX

That He Died Voluntarily, and What It Means to Say that "He Became Obedient Unto Death," and "For Which Cause God Also Hath Exalted Him," and "I Came Not to Do Mine Own Will," and "God Spared Not His Own Son," and "Not as I Will, but as Thou Wilt."

A. It seems to me that you fail to distinguish what he did as the requirement of obedience from what he endured, apart from any requirement of obedience, simply because he maintained his obedience.

B. I need to have this explained more clearly.

A. Why did the Jews persecute him even to death?

B. Simply because he constantly upheld truth and justice, in life and in word.

A. I think that God requires this from every rational creature, and that the latter owes this to God as a matter of obedience.

B. So we must acknowledge.

A. Then that Man owed this obedience to God the Father, and his manhood owed it to his divinity, and the Father required this from him.

B. Nobody can doubt this.

A. Now you see what he did as the requirement of obedience.

B. That is true, and I begin to see what he endured when it was brought on him by his perseverance in obedience. For death was inflicted on him because he persevered in obedience, and he endured it. But I cannot understand how his obedience did not require this.

A. If man had never sinned, ought he to suffer death, or ought God to require it of him?

B. According to our belief, man would not have died, and this would not have been required of him. But I want to hear what reason you give for this.

A. You do not deny that the rational creature was created just, in order that it might be blessed in the enjoyment of. God?

B. No.

A. And you will not think it at all fitting for God to compel the creature, whom he made just, with a view to blessedness, to be wretched by no fault of his own. Now it would be a wretched thing for a man to die against his will.

B. It is clear that if man had not sinned, it would not have been right for God to require him to die.

A. Therefore God did not compel Christ to die, when there was no sin in him, but Christ himself freely underwent death, not by yielding up his life as an act of obedience, but on account of his obedience in maintaining justice, because he so steadfastly persevered in it that he brought death on himself.

It can even be said that the Father commanded him to die, when he gave him the commandment through which he met death. In this sense, therefore, he did "as the Father gave" him "commandment," [40] and drank the "chalice" which his "Father gave him," [41] and became "obedient" to the Father "unto death," [42] and so "learned obedience by the things which he suffered" [43]—that is, how far obedience should be maintained. But the expression, "he learned," can be understood in two ways. For "he learned" may be used instead of "he made others learn," or it may mean that he learned by experience what he was not unaware of by knowledge. But when the apostle, after saying that "he humbled himself, becoming obedient unto death, even to the death of the cross," added, "For which cause God also hath exalted him, and hath given him a name which is above all names" [44]—David said something like this: "He drank of the brook in the way, therefore he lifted up his head" [45]—he did not mean to say that he could not possibly have reached this exaltation apart from this obedience unto death, or that this exaltation was granted only in return for this obedience. For before Christ suffered, he himself said that all things were "delivered" to him by his Father, [46] and that all that belonged to the Father was his. [47] The fact is that the Son, with the Father and the Holy Spirit, had determined to show the loftiness of his omnipotence by no other means than death. Now if it was determined that something would be done only through that death, when it is actually done by means of it, it is not unreasonable to say that it is done on account of it.

For if we intend to do anything, but plan to do something else first, by means of which the other may be done, then, if we

---

[40] Cf. John 14:31.

[41] Cf. John 18:11.

[42] Cf. Phil. 2:8.

[43] Cf. Heb. 5:8.

[44] Cf. Phil. 2:8 f.

[45] Ps. 109:7 (P.B.V., 110:7); the Vulgate reads: "He shall drink . . . shall lift up . . ."

[46] Cf. Luke 10:22.

[47] Cf. John 16:15.

do what we intend, having already done what we wanted to do beforehand, the second act is rightly held to be a consequence of the first, since it was delayed until the first was done, because it had been determined that it should take place only by means of the first. If I can cross a river on horseback or in a boat, but decide that I will cross only in a boat, and then delay my crossing because no boat is available, when a boat finally arrives, if I cross, it is right to say: The boat was ready, and so he went across. Indeed, we speak in this way, not only when we decide to do anything *by means of* something else that we want to have done first, but even when we simply do it *after* something else. For instance, if anyone puts off taking food because he has not yet assisted at the celebration of mass that day, it is not improper to say to him, when he has finished what he wanted to do first, "Now take your food, because you have done that for the sake of which you put off taking it." It is far less strange, then, to say that Christ was exalted because he endured death, since he resolved to bring about that exaltation through his death and after it. In the same way, we can understand the statement that the same Lord "advanced in wisdom and . . . grace with God"[48]—not because this was really the case, but because he conducted himself as if it were. For he was exalted after death, just as if it happened on account of the latter.

Furthermore, when he himself says, "I came not to do mine own will, but the will of him that sent me,"[49] this is the same kind of saying as, "My doctrine is not mine."[50] For if anyone possesses something, not of himself but from God, he should speak of it as God's rather than his own. But no man has the truth he teaches, or a just will, from himself; these come from God. Christ came, then, not to do his own will, but to do the Father's will, since the just will which he had came not from his humanity but from his divinity. But to say that God "spared not even his own Son, but delivered him up for us"[51] simply means that he did not set him free. Many statements like this are found in Holy Scripture. Again, when he says, "Father, if it be possible, let this chalice pass from me; nevertheless, not as I will, but as thou wilt,"[52] and, "If this chalice may not pass away, but I must drink it, thy will be done,"[53] by his own will he means the natural desire for safety, by which

---

[48] Cf. Luke 2:52.
[50] John 7:16.
[52] Matt. 26:39.

[49] John 6:38.
[51] Rom. 8:32.
[53] Matt. 26:42.

his human flesh shrank from the pain of death. It is true that he speaks of the Father's will, but not because the Father preferred the death of his Son to his life—rather, because the Father was unwilling for the human race to be restored unless man performed a great act, equal to the Son's death. Since reason did not demand what another could not do, the Son says that the Father wills his death, while he himself prefers to suffer death rather than leave the human race unsaved. It is as though he were to say: "Since thou dost not will that the reconciliation of the world should be brought about in any other way, I say that in this sense thou willest my death. Therefore, let this thy will be done; that is, let my death take place, that the world may be reconciled to thee." For we often say that someone wills something because he does not will something else, when, if he were to will the latter, what he is said to will could not happen. For instance, we say that a man wants to put out a lamp, when he does not want to shut the window through which the wind comes in and blows out the lamp. In this sense, then, the Father willed the Son's death, because he was not willing for the world to be saved unless a man were to do some great deed, as I have said. Since no one else could achieve this, for the Son, who willed the salvation of men, this amounted to the same thing as if the Father had commanded him to die. And thus he did "as the Father gave" him "commandment,"[54] and drank "the chalice which the Father gave" him,[55] "obedient unto death."[56]

CHAPTER X

ANOTHER CORRECT INTERPRETATION OF THE SAME STATEMENTS IS POSSIBLE

Another correct interpretation is possible, to the effect that through that holy will, by which the Son was willing to die for the salvation of the world, the Father (though without any compulsion) gave him the "commandment"[57] and the "chalice"[58] of his Passion, and did not spare him, but "delivered him up for us"[59] and willed his death—and that the Son himself was "obedient unto death"[60] and "learned obedience by the things which he suffered."[61] For according to

[54] Cf. John 14:31.   [55] Cf. John 18:11.   [56] Phil. 2:8.
[57] Cf. John 14:31.   [58] Cf. John 18:11.
[59] Cf. Rom. 8:32; Augustine, *Tr. in Ioan.*, 112, 5 (*PL*, 35, 1932).
[60] Cf. Phil. 2:8.   [61] Heb. 5:8.

his manhood he had the will to live justly from the Father, and not from himself; similarly, he could have the will by which he was willing to die, to achieve such a great good, only "from the Father of lights," from whom comes "every best gift, and every perfect gift."[62] And, just as the Father is said to draw men by giving them the will, it is not improper to assert that he moves them. For when the Son said of the Father, "No man cometh to me, except the Father draw him,"[63] he might just as well have·said, "Except he move him." And similarly he could have gone on, "No man runneth to death for my name's sake, except the Father move or draw him." For since everyone is drawn or moved by will to what he unchangeably wills, it is not unseemly to assert that God draws or moves when he gives such a will. This drawing or moving is not to be understood as violent necessity, but as the free and ready steadfastness of the good will that is received. If, then, in this sense we cannot deny that the Father drew or moved the Son to death, by giving him that will, who can fail to see, in the same terms, that he gave him "commandment" to endure death willingly, and gave him the "chalice" to drink, but not against his will.[64] And if it is right to say that the Son did not spare himself, but delivered himself up for us with a ready will, who can deny that it is right to say that the Father, from whom he received such a will, did not spare him, "but delivered him up for us" and willed his death?[65] In the same way, the Son, by keeping steadfastly and willingly the will which he received from the Father, became "obedient" to him "unto death"[66] and "learned obedience by the things which he suffered"[67]—that is, he learned what a great work is to be done through obedience. For this is simple and true obedience, when the rational nature, not of necessity but willingly, keeps the will that it has received from God.

There are other possible interpretations of the statement that the Father willed the Son's death, although we may already have offered enough explanations. For we not only say that a man wills something if he makes another will it, but we even say that someone wills a thing, if he approves when another wills it, without actually making him will it. For instance, when we see someone who is prepared to suffer hardship in order to achieve something good, although we admit that we want him to suffer the pain, it is not the pain but the will that

62 James 1:17.
64 Cf. John 14:31, 18:11.
66 Phil. 2:8.

63 John 6:44.
65 Cf. Rom. 8:32.
67 Heb. 5:8.

we desire and love. Then too, when a man can prevent something, but does not do so, we commonly say that he wills what he does not prevent.[68] Since, then, the Son's will pleased the Father, and he did not prevent him from willing what he willed, or from carrying it out, it is correct to state that he willed that the Son should endure such a dutiful and fruitful death, even though he did not love the Son's suffering. Moreover, when he said that the "chalice" could not pass away unless he drank it,[69] he did not mean that he could not avoid death if he wished. But because (as has been said) the world could not be saved in any other way, he steadfastly determined to suffer death rather than leave the world unsaved. It was with this in mind that he said these words—not to show that he could not possibly escape death, but to teach that the human race could be saved only through his death. For whatever is said about him in similar terms is to be explained as meaning that he died by free choice, and not by any necessity. For he was almighty, and we read of him that "he was offered because it was his own will."[70] And he himself says: "I lay down my life, that I may take it again. No man taketh it away from me: but I lay it down of myself, and I have power to lay it down: and I have power to take it up again."[71] Thus it cannot rightly be said that he is forced into this in any way, since he does it by his own power and his own will.

B. But this single fact, that God allowed him to be so treated, does not seem fitting for such a Father with respect to such a Son, even though he was willing.

A. On the contrary, it is supremely fitting for such a Father to permit such a Son to do what he wills to do to the praise and honor of God and the benefit and salvation of men, when the latter could not be saved in another way.

B. We are still pondering the problem of showing how that death is reasonable and necessary. Failing this, it seems that the Son should not have willed it, and that the Father should neither have compelled nor permitted it. For the question is, why God could not have saved man in some other way, or, if he could have, why he chose to save him in this way.[72] Not only does it seem unfitting for God to have saved man in this way, but it is not clear why that death should avail for man's

---

[68] Cf. *De casu diaboli*, 28 (Schmitt, I, 276).
[69] Cf. John 18:11.   [70] Isa. 53:7.
[71] John 10:17 f.; cf. Augustine, *De trin.*, IV, 13:16 (*PL*, 42, 898 f.).
[72] Cf. Chapters VI and VIII, above.

salvation. For it is an extraordinary thing if God so delights in or stands in need of the blood of the innocent that apart from his death he cannot or will not spare the guilty.

A. Since in this inquiry you are taking the part of those who will believe nothing unless it is first proved by reason,[73] I want to make an agreement with you. We shall attribute to God nothing that is at all unfitting, and we shall reject no reason, even the slightest, unless a weightier one is opposed to it. For just as nothing that is in the least degree unseemly can be acknowledged in God,[74] so even the slightest reason has the force of necessity, unless it is outweighed by a greater.

B. I accept nothing more willingly in this whole discussion than this agreement, which we are both to keep.

A. The only question at issue is the incarnation of God, together with the things we believe about the manhood assumed by him.

B. That is right.

A. Then let us suppose that the incarnation of God and the things we say about this Man have never happened. Let us agree that man was made for blessedness, which cannot be attained in this life, and that, while no man can reach it unless his sins are forgiven, no man passes through this life without sin. And let us agree on the other points which we must believe for eternal salvation.[75]

B. All right; nothing in all this seems impossible or unseemly for God.

A. Then remission of sins is necessary for a man, if he is to arrive at blessedness.

B. So we all hold.[76]

CHAPTER XI

THE MEANING OF SIN, AND OF SATISFACTION FOR SIN

A. We are to ask, then, on what ground God forgives men their sins. In order to do this more clearly, let us first see what it means to sin and to make satisfaction for sin.

B. It is for you to explain, and for me to listen.

[73] Cf. Chapter III, above.
[74] Cf. *Epist. de incarn. verbi*, 10 (Schmitt, II, 26).
[75] Cf. Preface, above.
[76] On Chapters IX, X, cf. Ambrosiaster, *Comm. in ep. ad Ephes.*, 5:2 (*PL*, 17, 416).

A. If an angel or a man always rendered to God what is due to him, he would never sin.

B. I cannot contradict you.

A. Thus to sin is the same thing as not to render his due to God.

B. What is the debt which we owe to God?

A. Every inclination of the rational creature ought to be subject to the will of God.

B. Nothing could be truer.

A. This is the debt which angels and men owe to God. No one who pays it sins; everyone who does not pay it sins. This is the justice or rectitude of the will, which makes men just or upright in heart, that is, in will.[77] This is the sole and entire honor which we owe to God, and God requires from us. For only such a will does works pleasing to God, when it is able to act; and when it cannot act, it pleases by itself alone, since apart from it no work is pleasing. One who does not render this honor to God takes away from God what belongs to him, and dishonors God, and to do this is to sin. Moreover, as long as he does not repay what he has stolen, he remains at fault. And it is not enough merely to return what was taken away; in view of the insult committed, he must give back more than he took away. For it is not enough for someone who has injured another's health to restore his health without making some recompense for the pain and injury suffered, and, similarly, it is not enough for someone who violates another's honor to restore the honor, unless he makes some kind of restitution that will please him who was dishonored, according to the extent of the injury and dishonor. We should also note that, when someone pays back what he unjustly took away, he ought to give something that could not be required of him if he had not stolen another's property. So, then, everyone who sins must repay to God the honor that he has taken away, and this is the satisfaction that every sinner ought to make to God.

B. Although you frighten me a little, I have nothing to say against any of these statements, since we promised to follow reason.

[77] Cf. *De veritate,* 12 (Schmitt, I, 194); Ps. 35:11 (A.V., 36:10).

CHAPTER XII

WHETHER IT WOULD BE FITTING FOR GOD TO FORGIVE SINS BY
MERCY ALONE, WITHOUT ANY PAYMENT OF MAN'S DEBT

A. Let us go back and see whether it is fitting for God to remit sins by mercy alone, without any payment for the honor taken away from him.

B. I do not see why it is not fitting.

A. To remit sin in this way is the same thing as not to punish it. And since to deal rightly with sin without satisfaction is the same thing as to punish it, if it is not punished it is remitted irregularly.

B. What you say is reasonable.

A. But it is not fitting for God to remit any irregularity in his Kingdom.

B. I am afraid of sinning, if I want to say anything different.

A. Then it is not fitting for God to remit sin thus unpunished.

B. That follows.

A. Something else follows, if sin is thus remitted unpunished. He who sins and he who does not sin will be in the same position with God. But this is unseemly for God.

B. I cannot deny it.

A. And look at this. Everyone knows that the justice of men is under a law, so that the recompense paid by God is measured by the quantity of justice.

B. So we believe.

A. But if sin is neither paid for nor punished, it is subject to no law.

B. I cannot suppose anything else.

A. Then injustice is more free than justice, if it is remitted by mercy alone, and this seems very incongruous. This incongruity reaches the point of making injustice resemble God, since injustice will be no more subject to anyone's law than God is.

B. I cannot stand up to your reasoning. But when God commands us to forgive altogether those who sin against us,[78] it seems inconsistent for him to enjoin this on us if it is not proper for him to do it himself.

A. There is no inconsistency here, because God enjoins this on us lest we presume to do what belongs to God alone. For it belongs to no one to execute vengeance save to him who is Lord of all.[79] For when earthly authorities do this rightly, God

78 Cf. Matt. 6:12.   79 Cf. Rom. 12:19.

himself, who appointed them for this purpose, really does it.[80]

B. You have removed the inconsistency that I thought was present, but I should like to have your reply to another difficulty. For God is so free that he is subject to no law and to no one's judgment, and so kind that nothing kinder can be conceived, and nothing is right or fitting save what he wills. But that makes it seem extraordinary to say that he does not wish, or is not at liberty, to forgive wrong done to him, when we are accustomed to seek pardon from him even for wrongs we do to others.

A. What you say about his freedom and will and kindness is quite true, but we must interpret all these by reason in a way that will not seem to contradict his dignity. For liberty only extends to the beneficial and fitting, and nothing that does something unseemly to God can be called kindness. But when it is said that what he wills is just, and what he does not will is not just, this must not be taken to mean that if God were to will something unfitting, it would be just because he willed it. For it does not follow that if God wills to lie, it is just to lie, but, rather, that he is not God. For the will cannot possibly will to lie, unless the truth has been falsified in it, or, rather, unless it has been falsified by forsaking the truth. Thus, to say, "If God wills to lie," is the same thing as to say, "If God's nature is such that he could will to lie," and it does not follow from this that a lie is just. Unless, indeed, we interpret it in the sense in which we say of two impossibilities, "If this is, that is," when neither this nor that is really the case. For example, someone may say, "If water is dry, then fire is wet," when neither is true. Thus it is only true to say, "If God wills this, it is just," of those things which it is not unfitting for God to will.[81] For if God wills it to rain, it is just for it to rain, and if he wills that some man should be killed, it is just for him to be killed. Therefore, if it is not fitting for God to do anything unjustly or without due order, it does not belong to his freedom or kindness or will to forgive unpunished the sinner who does not repay to God what he took away.

B. You have removed every objection that I thought I could bring against you.

A. See further why it is not fitting for God to do this.

B. I listen willingly to whatever you say.[82]

[80] Cf. Rom. 13:1.   [81] Cf. Augustine, *De symbolo*, 1:2 (*PL*, 40, 627).
[82] On this chapter, cf. Augustine, *Enarr. in Ps.* 50:11 (*PL*, 36, 592).

CHAPTER XIII

Nothing Is Less Tolerable in the Order of Things than for the Creature to Take Away the Honor Due to the Creator and Not Repay What He Takes Away

A. Nothing is less tolerable in the order of things, than for the creature to take away the honor due to the Creator and not repay what he takes away.

B. Nothing is clearer than this.

A. But nothing is more unjustly tolerated than that which is most intolerable.

B. This is not obscure, either.

A. I think, then, that you will not say that God ought to tolerate that than which nothing is more unjustly tolerated— namely, that the creature should not restore to God what he takes away.

B. Quite the opposite; I realize that it must be denied.

A. Again, if nothing is greater or better than God, then the highest justice, which is none other than God himself, maintains nothing more justly than his honor, in the ordering of things.[83]

B. Nothing can be plainer than this.

A. Then God maintains nothing more justly than the honor of his dignity.

B. I must grant this.

A. Does it seem to you that he preserves it wholly if he permits it to be taken away from him, and neither receives recompense nor punishes him who took it away?

B. I dare not say so.

A. Therefore, either the honor that was taken away must be repaid or punishment must follow. Otherwise, God will be either unjust to himself or powerless to accomplish either; but it is impious even to imagine this.

CHAPTER XIV

How God Is Honored in the Punishment of the Sinner

B. I think that nothing more reasonable can be said. But I want to hear from you whether the punishment of the sinner brings honor to God, and what sort of honor this is. For when the

[83] Cf. *Monologion*, 16 (Schmitt, I, 30 f.).

sinner does not repay what he took away, but is punished, if the punishment of the sinner is not to the honor of God, then God loses his honor and does not regain it. But this seems contrary to what has been said.

A. It is impossible for God to lose his honor. For if a sinner does not freely pay what he owes, God takes it from him against his will. In the one case, a man of his own free will manifests due subjection to God, either by avoiding sin or by making payment for it; in the other, God subjects him to himself against his will by torment, and in this way shows that he is man's Lord, even though the man himself refuses to admit it of his own will. In this matter we should observe that, just as man in sinning seizes what belongs to God, so God in punishing takes away what belongs to man. For not only what a man already possesses is said to belong to him, but also what he has it in his power to possess. Thus, since man was so made that he could obtain blessedness if he did not sin, when he is deprived of blessedness and every good on account of sin, he pays from his own property, all unwillingly, what he stole. For even though God does not apply what he takes away to his own use and advantage—as a man puts the money he takes away from another to his own use—nonetheless he uses what he takes away for his own honor, by the very fact that he does take it away. For by taking it away he proves that the sinner and all that belongs to him are subject to himself.

CHAPTER XV

Whether God Suffers Even the Slightest Violation of His Honor

B. I am pleased with what you say. But there is still another question that I want you to answer. You prove that God ought to maintain his honor; why, then, does he allow it to be violated at all? For if something is allowed to suffer damage in any way, it is not completely and perfectly preserved.

A. As far as God himself is concerned, nothing can be added to his honor or subtracted from it. For to himself, he himself is honor incorruptible and absolutely unchangeable. But when the particular creature, either by nature or reason, keeps the order that belongs to it and is, as it were, assigned to it, it is said to obey God and to honor him, and this applies specially to the rational nature, to which it is given to understand what it owes. When it wills what it ought to will, it honors God—not because it bestows something on him, but because it willingly submits itself to God's will and direction, and keeps its own place in the universe of things, and maintains the beauty of that same universe, as far as in it lies. But when it does not will what it ought, it dishonors God, as far as it is concerned, since it does not readily submit itself to his direction, but disturbs the order and beauty of the universe, as far as lies in it, although of course it cannot injure or stain the power and dignity of God.

For if the things that are contained by the circle of heaven wished not to be under heaven or to be further removed from heaven, they could actually exist nowhere but under heaven, and could flee from heaven only by approaching heaven. For wherever they came from or went to, and however they went, they would still be under heaven, and the further they were removed from any given part of heaven, the closer they would approach to the opposite part. Hence, even though a man or a wicked angel does not want to be subject to the divine will and appointment, he is unable to escape it; if he tries to escape the will that commands, he runs into the power of the will that punishes. And if you ask how he crosses over, the answer is that he does it only under the will that permits it, and supreme wisdom redirects the very perversity of his will or action toward the order and beauty of the aforesaid universe. For the ready satisfaction for wrongdoing and the exaction of a penalty from him who does not give satisfaction—it being understood that God brings good out of evil in many ways—hold their own place in this universe and maintain the beauty of its order. If the divine wisdom did not add these requirements wherever wrongdoing tries to disturb right order, there would arise a certain ugliness, derived from the violation of the beauty of order, in the very universe which God ought to regulate, and God would seem to fail in his direction of the world.[84] Now, since both these things are unseemly, and therefore impossible, every sin is necessarily followed either by satisfaction or by punishment.[85]

B. You have satisfied my criticism.

A. It is evident, then, that no one can honor or dishonor God, as he is in himself; at the same time, anyone who submits his

---

[84] Cf. Augustine, *Enarr. in Ps.* 7:19 (*PL*, 36, 108); *Epist.* 140, 2:4 (*CSEL*, 34/3, 157 f.); *De lib. arbit.*, III, 9:26 (*PL*, 32, 1283 f.).
[85] Cf. Tertullian, *De pudic.*, 2 (*CSEL*, 20, 224).

will to God's will, or withdraws it, seems to do one or the other, as far as lies in him.

B. I do not know what I can say to the contrary.

CHAPTER XVI

THE REASON WHY THE NUMBER OF THE ANGELS WHO FELL IS TO BE MADE UP FROM AMONG MEN

A. I still have something to add.

B. Go on, until I am tired of listening.

A. It is certain that God intended to make up the number of the fallen angels from human nature, which he made without sin.[86]

B. We believe this, but I should like to have some reason for it.

A. You are trying to trick me. We planned to deal with nothing except the incarnation of God, and you are inserting other questions for me to answer.[87]

B. Do not be angry; "God loveth a cheerful giver."[88] For no one makes it clearer that he cheerfully gives what he promises than he who gives more than he promises. So, then, tell me freely what I ask.

A. We cannot doubt that the rational nature, which either is or is going to be blessed in the contemplation of God, was foreseen by God as existing in a particular reasonable and perfect number, so that its number cannot fittingly be greater or smaller. For it is false to say that God does not know in what number it would be best for it to be created; but if he knows, he will create it in the number that he knows to be most fitting for his purpose. Therefore, unless the angels who fell were made to be included within that number, they fell of necessity, because they could not persevere outside it; but it is absurd to suppose this.

B. What you say is the manifest truth.

A. Therefore, since they should have been in that number, either their number must necessarily be made up, or else the

---

86 Cf. *De casu diaboli*, 5; 23 (Schmitt, I, 243; 270). The idea appears in Augustine, *Enchir.*, 29 (*PL*, 40, 246); Gregory, *Homil. in evang.*, 21, 2 (*PL*, 76, 1171).

87 Cf. Chapter X, above.

88 II Cor. 9:7. Cf. Ecclesiasticus. 35:11.

rational nature will remain incomplete in number, although it was foreseen in a perfect number; but this cannot be.

B. Without doubt, their number is to be made up.

A. Then it is necessary for it to be made up from human nature, since there is no other possible source.[89]

CHAPTER XVII

OTHER ANGELS CANNOT REPLACE THEM

B. Why can they themselves not be restored, or other angels in their place?

A. When you see the difficulty of our restoration, you will see the impossibility of their reconciliation.[90] Moreover, apart from the fact that this would be inconsistent with the perfection of the first creation, other angels cannot replace them, because they ought not to do so, unless they could be what the first angels would have been if they had not sinned. But the latter would have persevered without witnessing any retribution for sin, and this would be impossible for any who replaced them after their fall. For he who knows no punishment for sin and he who forever witnesses its eternal punishment are not equally praiseworthy if they stand firm in truth. For we must suppose that the good angels were confirmed, not by the fall of the wicked, but by their own merit. For just as the good would have been condemned together with the wicked if they had sinned with them, so the unjust would have been confirmed as well as the just if they had stood with them. Indeed, if some of them were to be confirmed only by the fall of others, either none would ever have been confirmed or else it was necessary for one to fall so that he might be punished for the confirmation of the rest—but both these notions are absurd. Therefore, those who stood were confirmed in the same way in which all would have been confirmed if they had stood. I expounded this way as well as I could, when I dealt with the question why God did not grant perseverance to the devil.[91]

B. You have proved that the evil angels are to be replaced from human nature, and it is clear from this reasoning that elect men will not be fewer in number than the reprobate angels. But, if you can, indicate whether there will be more.

[89] Cf. Augustine, *De civ. dei*, XIV, 26 (*CSEL*, 40/2, 54 f.).
[90] Cf. Book II, Chapter XXI, below.
[91] Cf. *De casu diaboli*, 2–3; 24 (Schmitt, I, 235 ff.; 271 f.).

CHAPTER XVIII

WHETHER THERE WILL BE MORE HOLY MEN
THAN THERE ARE WICKED ANGELS

A. If the angels, before any of them fell, existed in the perfect number of which we have spoken,[92] men were made for the sole purpose of replacing the lost angels, and it is evident that there will not be more of them. But if that number was not found in all the angels together, both what was lost and what was originally lacking are to be filled up from among men, and there will be more elect men than reprobate angels. In this case, we shall say that men were made, not simply to make up the diminished number, but also to complete the still imperfect number.

B. Which view should we hold? Were the angels created in a perfect number to begin with, or not?

A. I shall tell you what I think.

B. I can hardly ask you to do more.

A. If man was made after the fall of the wicked angels, as some interpret Genesis to mean, I do not see how I can prove either position decisively. For it could be, I think, that the angels were in a perfect number to begin with, and that man was created afterward to fill up their depleted number. It could be also that they were not in a perfect number, because God put off—as he still puts off—completing that number, intending to make man in his own time. On this showing, God might only perfect the still incomplete number, or also, if it were diminished, he might make it up. But if the whole creation was produced at once,[93] and the "days" of Moses' account, where he seems to say that the world was not made all at once, are not to be equated with the days in which we live,[94] I cannot understand how the angels were made in that complete number. Certainly, if this were so, it seems to me to follow that, unless some angels and men were necessarily going to fall, there would be more in the Heavenly City than the appropriateness of the perfect number required. Therefore, if all things were created at once, the angels and the first two human beings seem to have been in an imperfect number, so that, if no angel were to fall, only what was lacking would be made up, while, if any were

92 Cf. Chapter XVI, above.
93 Cf. Augustine, *De Genes. ad litt.*, IV, 33 (*CSEL*, 28, 131 ff.); John Scotus Erigena, *De divis. nat.*, V (*PL*, 122, 1006 ff.).
94 Cf. Augustine, *De civ. dei.* XI, 9 (*CSEL*, 40/1, 524).

lost, what was lost would also be replaced. In this way human nature, which was weaker, would, so to speak, vindicate God and confound the devil, if the latter tried to blame his fall on his weakness while the weaker nature remained upright. And even if it too were to fall, it would justify God much more against the devil and against itself, since, though made much weaker and mortal, it would rise in the elect from such great weakness to a height loftier than that from which the devil had fallen—to the height to which the good angels, with whom it ought to be equal, had advanced after the ruin of the wicked angels, because they persevered.

For these reasons it seems likely to me that the angels did not constitute the perfect number by which the city on high should be perfected. This is possible, even if man was not created at the same time as the angels, and it seems necessary if they were created together—as the majority think, because it is written, "He that liveth forever created all things together."[95] But even if the perfection of the created world is to be found in the number of natures rather than the number of individuals, human nature must have been made to round out that perfection—unless it is superfluous, a thing we dare not say of the nature of the smallest little worm. It was made, therefore, for its own sake, and not simply to replace individuals of another nature. Thus it is obvious that, even if no angel had perished, men would have had their own place in the Heavenly City. It follows, then, that the perfect number was not made up by the angels, before any of them fell. Otherwise, either men or some of the angels would have had to fall, since no one could remain there beyond the perfect number.[96]

B. You have accomplished something.

A. There is another reason which seems to me to give considerable support to the opinion that the angels were not created in that perfect number.

B. Tell me about it.

A. If the angels were created in that perfect number, and men were created purely and simply to replace the lost angels, it is obvious that men would never have risen to blessedness, unless some angels had fallen from it.

B. That is agreed.

A. Then, if anyone says that elect men will rejoice in the loss

---

[95] Ecclesiasticus 18:1. Cf. Augustine, *De Genes. ad litt. lib. imperf.*, 9:31 (*CSEL*, 28/2, 481 f.).
[96] Cf. Chapter XVI, above.

of the angels as much as in their own exaltation (since unquestionably the latter would not have come about apart from
the former), how can they be defended from this perverse joy?
Or how shall we say that the angels who fell were replaced by
men, if the former were to remain free from this defect, if they
had not fallen—free, that is, from joy in the fall of others—
whereas the latter cannot be free from it? How, indeed, can
they rightly be made blessed with this defect in them? Then
what temerity it is to say that God is neither willing nor able to
make this replacement without this defect!

B. Is this not just like the case of the Gentiles, who were
called to the faith because the Jews spurned it?

A. No. For even if all the Jews had believed, the Gentiles
would still have been called, because "in every nation, he that
feareth" God, "and worketh justice, is acceptable to him."[97]
But because the Jews despised the apostles, this was the occasion of their turning to the Gentiles.

B. I do not see what I can possibly say against this.

A. How does this joy over another's fall seem to you to arise?

B. Surely, just because each one will be certain that he would
never have been where he is if someone else had not fallen
from that height.

A. Then, if no one had this certainty, there would be no
occasion for joy in another's loss.

B. So it seems.

A. Do you think that any one of them will have this certainty,
if they are many more in number than those who fell?

B. It is quite impossible for me to suppose that he has it or
ought to have it. For how will anyone be able to know whether
he was created to make up what had been lost or to fill up
what was still short of the number required to constitute the
city? But all will be certain that they were created to complete
that city.

A. Then if they are more numerous than the reprobate
angels, none of them either will or ought to be able to know
that he was exalted to that city solely because of another's fall.

B. That is true.

A. Thus no one will have any reason to rejoice in another's
loss.

B. That follows.

A. Since, then, we see that, if there are more elect men than
reprobate angels, the unseemly result that otherwise would

[97] Acts 10:35.

necessarily follow does not follow, and since it will be impossible for anything unseemly to exist in that city, it seems that the angels cannot have been created in that perfect number, and that there will be more blessed men than wretched angels.

B. I do not see on what grounds this can be denied.

A. I think that still another reason for this conclusion can be stated.

B. Then you ought to bring it forward.

A. We believe that the corporeal structure of this world is to be renewed for the better,[98] and that this will neither take place before the number of elect men is completed and the blessed city perfected nor be postponed beyond its perfection.[99] From this we can infer that from the beginning God intended to perfect both together. In this way the lesser nature that did not perceive God would not be perfected before the greater, which ought to enjoy God, and yet, changed for the better, would, as it were, share in the joy of the perfection of the greater. Indeed, every creature would delight in its own glorious and wonderful consummation, eternally rejoicing in its Creator and itself and its fellows, each in its own way. Thus by God's direction even the unconscious creature would display by nature what the will does freely in the rational creature. For we are accustomed to rejoice in the exaltation of our forefathers —for instance, when we enjoy a festal celebration on the "birthdays" of the saints, rejoicing in their glory.[1] This opinion seems to be supported by the fact that if Adam had not sinned, God would still have put off the perfection of that city until the number he required was made up from men, and men themselves were transformed, so to speak, into the immortal immortality of their bodies.[2] For in paradise they had a kind of immortality, that is, the power of not dying, but this was not an immortal power, because it could die and leave them unable not to die.

But if it is true that God from the beginning intended to perfect that spiritual and blessed city and this earthly and

---

[98] Cf. II Peter 3:13; Rev. 21:1.

[99] Cf. Augustine, De civ. dei, XX, 14 (CSEL, 40/2, 461).

[1] On the use of natalicia for the anniversaries of saints, etc., cf. Ignatius, Ep. ad Rom., 6:1 (PG, 5, 692); Mart. Polycarpi, 18 (PG, 5, 1044); A. C. Rush, Death and Burial in Christian Antiquity (Studies in Christian Antiquity, Catholic University of America Press, Washington, 1941), Chapter 4; G. Dix, The Shape of the Liturgy (Dacre Press, Westminster, 1945), 369.

[2] Cf. Augustine, De Genes. ad litt., IX, 3:6 (CSEL, 28, 271 f.); De pecc. mer., I, 2 (CSEL, 60, 3 f.).

irrational nature together, three conclusions seem possible. Perhaps the number of the angels, before the ruin of the wicked, did not complete that city, but God was waiting to complete it from men, when he changed the nature of the corporeal world for the better. Or possibly it was complete as to number, but not complete as to its final confirmation, and its confirmation was to be put off, even if no one in it had sinned, until the renewal of the world, to which we look forward. Or perhaps, if that confirmation was not to be deferred any longer, the renewal of the world was to be hastened, so as to coincide with this confirmation. But for God to decide to renew the newly made world right away, and to destroy the things that will not exist after that renewal at the very beginning, before it was apparent why they had been created at all, would be utterly unreasonable. It follows, then, that the angels were not of a perfect number, so that their confirmation could not be delayed very long, since it would then have been necessary for the renewal of the new world to take place immediately; but this is not fitting. But it also seems incongruous that God should have wished to put off their confirmation to the future renewal of the world, especially since he accomplished that confirmation so quickly in some; moreover, we may suppose that, if they had not sinned, he would have confirmed the first human beings at the time when, in fact, they did sin, as he did the angels who persevered. Of course, they would not then have been raised to that equality with the angels to which men were to attain when the number to be taken from among them was complete. Nevertheless, it seems that, if they had conquered and not sinned when they were tempted, they would have been confirmed, with all their posterity, in the justice that was theirs, so that they would no longer have been able to sin—just as, because they were conquered and sinned, they were so weakened that of themselves they could not exist without sin. For who dares to say that injustice has more power to bind a man in slavery, when he yields to it at its first suggestion, than justice would have had to confirm him in liberty, if he had adhered to it in this same first temptation? For because the whole of human nature was in our first parents, the whole of human nature was conquered for sin in them, with the sole exception of that man whom God determined to make from a virgin without man's seed, and thus to set apart from the sin of Adam; similarly, the whole of human nature would have conquered in them, if they had not sinned. It remains to be said, then, that the city on high was not complete with the original number of the angels, but was to be completed from among men. If this is accepted, it follows that there will be more elect men than there are reprobate angels.

B. What you have to say seems most reasonable to me. But what is meant by the statement that God "appointed the bounds of the peoples according to the number of the children of Israel"[3]? Some take this to mean that the number of elect men to be taken up is to correspond to the number of the good angels,[4] because they read "angels of God" instead of "children of Israel."[5]

A. This is not contrary to the previous statement, as long as it is not certain that just as many angels fell as persevered. For if there are more elect than reprobate angels, it is both necessary for elect men to replace the latter, and possible for them to equal the number of the blessed angels, and thus there will be more just men than unjust angels. But remember the condition on which I undertook to answer your inquiry—namely, that if I say anything which a higher authority does not confirm, even though I seem to prove it by reason, it is to be taken as certain only in the sense that it seems to me to be true, until God in some way reveals something better to me. For I am sure that if I say anything that unquestionably contradicts Holy Scripture, it is false, and if I am aware of this I do not want to hold it. But we may (as we are doing now) deal with matters where different opinions can be held without danger. For example, if we do not know whether there will be more elect men than lost angels, or not, but regard one of these views as more probable than the other, I do not think that this involves any danger to the soul. In such cases, if we expound the divine oracles so that they seem to favor divergent opinions, and there is no other passage where they definitely determine what is to be held, I do not think that we should be censured.

But as to the text you quoted, to the effect that "he set the bounds of the peoples" or nations "according to the number of the angels of God," where another translation reads, "According to the number of the children of Israel,"[6] since both translations have either the same meaning or different but compatible meanings, the passage is to be interpreted as follows.

---

[3] Deut. 32:8.
[4] Cf. Gregory, *Homil. in evang.*, 34, 11 (*PL*, 76, 1252).
[5] Following the reading of the LXX.
[6] Cf. notes 1 and 3.

"Angels of God" and "children of Israel" may signify nothing but good angels, or elect men only, or angels and elect men together (that is to say, the whole city on high). Or perhaps "the angels of God" refers only to the holy angels, and "the children of Israel" only to just men—or "the children of Israel" to angels alone, and "the angels of God" to just men. If the good angels only are designated by both phrases, that is just as if the term "the angels of God" were used alone. If, on the other hand, the reference is to the whole Heavenly City, the point is that peoples —that is, multitudes of elect men—will be taken into it, or that there will be peoples in this world until the predestined but not yet perfect number of that city is completed from among men.

But at present I do not see how "the children of Israel" can mean angels alone, or angels and holy men together. It is not strange, however, that men should be called "children of Israel" as well as "children of Abraham."[7] They can also rightly be called "angels of God," because they imitate the angelic life, and a likeness to the angels, and equality with them, is promised to them in heaven; furthermore, all who live justly are angels of God, and on that account are called "confessors"[4] or "martyrs." For whoever confesses and witnesses to the truth of God is his messenger, that is, his angel. And if a wicked man is called a devil, as Judas was by our Lord,[8] on account of his likeness in wickedness, why shall a good man not be called an angel, on account of his imitation of righteousness? Thus we can, I think, say that God set the bounds of the peoples according to the number of elect men, because peoples and the procreation of men will continue in this world until the number of those elect men is completed, and when it is completed, the generation of men, which takes place in this life, will cease.

On the other hand, if by "the angels of God" we understand the holy angels only, and by the "children of Israel" just men alone, we can interpret the statement that God "set the bounds of the peoples according to the number of the angels of God"[9] in two ways. It may mean that as great a people—that is, as many men—will be taken up as there are angels of God, or, alternatively, that the peoples will continue until the number of the angels of God is completed from among men. In the same context, I think that we can expound the words, "He set the bounds of the peoples according to the number of the children of Israel,"[10] in only one way—namely, to the effect

7 Cf. Gal. 3:7.   8 Cf. John 6:71 (A.V., 6:70).
9 Cf. note 3.   10 Deut. 32:8.

that (as has been said above) the peoples will continue in this world until the number of holy men is taken. And we shall gather from both translations that as many men will be taken up as there were angels that persevered. But it still does not follow, even though the lost angels are to be replaced from among men, that as many angels fell as persevered. If anyone asserts this nonetheless, he will have to indicate how the reasons put forward above are not valid. For they seem to prove that before some of the angels fell that perfect number, to which I referred above,[11] did not exist among them, and also that there will be more elect men than there are wicked angels.

B. I am not sorry that I made you say these things about the angels, for it has not been without profit. But now go back to the point from which we digressed.[12]

CHAPTER XIX

MAN CANNOT BE SAVED WITHOUT SATISFACTION FOR SIN

A. It is agreed that God intended to replace with men the angels who fell.[13]

B. That is certain.

A. It is necessary, then, for the men who are taken into that Heavenly City in place of the angels to be in the same state as those whom they replace would have been—that is, as the good angels are now.[14] Otherwise, those who fell will not be replaced, and it will follow, either that God will be unable to complete the good work that he began or that he will regret that he began so great a good work. But both these suggestions are absurd.

B. Certainly men must be equal to the good angels.

A. Have the good angels ever sinned?

B. No.

A. Can you suppose that a man who has once sinned, and has never made satisfaction to God for his sin, but is simply let off unpunished, is equal to an angel who has never sinned?

B. I can think and say the words, but I cannot think their real meaning any more than I can suppose falsehood to be the truth.

A. Then it is unfitting for God to take sinful man, without satisfaction, to replace the lost angels, since truth does not allow him to be raised to equality with the blessed.

[11] Cf. Chapter XVI, above.
[12] On this chapter, cf. Augustine, *Enchir.*, 29 (*PL*, 40, 246).
[13] Cf. Chapter XVI, above.   [14] Cf. Chapter XVII, above.

B. Reason proves this.

A. Also consider man alone, apart from the question of his being made equal to the angels; should God raise him on these terms to any blessedness, even such as he had before he sinned?

B. You tell me what you think, and I shall consider it as well as I can.

A. Let us suppose that some rich man is holding a precious pearl in his hand. No defilement has ever touched it, and no one else can take it out of his hand unless he allows it. He decides to store it in his treasury, where he keeps his dearest and most precious possessions.

B. I am imagining this, as if it were before us.

A. What if he himself, although he could prevent it, allows some envious person to knock this pearl out of his hand into the mud, and afterward takes it from the mud and stores it, dirty and unwashed, in some clean and costly receptacle of his, with the intention of keeping it in that state? Will you think that he is wise?

B. How could I? For would it not be much better for him to keep and preserve his pearl clean rather than polluted?

A. But God kept man in paradise, as it were in his own hand, without sin, to be joined to the angels, and yet permitted the devil, inflamed by envy, to cast him down (though with man's own consent) into the mire of sin. For if God had willed to prevent him, the devil could not have tempted man. Would he not behave like our rich man if he restored man, stained by the dirt of sin and without any washing—that is, without any satisfaction—to remain in such a condition forever, at the very least in paradise, from which he had been cast out?

B. I dare not deny the resemblance, if God were to do this, and therefore I will not grant that he can do it. For it would seem either that he could not carry out what he planned or that he regretted his good plan; but neither of these things can happen to God.

A. Then hold it as most certain that without satisfaction, that is, without the willing payment of man's debt, God cannot remit sin unpunished, any more than the sinner can attain even to such blessedness as he had before he sinned. For in this way man would not be restored even to the state he enjoyed before sin.

B. I find it quite impossible to contradict your reasoning. But how is it that we say to God, "Forgive us our debts,"[15] and that every nation prays to the god it believes in to forgive its

15 Matt. 6:12.

sins? For if we pay what we owe, why do we pray him to forgive? Is God unjust, so that he demands again what has already been paid? On the other hand, if we do not pay, why do we vainly pray for him to do what he cannot do, because it is unfitting?

A. He who does not pay says, "Forgive," in vain. But he who pays prays, because the very prayer itself is part of the payment. For God is in debt to no one, but every creature is in debt to him, and therefore it is not proper for a man to deal with God as an equal with an equal. But I do not need to answer this question for you now. For when you know why Christ died, perhaps you will see the answer for yourself.

B. I am satisfied for the moment with the answer you give. Moreover, I could not possibly doubt that no man can attain to blessedness in the state of sin, or be loosed from sin without repaying what he has stolen by sinning, for you have proved it all so clearly.

CHAPTER XX

There Must Be Satisfaction According to the Measure of Sin, and Man Cannot Make It by Himself

A. Nor will you, I suppose, doubt that satisfaction must be made according to the measure of sin.

B. Otherwise sin would remain to some extent outside due order, but this cannot be the case, if God leaves nothing disordered in his Kingdom.[16] But it has already been settled that even the slightest incongruity is impossible in God.[17]

A. Tell me, then, what will you pay to God for your sin?

B. Repentance, a contrite and humble heart, fastings and all sorts of bodily labors, mercy in giving and forgiving, and obedience.

A. In all this what do you give to God?

B. Do I not honor God, when for fear and love of him I abandon temporal delight with contrition of heart; when by fastings and labors I trample on the pleasures and repose of this life; when I freely spend what is mine, giving and forgiving; when I subject myself to him in obedience?

A. When you pay what you owe to God, even if you have not sinned, you must not count this as part of the debt you owe for sin. But you owe God all those things you have mentioned. For in this mortal life there ought to be such great love,

[16] Cf. Chapter XII, above.   [17] Cf. Chapter X, above.

and longing to reach that for which you were made—it is with this that prayer has to do—and sorrow because you are not yet there, and fear lest you fail to reach it, that you should feel no delight save in the things that either help you on your way or give you the hope of attaining it. For you do not deserve to have what you do not love and desire for its true worth, and for which you do not grieve, because you do not yet possess it and are still in great danger of not possessing it at all. With this in mind, you must flee from repose and worldly pleasures, which hold back the mind from the true repose and pleasure, save in so far as you know that they support your purpose of attaining that end. As for what you give, you ought to consider it part of what you owe, since you understand that you do not possess what you give of yourself, but from Him whose servants both you and he to whom you give are. Nature also teaches you to do to your fellow-servant, as man to man, what you wish him to do to you,[18] and also shows that he who is not willing to give what he has should not receive what he does not have. As for vengeance, let me say briefly that vengeance in no sense belongs to you, as we said above.[19] You are not your own, nor is he who did you injury your own or his own, but you are servants of one Lord, created by him out of nothing. And if you revenge yourself on your fellow-servant, you proudly claim over him the right of judgment which is proper to the Lord and Judge of all. As for obedience, what do you give God that you do not owe him, to whose command you owe all that you are and have and can do?

B. I do not dare now to say that in all these things I give God anything that I do not owe.

A. What, then, will you pay to God for your sin?

B. If I owe him myself and all that I can do, even when I do not sin, lest I should sin, I have nothing to repay him for sin.

A. Then what will become of you? How are you going to be saved?

B. If I think over your reasons, I cannot see how. But if I turn back to my faith, I hope that in the Christian faith, "that worketh by love,"[20] I can be saved. Also, we read that "if the unjust be turned from his injustice and do justice,"[21] all his injustices are forgotten.[22]

---

[18] Cf. Matt. 7:12.   [19] Cf. Chapter XII, above.
[20] Gal. 5:6 (*dilectionem* in place of Vulgate, *caritatem*).
[21] Ezek. 18:27 (not quoted according to the Vulgate).
[22] Cf. Ezek. 18:22; 33:16.

A. This is said only to those who looked for Christ before he came, or to those who believe in him now he has come. But we set aside Christ and the Christian faith as though they had never existed, when we undertook to inquire by reason alone whether his advent was necessary for the salvation of men.[23]

B. So we did.

A. Then let us proceed by reason alone.

B. Although you lead me into some difficulties, still I am anxious for you to go forward as you began.

CHAPTER XXI

What a Great Weight Sin Is

A. Let us assume that you do *not* owe all the things that you have just stated you are able to pay for sin, and let us see whether they can suffice as satisfaction even for one small sin—for instance, for a single glance in opposition to the will of God.

B. If it were not for the fact that I hear you question it, I should suppose that I could blot out this sin by a single act of sorrow.

A. You have not yet considered what a heavy weight sin is.

B. Show me now.

A. Picture yourself in God's presence. Someone says to you, "Look this way," but God, on the contrary, says, "I wish you on no account to look." Now ask yourself, in your own heart, what there is among all the things that exist for whose sake you ought to cast that glance in opposition to God's will.

B. I can find nothing for whose sake I ought to do this, unless perhaps I were to be placed under the necessity of committing either this or some greater sin.

A. Setting aside this necessity, consider this sin alone, and ask whether you can commit it even to redeem yourself.

B. I see clearly that I cannot.

A. Not to keep you too long—what if it were necessary for the whole world and all that is not God to perish and be reduced to nothingness, if you would not do such a small thing against God's will?

B. When I consider the act itself, I realize that it is a very trifling thing, but when I see how it is against God's will, I recognize that it is of the greatest weight, and cannot be compared with any loss. But sometimes we act against some-

[23] Cf. Chapter X and Preface, above.

one's will, yet without blame, in order to preserve his property, and afterward he is pleased with what we did against his will.

A. This is done for a man who sometimes does not understand what is to his advantage, or who cannot replace what he loses. But God is in need of nothing, and, if all things were to perish, he could replace them, just as he made them.

B. I must admit that I should do nothing against God's will, even to preserve the whole creation.

A. What if there were more worlds full of creatures, as this is?

B. If they were infinitely multiplied and spread before me in the same way, I should make the same reply.

A. You can do nothing better. But consider also what you could pay for this sin, if you did happen to cast that glance against God's will.

B. I have nothing further to say than I have already said.[24]

A. We sin thus gravely, every time we knowingly do even the slightest thing against God's will, because we are always in his sight, and he is always commanding us not to sin.

B. As I understand it, we live in a very dangerous state.

A. It is clear that God requires satisfaction according to the greatness of the sin.

B. I cannot deny it.

A. Therefore, you do not make satisfaction unless you repay something greater than that for the sake of which you were obliged not to commit the sin.[25]

B. I see that reason requires this, and at the same time that it is quite impossible.

A. Nor can God take to blessedness anyone who is bound in any way by the debt of sin, because he ought not to do so.

B. This is a very painful conclusion.

CHAPTER XXII

THE OUTRAGE THAT MAN DID TO GOD WHEN HE LET HIMSELF BE OVERCOME BY THE DEVIL, AND HOW HE CANNOT MAKE SATISFACTION FOR IT

A. Listen to still another reason why it is not less difficult for man to be reconciled to God.

B. Unless faith comforted me, this reason alone would drive me to despair.

[24] In the preceding chapter.
[25] I.e., greater than the simple maintenance of obedience to God's will.

A. Listen, nonetheless.

B. Go on.

A. When man was created in paradise without sin, he was set, as it were, for God between God and the devil, in order to overcome the devil by not consenting to his persuasions to sin. This would have vindicated and honored God and confounded the devil, since man, though the weaker, would have refused to sin on earth at the instance of that very devil who, though the stronger, sinned in heaven without persuasion. But though man could easily have done this, and was coerced by no force, he readily allowed himself to be overcome by persuasion alone, in accordance with the will of the devil, and contrary to the will and honor of God.

B. What are you driving at?

A. Judge for yourself if it is not contrary to God's honor for man to be reconciled to him still bearing the reproach of the outrage he inflicted on God, without first honoring God by conquering the devil, just as he dishonored him when he was conquered by the devil. But the victory ought to be like this. Strong and immortal in power, man freely accepted the devil's temptation to sin, and thus justly incurred the penalty of mortality; now, weak and mortal as he made himself, he ought through the distress of death to conquer the devil, so as not to sin at all. But this is what he cannot do as long as, through the wound of the first sin, he is conceived and born in sin.[26]

B. Once more I say that reason proves what you say, and at the same time that it is impossible.

CHAPTER XXIII

WHAT MAN TOOK AWAY FROM GOD WHEN HE SINNED, AND CANNOT REPAY

A. You must admit still another point, which is equally impossible, but apart from which man may not justly be reconciled.

B. You have already put forward so many things that we ought to do, that nothing else you add can frighten me any more.

A. Listen, nonetheless.

B. I am listening.

A. What did man take away from God when he let himself be vanquished by the devil?

26 Cf. Ps. 50:7 (P.B.V., 51:5).

B. You tell me, as you have begun, for I do not see what can be added to the evils that you have pointed out.

A. Did he not take away from God whatever he had planned to make out of human nature?[27]

B. That cannot be denied.

A. Consider strict justice, and judge by that whether man makes to God a satisfaction equal to his sin, unless by conquering the devil he restores to God precisely what he took away from him when he let himself be conquered by the devil. For, then, just as, by the very fact that man was conquered, the devil stole what belonged to God and God lost it, so, by the very fact that man conquers, the devil loses it and God regains it.

B. Nothing more strict or just could be imagined.

A. Do you think that supreme justice can violate this justice?

B. I dare not think so.

A. Then man should not and cannot possibly receive from God what God intended to give him, unless he repays to God the whole of what he took from him, so that as through him God lost it, through him he may regain it. But there is only one way in which this can be done. Through him who was overcome the whole of human nature was corrupted and, as it were, leavened by sin, and God takes no one who is stained by sin to perfect the Heavenly City. But through him who overcomes, as many men must be justified as would be needed to fill up that number which man was created to complete. Sinful man, however, is quite incapable of doing this, because a sinner cannot justify a sinner.

B. Nothing is more just, and yet nothing is more impossible. But in view of all this the mercy of God and the hope of man seem to vanish, as far as that blessedness is concerned for which man was made.

CHAPTER XXIV

As Long as Man Does Not Restore What He Owes to God, He Cannot Be Blessed, and His Inability Does Not Excuse Him

A. Wait a little longer.

B. What more have you to say?

A. If a man is called unjust when he does not restore what he owes to a man, surely he who does not restore what he owes to God is much more unjust.

[27] Cf. Chapter XVI, above.

B. If he can restore it, and does not, he certainly is unjust. But if he cannot, how can we call him unjust?

A. Perhaps if his inability has no cause in himself, he can be partially excused. But if there is any guilt in that inability, it neither lightens the sin nor excuses him when he fails to pay his debt. Suppose that a man enjoins some task on his servant, and charges him not to throw himself into a pit which he points out to him, out of which he cannot possibly escape. But that servant despises the command and the warning of his master and, of his own free will, throws himself into the pit that has been shown him, so that he is unable to carry out his assigned task. Do you think that this inability is worth anything as an excuse for not performing the assigned task?

B. Not at all. On the contrary, it increases his guilt, since he brought this inability on himself. For he sinned doubly, because he did not do what he was ordered to do, while what he was commanded not to do he did.

A. Thus man is inexcusable, because he willingly incurred that debt, which he cannot pay, and by his own fault involved himself in this inability, so that he can pay neither what he owed before sin—namely, to refrain from sin—nor what he owes on account of sin. For the very inability is a fault, because it is wrong for him to suffer from it, or rather, he is obliged not to have it. For just as it is a fault not to have what one ought to have, so it is a fault to have what one ought not to have. Therefore, just as it is a fault for man not to have the power that he received for the sake of avoiding sin, so it is a fault for him to have this inability to maintain justice and avoid sin, or to repay what he owes for sin. For he freely performed the action by which he lost that power and brought this inability on himself. For it is the same thing not to have the power one ought to have and to have the inability one ought not to have. For this reason, the inability to repay to God what a man owes, which is the cause of his not repaying it, does not excuse him when he fails to make repayment, since the effect of sin does not excuse the sin that causes it.

B. This is a very serious thing, and yet it must be so.

A. Then a man is unjust when he does not repay what he owes to God.

B. That is only too true, for he is unjust because he does not repay, and unjust because he cannot.

A. But no unjust man will be admitted to blessedness, for blessedness is a condition of sufficiency in which nothing is lacking,[28] and it is only suitable for him whose justice is so pure that there is no injustice in him.

B. I dare not believe otherwise.

A. Then it will not be possible for anyone to be blessed if he does not pay God what he owes.

B. I cannot deny that this follows as well.

A. But if you want to say that the merciful God forgives the suppliant what he owes, precisely because he cannot repay it, he can only be said to forgive one of two things. He either forgives what man should willingly repay but cannot, namely, some recompense for the sin which he ought not to have committed even for the preservation of everything that is not God,[29] or else he remits the punishment which (as I said above) he was going to inflict on man by depriving him of blessedness against his will.[30] But if he forgives what man ought freely to repay, because he cannot pay it, surely that is to say that God remits what he cannot get. But it is mockery to ascribe such mercy to God. And if he remits what he was going to take from man against his will, because man is powerless to repay what he ought readily to repay, then God eases the punishment and makes a man blessed on account of his sin (that is, because he has what he ought not to have). For he ought not to have this inability, and, therefore, as long as he does have it without making satisfaction, it is a sin for him. But this kind of divine mercy is too directly opposed to God's justice, which allows nothing but punishment to be repaid for sin. Therefore, since God cannot be in opposition to himself, it is impossible for him to be merciful in this way.

B. I see that we must search for another kind of divine mercy.

A. But suppose it were true that God forgives him who does not pay what he owes, just because he cannot.

B. That is what I should wish.

A. But as long as he does not repay, he either will or will not wish to repay. But if he wishes to do what he cannot do, he will be in want, and if he does not wish to do it, he will be unjust.

B. Nothing is clearer than this.

A. But if he is either in need or unjust, he will not be blessed.

B. That is evident also.

A. Then as long as he does not repay, he cannot be blessed.

B. If God follows the rule of justice, wretched little man can

28 Cf. Boethius, *De consol. philos.*, III, prosa 2 (*CSEL* 67, 49).
29 Cf. Chapter XXI, above.
30 Cf. Chapter XIV, above.

find no way of escape, and the mercy of God seems to come to nothing.

A. You have asked for a reason; now accept a reason. I do not deny that God is merciful, because he saves "men and beasts," even as he has "multiplied" his mercy.[31] But we are speaking of that ultimate mercy by which, after this life, he makes man blessed. I think that I have adequately proved, by the reasons stated above,[32] that this blessedness should be given to no one save to him whose sins are completely forgiven, and that this forgiveness should be granted only when the debt that is due for sin according to the greatness of the sin has been repaid. But if you think that any objection can be brought against these arguments, you should say so.

B. I, at any rate, do not see how any of your arguments can be shaken at all.

A. Nor do I, if they are properly considered. Nevertheless, if only one out of all the arguments I have presented is confirmed by indisputable truth, that should be enough. For whether the truth is demonstrated beyond question by one argument or by many, it is equally secure against all doubt.

B. That is quite right.

CHAPTER XXV

Of Necessity, Man Is Saved Through Christ

How, then, will man be saved if he himself does not pay what he owes and he ought not to be saved unless he pays it? Or with what shame shall we declare that God, who is rich in mercy[33] beyond man's understanding, cannot do this work of mercy?

A. What you should do now is to require those for whom you speak, who do not believe that Christ is necessary for man's salvation, to tell us how man can be saved apart from Christ. And if they cannot do this at all, let them stop mocking us, and come and join themselves to us, who do not doubt that man can be saved through Christ—or else let them despair of the very possibility of salvation. If they shrink from this, then let them believe in Christ with us, so that they may be saved.

B. I shall ask you (as I began) to show me in what way man is saved through Christ.

---

[31] Cf. Ps. 35:7 f. (P.B.V., 36:7).   [32] Cf. Chapters XIX, XX, above.
[33] Cf. Eph. 2:4.

A. Even unbelievers do not deny that man can in some way be made blessed. Since it has been adequately proved that no salvation whatever can be found for man if we assume that Christ does not exist, is this not enough to show that man can be saved through Christ? For man can be saved either through Christ, or in some other way, or in no way at all. Therefore, if it is wrong to say that this is impossible, or that it can be brought about in some other way, it must necessarily be done through Christ.

B. Suppose that someone sees why man cannot be saved in some other way, but does not understand how he can be saved through Christ. If he chooses to assert that it cannot be accomplished through Christ or in any way at all, what shall we reply to him?

A. How should we answer a man who asserts that what must be cannot be, simply because he does not know how it happens?

B. Tell him that he is a fool.

A. Then what he says should be held in contempt.

B. That is true. But we should show him how what he regards as impossible can happen.

A. Do you not understand from what we have said before[34] that some men must attain to blessedness? It is true that it is unfitting for God to bring man with any stain on him to the end for which he made him without any stain, lest he seem either to regret his good undertaking or to be unable to carry out his plan. But, on account of the same incongruity, it is much more impossible that no man at all should be raised to the end for which he was created.[35] Therefore, some such satisfaction for sin, as we have already shown[36] to be necessary, must be found outside the Christian faith—though no reasoning can point out such a thing—or else we must unhesitatingly believe that it exists within the Christian faith. For if we conclude, on the basis of a necessary reason, that something is really true, we should not bring it into any doubt, even if we do not perceive the reason why it is true.[37]

B. What you say is quite right.

A. What, then, do you ask further?

B. I did not come to you to have any doubt of mine concerning the faith taken away, but to be shown the reason for my certainty. Therefore, now that you have led me by reasoning to see that sinful man owes God a debt for sin which

---

[34] Cf. Chapter XVI, above.
[35] Cf. Chapter IV, above.
[36] Cf. Chapters XIX, XX, above.
[37] Cf. *Monologion*, 64 (Schmitt, I, 75).

he cannot repay, and at the same time that he cannot be saved without repaying it, I want you to lead me further. Help me to understand by rational necessity how all that the Catholic faith bids us believe about Christ, if we wish to be saved, must be true,[38] and how it all avails for man's salvation,[39] and how God saves man by mercy, when he does not forgive him his sin unless he repays what he owes on its account.[40] And to make your arguments more certain, begin far enough back to place them on a firm foundation.[41]

A. May God help me now, for you show me no pity, and do not take into account the weakness of my knowledge when you impose such a great undertaking on it. But I shall try, now that I have begun, with trust in God rather than myself, and I shall do what I can with his help. But lest we arouse distaste in anyone who wants to read this, by presenting too long and continuous an argument, let us mark off what is still to be said from what has already been said, by a new introduction.

BOOK TWO

CHAPTER I

Man Was Created Just, So that He Might Be Blessed

A. We should not doubt that the rational nature was created just by God, so that it might be blessed in the enjoyment of him. For it is rational for the very purpose of distinguishing the just from the unjust, and good from evil, and the greater good from the lesser good; otherwise it would have been created rational to no purpose. But God did not create it rational to no purpose. Thus there is no doubt that it was made rational for this purpose. By a similar argument it can be proved that it received the power of discernment so that it might hate and shun evil, and love and choose the good—and love and choose the greater good most of all. For otherwise God would have given it the power of discernment in vain, since it would distinguish in vain if it did not love and avoid in the light of its discrimination. But it would not be fitting for God to give so great a power in

---

[38] Cf. Book II, Chapters V–XVIII, below.
[39] Cf. Book II, Chapter XIX, below.
[40] Cf. Book II, Chapter XX, below.
[41] Cf. Book II, Chapters I–IV, below.

vain. Thus it is certain that the rational nature was created to love and choose the supreme good above all things, not for the sake of another good, but for its own sake. For it does not love the good itself, but the other thing, if it loves the good for the sake of the other.[1] But unless it is just, it cannot love the supreme good. Therefore, so that it should not be rational to no purpose, it was created rational and just at the same time, for this purpose. Now if it was created just, in order to choose and love the highest good, either this was done so that at some time it might attain to what it loved and chose, or it was not. But if it was not made just, for the sake of attaining what it thus loves and chooses, it was made what it is in vain. For it was made to love and choose the supreme good, but there will be no reason why it should ever attain to it. Therefore, as long as it acts justly, by loving and choosing the supreme good (which it was created to do), it will be miserable. For it will be in need against its will, since it will not possess what it longs for. But this is too absurd. The rational nature, then, was created just, so that it might be blessed in the enjoyment of the highest good, that is, God. Man, therefore, who is of a rational nature, was made just, in order that he might be blessed in the enjoyment of God.[2]

CHAPTER II

MAN WOULD NOT HAVE DIED IF HE HAD NOT SINNED

Moreover, it is easy to prove that he was made of such a nature that he would not have to die, because, as we have already said,[3] it is contrary to God's wisdom and justice to compel man to suffer death without any fault, since he made him just, with a view to eternal blessedness. It follows, therefore, that if he had never sinned, man would never have died.[4]

CHAPTER III

MAN WILL RISE AGAIN WITH THE BODY IN WHICH HE LIVES IN THIS LIFE

From this we can clearly prove the resurrection of the dead at some future time. For if man is to be perfectly restored, he

---

[1] Cf. *Monologion*, 68 (Schmitt, I, 78 f.). [2] Cf. *ibid.*, 69 (I, 79 f.).
[3] Cf. Book I, Chapter IX, above. [4] Cf. note 2.

ought to be restored to the condition he was going to be in if he had not sinned.[5]

B. It cannot be otherwise.

A. If he had not sinned, man was to have been transformed into incorruptibility with the very body that he possessed.[6] When he is restored, then, he must be restored with his own body in which he lives in this life.

B. What shall we answer, if anyone says that this should be done for those in whom the human race will be restored, but that it is unnecessary in the case of the reprobate?

A. If man had persevered in justice, he would have been eternally blessed in his entire being, soul and body. Thus we can conceive nothing more just and appropriate than for him to be eternally and entirely miserable in soul and body, if he persists in injustice.

B. You have satisfied me on these points in a short time.

CHAPTER IV

God Will Complete What He Began with Human Nature

A. It is easy to see from all this that, unless God is going to complete what he began with human nature, he made so sublime a nature for so great a good all to no purpose. But if we know that God made nothing more precious than the rational nature, created to rejoice in him, it is certainly incongruous for him to let any rational nature perish altogether.[7]

B. No rational mind could think otherwise.

A. Then it is necessary for him to complete what he began with human nature. But, as we have said,[8] this can be done only by means of a complete satisfaction for sin, which no sinner can make.

B. I understand now how it is necessary for God to carry out what he began; otherwise he would appear to fail in his undertaking, and this is not fitting.[9]

[5] Cf. Book I, Chapter XIX, above.
[6] Cf. Book I, Chapter XVIII, above.
[7] Cf. Book I, Chapter IV, above.
[8] Cf. Book I, Chapter XIX, above.
[9] On this chapter, cf. Irenaeus, *Adv. Haer.*, III, 23:1 (*PG*, 7, 960).

CHAPTER V

ALTHOUGH THIS MUST BE DONE, GOD WILL NOT DO IT UNDER
ANY COMPULSION OR NECESSITY. THE KIND OF NECESSITY THAT
TAKES AWAY OR DIMINISHES GRATITUDE, AND THE KIND THAT
INCREASES IT

But if this is the case, God seems to be compelled, as it were,
to attend to man's salvation, by the necessity of avoiding the
unseemly. How, then, can it be denied that he does this more
for his own sake than for ours? But if this is so, what thanks do
we owe him for what he does for his own sake? How shall we
even ascribe our salvation to his grace if he saves us of necessity?

A. There is a kind of necessity that takes away or lessens
gratitude to a benefactor, and there is another kind of necessity
that increases our debt of gratitude for the benefit. When someone confers a benefit unwillingly, simply because he is subject
to necessity, little or no gratitude is due to him. But when he
freely submits himself to the necessity of doing a kindness,
instead of enduring it unwillingly, he certainly deserves greater
gratitude for the favor. For this is not to be called necessity, but
grace, since he undertook it and holds fast to it freely, and under
compulsion from no one. It is true that if you promise today
of your own free will to give something tomorrow, and give it
tomorrow by the same free will, you have to do the latter, if
you can, just as you promised, unless you are to be a liar. And
yet the person to whom you give it does not owe you any less
for the costly favor than he would if you had made no promise,
since you did not hesitate to make yourself a debtor to him
before the time of the actual giving. It is just the same when
someone freely takes a vow to live in the religious state.[10] Once
the vow is made, of course, he is necessarily bound to keep it,
if he is not to incur the condemnation of an apostate; indeed,
he can be compelled to keep it if he is unwilling to do so.

10 I have translated Anselm's phrase *sancta conversatio* by the term "religious
state," in the technical sense of the common life under vows. For the theory
of the religious life assumed by Anselm, cf. Thomas Aquinas, *Sum. theol.*,
IIa–IIae, 186, 1, and S. C. Hughson, *The Fundamentals of the Religious
State* (New York, 1915), Chapter I. For a full discussion of the meaning
of *conversatio* and *sancta conversatio*, cf. J. McCann, *Saint Benedict* (Sheed and
Ward, London, 1937), 148–167, which terminates a long debate on
conversatio (the correct reading, rather than *conversio*) in Benedict, *Regula*,
58. Cf. C. Butler, *Benedictine Monachism* 2d ed., London, 1924), 134–139,
405.

Nevertheless, if he keeps his vow with a ready will, he is not less but more pleasing to God than he would be if he had not made the vow. For he has renounced, for God's sake, not only ordinary life but even his freedom to live it, and we must say that he lives this holy life, not by necessity, but rather by the same freedom by which he made the vow.

Much more, then, if God performs for man the good work which he has begun, we should ascribe the whole to grace, even though it does not befit him to fail in a good undertaking, because he undertook it all for our sake, and not for his own, since he is in need of nothing. For what man was going to do was not concealed from him when he made him, but despite this, in creating man of his own goodness, he freely bound himself, as it were, to complete the good work once begun.[11] In short, God does nothing of necessity, since nothing whatever can coerce or restrain him in his actions. And when we say that God does something by necessity, as it were, of avoiding dishonor—which, in any case, he need not fear—it is better to interpret this as meaning that he does it from the necessity of preserving his honor. Now this necessity is nothing but his own changeless honor, which he has from himself and not from another, and on that account it is improper to call it necessity. Nevertheless, let us say that it is necessary, on account of his own changelessness, for God's goodness to complete what he undertook for man, even though the whole good that he does is of grace.

B. I grant this.

CHAPTER VI

Only a God-Man Can Make the Satisfaction by Which Man Is Saved

A. But this cannot be done unless there is someone to pay to God for human sin something greater than everything that exists, except God.

B. So it is agreed.[12]

A. If he is to give something of his own to God, which surpasses everything that is beneath God, it is also necessary for him to be greater than everything that is not God.

B. I cannot deny it.

---

[11] Cf. Augustine, De catech. rud., 18:30 (PL, 40, 332).
[12] Cf. Book I, Chapter XXI, above.

A. But there is nothing above everything that is not God, save God himself.

B. That is true.

A. Then no one but God can make this satisfaction.

B. That follows.

A. But no one ought to make it except man; otherwise man does not make satisfaction.[13]

B. Nothing seems more just.

A. If then, as is certain,[14] that celestial city must be completed from among men, and this cannot happen unless the aforesaid satisfaction is made, while no one save God can make it and no one save man ought to make it, it is necessary for a God-Man to make it.

B. "Blessed be God!"[15] We have already found out one great truth about the object of our inquiry. Go on, then, as you have begun, for I hope that God will help us.[16]

CHAPTER VII

IT IS NECESSARY FOR THE SAME PERSON TO BE PERFECT GOD AND PERFECT MAN

A. Now we must inquire how there can be a God-Man. For the divine and human natures cannot be changed into each other, so that the divine becomes human or the human divine. Nor can they be so mingled that a third nature, neither fully divine nor fully human, is produced from the two.[17] In short, if one could really be changed into the other, the person would be God only and not man, or man alone and not God. Or if they were mingled in such a way that a third nature was made out of two corrupted natures—just as from two individual animals, a male and a female, of different species, a third is born, which does not preserve the entire nature either of father or of mother, but possesses a third composed of both—the result would be neither man nor God. Therefore, the Man-God we are seeking cannot be produced from divine and human

---

13 Cf. Augustine, *Enarr. in Ps.* 63:13 (*PL*, 36, 766).
14 Cf. Book I, Chapters XVI and XIX, above.
15 Ps. 67:36 (P.B.V., 68:35).
16 On this chapter, cf. Leo, *Sermo* 56, 1 (*PL*, 54, 326 f.).
17 Cf. "The Chalcedonian Definition of the Faith," in T. H. Bindley, *The Oecumenical Documents of the Faith*, revised ed. (ed. F. W. Green, Methuen, London, 1950), 183–199, 232–235.

nature, either by the conversion of one into the other or by the destructive commingling of both into a third, because these things cannot be done, and if they could they would be of no avail for the end we seek.

Moreover, even if these two complete natures are said to be united in some way, but still man is one person and God another, so that the same person is not both God and man, the two natures cannot do what needs to be done. For God will not do it, because he does not owe it, and man will not do it, because he cannot. Therefore, for the God-Man to do this, the person who is to make this satisfaction must be both perfect God and perfect man, because none but true God can make it, and none but true man owes it. Thus, while it is necessary to find a God-Man in whom the integrity of both natures is preserved, it is no less necessary for these two complete natures to meet in one person—just as body and rational soul meet in one man—for otherwise the same person could not be perfect God and perfect man.

B. I am pleased with everything you say.

CHAPTER VIII

God Ought to Take Manhood of Adam's Race, and from a Virgin

A. Now it remains for us to ask from what source God will take human nature, and how. For he will either take it from Adam or create a new man, just as he created Adam from no other man.[18] But if he creates a new man, who is not of the race of Adam, he will not belong to the human race which was born of Adam. In that case he will not be obliged to make satisfaction for it, because he will not come from it. For just as it is right for man to make satisfaction for man's fault, it is necessary that the sinner himself, or one of the same race, should be the person who makes satisfaction. Otherwise neither Adam nor his race will make satisfaction for themselves. Thus, just as sin was transmitted to all men from Adam and Eve, only they or someone born from them ought to make satisfaction for the sin of men. Therefore, since they themselves cannot, he who is to make it must be born from them.

Further, Adam and his whole race would have stood by themselves, without support from any other creature, if they

[18] Cf. Book I, Chapter V, above.

had not sinned, and the same race must rise and be lifted up
through itself, if it rises again after the fall. For if anyone
restores it to its own state, so that it recovers that state through
him, it will certainly stand through him. Moreover, when God
first created human nature in Adam alone, and did not choose
to create the woman—so that mankind might be mutliplied
from the two sexes—except from him, he showed clearly that
he wished to create what he was going to create from human
nature, from Adam alone. Therefore, if the race of Adam
is raised up through some man who is not of the same race,
it will not be restored to the dignity it was to have had if
Adam had not sinned. But in that case it will not be entirely
restored, and God's purpose will seem to fail, and these two
things are unfitting. It is necessary, therefore, for the man
through whom Adam's race is to be restored to be taken from
Adam.[19]

B. If we follow reason, as we planned, this is inevitable.

A. Let us now inquire whether God is to take human nature
from a father and mother, as is the case with other men, or
from a man without a woman, or from a woman without a
man. For if it is taken in any of these three ways, it will be taken
from Adam and Eve, since every human being of either sex
comes from them. Moreover, no one of these three ways of
taking human nature is easier for God than the others, so as to
be preferable to them.

B. You are making progress.

A. But it will not take much effort to show that this man will
be brought forth more purely and honorably from a man or
woman alone than from the union of both, like all the other
sons of men.

B. This is enough to go on with.

A. Then he is to be taken either from a man alone or from a
woman alone.

B. He cannot be taken from any other source.

A. God can make a man in four ways: from man and woman,
as constant experience shows; neither from man nor from
woman, as he created Adam; from a man without a woman, as
he made Eve; or from a woman without a man, which he has
yet to do. Therefore, in order to prove that this way is also
within his power, and was deferred for this very purpose,
nothing is more fitting than for him to take that man whom we
are seeking from a woman without a man. Moreover, we need

[19] Cf. *ibid.*

not discuss whether this is more worthily done from a virgin or from one who is not a virgin, but we must affirm without the slightest doubt that the God-Man ought to be born of a virgin.[20]

B. You say what my own heart believes.

A. Is what we have said substantial, or is it something empty like the clouds, as unbelievers complain that it is, according to you?[21]

B. Nothing could be more substantial.

A. Then paint on the solid truth, not on empty fancies, and say that it is most fitting for the medicine for sin and the cause of our salvation to be born of a woman, just as the sin of man and the cause of our condemnation took its beginning from a woman.[22] Also, lest women despair of sharing in the lot of the blessed, since such great evil came from a woman, it is right that such great good should come from a woman, to renew their hope. And paint this too: if the cause of all evil for the human race was a virgin, it is still more fitting for the cause of all good to be a virgin. And paint this as well: if the woman whom God made from a man without a woman was made from a virgin, it is also very appropriate for the man who is made from a woman without a man to be made from a virgin. But for the present let these be enough of the pictures that can be painted on the truth that the God-Man ought to be born of a virgin woman.

B. These pictures are very beautiful and reasonable.[23]

CHAPTER IX

It Is Necessary for the Word Alone and Man to Meet in One Person

A. Now we must inquire in which person God (who is three persons) should take manhood. For several persons cannot take one and the same man into a unity of person, so that this must necessarily be done in one person only. But I have spoken of this unity of person of God and man, and of the divine person in whom it is most fitting for this to be brought about, as far

---

[20] Cf. Tertullian, *De carne Christi*, 17 (*PL*, 2, 827).
[21] Cf. Book I, Chapter IV, above.
[22] Cf. Book I, Chapter III, above.
[23] On this chapter, cf. Augustine, *De trin.*, XIII, 18 (*PL*, 42, 1032 f.); Leo, *Sermo* 22, 2 (*PL*, 54, 195).

as the present investigation seems to require, in the letter *On the Incarnation of the Word*, addressed to the Lord Pope Urban.[24]

B. Nevertheless, at least touch briefly on the question why the person of the Son should be incarnate, rather than the Father or the Holy Spirit.

A. If any other person is incarnate, there will be two Sons in the Trinity, namely, the Son of God, who is Son even before the incarnation, and he who will be Son of the Virgin through the incarnation; and in the persons who ought always to be equal there will be inequality with respect to the dignity of their births. For he who is born of God will have a worthier birth than he who is born of the Virgin. Again, if the Father is incarnate, there will be two grandsons in the Trinity, because the Father will be grandson of the Virgin's parents, through the manhood he assumes, while the Word, though he has no share in human nature, will nevertheless be the grandson of the Virgin, because he will be Son of her Son. All these things are incongruous, and do not occur in the incarnation of the Word. And there is another reason why it is more fitting for the Son than for the other persons to be incarnate; it sounds more fitting for the Son to pray to the Father than for another person to pray to either of the others. Furthermore, man, for whom he was to pray, and the devil, whom he was to conquer, had both, through self-will, laid claim to a false likeness to God. Thus, in a special way they had sinned against the person of the Son, who is believed to be the true likeness of the Father.[25] To him, then, against whom the wrong is more specially done, the avenging or the pardon of the crime is more suitably attributed. Therefore, since reason has led us inescapably to the conclusion that it is necessary for divine and human nature to meet in one person, that this cannot be done in more than one divine person, and that obviously this is more fittingly done in the person of the Word than in the other persons, it is necessary for God the Word and man to meet in one person.

B. The way by which you are leading me is so thoroughly guarded by reason that I do not see how I can turn aside from it either to right or to left.

A. I am not leading you; rather, he of whom we are speaking, without whom we can do nothing, leads us whenever we hold to the way of truth.[26]

24 Cf. *Epist. de incarn. verbi*, 6–11 (Schmitt, II, 20 ff.).
25 Cf. II Cor. 4:4; Col. 1:15; Thomas Aquinas, *Sum. Theol.*, Ia, 35.
26 On this chapter, cf. *Epist. de incarn. verbi*, 10 (Schmitt, II, 25 ff.).

CHAPTER X

That This Man Is Not Obliged to Die; How He Can and
Yet Cannot Sin; and Why He and an Angel Are to Be
Praised for Their Justice, Though They Cannot Sin

And now we must ask whether this Man is bound to die, as
all other men are obliged to die. If Adam was not going to die,
if he had not sinned,[27] much more will that Man not be obliged
to suffer death, since sin will be impossible for him because he
is God.

B. I want you to linger a little over this point. For whether
we say that he can or cannot sin, a far from small question
presents itself to me. For if we say that he cannot sin, it seems
hard to believe. To speak for a little while, not, as we have done
till now, of someone who never existed, but of him whose
person and acts we know, who will deny that he could do many
things that we call sins? For instance—not to mention anything
else—how shall we say that he could not have lied, though this
is always a sin? For when he says to the Jews concerning the
Father, "If I shall say that I know him not, I shall be like to
you, a liar,"[28] and in the middle of this sentence pronounces the
words, "I know him not," who will say that he could not have
spoken these words and no others, so as to say simply, "I know
him not"? But if he did this, as he says himself, he would be a
liar, that is, a sinner. Therefore, since he could have done this,
he could have sinned.

A. He could have said this, and still he could not have sinned.

B. Make this plain.

A. All power follows the will. For when I say that I am able
to speak or walk, "if I will" is understood; for if will is not taken
for granted, it is a case of necessity, not of power. Thus when
I say that I can be carried off or conquered against my will,
this is not my power, but my necessity and another's power. For
to say, "I can be carried off or conquered," is the same thing as
to say, "Someone else is able to carry off or conquer me." Thus
we can say that Christ was able to lie, if we understand, "if he
willed." But since he could not lie against his will, and could
not will to lie, it is no less possible to say that he was unable to
lie. So, then, he both could and could not lie.[29]

27 Cf. Chapter II, above.   28 John 8:55.
29 Cf. *Proslogion*, 7; *De casu diaboli*, 7 (Schmitt, I, 253).

B. Now let us go back to inquiring about him as if he did not yet exist, just as we began. I say, then, that if he cannot sin, because (as you assert) he cannot will to sin, he will maintain his justice of necessity. Therefore, he will not be just by free choice. What thanks, then, will be due to him for his justice? For we commonly say that God made both angels and men capable of sinning precisely so that, when they could abandon justice and yet kept it by free choice, they should deserve thanks and praise, which would not be due to them if they were just by necessity.

A. Are not the angels who now cannot sin to be praised?

B. Certainly they are, because they earned their present inability to sin by not willing to sin when they were able.

A. What do you say about God, who cannot sin, but did not earn this through being able to sin and not sinning? Is he not to be praised for his justice?

B. At this point I want you to answer for me. For if I say that he is not to be praised, I know that I am lying. But if I say that he is to be praised, I am afraid of weakening the argument I put forward concerning the angels.

A. Angels are not to be praised for their justice because they were able to sin, but because as a result of this they possess their present inability to sin from themselves in some respects. In this they are in some sense like God, who has whatever he possesses from himself. For a person may be said to give something if he does not take it away when he can, and to make something if he does not prevent its being when he can. So then, when an angel could have deprived himself of justice and did not, and could have made himself unjust and did not, it is correct to say that he gave himself justice and made himself just. In this way, then, he possesses justice from himself—since the creature cannot possess it from himself in any other way— and for that reason he is to be praised for his justice. And he is just by liberty, not by necessity, since it is improper to speak of necessity where there is neither compulsion nor restraint. Since God, therefore, perfectly possesses from himself whatever he has, he is to be praised above all for the excellences which he has and keeps, not by any necessity but, as I said above,[30] by his own eternal changelessness. So, then, this Man who will also be God will possess of himself, not by necessity but freely, every good that he has, and thus will be just of himself and, for that very reason, worthy of praise. For although his human nature

[30] Cf. Chapter V, above.

will have whatever it possesses from the divine nature, nevertheless he will have it from his very self, since the two natures will be one person.

B. You have satisfied me with this argument, and I see clearly that he will be praiseworthy for his justice, even though he will not be able to sin.

But now I think that we should inquire why, when God was able to make such a man, he did not make the angels and the two first human beings in such a way that they also would be unable to sin, and yet would be worthy of praise for their justice.

A. Do you understand what you are saying?

B. I think I understand, and therefore I ask why he did not make them like this.

A. Because it was neither right nor possible for one of them to be the selfsame person as God, as we say that this Man is to be. And if you ask why he did not do this for as many beings as there are persons in God, or at least for one being, I answer that reason in no sense required that this should be done then. On the contrary, since God does nothing without reason, it forbade it.

B. I am ashamed that I raised this question. Tell me what you were going to say.

A. Let us say, then, that he will not be obliged to die, because he will not be a sinner.

B. I must grant this.[31]

CHAPTER XI

He Dies of His Own Power, and Mortality Does Not Belong to the Pure Nature of Man

A. But now it remains for us to inquire whether he can die in his human nature, since in his divine nature he will always be incorruptible.

B. Why should we be doubtful about this, since he is to be true man, and every man is naturally mortal?

A. In my view mortality belongs to the corrupt, not to the pure nature of man.[32] For if man had never sinned, and his

---

[31] On this chapter, cf. Book I, Chapters IX, X, above.

[32] Cf. Augustine, *Contra Iulian. op. imperf.*, I, 96 (*PL*, 45, 1112). This was one of the sharply debated points of the Pelagian controversy; cf. J. Tixeront, *History of Dogmas*, 2d ed. (St. Louis, 1923), II, 432–476.

immortality had been unchangeably established, he would not have been any less a true man, and when mortals rise again to incorruption,[33] they will not be any less true men. For if mortality belonged to the true nature of man, there could not possibly be a man who was immortal. Neither corruptibility nor incorruptibility, then, belongs to the integrity of human nature, since neither one makes or destroys a man, but one avails for his wretchedness, the other for his blessedness. But since there is no man who does not die, mortality is laid down by the philosophers in their definition of man, because they did not believe that the whole man ever could have been or can be immortal.[34] Thus, we cannot prove that this Man ought to be mortal, simply on the ground that he will be true man.

B. Then look for another argument to prove that he can die, since I do not know of any, unless you do.

A. There is no doubt that, as he will be God, he will also be almighty.

B. That is true.

A. Then if he wills it he will be able to lay down his life and take it again.[35]

B. If he cannot do this, he does not seem to be almighty.

A. Then he will be able never to die, if he wills it, and he will be able to die and rise again. But whether he lays down his life without another's action, or lays it down through another's action, which he permits, makes no difference as far as his power is concerned.

B. There is no doubt of that.

A. Therefore, if he wills to permit it, it will be possible for him to be killed, and if he does not will it, it will not be possible.

---

33 Cf. I Cor. 15:42.
34 Cf. De grammatico, 8 (Schmitt, I, 152 f.); Augustine, De ordine, II, 11:31 (PL, 32, 1009); Boethius, In Isagogen Porphyrii commenta, edit. la, I, 20 (CSEL, 48, 60). The term philosophi is applied, here and elsewhere in medieval writers, to non-Christian thinkers who have attempted, on the basis of natural reason alone, to understand the world, and have sought the ordering of man's moral life in terms of temporal good. In contrast to the philosophi are the sancti (sometimes called theologi), the authoritative Christian writers—"Fathers of the Church," although the term patres ordinarily refers specifically to members of a council—whose speculations and moral ideals have been formulated in the light of their faith, and thus with an understanding of man's destiny not fully possible for the philosophi. For a discussion of this subject, with illustrative texts, cf. M. D. Chenu, "Les 'Philosophes' dans la philosophie chrétienne médiévale," Revue des sciences philos. et théol., 26 (1937), 27–40 (R.D.C.).
35 Cf. John 10:17 f.

B. Reason inevitably leads us to this conclusion.

A. Reason also has taught us that he should have something greater than anything under God, to give to God freely, and not as a debt.[36]

B. That is right.

A. But this cannot be found beneath him or apart from him.

B. That is true.

A. Then it must be found in himself.

B. So it follows.

A. Then he will either give himself or something that belongs to him.

B. I cannot think anything else.

A. Now we must ask what sort of gift this must be. For he will not be able to give himself or anything that belongs to him to God as if he were not God's own possession, since every creature belongs to God.

B. That is so.

A. So, then, we must understand that in this gift he devotes himself or something that belongs to him to the honor of God, in some way in which he is not bound to act.

B. That follows from what has already been said.[37]

A. If we say that he will give himself to obey God, so that in steadfastly maintaining justice he submits himself to his will, this will not be to give what God does not require of him as an obligation. For every rational creature owes this obedience to God.

B. This cannot be denied.

A. Then he must give himself or something that belongs to him to God in another way.

B. Reason drives us to this conclusion.

A. Let us see whether he may do this by giving his life, or laying down his life, or giving himself up to death for the honor of God. For God will not require this from him as a debt, because, as we have said,[38] since there will be no sin in him he will not be bound to die.

B. I cannot think otherwise.

A. Let us consider further whether this is congruous with reason.

B. Tell me, and I will gladly listen.

[36] Cf. Book I, Chapter XXI; Book II, Chapter VI, above.
[37] Cf. Book I, Chapter XX, above.
[38] Cf. preceding chapter.

A. If man sinned through pleasure, is it not fitting for him to make satisfaction through adversity? And if he was so easily overcome by the devil that in sinning he dishonored God in the easiest possible way, is it not just for man, when he makes satisfaction for sin, to honor God by overcoming the devil with the greatest possible difficulty? Is it not right for him who, by his sin, stole himself from God as completely as possible, to make satisfaction by giving himself to God as fully as he can?

B. Nothing could be more reasonable.

A. But nothing that man can suffer for God's honor, freely and not as an obligation, is more bitter or harder than death. Nor can a man give himself more fully to God than he does when he surrenders himself to death for His honor.

B. All this is true.

A. Then he who wishes to make satisfaction for man's sin must be able to die if he wills it.

B. I see plainly that the man we are seeking ought to be one who dies neither by necessity (since he will be almighty) nor out of obligation (since he will never be a sinner), but who can die of his own free will (since it will be necessary).

A. There are many other reasons why it is most fitting for him to be like men and to dwell among them without sin,[39] but these are more easily and clearly seen by themselves in his life and actions than by rational demonstration alone before any experience. For who can set forth how necessarily, how wisely, it was done, when he, who was to redeem men and to lead them back by his teaching from the way of death and ruin to the way of life and blessedness, moved among men,[40] and, in that very association, presented himself as an example, while by word he taught them how to live? But how could he give himself as an example to the weak and mortal, to teach them not to draw back from justice on account of injuries or insults or sufferings or death, if they did not recognize that he himself felt all these things?

CHAPTER XII

Although He Shares All Our Misfortunes, He Is Not Wretched

B. All these things show plainly that he must be mortal and a sharer in our misfortunes. But all these things are our miseries. Is he, then, to be miserable?

[39] Cf. Heb. 4:15.   [40] Cf. Baruch 3:38 (A.V. 3:37).

A. By no means. For just as an advantage someone may possess against his will does not constitute happiness, so it is no misery to experience some disadvantage of our own free will, prudently and under no compulsion.

B. That must be conceded.

CHAPTER XIII

HE DOES NOT SUFFER FROM IGNORANCE ALONG WITH OUR OTHER INFIRMITIES

But tell me whether, in this resemblance that he ought to have to men, he is to suffer from ignorance as well as from our other infirmities.

A. Why do you doubt that God knows all things?

B. Because, although he is to be immortal by his divine nature, he will be mortal by his human nature. Then why should that Man not be truly ignorant, just as he will be truly mortal?

A. That taking of manhood in the unity of a divine person can only be done wisely by the supreme wisdom. Therefore he will not take in his manhood anything that, far from being of any use, is highly prejudicial to the work he is going to do. Now ignorance would not only be useless to him, but would be harmful in many ways. For how can he do all the great works that he is to do without boundless wisdom? Or how will men believe him, if they know that he is ignorant? But if they do not know this, of what use will his ignorance be to him? Furthermore, nothing is loved save what is known; thus, as there will be no good thing that he does not love, there will be no good that he does not know. But no one knows the good perfectly except the person who knows how to distinguish it from evil. And no one who is ignorant of evil knows how to make this distinction. Therefore, he of whom we are speaking will be ignorant of no evil, just as he knows all good perfectly. Thus he will have all knowledge, even if he does not show it publicly in his dealings with men.

B. What you say seems to apply to his grown manhood, but his childhood will not be a suitable time for wisdom to appear in him, and it will be unnecessary (and consequently unfitting) for him to possess it.

A. Did I not say that this incarnation will be brought about wisely? God will wisely assume mortality, and will use it wisely, since it is most useful for his purpose. But he cannot assume

ignorance wisely, since it is always harmful and never useful—
except perhaps when by it some wicked intention, such as he
can never form, is frustrated. For even though it may do no
further harm, ignorance is harmful inasmuch as it deprives man
of the benefit of knowledge. And to settle your question briefly,
from the moment this Man exists he will always be full of God
as he is of himself. Thus he will never lack God's power and
might and wisdom.

B. Although I did not doubt that this was always true of
Christ, I raised the question in order to hear the reason for this
as well. For we are often quite certain of something, and yet do
not know how to prove it by reason.

CHAPTER XIV

How His Death Outweighs All Sins, Great as They Are in Number and Magnitude

Now I pray you to teach me how his death outweighs the
number and greatness of all sins, since you show how one
trifling sin (as we reckon it) is so infinite that if an infinite
number of worlds is spread before us, as full of creatures as our
own, and they cannot be kept from returning to nothingness
unless someone takes a single glance against God's will, that
glance still should not be taken.[41]

A. If that Man were present, and you knew who he was, and
someone said to you, "Unless you kill this man, the whole world
and everything that is not God will perish," would you do this
for the sake of preserving every other creature?

B. I would not do it, even if an infinite number of worlds
were spread before me.

A. What if someone said to you again, "Either kill him or all
the sins of the world will come upon you"?

B. I would answer that I should prefer to bear all other sins
—not only those that have been and will be in this world, but
whatever else can be imagined beyond these—rather than that
one alone. I think that I ought to give the same answer with
respect not only to his death, but also to the slightest injury
that might touch him.

A. You are right in thinking this. But tell me why your heart
judges that one sin that injures this Man is more dreadful than

41 Cf. Book I, Chapter XXI, above.

all the others that can be imagined, when every sin that is committed is committed against him.

B. Because a sin committed against his person is incommensurate with every conceivable sin that does not touch his person.

A. What will you say to this? Often someone willingly suffers some injuries to his own person, in order to avoid more serious damage to his property.

B. I will say that God, to whose power all things are subject, does not need to bear this loss, as you have already said in answer to one of my questions.[42]

A. That is a good answer. We see, then, that no greatness or multitude of sins apart from God's person can be compared to an injury done to the bodily life of this Man.

B. That is quite evident.

A. How great a good does this seem to you, when its destruction is so evil?

B. If every good is as good as its destruction is evil, it is incomparably more good than those sins, which his slaying surpasses beyond all reckoning, are evil.

A. You speak the truth. Consider also, that sins are as hateful as they are evil, and that that life is as lovable as it is good. It follows that this life is more lovable than sins are hateful.

B. I cannot help seeing this.

A. Do you think that so great and lovable a good is enough to pay what is owing for the sins of the whole world?

B. It is infinitely more than enough.

A. You see, then, how this life overcomes all sins, if it is given for them.

B. Clearly.

A. Therefore, if to give one's life is to accept death, the acceptance of death, like the giving of this life, outweighs all the sins of men.

B. That is certainly true for all sins that do not touch God's person.

CHAPTER XV

How the Same Death Can Wipe Out Even His Murderers' Sins

But now I see another problem. For if to kill him is as evil a thing as his life is good, how can his death overcome and wipe

---

[42] Cf. *ibid.*

out the sins of those who killed him? Or if it wipes away the sin of any one of them, how can it also blot out any of the sins of other men? For we believe that many of them have been saved, and that countless others are saved as well.

A. The apostle solved this problem when he said that "if they had known it, they would never have crucified the Lord of glory."[43] For a sin knowingly committed and one done through ignorance differ so greatly that an evil which they never could have done if they had recognized its enormity is venial, because it was done in ignorance. For no man could ever wish, at least knowingly, to kill God, and thus those who killed him in ignorance did not rush into that infinite sin, to which no other sins can be compared. For in considering its greatness, in order to see how good that life was, we have been thinking of it, not as something done in ignorance, but as if it had been committed knowingly—a thing that no one has ever done or could have done.

B. You have given good reason to suppose that the slayers of Christ could attain to the pardon of their sin.[44]

A. What more do you want now? After all, you already see how rational necessity shows that the city on high is to be completed from among men, and that this can be accomplished only through the remission of sins, which a man can gain only through the Man who is himself God and who reconciles sinful men to God through his death. Clearly, then, we have found Christ, whom we confess as God and Man who died for us. But when this is acknowledged beyond all doubt, we cannot doubt that whatever he says is certain, since God cannot lie, and that whatever he has done has been wisely done, even though we do not understand the reason.

B. What you say is true, and I do not have the slightest doubt that what he said was true, or that what he did was done with a good reason. But I do ask you to show me on what grounds those aspects of the Christian faith that seem wrong or impossible to unbelievers are really right and possible. I do not ask to be established in the faith, but I want to be made joyful by the understanding of the truth itself which I already hold.

[43] I Cor. 2:8.
[44] Cf. Augustine, *Tr. in Ioan.*, 93, 1 (*PL*, 35, 1863); Leo, *Sermo* 54, 2 (*PL*, 54, 320).

CHAPTER XVI

How God Took Manhood Out of the Sinful Mass, Yet Without Sin; the Salvation of Adam and Eve

So, then, since you have made clear the reason for what has already been stated, I beg you to show me the ground of the things I am still going to ask about. In the first place, I shall ask how God took manhood without sin from the sinful mass, that is, from the human race which was totally infected by sin, as if he were to take something unleavened from a lump of fermented dough.[45] For even though the conception of this Man is pure and free from the sin of carnal delight, nevertheless the Virgin herself, from whom he was taken, was "conceived in iniquities" and her mother conceived her "in sins,"[46] and she was born with original sin, since she also sinned in Adam,[47] "in whom all have sinned."[48]

A. Once it is established that this Man is God and the reconciler of sinners, there can be no doubt that he is completely free from sin.[49] But this cannot be the case, unless he was taken from the sinful mass without sin. If we cannot grasp the way in which the wisdom of God did this, we must not be astonished, but must with reverence accept the fact that in such a great matter there is something hidden of which we are ignorant. In fact, God has restored human nature even more wonderfully than he created it.[50] For both works are equally easy for God, but before man existed he did not sin and unfit himself for being made, while after he was made he deserved, because of sin, to lose both his being and the end for which he was made. He did not, however, lose his very being, but exists to be either punished or pitied by God—for neither of these would be possible if he had been reduced to nothingness. Yet his restora-

---

[45] Cf. p. 106, n. 13.   [46] Cf. Ps. 50:7 (P.B.V., 51:5).
[47] Cf. Augustine, *Contra Iulian. Pel.*, V, 15 (*PL*, 44, 813); *Contra Iulian. op. imperf.*, VI, 22 (*PL*, 45, 1552 f.). On the origins and history of the doctrine of the immaculate conception of Mary, and the attitude of Anselm and other medieval theologians, cf. X. Le Bachelet and M. Jugie, art. "Immaculée conception," *DTC*, 7, 845–1218.
[48] Rom. 5:12. Cf. p. 85, n. 51.
[49] Cf. Gregory, *Moralia*, XXIV, 2:4 (*PL*, 76, 289); Bede, *In I Epist. Ioan.*, 3 (*PL*, 93, 100).
[50] Cf. *Missale Romanum*, prayer at the mixing of the chalice: "O God, who didst wonderfully create and yet more wonderfully renew the dignity of the substance of man . . ."

tion by God was more wonderful than his creation, since the former was done to a sinner against his desert, but the latter neither to a sinner nor against his desert. Again, what a great thing it is for God and man to meet in one person, so that, while the integrity of both natures is preserved, the same person is man and God! Who, then, will dare even to imagine that human understanding is able to discern how wisely, how wonderfully, such an unsearchable deed was done?

B. I agree that in this life no man can fully explain so great a secret, and I do not ask you to do what no man can do, but only to do as much as you can. For you will more readily convince me that deeper reasons lie hidden in this matter,[51] if you show that you see some reason in it, than if you say nothing, and so prove that you really cannot make sense of it at all.

A. I see that I cannot escape from your persistence. But if I can even begin to prove what you ask, let us thank God. However, if I cannot, let what has been proved before suffice. For when it is admitted[52] that God ought to be made man, it is unquestionable that his wisdom and power will not fail to accomplish this without sin.

B. I willingly admit this.

A. It was certainly necessary for the redemption that Christ effected to benefit not only those who were alive at that time, but others as well. For suppose that there is a king, and that the whole population of one of his cities—with the sole exception of one man, who nonetheless belongs to their race—has sinned against him, so that none of them can manage to escape condemnation to death. But suppose too that the one innocent man is in such favor with the king that he is able—and so kindly disposed toward the guilty that he is willing—to reconcile all who believe in his plan by some service, sure to please the king greatly, which he will perform on a day set by the king's decision. And since all who need to be reconciled cannot meet on that day, the king grants absolution from every past fault, because of the greatness of this service, to everyone who either before or after that day confesses his readiness to seek pardon through the deed done that day, and to ratify the agreement then made. And if they happen to sin again after this pardon, he is ready to grant them pardon again because of the efficacy of this agreement, if they are willing to make due satisfaction and then amend their conduct. No one, however, is to enter his palace until the deed through which faults are remitted is done.

[51] Cf. Book I, Chapter II, above.   [52] Cf. Chapter VI, above.

As this illustration suggests, since all the men who were to be saved could not be present when Christ effected their redemption, his death had such power that its effect reaches even to those who lived in another place or at another time.[53] Moreover, it is easy to see that it ought not only to benefit those who were present, from the fact that all who are needed to build up the city on high could not be present at his death, even if all who were living anywhere at the time of his death were to share in that redemption. For there are more demons than there were men (from whom their number is to be made up) living that day.

Nor should we believe that there has been any time since man was created when this world, with the creatures made for man's use, has been so empty that it contained no one with a part in this destiny for which man was made. For it seems incongruous that God should even for a single moment have permitted the human race, and the things he made for the use of men, from whom the city on high is to be completed, to exist, as it were, in vain. For they would seem, in some sense, to exist in vain, as long as they did not appear to be serving the purpose for which, above all, they were created.

B. You have given a fitting reason, which nothing seems to contradict, to show how there has never been a time, since man was made, when no one existed who had a part in this reconciliation, without which every man would have been made in vain. We can conclude that this was not only fitting, but even necessary. For this is more fitting and reasonable than the view that at some given time there was no one in whom God's purpose, for which he made man, was to be carried out. Thus, since nothing opposes this reasoning, there must always have been someone who had a part in the aforesaid reconciliation. There is no doubt, then, that Adam and Eve had a share in this redemption, even though divine authority does not proclaim this openly.

A. It also seems incredible that God should have excluded these two from his purpose, when he made them and steadfastly purposed to produce from them all the men whom he was to take to the Heavenly City.

B. On the contrary, we should believe that he made them especially to be included among those for whose sake they were created.

---

[53] On the sole and universal efficacy of faith in Christ's death, cf. Leo, *Sermo* 52, 1 (*PL*, 54, 314).

A. You are right. But still, no man could enter paradise before Christ's death, as I said before in connection with the king's palace.

B. So we hold.

A. But that Virgin from whom the Man we are speaking of was taken was among those who, before his birth, were purified from sins through him, and he was taken from her in this very state of purity.

B. What you say would please me very much. But, although he ought to have purity from sin from his own person, he would seem to have it from his mother, and thus to be pure, not by himself but by her.

A. That is not the case. Since his mother's purity, by which he is pure, came from him alone, he also was pure by himself and from himself.

B. That is all right then.

But still another question must be asked. For we said before[54] that he was not to die of necessity, and now we see that his mother was pure by virtue of his future death; but if she had not been pure, he could not have taken being from her. How can we say, then, that he did not die of necessity, when he could not have existed if he had not been going to die? For if he had not been going to die, the Virgin from whom he was taken would not have been pure, since this was only possible through belief in his real death; but if she had not been pure, he could not have been taken from her. Therefore, if he did not die of necessity after he was taken from the Virgin, he could not have been taken from the Virgin after he *was* taken from her—but this is impossible.

A. If you had seriously considered what was said before, I think that you would have realized that your question has been answered already.

B. I do not see how.

A. When we asked whether he could lie, did we not show that two powers are involved in lying, namely, the power of willing to lie, and the power of telling a lie, and that, although he had the power of telling a lie, he was of himself incapable of wishing to lie, so that he is to be praised for his own justice, by which he maintained the truth?[55]

B. That is so.

A. In the same way, when it comes to preserving one's life, there is the power of willing to preserve it, and the power of

[54] Cf. Chapters X, XI, above.   [55] Cf. Chapter X, above.

preserving it. Thus, when someone asks whether this God-Man could have preserved his life so as never to die, we must not doubt that he always had the power of preserving it, even though he could not have willed to preserve it so as never to die. And since he was of himself incapable of willing to preserve his life, he laid it down by his own free power, and not of necessity.

B. Those two powers he had, of lying and of preserving his life, were not quite alike. For in the one case it follows that if he willed it he could lie. But in the other case, even if he willed not to die he could no more avoid death than he could help being what he was. For he became man for the express purpose of dying, and it was on account of her faith in his future death that he could be taken from the Virgin, as you said before.

A. You think that he could not avoid dying, or that he died of necessity, because he could not help being what he was. In the same way, you might assert that he could not will not to die, or that he necessarily willed to die, because he could not help being what he was. For he was no more made man for the purpose of dying than for the purpose of willing to die. Therefore, just as you should not say that he could not have willed not to die, or that he necessarily willed to die, so you must not say that he was unable to avoid dying, or that he died of necessity.

B. Yes, but since both dying and willing to die come under the same principle, both seem to have been necessary in his case.

A. Who was it that freely willed to make himself man, that by the same unchangeable will he might die, and that by faith in this certainty the Virgin from whom that Man was to be taken might be made pure?

B. God, the Son of God.

A. Was it not shown above that God's will is not constrained by any necessity, but that it maintains itself by its own free changelessness, when it is said to do anything by necessity?[56]

B. That was certainly shown. But we see, on the other hand, that what God unchangeably wills cannot help happening, but must necessarily happen. If, then, God willed that this Man should die, he could not help dying.

A. From the fact that the Son of God took manhood with the intention of dying, you deduce that this same Man could not avoid dying.

B. That is how I understand it.

56 Cf. Chapters V and X, above.

A. Was it not made equally clear, by what was said,[57] that the Son of God and the Man taken by him are one person, so that the same being is God and man, Son of God and son of the Virgin?

B. That is so.

A. Then it was by his own will that this Man was unable to avoid death, and actually died.

B. I cannot deny it.

A. Then since the will of God does a thing, not by necessity, but by its own power, and this Man's will was the will of God, he died by no necessity, but only by his own power.

B. I cannot answer your arguments. For I am quite incapable of weakening either the premises you lay down or the conclusions you draw.

And yet I keep running into the same difficulty. Even if he willed not to die, he could no more avoid dying than he could help being what he was. For he *was* going to die, since if he had not really been going to die, the faith in his future death, through which both the Virgin from whom he was born and many others were cleansed from sin, would not have been true. But if it had not been true, it could not have been of any benefit. Therefore, if he could have avoided death, he could have turned the truth into untruth.

A. Why was it true, before he died, that he was going to die?

B. Because he willed it freely, by an unchangeable decision.

A. If, then, as you say, he was unable to avoid death, because he was really going to die, and if he was going to die, because he freely and unalterably willed it, it follows that he was unable to avoid dying for the sole reason that by his unchangeable decision he chose to die.

B. That is so. But whatever the cause was, it is still true that he could not avoid dying and that it was necessary for him to die.

A. You are excessively perplexed about nothing and, as the saying goes, "You are looking for a knot in the bulrush."[58]

B. Have you forgotten the objection I brought against your excuses at the beginning of this discussion of ours? I was asking you to do something for me and for those who made the same

---

[57] Cf. Chapter VII, above.

[58] Cf. Plautus, *Menaechmi*, Act 2, Sc. 1, l. 247 (Loeb Classical Library ed. [Heinemann, London, 1932], II, 390); Terence, *Andria*, Act. 5, l. 941 (Loeb ed. [Heinemann, London, 1931], I, 102). The expression is obviously proverbial.

request with me, and not for the learned.[59] Bear with me, then, when I put questions appropriate to the slowness and dullness of our capacity, and give satisfaction to me and to them even in childish questions, as you began to do.

CHAPTER XVII

There Is No Necessity or Impossibility in God, and There Is a Necessity That Compels and a Necessity That Does Not

A. We have already stated that it is improper to say that God cannot do something, or that he does it by necessity.[60] Rather, every necessity and impossibility is subject to his will, while his will is subject to no necessity or impossibility. For nothing is necessary or impossible save because he himself so wills it, but it is altogether untrue to say that he wills or does not will something because of its necessity or impossibility. Therefore, since he does all that he wills and only what he wills, no necessity or impossibility is prior to his acting or not acting, any more than to his willing or not willing, although he may unalterably will many things, and do them. And when God does anything, once it is done it is impossible for it not to have been done, but it is always true that it has been done; and yet it is not right to say that it is impossible for God to make what is past not to be past. For there the necessity of not doing something or the impossibility of doing it has no effect, but only the will of God, who, since he himself is truth, wills that the truth should be always unchangeable, as it is. Similarly, if he unalterably decides to do something, although it is necessarily true, even before it is done, that it is going to be done, still he is subject to no necessity of doing it or impossibility of not doing it, since his will alone works in him. For whenever it is said that God cannot do something, there is no denial of his power, but rather an indication of his unconquerable might and strength. For this way of speaking simply means that no circumstance can make him do what it is said that he cannot do.

For an expression like this is often used, for instance, when we say that something is possible, not because there is any power in the thing, but because power is in something else— or is impossible, not because the lack of power is in itself, but because it is in something else. For we say, "That man can be

---

[59] Cf. Book I, Chapter I, above.   [60] Cf. Chapter V, above.

conquered," meaning, "Someone can conquer him," and we say, "He cannot be conquered," meaning, "No one can conquer him." For the possibility of being conquered is not power, but lack of power, and the inability to be conquered is not lack of power, but power.[61] Nor do we say that God does something by necessity, as if there were any necessity in him, but because there is necessity in something else—as I remarked concerning lack of power, with reference to the statement that he cannot do something. For every necessity is either compulsion or prevention, and these two necessities are mutually exclusive, like necessity and impossibility. For whatever is compelled to exist is prevented from not existing, and whatever is compelled not to exist is prevented from existing, just as it is impossible for what necessarily exists not to exist, and impossible for what necessarily does not exist to exist, and vice versa. But when we say that something is or is not necessary in God, we do not suppose that there is any necessity in him, either by way of compulsion or by way of restraint; rather, we mean that in all other things there is a necessity that prevents them from doing, and compels them not to do, anything contrary to what is said about God. For example, when we say that it is necessary for God always to speak the truth, and necessary for him never to lie, we are simply saying that in him there is such great consistency in maintaining truth, that of necessity nothing can have the power to make him either not speak the truth or lie.

Therefore, when we say that this Man who, according to the unity of his person—as has already been said[62]—is the same as God, the Son of God, could not avoid death, or will not to die, after he was born of the Virgin, we do not mean that in himself he was unable to preserve (or to will to preserve) his immortal life; rather, we refer to his unchangeable will, by which he freely made himself man, in order to die by persisting in the same decision, and we say that nothing can change that decision. For it would be powerlessness rather than power if he could choose to lie or deceive or change his decision, which he had already willed to be changeless. As I said before,[63] when anyone freely plans to do some good deed, and afterward by the same will carries out what he planned, we are not to say—even though he could be forced, if he were unwilling, to keep his promise—that he does what he does by necessity, but that

---

[61] Cf. *De casu diaboli*, 12 (Schmitt, I, 253); *De veritate*, 8 (I, 188).
[62] Cf. Chapters VII and IX, above.
[63] Cf. Chapter V.

he does it by the same free will by which he planned it. For a thing should not be said to be done or not done by necessity or inability, when neither necessity nor inability has anything to do with it, but the will alone acts. If, I say, this is the case with man, much more are necessity and inability not to be mentioned in God's case, since he does only what he wills, and no force can compel or restrain his will. For in Christ the diversity of natures and unity of person meant that, if the human nature could not do what was required for the restoration of men, the divine nature did it, while when it was incongruous with the divine nature the human nature performed it. Yet it was not first one person and then another, but the selfsame being who, existing perfectly in both natures, would through the human nature pay what it owed, and would through the divine nature be able to do what was needed.[64] Finally the Virgin, who was made pure by faith, so that he might be taken from her, believed that he was going to die only because he willed it, just as she had learned through the prophet who said of him, "He was offered because it was his own will."[65] Therefore, since her faith was true, it was necessary that it should be as she believed. But if you are bothered again because I say, "It was necessary," remember that the Virgin's faith was not the cause of his voluntary death; on the contrary, it was because this was going to take place that her faith was true. Therefore, if it is said, "It was necessary for him to die of his free will alone, because the faith or the prophecy which anticipated his death was true," this amounts to saying, "it was necessary for this to happen, because it was going to happen." But this sort of necessity does not compel something to exist; on the contrary, the existence of the thing causes the necessity.

For there is an antecedent necessity which is the cause of a thing's existence, and there is a consequent necessity produced by the thing itself. It is a matter of antecedent and effectual necessity when we say that the sky revolves because it is necessary for it to revolve, but it is a case of consequent necessity, which effects nothing but is itself produced, when I say that you necessarily speak because you are speaking. For when I say this, I mean that nothing can make it true that you are not speaking, at the moment when you are speaking—not that something compels you to speak. For the force of its natural state compels the sky to revolve, but no necessity makes you

---

[64] Cf. Leo, *Sermo* 52, 2 (*PL*, 54, 314 f.).
[65] Isa. 53:7 (as rendered in Vulgate).

speak. Wherever there is antecedent necessity, there is consequent necessity as well, but it is not true that there is any
antecedent necessity simply because there is consequent
necessity. For we can say that it is necessary for the sky to
revolve, because it is revolving, but it is not similarly true that
you speak because it is necessary for you to speak. That
consequent necessity applies to all times in this way: Whatever
has been, must have been; whatever is, must be, and will
necessarily have been; whatever is going to be is necessarily
going to be. (This is the necessity which in Aristotle's treatment
of singular and future propositions seems to destroy the possibility of choice and to build up everything on necessity.[66]) It was
by this consequent necessity, which effects nothing—since the
faith and the prophecy concerning Christ were true, *because*
he was going to die by free choice, not by necessity—that it
was necessary for things to happen as they did. By this necessity
he was made man; by this he did and suffered whatever he did
and suffered; by this he willed whatever he did will. For these
things were necessary because they were going to be, and they
were going to be because they were, and they were because they
were. And if you want to know the real necessity of everything
he did and suffered, you must understand that everything
happened necessarily because he himself willed it. But no
necessity preceded his willing. Thus, if these things happened
only because he willed it, they would not have happened if he
had not willed it. So, then, no one took his life from him, but
he himself laid it down and took it again, because he had
"power" to lay down his life and to "take it again," as he
himself says.[67]

B. You have convinced me that it cannot be proved that he
underwent death by any necessity, and I am not sorry that I
seemed so insistent that you should do this.

A. In my opinion, we have shown a sure way by which God
might have taken manhood without sin from the sinful mass.
But I do not think that we can possibly deny that there is some
other way than the one we have spoken of, on the supposition
that God can do what human reason cannot comprehend. But
this one seems sufficient to me; besides, if I wanted to look for
another now, I should have to investigate the meaning of
original sin, and the manner of its diffusion from our first

---

[66] Cf. Aristotle, *De interpret.*, 9 (18ª 28–19ᵇ4); Boethius, *In lib. Arist. de
interpret.*, edit. 1a, I (*PL*, 64, 329 ff.); edit. 2a, III (495 ff.).
[67] John 10:18.

parents into the entire human race (with the exception of that Man with whom we are dealing), and to touch on some other problems that demand separate treatment. Let us go on, then, with what is left of the task we have undertaken, and be satisfied with the explanation we have put forward.

B. Do what you like, but on the condition that sometime you will discharge your debt by discussing, with God's help, the other reason that you do not want to look into now.

A. Since I know that I cherish this intention, I do not refuse your request. But since I am uncertain about the future, I do not dare to promise anything, but I leave it all to God's disposal.[68]

CHAPTER XVIII

How the Life of Christ Is Paid to God for the Sins of Men, and How Christ Should and Should Not Have Suffered

But now tell me what you think remains to be answered of the question you put at the beginning, which forced so many other questions on us.

B. The heart of the question was this: Why did God become man, to save man by his death, when it seems that he could have done this in some other way? You have answered this by showing, by many necessary reasons, how it would not have been right for the restoration of human nature to be left undone, and how it could not have been done unless man paid what was owing to God for sin. But the debt was so great that, while man alone owed it, only God could pay it, so that the same person must be both man and God. Thus it was necessary for God to take manhood into the unity of his person, so that he who in his own nature ought to pay and could not should be in a person who could. Then you showed that the Man who also was God was to be taken from a virgin, and by the person of the Son of God, and how he could be taken from the sinful mass without sin. Moreover, you have proved most straightforwardly that the life of this Man was so sublime, so precious, that it can suffice to pay what is owing for the sins of the whole world, and infinitely more. It now remains, therefore, to be shown how it is paid to God for the sins of men.

---

[68] Anselm realized his intention in *De conceptu virginali et de originali peccato* (Schmitt, II, 135–173; partial translation in this volume).

A. If he let himself be killed for the sake of justice, did he not give his life for the honor of God?

B. If I can understand what I do not doubt, even though I do not see how he did this with good reason (since he was able both to maintain justice unalterably and to preserve his life everlastingly), I shall admit that he freely gave to God, for his honor, a gift to which nothing that is not God can be compared, and which can compensate for all the debts of all men.

A. Do you not understand that by enduring with gentle patience the injuries and insults and death on the cross with thieves—all brought on him, as we said above, [69] by his obedience in maintaining justice—he gave an example to men, to teach them not to turn away from the justice they owe to God on account of any trials which they can experience? But he would not have given this kind of example at all if, by using his own power, he had turned away from the death brought on him for such a cause.

B. It seems to me that there was no need for him to give this example, since many before his coming, and John the Baptist after his coming but before his death, admittedly set an adequate example by bravely enduring death for the truth's sake.

A. No man besides him ever gave to God, by dying, what he was not necessarily going to lose at some time, or paid what he did not owe. But this Man freely offered to the Father what he would never have lost by any necessity, and paid for sinners what he did not owe for himself. Therefore he gave us a more striking example, to the effect that each man should not hesitate to surrender to God for himself, when reason demands it, what he is going to lose very soon. For although he did not need to do it for himself, and was not compelled to do it for others, since he owed them nothing but punishment, he gave up such a precious life—yes, nothing less than himself—surrendering so great a person with such willingness.

B. You are coming very close to what I want to know.

But allow me to ask something that I could not readily answer if it were presented to me, even though you may think that it is a foolish thing to ask. You say that when he died he gave what he did not owe. But no one will deny that when he set this example in this way he did something better and more pleasing to God than if he had not done it. And no one will say that he was not obliged to do what he knew was better and

[69] Cf. Chapter IX, above.

more pleasing to God. How, then, can we assert that he did not owe to God what he did, that is, what he knew was better and more pleasing to God, especially since the creature owes to God all that it is and knows and can do?

A. Even though the creature possesses nothing of itself, when God permits it either to do or not to do something he puts both alternatives in its power, so that, although one course may be preferable, neither is definitely required. Thus, whether a man does what is better, or does the other, we may say that he ought to do what he does, while if he does what is better, he should have a reward, since he freely gives what is his own to give. For instance, although celibacy is better than marriage, neither one of them is definitely required from a man, but whether he prefers to use marriage or to preserve virginity, we may say that he ought to do what he does. No one, indeed, says that a choice must not be made between celibacy and marriage, but we do say that a man ought to do what he prefers, *before* he decides on one or other of these states, while if he keeps his virginity, he expects a reward for the free gift which he offers to God. Thus, when you say that the creature owes to God what he knows is best, and is able to do, this is not always true, if you interpret it as a debt, and do not understand, "If God commands it." As I have pointed out by way of illustration, a man does not owe virginity as a debt, but rather, if he prefers it, he ought to use marriage.

But if the word "ought" bothers you, and you cannot understand it without some reference to "debt,"[70] you should realize that "ought," like "to be able" or "unable" and "necessity," is sometimes used, not because any of these terms really refer to the things to which they are applied, but because they are found in something else.[71] For example, when we say that the poor ought to receive alms from the rich, this is the same thing as saying that the rich ought to give alms to the poor, since this is a debt to be exacted, not from the poor, but from the rich.[72] Again, we say that God ought to be above all things, not because he is really a debtor in any sense, but because all things ought to be subject to him, and we say that he ought to do what he wills, because what he wills ought to be. So when some creature wills to do what it has the right to do or not to do, it is said that it ought to do it, because what it

---

[70] *debitum* (debt or duty) is derived from *debere* (to owe, to be bound; *debeo*, I ought).

[71] Cf. Chapter XVII, above.   [72] Cf. *De veritate*, 8 (Schmitt, I, 188).

wills ought to be. Thus when the Lord Jesus willed to endure death (as we have said[73]), because he had the right either to suffer or not to suffer, he ought to have done what he did, because what he willed ought to be done, and yet he was not obliged to do it, because there was no indebtedness involved. For in his human nature (since he himself is God and man), from the time that he became man, he received from the divine nature, which is different from the human, the right to claim as his own whatever he possessed, so that he was bound to give only what he willed to give. But in his person he had all that he possessed so completely from himself, and was so perfectly self-sufficient, that he neither owed any recompense to anyone else nor needed to give in order to have something repaid to him.

B. Now I see clearly that it was in no sense as a matter of obligation that he gave himself up to death for the honor of God—as my reasoning seemed to show—and yet that he ought to have done what he did.

A. In fact, that honor belongs to the whole Trinity. Therefore, since he himself is God, the Son of God, he offered himself for his own honor to himself, as he did to the Father and the Holy Spirit. That is, he offered his humanity to his divinity, which is itself one of the three persons. However, in order to say what we want to say more plainly, while continuing in the same truth, let us say, as usage has it, that the Son freely offered himself to the Father. For it is in this way that we most aptly express it, both because the whole Godhead, to whom as man he offered himself, is understood in the reference to the one person, and because when we hear the names of Father and of Son we feel a certain boundless gratitude in our hearts, when it is said that the Son entreats the Father in this way for us.

B. I admit this most readily.

CHAPTER XIX

The Great Reason Why Human Salvation Follows from His Death

A. Now let us consider, as fully as we can, the great reason why man's salvation follows from his death.

B. My heart is struggling toward this. For although I seem to myself to understand it, I want to have the whole structure of the argument outlined by you.

[73] Cf. Chapter XI, above.

A. There is no need to explain what a great gift the Son gave freely.

B. That is clear enough.

A. You will not suppose that he who freely gives God so great a gift ought to be left unrewarded.

B. On the contrary, I see how necessary it is for the Father to reward the Son. Otherwise, he would seem unjust if he were unwilling and powerless if he were unable to reward him; but both these things are foreign to God.

A. He who rewards someone either gives what the latter does not have or foregoes what can be required from him. But before the Son did this great work, all that belonged to the Father belonged to him,[74] and he never owed anything that could be remitted to him. What, then, will be given him as a reward, when he is in need of nothing and there is nothing that can be given or forgiven him?

B. I see on the one hand that a reward is necessary, and on the other that it is impossible. For it is necessary for God to repay what he owes, and there is no way of making repayment.

A. If such a great and merited reward is paid neither to him nor to anyone else, it will seem that the Son performed such a great work in vain.

B. It is impious to think this.

A. Then it must be paid to someone else, since it cannot be paid to him.

B. That inevitably follows.

A. If the Son willed to give to another what is owing to himself, could the Father rightly forbid him, or deny it to the other?

B. On the contrary, I think that it is both just and necessary for the Father to pay it to anyone to whom the Son wills to give it, because the Son has a right to give what belongs to him, and the Father can only give what he owes him to someone else.

A. To whom would it be more fitting for him to assign the fruit and recompense of his death than to those for whose salvation (as truthful reasoning has taught us) he made himself man, and to whom (as we have said[75]) by dying he gave an example of dying for the sake of justice? For they will be his imitators in vain if they do not share in his merit. Or whom will he more justly make heirs of the debt which he does not need, and of the abundance of his own fullness, than his kinsmen and brethren, whom he sees bound by so many great debts,

[74] Cf. John 16:15.   [75] Cf. preceding chapter.

languishing in poverty and deepest misery—so that what they owe for their sins may be forgiven them, and what they need, on account of their sins, may be given them?

B. The world can hear nothing more reasonable, nothing more delightful, nothing more desirable. Indeed, I gain such great confidence from this, that already I cannot say how great the joy is that makes my heart leap. For it seems to me that God can repel no man who draws near to him in this name.

A. That is true, if he draws near as he ought to. But Holy Scripture everywhere teaches us the way to attain to a share in such great grace, and how we are to live under it—Holy Scripture, founded upon immovable truth (which we have examined to a certain extent, with God's help) as upon a firm foundation.[76]

B. Certainly whatever is built on this foundation is founded on a solid rock.

A. I think that I have now answered your question, at least in a small way, although a better than I could do it more fully, and there are more and greater reasons for this truth than my own or any mortal ability can comprehend. Moreover, it is clear that God did not need in any way to do the act we have been speaking of, but that his unchanging truth required it. For while God is said to have done what that Man did, on account of the unity of person, God did not need to descend from heaven to conquer the devil, or to act against him by justice to deliver man. But God did require from man that he should conquer the devil, and that he who had offended God by sin should make satisfaction by justice. For God owed the devil nothing but punishment, and man owed him nothing but retaliation, reconquering him by whom he had been conquered; but whatever was required from man was due to God, not to the devil.[77]

CHAPTER XX

How Great and How Just God's Mercy Is

When we were considering God's justice and man's sin, God's mercy seemed to you to vanish.[78] But we have found how great it really is, and how it is in such harmony with his justice that it cannot be conceived to be greater or more just. For, indeed, what greater mercy could be imagined, than for

[76] Cf. Luke 6:48.   [77] Cf. Book I, Chapters VI, VII, above.
[78] Cf. Book I, Chapter XXIV, above.

God the Father to say to the sinner, condemned to eternal torments, and without any power of redeeming himself from them, "Receive my only-begotten Son, and give him for yourself," and for the Son himself to say, "Take me, and redeem yourself"? For they as much as say this when they call us and draw us to the Christian faith. And what could be more just, than for Him to whom the price more valuable than every debt is paid to forgive every debt (if the price is given with the right disposition)?

CHAPTER XXI

It Is Impossible for the Devil to Be Reconciled

But you will understand that the devil's reconciliation, about which you asked,[79] is impossible, if you carefully consider man's reconciliation. For man could be reconciled only by a Man-God who could die, by whose justice what God had lost through man's sin might be restored to him. Similarly, the condemned angels can be saved only by an Angel-God who can die, and by his justice can restore to God what the sins of the others took away. Moreover, it would not have been right for man to be raised up by another man who was not of the same race, even if he were of the same nature. Similarly, no angel ought to be saved by another angel, even though they are all of one nature, because they are not of the same race, as men are. For all the angels are not descended from one angel, as all men are from one man. Then their restoration is also ruled out by the fact that they ought to rise again without anyone's help, just as they fell without being made to fall by any injury inflicted by another. But this is impossible for them. For they cannot be restored in any other way to the dignity they were to have had, since if they had not sinned they would have stood firm in the truth[80] by their own power which they had received, without another's help. Therefore, if anyone supposes that redemption through our Saviour ought at length to be extended even to them, reason convicts him of being unreasonably deceived. I say this, not as if the price of his death might not, by its greatness, avail for all the sins of men and angels, but simply because an unchangeable reason is opposed to the raising up of the lost angels.[81]

[79] Cf. Book I, Chapter XVII, above.   [80] Cf. John 8:44.
[81] Cf. Augustine, *Enarr. in Ps.* 54:4 (*PL*, 36, 630).

CHAPTER XXII

The Truth of the Old and New Testaments Has Been Proved in What Has Been Said

B. Everything you say seems reasonable to me, and I cannot gainsay it. Also, I think that whatever is contained in the New and Old Testaments has been proved by the solution of the one question we put forward. For you prove that God was necessarily made man, in such a way that even if the few things you have cited from our books—for instance, in touching on the three persons of the Godhead,[82] or on Adam[83]—were taken away, you would satisfy not only Jews, but even pagans, by reason alone. And the God-Man himself establishes the New Testament and proves the truth of the Old. Therefore, just as we must confess his own truthfulness, so no one can refuse to confess the truth of everything that is contained in them both.[84]

A. If we have said anything that should be corrected, I do not refuse correction, if it is done with good reason. But if what we think we have discovered by reason is confirmed by the testimony of the truth, we should ascribe this, not to ourselves, but to God, who is blessed forever. Amen.

[82] Cf. Chapter IX, above. [83] Cf. Chapter XVI, above.
[84] Cf. Chapter XV, above.

The Virgin Conception and Original Sin

THE TEXT

[Preface omitted. See Schmitt, Vol. II, p. 139.]

CHAPTER I

WHAT IS ORIGINAL AND WHAT IS PERSONAL JUSTICE OR INJUSTICE

To see, then, how God took manhood without sin from the sinful mass of the human race, we must first inquire about original sin, since our question arises only from the latter. For if we see how Christ could not be subject to this, it will be evident in what way the assumption or conception of that manhood was free from all sin.

Without doubt, the term "original" is derived from "origin." Therefore, if original sin is found only in man, it seems to take its name either from the origin of human nature, since it is original from its beginning, being derived from the very origin of human nature, or from the origin or beginning of each and every person, since it is contracted in his very origin. But it does not appear to descend from the beginning of human nature, since the latter's origin was just, our first parents having been created just, without any sin.[1] Thus it seems to be called original from the origin of each particular human person. However, if anyone says that sin is called original because it descends to individuals from those from whom their nature takes its origin, I shall not contradict him, provided that he does not deny that original sin is contracted with the very origin of each person. For in each man there are at once the nature, by which he is a man like all the others, and the person, by which he is distinguished from others, and to which we apply "that" or "this" or a proper name, like Adam or Abel,[2] and each one's sin is in the nature and the person—for Adam's sin was in man, because it is in the nature, and in him who was called Adam, because it is in the person. And yet there is a sin which each derives with his nature in his own origin, and there is a sin which he does not

---

[1] Cf. *Cur deus homo*, II, 1.   [2] Cf. *Epist. de incarn. verbi*, 11 (Schmitt, II, 29).

contract with nature itself, but commits himself after he has become a person distinct from other persons. Now that which is contracted in his very origin is called "original," and can also be called "natural," not because it comes from the essence of the nature, but because it is received with the latter on account of its corruption. But the sin which each commits after he is a person can be named "personal," because it is done by the fault of the person. For a similar reason we can speak of original and personal justice, since Adam and Eve were "originally" just—that is, they were just at their very beginning, as soon as they existed as human beings, without any interval. But justice can be called "personal" when the unjust receives the justice which he did not have from the beginning.[3]

CHAPTER II

How Human Nature Was Corrupted

If Adam and Eve, then, had preserved their original justice, those who were born of them would have been originally just, as they were. But since they sinned personally, even though, being originally strong and uncorrupted, they had the power of always keeping justice without difficulty, all that they were was enfeebled and corrupted. The body was weakened, because after sin it was like the bodies of brute animals, subject to corruption and carnal appetites. The soul was weakened, because from the corruption of the body and from those appetites, as well as from the want of the goods it lost, it was tainted by carnal affections. And since the whole of human nature was in Adam and Eve, and nothing belonging to it was outside them, it was weakened and corrupted as a whole.

There remained in it, therefore, three things: the obligation of possessing unimpaired justice without any injustice, as it received it; the obligation of making satisfaction because it deserted justice; and the corruption itself which it incurred on account of sin. Thus, just as it would have been propagated as God made it, if it had not sinned, after sin it is propagated as it made itself by sinning. By itself, then, it can neither make satisfaction for sin nor recover its abandoned justice,[4] and "the corruptible body is a load upon the soul"[5]—more especially when it is weaker, as in infancy or in its mother's womb—so

3 On this chapter, cf. Augustine, *De pecc. mer.*, I, 10:11 (*CSEL*, 60, 12).
4 Cf. *Cur deus homo*, I, 20–23.   5 Wisdom of Solomon 9:15.

that it cannot even understand justice. For this reason it seems necessary for human nature to be born in infants with the obligation of making satisfaction for the first sin (which it could always have avoided), as well as the obligation of having original justice (which it could always have kept). Nor does lack of power excuse it even in infants, when in them it does not pay what it owes, since it brought that lack of power on itself by abandoning justice in our first parents (in whom it was complete), and is always obligated to have the power which it received with a view to the perpetual preservation of justice. This state, then, is original sin even in infants.

Let us also add the sins of nearer ancestors, which are repaid "unto the third and fourth generation."[6] It is true that it is an open question whether all these things are to be interpreted as part of original sin, or not; at the same time, lest I seem to lighten the latter for the sake of the solution I am seeking, I shall present it as so weighty that no one can show it to be weightier.

CHAPTER III

There Is No Sin Save in the Rational Will

But whether original sin is all this, or something less, I do not think that we can ascribe it to the infant in any way, before it has a rational soul, any more than we could say that justice was in Adam before he became a rational man. For even if Adam and Eve had begotten children before they sinned, justice would not and could not have been in the seed before it was formed into a living man. Therefore, if man's seed is unable to receive justice before it becomes man, it cannot receive original sin before it is man.

Certainly we must not doubt that original sin is injustice. For if every sin is injustice, and original sin is sin, it must undoubtedly be injustice also. But if someone says, "Not every sin is injustice," let him say that there can at the same time be some sin and no injustice in anyone; but this seems incredible. Yet if it is said that original sin is not to be called sin absolutely, but sin with the addition of "original," as a painted man is not really a man, but a painted man, it will follow immediately that an infant who has no sin save original sin is pure from sin. In that case, the Son of the Virgin was not unique among men, in being without sin both in his mother's womb and when he

---

[6] Ex. 20:5.

was born of his mother. Also, the infant who dies without baptism, sinless except for original sin, either is not condemned at all or is condemned without sin. But we do not accept any of this. Therefore, every sin is injustice, and original sin is sin absolutely. It follows, then, that it is injustice also. Again, if God condemns a man for injustice only, but condemns someone for original sin, original sin cannot be something other than injustice. But if this is the case, and injustice is the same thing as the absence of due justice[7]—for injustice seems to lie only in the nature which does not possess justice when it ought to do so—then original sin is included under the definition of injustice.

Now if justice is "the rectitude of the will maintained for its own sake,"[8] and that rectitude can be found only in the rational nature, then only the rational nature is debtor to justice, just as no nature but the rational can receive justice. Then, since there can be no injustice except where there ought to be justice, original sin, which is injustice, is in the rational nature only. Now the rational nature is found only in God and the angel and the human soul, for which a man is called rational, and without which he is not man. Since, then, there is no original sin either in God or in an angel, it can be only in the rational soul of man.

We should realize also that justice can be found only in the will, if justice is the rectitude of the will maintained for its own sake. This applies, of course, to injustice also. For the absence of justice is called injustice only when justice ought to be present. Nothing, therefore, except justice itself or injustice is called just or unjust save the will, or something else for the sake of a just or unjust will. For this we call a man or an angel just or unjust, a soul or an action just or unjust.

CHAPTER IV

NOTHING IS JUST OR UNJUST BY ITSELF SAVE JUSTICE ITSELF OR INJUSTICE, AND ONLY THE WILL IS PUNISHED

For nothing, whether substance or action or anything else, is just, considered in itself, save justice, and nothing unjust or sinful, save injustice—not even the will itself in which justice or injustice is to be found. For the power of the soul by which the

[7] Cf. *De casu diaboli*, 16 (Schmitt, I, 259 ff.).
[8] Cf. *De veritate*, 12 (I, 191 ff.).

soul itself wills anything, which we call the "will"—the power that can be called the "instrument" of willing, as sight is the instrument of seeing—is one thing, and justice, whose presence or absence makes the will just or unjust, is another. (The affections and uses of this instrument are also called "wills," but this is too big a question to introduce here.[9])

The appetites themselves—which the apostle calls the "flesh," which "lusteth against the spirit,"[10] and the "law of sin,"[11] which is in the "members, fighting against the law of my mind"[12]—are neither just nor unjust, considered in themselves. For they do not make a man just or unjust simply because he feels them, but make him unjust only if he voluntarily consents to them when he should not. For the same apostle says that there is "no condemnation to them that are in Christ Jesus, who walk not according to the flesh,"[13] that is, who do not consent in their will to the flesh. Now if they made a man who felt them, even without consent, unjust, condemnation would follow. Therefore, it is not feeling them but consenting to them that is sin. For if they were unjust in themselves, they would produce injustice whenever they were consented to. But when brute animals consent to them, we do not call them unjust. Again, if they were sins, they would be removed in baptism, when every sin is wiped away, but it is obvious that they are not. Thus there is no injustice in their essence, but injustice lies in the rational will which follows them inordinately. For when the will resists them, rejoicing in the law of God according to the inner man, then the will is just. For the apostle calls the justice which the law orders both the "law of God,"[14] because it comes from God, and the "law of the mind,"[15] because it is understood by the mind—just as the old law is called the "law of God,"[16] because it comes from God, and the "law of Moses,"[17] because it was given through Moses.

I said that an action is called unjust not in itself but on account of an unjust will. This is plain in those acts that can sometimes be done without injustice—for instance, to kill a man, as Phinehas did,[18] or to have sexual intercourse, as in marriage or among brute animals. But those actions that can never be done justly, such as perjury, and certain other things that should

9 Cf. *De concordia praescientiae*, etc., III, 11 (II, 278 ff.).
10 Gal. 5:17.   11 Rom. 7:25.   12 Rom. 7:23.
13 Rom. 8:1.   14 Rom. 7:22, 25.   15 Rom. 7:23.
16 I Esdras 7:21 (A.V., Ezra 7:21).
17 Josh. 8:31.   18 Num. 25:7 ff.

not be named,[19] are not easy to understand in this way. But suppose that the act of doing something—an act that only lasts as long as something is being done, and when that is completed passes away and no longer has any reality—or the product that is made and remains were a sin. (The fact that, when we write something that should not be written, the act of writing passes away, while the signs produced by it remain, will serve as an example.) Then, when the action completely passed away, the sin would likewise completely pass away, or, in the other case, the sin would never be wiped out as long as what had been produced remained. But we see that sins often are not wiped out when the action is, and that they often are wiped out when the product is not. Therefore, neither the action that passes away nor the product that remains is now a sin.

Finally, if we censure voluntary actions which are unjustly done, the members and senses by which they are done can reply: "God subjected us and the power that is in us to the will, so that we cannot help moving ourselves and doing what it wills, at its command. Or rather, it moves us as its instruments, and does the works that we seem to be doing. We cannot resist it by ourselves, and the works which it does cannot fail to be done. It is neither right nor possible for us to disobey the mistress whom God has given us. When we obey her, we obey God, who gave us this law." How, then, do members or senses or works sin, when God has subjected them to the will in this way, if they observe what God appointed for them? Whatever they do, therefore, is to be attributed totally to the will.

But perhaps, since this is the case, someone may wonder why the members and the senses are punished for the fault of the will. But this does not really happen, for only the will is punished. For only what happens against his will is punishment for anyone,[20] and no being that does not possess a will feels punishment. But the members and the senses will nothing by themselves. Thus, just as the will works in the members and the senses, so it is tormented or given pleasure in them. If anyone does not accept this, he should recognize that only the soul, which includes the will, feels and acts in the senses and the members, so that the soul alone is tormented or given pleasure in them. Nonetheless, it is customary for us to call the actions which the unjust will performs sins, because there is sin in the will by which they are performed. We even give names to some of them, to signify that they are done unjustly (for instance,

[19] Cf. Eph. 5:3.   [20] Cf. *Cur deus homo*, II, 12.

fornication, lying). But one thing is understood when the action or speech itself is considered, and another thing when we examine it to see whether it is justly or unjustly done. Finally, every essence is from God, from whom nothing unjust comes. Thus no essence is unjust in itself.[21]

CHAPTER V

Evil, Which Sin or Injustice Is, Is Nothing

Moreover, injustice is absolutely nothing, just like blindness. For blindness is simply the absence of sight where it ought to be, but this is no more something real in the eye where sight ought to be than it is in wood where it ought not to be. For injustice is not a kind of thing by which the soul is infected and corrupted, as the body is by poison, or which really does something—as seems to happen when the wicked man does evil works. When an untamed beast breaks its chains and runs about in a fury, or when a ship, if the pilot leaves the helm and abandons it to the winds and the motion of the sea, goes to and fro and is drawn into all kinds of dangers, we do indeed say that the absence of a chain or a rudder does this—not, however, because their absence is something or does anything, but because, if they were present, they would keep the beast from raging or the ship from being lost. Similarly, when a wicked man rages and is driven into any evil deeds which constitute a peril to his soul, while we do declare that injustice performs these actions, we do not mean that it is a real essence or does something. We mean, rather, that when the will, to which all the voluntary movements of the whole man are subject, is driven, in the absence of justice, by diverse appetites, inconstant and unrestrained and masterless, it casts itself and everything subject to it down into manifold evils, while justice, if it were present, would prevent it from doing all this.

From all this, then, it is easy to learn that injustice has no essence, even though the affections and acts of an unjust will, which, considered in themselves, are something, are commonly called "injustice." By the same reasoning we understand that evil is nothing. For just as injustice is nothing but the absence of due justice, so evil is nothing but the absence of due good. But no essence, though it may be called evil, is nothing, nor

[21] Cf. *De casu diaboli*, 7 (Schmitt, I, 244 f.).

does being evil mean being something for it. For being evil does not mean anything for any essence, except that it lacks the good which it ought to have. But the lack of a good which ought to be present is not some kind of being. Therefore, being evil does not mean being something for any essence.

I have made these brief statements concerning evil which, in so far as it is injustice, is always nothing, beyond any doubt. Misfortune, indeed, is an evil, and thus particular misfortunes are called evils; while sometimes it is nothing, as in the case of blindness or deafness, at other times it seems to be something, as in the case of pain and grief. [22] But that justice is the rectitude of the will maintained for its own sake, and that injustice is nothing but the absence of due justice, and has no essence, is proved sufficiently, I think, in the treatise I produced called *On the Fall of the Devil,* [23] though I may have proved it more fully, as far as justice is concerned, in the treatise I published *On Truth.* [24]

CHAPTER VI

Nevertheless, When God Punishes for Sin, He Does Not Punish for Nothing

When some people hear that sin is nothing, they usually say, "If sin is nothing, why does God punish man for sin, when no one should be punished for nothing?" Although their question is slight enough, some brief reply should be given, since they do not know what they are asking.

Although it is equally true that the absence of justice is nothing, both where justice is due and where it is not due, God rightly punishes sinners because of something, and not for nothing, because—as I said in the above-mentioned book [25]—he exacts from them against their will the due honor which they were unwilling to repay freely, and by a suitable order sets them apart from the just, lest there be something disordered in his kingdom. But he does not punish creatures in whom no justice is due for the absence of justice—that is, for nothing—since there is nothing that he can exact from them, and the fitting order of the universe of things does not require their punishment. So then, when God punishes for sin, that is, for the absence

---

22 Cf. *ibid.*, 26 (I, 274).
23 Cf. *ibid.*, 9–11, 15–16, 19, 26 (I, 246 ff.).
24 Cf. *De veritate*, 12 (I, 191 ff.).
25 Cf. *Cur deus homo*, I, 12; 14.

of due justice—which is nothing—he does not punish for nothing at all, and it is true that unless there is something for which he ought to administer punishment he simply does not punish for nothing.

CHAPTER VII

How the Seed of Man is Called Unclean and Is Said to Be Conceived in Sins, Although There Is No Sin in It

It is, I think, already evident from what has been said that sin and injustice are nothing, that they are only to be found in the rational will, and that no essence save the will is properly called unjust. It seems, then, that an infant has a rational soul (without which it cannot have a rational will) from the very moment of its conception, or else that there is no original sin in it as soon as it is conceived. But no human mind admits that it has a rational soul from the instant of its conception. For it would follow that as often as conceived human seed is lost—even from the very moment of conception—before it attains to human form, a human soul is condemned in it, since it is not reconciled through Christ; but this is too absurd. Therefore this alternative must be given up altogether.

But if the infant does not have sin from the very instant of its conception, what does Job mean when he says to God: "Who can make him clean that is conceived of unclean seed? is it not thou who only art?"[26] And how is what David says true: "I was conceived in iniquities; and in sins did my mother conceive me"?[27] If I can, therefore, I shall ask how, although sin is not in infants from the very moment of their conception, they may be said to be conceived from unclean seed, in iniquities and in sins.

Certainly divine Scripture often asserts that something is when it is not, simply because it is certain to come about. Thus, for instance, God said to Adam concerning the forbidden tree, "In what day soever thou shalt eat of it, thou shalt die the death"[28]; not that he would die bodily on that day, but because on that day he became subject to the necessity of dying at some time. And Paul speaks in the same way of the necessity of dying at some time: "And if Christ be in you, the body indeed is dead, because of sin; but the spirit liveth, because of justification."[29] For the bodies of those to whom he was speaking were not dead, but they were going to die because of sin, since "by one man sin entered into this world, and by sin

26 Job 14:4.   27 Ps. 50:7 (P.B.V., 51:5).
28 Gen. 2:17.   29 Rom. 8:10.

death."[30] Thus we all sinned in Adam when he sinned, not because we ourselves, who did not yet exist, sinned then, but because we were going to come from him, and it was then made necessary that, when we existed, we should sin, because "by the disobedience of one, many were made sinners."[31]

In the same way, we can understand that man is conceived of unclean seed, in iniquities and sins; not that there is any uncleanness of sin or sin or iniquity in the seed, but because from the very seed and the very conception by which he begins to be a man he derives the necessity of having the uncleanness of sin—which is the same thing as sin and iniquity—as soon as he has a rational soul. For even if an infant is begotten by corrupt concupiscence, there is no more fault in the seed than there is in spittle or blood if a man spits or throws out some of his blood with an evil will. For the evil will is censured, and not the spittle or blood. It is clear, then, how there is no sin in infants in the very instant of their conception, and at the same time how the things I adduced from the divine Scripture are true. There is certainly no sin in them, because they do not yet possess the will, apart from which there cannot be any sin in them, and yet it is said to be in them, because they contract in the seed the necessity of sinning, as soon as they are men.

[Chapters VIII–XXI, on Christ's freedom from original sin, omitted. See Schmitt, Vol. II, pp. 149–161.]

CHAPTER XXII

The Magnitude of Original Sin

Moreover, original sin can be neither greater nor less than I said[32] because, as soon as the infant is rational, human nature does not possess in it the justice which it received in Adam and ought always to possess. Nor does its inability excuse it for not having it, as was said above.[33] Nevertheless, I think that it is not in all respects as weighty as I suggested above. For since I wanted to show that it does not extend to the Man conceived of the Virgin, I defined it in such a way that nothing could be added to it, lest—as I said—I should seem to lessen its weight in the interests of the solution I was looking for. I shall briefly disclose what I now think about it.

[30] Rom. 5:12.
[32] Cf. Chapter II, above.

[31] Rom. 5:19.
[33] Cf. ibid.

I do not think that the sin of Adam descends to infants in such a way that they ought to be punished for it, as if they themselves had each committed it personally, as Adam did, even though, because of Adam's sin, it has come about that none of them can be born without sin—while the latter is followed by condemnation. For when the apostle says that "death reigned from Adam into Moses, even over them also who have not sinned after the similitude of the transgression of Adam,"[34] he seems to signify clearly that the very transgression of Adam, or something just as great, is not personally imputed to them, even though in his writings he declares that all the children of Adam—except the Virgin's Son—are "sinners" and "children of wrath."[35] For when he says, "Even over them also who have not sinned after the similitude of the transgression of Adam," this can be construed as if he had said, "Even over them who have not sinned as greatly as Adam sinned by transgressing." And when he says, "The law entered in, that sin might abound,"[36] we may understand either that before the law, in those "who have not sinned after the similitude of the transgression of Adam," sin was less than Adam's sin, or that, if it was not less, sin abounded in them after the law, beyond Adam's sin; but I cannot understand this when I think about it. As you have already read, I have expounded my view of the weight of Adam's sin and the satisfaction for it in *Why God Became Man.*[37] It is true, nonetheless, that no one is restored to the end for which man was made and the power of propagation given to him, and that human nature is not brought out of the evils into which it fell, except by satisfaction for the sin by which it hurled itself down into those same evils.

Someone will say: "If they do not each have the sin of Adam, how can you assert that no one is saved without satisfaction for the sin of Adam? For how can a just God require satisfaction from them for a sin that is not theirs?" God, however, does not require more than he really owes from any sinner; but since no one can repay as much as he owes, Christ alone pays more than they owe for all who are saved, as I have already said in the frequently mentioned little work.

It remains to be seen in another way for what reason sin is less in infants than in Adam, although it descends from him to all. For "by one man sin entered into this world, and by sin death."[38]

34 Rom. 5:14.   35 Cf. Rom. 5:8; Eph. 2:3.
36 Rom. 5:20.   37 Cf. *Cur deus homo,* I, 21 ff.
38 Rom. 5:12.

CHAPTER XXIII

WHY AND HOW IT DESCENDS TO INFANTS

But we cannot know why it is less, if we do not understand why and how it is in them at all. Although this has already been stated,[39] as far as was necessary for what was being sought after, it will not be superfluous to repeat it briefly here. Now it cannot be denied that infants were in Adam when he sinned. But they were in him causally or materially, as though in his seed,[40] while they are personally in themselves, because in him they were the seed itself, while in themselves each is a different person. In him they were not distinct from himself; in themselves they are other than he. In him they were himself; in themselves they are themselves. Thus they were in him, but not as themselves, since they were not yet themselves.

Perhaps someone will say, "The being by which other men are said to have been in Adam is almost nothing, and an empty thing, and it should not be called 'being' at all." Let him say, then, that the being by which Christ was in Abraham, in David, and in the other fathers, according to the seed—and by which all things that come from seed were in the seeds—was nothing or empty or false. And let him say that God made nothing when he made everything that is begotten from seed in the seeds themselves to begin with. And let him call this being nothing or an empty thing, when the things that we see existing would not exist if it were not real. For if it is not true that the things which nature begets from seeds were something in them to begin with, they would not come from them in any way. But if it is most stupid to say this, then it was by true and genuine being—and not false or empty being—that all other men were in Adam, and God did not do something empty when he gave them being in him. But (as has been said) in him they were not distinct from himself, and therefore were quite different from what they are in themselves.

But although it is established that they were all in him, the Virgin's Son alone was in him in a quite different way. For all the others were in him in such a way that they came from him by natural propagation, which was subject to his power and will; but Christ alone was not in him in such a way as to be

---

[39] Cf. Chapter 10 (Schmitt, II, 151 f.).
[40] Cf. Ambrose, *In Luc.*, 7, 234 (*CSEL*, 32, 387); Augustine, *De civ. dei*, XIII, 13 (*CSEL*, 40/1, 632).

made of him by nature or will. For when Adam sinned, it had been settled that he would be the source from which the others were to have their being, and that they should come from him; but as for that Man, though Adam was that from which he was to come, he was not to take being from him, because it was not in his power that this Man should be begotten from him. But it was not in his power, either, that he should be made of another essence or from nothing. Therefore, it did not lie in Adam that this Man should exist in any way. For it was neither in the power of nature nor in the power of his will that he should exist in any way. Nevertheless, Adam did possess the nature from which he was to be begotten, not by the former's power but by God's. For although in his ancestors, down to the Virgin Mother, the will engendered and nature brought forth, so that the Virgin herself looked back to Adam as the source of her being, by a partly natural and partly voluntary process, like everyone else, nevertheless the will of the creature did not engender offspring in her, and nature did not bring forth, but the "Holy Ghost" and the "power of the Most High"[41] wonderfully begat a Man from a Virgin Mother. Thus with respect to the others it lay in Adam, that is, in his power, that they should have being from him, but with respect to this Man it did not lie in Adam that he should exist in any way, any more than it lay in the slime that the first man, who was made from it, should come from it in a wonderful way, or in the man, that Eve should be of him, as in fact she was made. But it did not lie in any of them, in whom he was from Adam to Mary, that he should exist. Nonetheless, he was in them, because that from which he was to be taken was in them, just as that from which the first man was made was in the slime, and that from which Eve was made in him. He was in them, however, not by the creature's will or strength, but by divine power alone. But he was taken so much more wonderfully and with greater grace, in so far as they were made mere men but he was made the Man-God. Thus he was in Adam, when the latter sinned, in a quite different way from those who are procreated by a voluntary and natural process. Therefore, in a certain way Adam produces them whom the human will begets and nature brings forth by the power of procreation which they have received. But God alone made that Man, even though he came from Adam, because he was not made through Adam but through himself, as it were of his own.

[41] Luke 1:35.

What, then, could be more fitting for the revelation of God's great goodness, and for the fullness of grace which he granted to Adam, than for those whose being was so fully in his power that through him they were what he was by nature, to depend also on his freedom of choice, so that he might beget them with the justice and happiness he himself possessed? This, then, was given to him. Therefore, since he freely abandoned the goods he had received to be kept for himself and for them, when he was set on so great a height of grace, the sons lost what their father took away from them by not preserving it, though by preserving it he could have given it to them. This seems to me a sufficient reason for the descent of Adam's sin and evils to infants, if we consider pure justice itself, carefully setting aside our own will, since the latter often seriously hinders the mind in the attempt to understand rectitude. But I shall indicate briefly how I think that sin descends to them.

As I said,[42] there is a sin that comes from the nature, and a sin that comes from the person. Thus, what is from the person can be called "personal," and what is from the nature "natural" —otherwise, "original." And the personal passes over into the nature, and the natural into the person, in this way. Nature required what Adam used to eat, because it had been created to require this. But when he ate from the forbidden tree, this was not done by natural will, but by a personal will—his own. And yet, the person did not do what it did without the nature. For the person was what was called Adam, and the nature, what was called man. The person, therefore, made the nature sinful, because when Adam sinned, man sinned. Notwithstanding, it was not because he was man that he was impelled to take the forbidden thing, but he was drawn by his own inclination, which was not required by the nature but was harbored by the person. In infants the reverse process takes place. For the fact that they do not have the justice they ought to possess is the result, not of a personal inclination, as with Adam, but of a natural indigence, which the nature itself inherited from Adam. For in Adam, in whom the totality of human nature was to be found, it was stripped of the justice which it possessed, and unless it is helped it always lacks it. In this way, since the nature subsists in persons and there are no persons without the nature, the nature makes the persons of infants sinful. Thus in Adam the person despoiled the nature of the good of justice, and the nature, once impoverished, makes every person it engenders from itself

42 Cf. Chapter I, above.

sinful and unjust, by virtue of that same poverty. In this way the personal sin of Adam passes over into all those who are naturally propagated from him, and becomes original or natural in them.

But it is obvious that there is a great difference between Adam's sin and theirs, since he sinned by his own will, but they sin by natural necessity, merited by his own personal will. But although no one doubts that unequal sins are not followed by equal punishment, the condemnation of personal and of original sin is alike in this respect, that no one is admitted to the Kingdom of God, for which man was made, save by the death of Christ—apart from which what is due for Adam's sin is not repaid—even if all are not equally deserving of torment in hell. For after the Day of Judgment there will be neither angel nor man who is not in the Kingdom of God or in hell, one or the other. So, then, the sin of infants is less than the sin of Adam, and yet no one is saved without that universal satisfaction by which both great and small sins are remitted. But why there is no satisfaction apart from that death, and how salvation comes to men through it, I have inquired and stated, as God gave me ability, in the book that has already been mentioned.[43]

[Chapters XXIV, XXV, on the sins of ancestors after Adam, omitted. See Schmitt, Vol. II, pp. 166–169.]

CHAPTER XXVI

How Despite All This No One Bears His Father's Sins, but Each Bears His Own

But if anyone objects that all who are not saved through faith in Christ bear Adam's iniquity and burden, and wants to prove by this that infants ought to bear the iniquities of other ancestors as well, in the same way, or else should not bear his, let him consider carefully that infants do not bear Adam's sin, but their own. For the sin of Adam was one thing, and the sin of infants is another, because they differ, as was said.[44] For one was the cause, and the other is the effect. Adam lacked due justice, because he himself abandoned it, and not another; infants lack it, because another forsook it, and not they them-

---

[43] I.e., *Cur deus homo*.   [44] Cf. Chapter XXIII, above.

selves. Therefore the sin of Adam and the sin of infants are not the same. And when the apostle says, as I noted above,[45] that "death reigned from Adam unto Moses, even over them also who have not sinned after the similitude of the transgression of Adam,"[46] by indicating that the sin of infants is less than that of Adam he clearly shows that it is something different.

When the infant, then, is condemned for original sin, he is condemned, not for Adam's sin, but for his own. For if he did not have his own sin, he would not be condemned. So, then, he does not bear Adam's iniquity, but his own, although he may be said to bear it because the former's iniquity was the cause of his own sin. But if the cause of the birth of infants in sin was in Adam, it is not to be found in their other ancestors, because, as I have said,[47] human nature does not possess in them the power of engendering just sons. Thus it does not follow that there is sin in infants for their sin, as there is for the sin of Adam.

CHAPTER XXVII

What Original Sin Is, and that It Is Equal in All

Therefore, by original sin I do not understand anything different from what is in the infant as soon as it has a rational soul, whatever may have happened in its body before it was animated—for instance, some corruption of the members— or whatever is to befall it afterward, either in soul or in body. For the reasons given above, I think that this is equal in all infants naturally begotten, and that all who die in it alone are condemned equally. Whatever sin is added in man beyond this is personal, and just as the person is born sinful because of the nature, so the nature is made more sinful by the person, because when any person sins, man sins.

In these infants, I cannot interpret this sin, which I call original, as anything but that deprivation of due justice, which, as I said above,[48] is the outcome of Adam's disobedience. By this deprivation they are all children of wrath,[49] since nature's ready abandonment of justice in Adam accuses it, while, as has been said,[50] the inability to regain justice does not excuse the persons. This deprivation is accompanied by the deprivation of justice, so that they are altogether lacking in blessedness,

[45] Cf. Chapter XXII, above.
[46] Rom. 5:14.
[47] Cf. Chapter X (Schmitt, II, 151 f.).
[48] Cf. Chapter XXIII, above.
[49] Cf. Eph. 2:3.
[50] Cf. Chapter II, above.

as well as in justice. These two deprivations leave them un-protected in this life's exile, and open to the sins and miseries which ceaselessly befall them everywhere and attack them on every side, except in so far as they are protected by the divine government.

[Chapters XXVIII, XXIX, on the condemnation of infants and their salvation through baptism, omitted. See Schmitt, Vol. II, pp. 170–173.]

A Prayer to Saint Mary to Obtain Love for Her and for Christ

THE TEXT

Mary, thou great Mary, thou who art great among blessed Marys, thou greatest of women: thee, O Lady great and very great, thee my heart wishes to love, thee my mouth longs to praise, thee my mind desires to reverence, thee my soul aspires to entreat, because my whole being commits itself to thy keeping.

Make an effort, depth of my soul, make what effort you can— if you can do anything—all my inmost self, to praise her merits, to love her blessedness, to wonder at her loftiness, to beseech her kindness. It is her protection that you daily need, and desire as you need it, and implore as you desire it, and obtain as you implore it. (Even if you do not obtain it according to your desire, you obtain it beyond or even in contrast to your merit.)

Queen of angels, Mistress of the world, Mother of Him who cleanses the world, I confess that my heart is most unclean, so that it is rightly ashamed to turn to such a pure one, and cannot worthily touch such a pure one in turning to her. Thee, therefore, Mother of my heart's illumination,[1] thee, Nurse of my mind's salvation,[2] thee my breast implores, as best it can. Hear, O Lady; be present, gracious one; help, O most mighty one. May the filth of my mind be cleansed, my darkness lightened,[3] my coldness kindled, my listlessness roused. Thy blessed holiness is exalted above all things after the highest of all, thy Son, through thy almighty Son, for the sake of thy glorious Son, by thy blessed Son. May my heart, therefore, know and reverence thee above all things after my Lord and God, the Lord and God of all things, thy Son. May it love and beseech thee, not with the affection with which my imperfection longs, but with that

---

[1] Cf. Ps. 26:1 (P.B.V., 27:1).   [2] Cf. *ibid.*
[3] Cf. Ps. 17:29 (P.B.V., 18:28).

which is due from one created and saved, redeemed and revived, by thy Son.

O Mother of the life of my soul, O Cherisher of the restorer of my flesh, O Nurse of the Saviour of my whole being! But what shall I say? Language fails me, because my mind lacks strength. O Lady, Lady, all my inmost self is stirred to give thee thanks for such great benefits, but it cannot conceive worthy thanks, and it is ashamed to bring forth unworthy thanks. For what shall I say worthily to the Mother of my Creator and Saviour, when through her holiness my sins are purged, through her integrity incorruption is given to me, through her virginity my soul is deeply loved by its Lord and betrothed to its God? What, I say, shall I worthily repay to the Mother of my God and Lord, by whose fruitfulness I was redeemed from captivity, by whose childbearing I was released from eternal death, by whose Offspring I was restored from ruin and brought back from the exile of misery to the homeland of blessedness?

O "blessed among women,"[4] the "blessed fruit of thy womb"[5] gave me all these things in my regeneration by his baptism[6]— some in hope, others in actuality—although I have so deprived myself of all these things by sin that I do not possess the actuality, and scarcely hold to the hope. What now? If they have disappeared by my fault, shall I be ungrateful to her through whom such great goods freely befell me? Far be it from me to add this iniquity upon iniquity![7] Rather, I give thanks because I had, I grieve because I have not, I pray that I may have. For I am certain that, as through the Son's grace I could receive them, so through the Mother's merits I can recover the same goods. Therefore, O Lady, Gate of life, Door of salvation, Way of reconciliation, Entrance to restoration, I beseech thee by thy saving fruitfulness, see that the pardon of my sins and the grace to live well are granted to me, and that this thy servant is guarded even to the end under thy protection.

O Palace of universal propitiation, Cause of general reconciliation, Vessel and Temple of the life and salvation of all, I lessen thy merits too much when I recount thy benefits to me separately, worthless little man that I am—though the world itself with love rejoices in them, and rejoicing cries that they are thine. For thou, O Lady admirable for matchless virginity, lovable for saving fruitfulness, venerable for inestimable

4 Cf. Luke 1:42.   5 *Ibid.*
6 Cf. Titus 3:5.   7 Cf. Isa. 30:1.

sanctity, thou hast shown to the world its Lord and its God, whom it knew not; thou hast displayed to the world its visible Creator, whom formerly it saw not; thou hast borne to the world the Restorer it craved in its ruin; thou hast brought forth to the world the Reconciler it possessed not in its guilt. By thy fruitfulness, Lady, the sinful world has been justified, the condemned saved, the exile brought home. Thy childbearing, Lady, redeemed a captive world, healed a sick world, revived a dead world. Wrapped in darkness, the world lay subject to the snares and cruelties of demons; now, enlightened by the Sun risen from thee, it avoids their craft and treads down their power.

Heaven, stars, earth, floods, day, night, and whatever else is subject to human power or use, congratulate themselves on their lost glory, Lady, revived as they are in some way through thee, and endued with a new and ineffable grace. For it was as if they all had died when they lost the inherited dignity of furthering the mastery and the benefit of the worshipers of God, for which they had been made, and were overwhelmed by oppression and defaced by the use of the servants of idols, for which they had not been made. But they rejoice, as if revived, now that they are ruled by the mastery of those who acknowledge God, and are adorned by their use. Moreover, they exulted, as it were, in a new and ineffable grace, when they not only perceived God himself, their own Creator, ruling them invisibly from above, but also saw him in their midst, visibly sanctifying them by his use of them. These great goods came to the world through the blessed fruit of the blessed womb of blessed Mary.[8]

But why do I only say, Lady, that the world is full of thy benefits? They pierce into hell, they rise above the heavens. For through the fullness of thy grace the things that were in hell rejoice in their deliverance, and the things that are above the world joy in their restoration. In fact, through the same glorious Son of thy glorious virginity, all the just who died before his life-giving death exult in the breaking of their captivity, and the angels give thanks for the restoration of their half-ruined city.

O Woman wonderfully matchless and matchlessly wonderful, through whom the elements are renewed, hell is remedied, demons are trampled on, men are saved, angels are replaced! O Woman full and more than full of grace,[9] from whose fullness

8 Cf. Luke 1:42.   9 Cf. Luke 1:28.

in its sprinkled superabundance every creature flourishes again! O Virgin blessed and more than blessed, through whose blessing every nature is blessed, not only the created nature by the Creator, but also the Creator by the creature! O thou exalted beyond measure, whom my soul's affection strives to follow, whither dost thou flee from my mind's vision? O beautiful to behold, lovable to contemplate, delightful to love, whither dost thou escape from the grasp of my heart? Lady, wait for the feeble soul that follows thee. Do not hide thyself, Lady, from the soul that sees too little when it seeks thee.[10] Take pity, Lady, on the soul that faints in panting after thee.

Wonderful fact, in what a lofty place do I contemplate Mary! Nothing is equal to Mary, nothing save God is greater than Mary. To Mary, God gave his own Son, equal to himself,[11] begotten from his heart, whom he loved as himself, and from Mary he made a Son for himself—not another Son, but the very same, so that by nature one and the same person should be the common Son of God and of Mary. Every nature was created by God, and God was born of Mary. God created all things, and Mary brought forth God. God, who made all things, made himself of Mary, and so remade all that he had made. He who was able to make all things of nothing was unwilling, when they had been profaned, to remake them without first becoming Mary's Son. God, therefore, is the Father of created things, and Mary is the Mother of re-created things. God is the Father of the establishment of all things, and Mary is the Mother of the re-establishment of all things. For God begat Him through whom all things were made,[12] and Mary bore Him through whom all things were saved. God begat Him without whom nothing exists at all, and Mary bore Him without whom there is no well-being for anything. O truly "the Lord is with thee,"[13] since by the Lord's gift every nature owes so much to thee, along with him.

Mary, I beseech thee by the grace by which the Lord thus willed to be with thee, and to have thee with him: according to the very same grace, deal with me for thy mercy's sake. See that thy love is always with me, and my concern always with thee. See that the cry of my necessity is with thee, as long as my necessity continues, and that the regard of thy kindness is with me, as long as I subsist. See that joy in thy blessedness is

10 Cf. Lam. 3:25.　　　　　　　　11 Cf. Phil. 2:6.
12 Cf. John 1:3, and the Nicene Creed.　　13 Luke 1:28.

always with me, and compassion for my misery—as far as it is fitting for me—is always with thee.

For, O most blessed one, just as everyone alienated from thee and disdained by thee must necessarily perish, so everyone turned to thee and cared for by thee cannot possibly be lost. For as God, O Lady, begat him in whom all things live, so thou, O Flower of virginity, hast begotten Him through whom the dead live again. And as God through his Son preserved the blessed angels from sin, so, O thou Splendor of purity, he has saved wretched men from sin through thy Son. For just as God's Son is the blessedness of the just, so thy Son, O thou Salvation of fruitfulness, is the reconciliation of sinners. For there is no reconciliation save that which thou hast chastely conceived; there is no justification save that which thou hast spotlessly cherished in thy womb; there is no salvation save that which thou, a virgin, hast borne. Therefore, O Lady, thou art the Mother of justification and of the justified, thou art the Bearer of reconciliation and of the reconciled, thou art the Parent of salvation and of the saved.

O blessed confidence, O safe refuge! The Mother of God is our Mother. The Mother of Him in whom alone we hope, and whom alone we fear, is our Mother. The Mother, I say, of Him who alone saves, who alone condemns, is our Mother.

But O blessed one, exalted not only for thyself but also for us, what is it, how great, how lovely is the thing that I see happens to us through thee! When I see it, I rejoice; when I rejoice, I dare not name it. For if thou, Lady, art his Mother, are not thy other sons his brethren? But who are the brethren, and whose are they? Shall I speak the reason of my heart's delight, or shall I be silent, lest my mouth be betrayed by my transport? But why should I not confess in praise what I believe in love? I shall speak, then, not with pride but with thanksgiving.

For He who so ordered things that he should belong to our nature by maternal generation, and that we should be his Mother's children through our restoration to life, himself invites us to confess ourselves his brethren.[14] Therefore, our Judge is our Brother. The Saviour of the world[15] is our Brother. In short, our God was made our Brother through Mary. With what certainty, then, should we hope, with what comfort can we fear, when our salvation or damnation hangs on the judgment of a good Brother and a kind Mother! With what affection, too, should we love this Brother and this Mother! With

14 Cf. Matt. 12:49; Heb. 2:11.   15 Cf. I John 4:14; John 4:42.

what intimacy shall we commend ourselves to them! With what safety shall we flee to them for refuge! With what graciousness shall we be received when we flee! Therefore, may our good Brother forgive us what we have done wrong; may he turn from us what by wrongdoing we have deserved; may he grant what we ask in penitence. May our good Mother pray and entreat for us; may she request and obtain what is fitting for us. May she pray to her Son for her sons, to the only-begotten for the adopted, to the Lord for the servants. May her good Son hear his Mother for his brethren, the only-begotten hear her for those whom he adopted,[16] the Lord for those whom he delivered.

Mary, how much do we owe thee! Lady Mother, through whom we possess such a Brother, what thanks, what praise, shall we return to thee?

O great Lord, thou who art our elder Brother,[17] O great Lady, thou who art our better Mother, teach my heart with what reverence it should think of you. Good one and good one, gracious one and gracious one, tell my soul with what affection it may delight in the remembrance of you, what pleasure it may find in its delight, what richness in its pleasure—and give all this to my soul. Enrich it and kindle it with your love. Let my heart faint with continual love for you,[18] let my soul melt,[19] let my flesh fail.[20] O that my inmost soul would blaze up with the sweet ardor of your love, that my inmost flesh would dry up! O that the depths of my spirit were so enriched with the sweetness of affection for you, that the marrow of my body would dry up altogether!

O Lord, Son of my Lady, O Lady, Mother of my Lord, if I am not worthy thus to be made blessed by your love, certainly you are not unworthy to be thus loved—yes, loved with greater love. Therefore, most bountiful, do not deny me when I ask that of which I confess myself unworthy, for then that of which you are worthy beyond contradiction will be taken away from you. Give then, most kind, give, I beseech you, to my suppliant soul, not for my merit but for your merit, give it love for you in proportion to your worthiness. Give me, I say, that of which I am unworthy, that you may be given back that of which you are worthy. For if you do not wish to let me have what I desire, at least do not hinder me from repaying to you what I owe.

[16] Cf. Gal. 4:5; Eph. 1:5. [17] Cf. Rom. 8:29.
[18] Cf. S. of Sol. 2:5. [19] Cf. S. of Sol. 5:6.
[20] Cf. Ps. 72:26 (P.B.V., 73:25).

Perhaps I shall be speaking with presumption, but in any case your goodness makes me bold. I shall still speak, then, to my Lord and my Lady, although "I am dust and ashes."[21] Lord and Lady, is it not better for you to make a free gift to one who asks what he does not deserve than for what is justly due to you to be taken away from you? In reality, the former is a mercy to be extolled, the latter an impious injustice. Spend your grace, then, O most kind, so that you may receive your due. Show such mercy on me as is good for me and fitting for you, lest I do you such injustice as is good for no one and fitting for no one. Be merciful to me while I pray lest I be unjust to you while I curse. Give, bountiful one and bountiful one, and be not hard to entreat; give my soul love for you, which it asks not unjustly and you require justly, lest it be ungrateful for your gifts—for it justly trembles at ingratitude and you not unjustly punish it.

Certainly, Jesus, Son of God, and Mary his Mother, you will—and rightly—that whatever you love should be loved by us. Therefore, good Son, I pray thee by the love with which thou lovest thy Mother that, as thou truly lovest her and willest that she be loved, thou wilt grant me truly to love her. Good Mother, I pray thee by the love with which thou lovest thy Son that, as thou truly lovest him and willest that he be loved, thou wilt obtain for me the gift of true love toward him. For behold, I ask what your will truly wills to be done; why then shall it not be done on account of my sins, even though it is in your power? Lover and pitier of men, thou couldest love thy guilty ones even unto death,[22] and wilt thou be able to deny love for thyself and for thy Mother to him who prays to thee? Mother of this our Lover, who wast worthy to bear him in thy womb and feed him at thy breast,[23] wilt thou be unable or unwilling to obtain love for him and for thyself for him who makes this request?

Therefore, let my mind venerate you as you are worthy, let my heart love you as is right. Let my soul love you as befits it, let my flesh serve you as it ought. Let my life be perfected in this, that my whole substance may sing for ever, "Blessed be the Lord for evermore! So be it, so be it!"[24]

21 Gen. 18:27.   22 Cf. Phil. 2:8; John 13:1.
23 Cf. Luke 11:27.   24 Ps. 88:53 (P.B.V., 89:50).

The Question of Investitures: Two Letters to Pope Paschal II

THE TEXT

EPISTLE 214

To the reverend Lord, the beloved Father Paschal, supreme Pontiff, Anselm, servant of the Church of Canterbury, pledges due submission and faithful prayers.

Since the policies and plans of the Church's sons depend on the authority of the Apostolic See, I turn again to the direction and counsel of Your Paternity. If you wish to know why I have been so long in writing something to Your Eminence, since my return to England,[1] you may learn the reason from the bearer of this message.[2]

On the death of King William,[3] by whose violence I was exiled from England for three years, my Lord King Henry and his nobles and the Church of the English urgently called me back, and received me with great joy. When they had understood the instruction, which I heard given in the Roman council[4] by your predecessor of venerable memory, Pope Urban,[5] to the effect that no one should accept investiture of a church from the hand of a layman, and that no bishop or abbot should become his man, I felt and heard that the King and his lords were by no means prepared to accept it. On this matter, then, I look for Your Eminence's advice, so necessary to me.

When I was in Rome, I discussed with the aforesaid Lord

---

1 September 23, 1100.
2 William Warelwast (d. 1137), who was deeply involved (largely as a royal agent) in the conflicts between William II and Henry I, on the one side, and Urban II, Paschal II, and Anselm, on the other. Cf. William Hunt, art. "William Warelwast," *DNB*, 59, 361 f.
3 William II was killed on August 2, 1100.
4 April 25, 1099.
5 Urban II (1088–1099).

Pope the question of the Roman legation over the Kingdom of England, and told him that the men of that Kingdom maintain that the Church of Canterbury has performed this function from ancient times down to our own time.[6] I explained how necessary it was for this to be done, and how any other action would be to the disadvantage of the Roman and of the English Church. Moreover, we have charged the present messenger to convey the reasons for this to you, at least in part. Now the legation, which this Church had held down to our time, according to the aforesaid testimony, was not taken away from me by the Lord Pope. And yet I have heard that, while I was in exile for fidelity to the Apostolic See, Your Authority entrusted this legation to the Archbishop of Vienne.[7] This is full of difficulty—indeed, of impossibility—as anyone will understand if he knows the long and perilous interval of the sea and the Kingdoms of France and Burgundy, lying between England and Vienne; for this must be crossed if the Archbishop of Vienne is to visit England, or the English are to visit Vienne, in connection with their cases. Wherefore I pray, suppliant servant and son of Your Paternity, as I am, that the Church which endured many adversities in suffering with me, while I was an impoverished exile because of my fidelity to the Roman Church, may not in my time be deprived of the dignity which it declares it possessed from your See in my predecessors before me.

[6] From early times the Roman Church made use of "legates" in the course of its dealings with other churches. Legatine visits to England date from 786, at the latest. The pontificate of Gregory VII gave new importance to the office, and in our period we find three types of legate playing a part in the life of the church: (1) the *legatus missus*, sent on a particular mission; (2) the *legatus a latere*, or papal plenipotentiary, sent to convene provincial councils or deal with affairs of state; (3) the *legatus natus*, or perpetual legate, holding the rank by virtue of his tenure of a privileged see. The archbishops of Canterbury held this office from 1220 (Stephen Langton) to 1534 (Thomas Cranmer), sharing the honors with York from 1352. *Legati nati* seem to have been important, not so much in terms of jurisdiction as because the prestige associated with the title furthered the claims of certain sees to primacy. Cf. H. W. C. Davis, art. "Legates," *DECH*, 321 f.; E. Amann and A. Dumas, *L'Eglise au pouvoir des laïques* (Fliche and Martin, VII), 172–174; A. Fliche, *La Réforme grégorienne et la reconquête chrétienne* (Fliche and Martin, VIII), 89–95; R. Foreville and J. Rousset, *Du Premier concile du Latran à l'avènement d'Innocent III* (Fliche and Martin, IX/2), 240. The traditional claim reported by Anselm would thus seem to be part of Canterbury's perpetual struggle for primacy in England.

[7] Wido (bishop from 1090), later Pope Calixtus II (1119–1124).

[The remainder of the letter deals with the misconduct of Ralph (Rannulfus) Flambard, bishop of Durham, 1099–1128, and with the election of Gerard, bishop of Hereford since 1096, as archbishop of York, 1101–1108.]

EPISTLE 217

[In the first paragraph, Anselm repeats his testimony to his fidelity to the Apostolic See. He then turns to the question of Investitures.]

After I was recalled by the present King of England, and had returned to my episcopal office, I set out the apostolic decrees that I had heard when I was present at the Roman council, to the effect that no layman should give investiture to churches, and that no one should receive it from his hand or become his man on this account, and that no one should consecrate anyone who presumed to do so—and also that anyone who disobeyed these decrees should be subject to the excommunication of this great council. When the King and his nobles, and even the bishops themselves, heard this, I hate to say what great evils they claimed would flow from these decrees, or what they declared they would do rather than accept them; but let the present legates,[8] who heard all this with me, tell you. Finally, they turned on me, and all together affirmed with one mind that I could get rid of every evil that, they claimed, would result from these decrees if I were willing to join my prayers to those of the bishops that it might please Your Eminence to modify the aforesaid decision. If I were to refuse to do this, they would judge that every evil that followed on my refusal was to be imputed to me without any excuse on my part.

Lest I seem, then, to disdain anything, or to do anything by my opinion alone or my own will, I do not dare not to listen to them, nor do I wish to depart in any way from the direction of Your Holiness. Therefore, maintaining all my reverence and obedience towards the Apostolic See, I pray you to condescend, according to your wisdom (as far as your dignity after God permits), to the aforesaid petition which the legates will explain to you. I also ask you to certify me by the present legates what you order me to do in this matter, whatever happens.

We pray Almighty God long to preserve Your Paternity safe in complete prosperity, for the strength and comfort of his Church.

[8] Three bishops sent by Henry I: Gerard of York, Herbert of Thetford, Robert of Chester.

Excerpt from Eadmer: History of Recent Events in England

THE TEXT

BOOK IV

THE SETTLEMENT OF THE CONTROVERSY

[Eadmer records a number of connected events, including the victory of Henry I over his brother, Count Robert, and the pacification of Normandy. He gives the texts of several letters looking toward a settlement of the controversy, including two from Paschal II to Anselm (in Anselm's *Epistolae*, 397; 422[1]). He continues as follows:]

On the first of August, then, an assembly of bishops, abbots, and nobles of the kingdom, was held in the king's palace in London. For three days in a row, while Anselm was absent, the matter of the investiture to churches was fully discussed by the king and the bishops. Some argued that the king should follow the practice of his father and brother, and should not act in obedience to the injunction of the Apostolic See. For the pope, in the sentence that had then been promulgated, had, while standing firm, conceded the homage which Pope Urban had forbidden equally with lay investiture, and in this way had brought the king to agree with him in the matter of investitures (as can be gathered from the letter which we quoted above[2]). Thereupon, in Anselm's presence, and with a large crowd at hand, the king agreed and ordered that from that time onward no one should ever receive investiture to a bishopric or abbacy in England by the giving of pastoral staff or ring by the king or by any lay hand whatever. Anselm in turn conceded that no one should be deprived of consecration to an honor which he had received, on the ground of any homage he had done to the king. When things had been settled

---

[1] Cf. Schmitt, V, 340–342; 368.
[2] I.e., *Epist.* 397; cf. previous note.

in this way, by the advice of Anselm and the nobles of the kingdom, fathers[3] were appointed by the king, without any investiture by pastoral staff and ring, for nearly all the churches[4] of England which had long been widowed of their pastors.[5] There and then certain persons were also appointed by the king himself to rule certain churches in Normandy, which likewise had been deprived of their fathers.

[3] I.e., bishops.
[4] Note, here and elsewhere, the ancient use of "church" to describe a local Christian community.
[5] Note the idea of the "marriage" of the bishop to his church. On this *spirituale connubium*, cf. F. Claeys-Bouuaert, art. "Evêques," in *Dictionnaire de droit canonique*, V (Letouzey et Ané, Paris, 1953), 578.

Excerpt from Eadmer: *The Life and Conversation of Saint Anselm*

THE TEXT

BOOK I

CHAPTER XXII

ON THE UPBRINGING OF BOYS

Once upon a time, then, when a certain abbot, who was looked upon as a very fine monk, was talking with Anselm about some of the problems of monastic life, he threw in some remarks about the boys who were being brought up in the cloister, and added: "What, I beg of you, is to be done with them? They are perverse and incorrigible. We beat them constantly, day and night, and they keep getting worse than they have ever been."

When Anselm heard this, he was astonished. "You never stop beating them?" he said. "And when they grow up, what are they like?"

"Dull," he replied, "and like brutes."

"With all your effort, you have been rather unfortunate in their upbringing, if you have only succeeded in turning human beings into beasts!"

"But what can we do?" the abbot asked. "What can we do about it? We restrain them in every way for their own benefit, and we get nowhere with it."

"You restrain them? I beg you, my lord abbot, tell me this. If you were to plant a young tree in your garden, and to hem it in right away on all sides, so that it could not stretch out its branches at all, if you released it after several years what kind of tree would result?"

"A quite useless one, of course, with gnarled and twisted branches."

"And whose fault would that be but your own, for shutting it in without using any judgment? But surely this is just what you are doing with your boys. By their parents' oblation[6] they have been planted in the Church's garden, to grow up and

---

6 Cf. *S. Benedicti regula monasteriorum*, cap. 59.

bear fruit to God. But you have bound them so, by terrors and threats and beatings everywhere they turn, that they are not allowed to enjoy any freedom at all. And so, because they are repressed without any discrimination, they fill their minds with thoughts that are crooked and twisted like thorns. Then they harbor those thoughts, they foster them, by fostering them they strengthen them, until finally their minds are so obstinate that they evade everything that could contribute to their correction. And so it happens, because they sense no kindness in you at all, no good will or gentleness toward them, that they come to lose all confidence in your goodness, and believe that all you do is the expression of hatred and ill-will toward them. The wretched result is this. As they keep on growing in body, hatred and suspicion and all kinds of evil grow in them, so that they are always inclined and bent toward vice. And since they were not trained for anything in true charity, they inevitably look at everything with frowns and averted eyes.

"But I should like to have you tell me, for God's sake, why you are so hostile to them. Are they not human? Are they not of the same nature as yourself? Would you want to be treated as you are treating them? You would, you say, if you were what they are? But be it so. Do you intend to form their character for goodness with nothing but blows and beatings? Did you ever see a craftsman form a beautiful image out of a plate of gold and silver by blows alone? I do not think so. What then? To form a suitable design from the plate, he now gently presses and strikes it with one of his tools, and now raises and shapes it more gently with careful support. It is the same with you. If you want your boys to have excellent characters, you cannot stop at beating them down with blows. You must also give them the support and help of fatherly kindness and gentleness."

To this the abbot protested: "What support? What help? Our task is to make them into serious and mature characters."

"Yes indeed," said Anselm. "And bread and other kinds of solid food are beneficial and good for him who can assimilate them. But take its milk away from a sucking child, and try to feed it with solids, and you will see that it chokes instead of getting any nourishment. And why? I shall not tell you why; the reason is clear. But be sure of this, that just as the body, whether it is weak or strong, has some food appropriate to its condition, so the soul, whether *it* is weak or strong, has its own sustenance suited to its capacity. The strong soul takes delight in being fed with solid food, such as being patient in tribula-

tion,[7] not desiring another's goods,[8] turning the other cheek
when one has already been struck,[9] praying for its enemies,[10]
loving those who hate it, and all sorts of things like this. But
the soul that is still weak and tender in God's service needs
milk,[11] in other words, gentleness from others, kindness, mercy,
cheerful comfort, and many things of this sort. If you will adapt
yourself in this way both to the strong and to the weak in your
care, then, as far as it lies in you, you will by God's grace gain
them all for God.[12]"

When the abbot heard all this he groaned, and said, "Truly
we have erred from the truth, and the light of good judgment
has not been shining on us." And falling on the ground before
his feet, he confessed that he had sinned and that he was guilty,
and he sought pardon for the past and promised amendment
for the future.

We have told all this so that by it we may learn how Anselm
was a man of kindly discrimination and discriminating kindness
toward all.

[7] Cf. Rom. 12:12.
[8] Cf. Ex. 20:17.
[9] Cf. Matt. 5:39.
[10] Cf. Matt. 5:44.
[11] Cf. I Cor. 3:2.
[12] Cf. I Cor. 9:22.

THEOLOGIANS OF THE TWELFTH
CENTURY

Theologians of the Twelfth Century: Introduction

I

ANSELM, ABAILARD, AQUINAS—FOR MANY CASUAL OBservers this alliterative list sums up medieval theology, and not without reason. Anselm, with his epoch-making study of the doctrine of our redemption, must be respected as one of the giants of intellectual history. Abailard also, even though it may be more difficult to assess his contribution, must at least be honored for his role in the development of theological method. Aquinas, with his impressive synthesis of Augustine and Aristotle, is not only the greatest thinker of his century but is also one of the most influential makers of the Christian mind. The three, taken together, provide a concrete symbol of the Christian thought of the Middle Ages.

And yet we both pay them a false compliment and do an unpardonable injustice to their contemporaries if we try to abstract them from the continuity of medieval thought. While recent studies have, if anything, deepened our awareness of the importance of their work, they have also illuminated the environment apart from which such an achievement would not have been possible, and have displayed the independent significance of a number of their contemporaries. In particular, we have been made more conscious of the importance of the doctrinal discussions of the twelfth century for the admittedly more finished and sophisticated work of the thirteenth. Indeed, it is only fair to point out that the later and more spectacular period could not have handled its weighty issues of faith and reason alike, if the ground had not been prepared by the "renaissance of the twelfth century."

The last phrase, which has become a classical description of the cultural achievements of the twelfth century, points to an age of advance and consolidation in Church and society, in literature and science, in philosophy and theology.[1] The reform of the Church and the reordering of human affairs showed real advances. The study of classical Latin literature was intensified, and sacred and profane poetry was created, of a depth and beauty that would do credit to any age. Thanks to economic and political development, and to the assimilation of Greek and Arabian science, medicine and other scientific disciplines made notable progress. Thanks both to rediscovery and to reflection on the rediscovered, philosophical issues of fundamental importance were aired. As for theology, the great questions of the Trinity and the incarnation, of sin and grace and redemption, were discussed, sometimes with genuinely creative results, almost always with a freshness and vigor unknown since the age of the Fathers.

II

The immediate setting of the theological work of the twelfth century was, of course, the ongoing life of the Church, and its effort to discipline both itself and society. Since the principal instrument of this discipline was the canon law, it is not surprising to find that the theologians were especially indebted to the canonists for an intellectual stimulus, for a good deal of important material, and for guidance in method. While the theologians did a good deal to repay this debt, the development of canon law has a certain priority in the story of medieval theology.

From the beginning, the Church had assumed the right to direct and discipline the conduct of its members,[2] and such direction early came to be embodied in rules or "canons."[3] In the "Dark Ages," when the Church found itself the one universal

---

[1] The idea of a twelfth century renaissance was popularized by the well-known books of Haskins and of Paré, Brunet, and Tremblay. For interesting comments on the idea, cf. the following articles: W. A. Nitze, "The So-called Twelfth Century Renaissance," *Speculum*, 23 (1948), 464–471; E. M. Sanford, "The Twelfth Century—Renaissance or Proto-Renaissance," *ibid.*, 26 (1951), 635–642; U. T. Holmes, Jr., "The Idea of a Twelfth Century Renaissance," *ibid.*, 643–651.

[2] Cf. the Pauline Epistles, particularly I Corinthians.

[3] Cf. W. Bright, *The Canons of the First Four General Councils* (2d ed., Oxford, 1892); E. G. Wood, *The Regal Power of the Church* (rev. ed., Dacre Press, Westminster, 1948), 66–69.

force making for social order, the canon law acquired new importance as a principle of cohesion in society as a whole. It followed that the canon law must itself be organized and codified, if it was to be effective in imposing order. It is no accident, then, that from the ninth century onward we find the systematic classification of canonical texts replacing the older chronological arrangement followed, for example, as late as the *Hispana*, associated with the name of Isidore of Seville.[4] Pioneering examples of such classification are to be found in the *Enchiridion* of Regino of Prüm,[5] and in the *Decretum* of Burchard of Worms,[6] which represents the movement of canonical codification associated with the imperial efforts to reform the Church.

Further stimulus was given to this trend by the movement for the autonomy and self-reform of the Church, to which the name of Gregory VII is commonly attached. The "Investiture Controversy," around which the struggle for the Church's freedom of action centered, evoked a number of systematic collections, which influenced theology partly because of their improved technique and partly on account of their emphasis on such canonico-theological questions as the validity of the sacraments[7] and the primacy and prerogatives of the Roman see. The climax of this canonical development can be seen in two writers who fall within the twelfth century—Ivo of Chartres and Gratian of Bologna.

Ivo has been described as "one of the most notable bishops of France at the time of the investiture struggles and the most important canonist before Gratian in the Occident."[8] A pupil of Lanfranc at Bec, Ivo, like his fellow student Anselm, took a loyally Roman but moderate line in the Church-State struggle[9] and, again like Anselm, anticipated the principles of the Concordat of Worms.[10] His contribution to theological advance was twofold. On the one hand, the "Prologue," prefixed both to his *Panormia*[11] and to the longer *Decretum* attributed to him[12]

---

[4] *PL*, 84, 93–848.
[5] C. 990; found in *PL*, 132, 186–400.
[6] Early eleventh century; *PL*, 140, 535–1058.
[7] This problem was raised, e.g., in connection with the question of simony.
[8] J. de Ghellinck, art. "Ivo of Chartres," *CE*, 8, 257.
[9] Cf. Ivo, *Epist.* 60 (to Hugh of Lyons); 189; 232; 236 f. (*PL*, 162, 70–75; 193–196; 235; 238–245).
[10] A.D. 1122.
[11] *PL*, 161, 1041–1344.
[12] *PL*, 161, 47–1022.

—both composed close to the end of the eleventh century—
suggests the method of conciliation of "authorities" practiced
by such later writers as Abailard and Gratian, as well as the
later Schoolmen. On the other hand, his extensive patristic
documentation of a wide range of theological issues, including
the doctrines of the Trinity and the Person of Christ, provided
the texts used by a whole generation of theologians, including
as original a thinker as Hugh of St. Victor.

In his *Concord of Discordant Canons*,[13] Gratian develops Ivo's
method with greater technical skill, thanks in part to the
advance of juristic studies, both Roman and canonical, and in
part to the influence of the theologians, notably Abailard. He
also provides a patristic dossier, reflecting that of Ivo, which is
to have great importance for theology, in view of the prestige
acquired by the *Decretum Gratiani*.[14] It is generally supposed that
this material was used by the Paris theologian, Peter Lombard,
and the dates usually assigned to the works of the two authors
would make this possible; at the very least, the interaction of
canonical and theological studies at this period is aptly symbol-
ized by the legend that Gratian and the Lombard were
brothers.[15]

The broader political and scholastic setting of twelfth
century thought is illustrated by a *chartrain* of a later generation
than Ivo. John of Salisbury, born c. 1120, at Old Sarum, studied
logic at Paris under Abailard and grammar at Chartres, later
pursuing further philosophical and theological studies at Paris.
After serving as secretary to Archbishop Theobald of Canterbury and to the latter's successor, Thomas Becket (whose
exile he shared and whose murder he witnessed), he became
bishop of Chartres,[16] whose humanistic traditions he worthily
upheld. His *Policraticus*, or "Statesman's Manual," not only
reveals his familiarity with the Latin classics and Fathers, but
also illustrates, among other things, the "hierocratic" outlook

---

13 Or *Decretum*, produced c. 1140 (cf. J. de Ghellinck, *Le Mouvement théologique
du XIIᵉ siècle*, 212). The title is *Concordia*, not *Concordantia*.
14 While this never attained the status of a law code, its prestige was
immense; as the first main section of the *Corpus iuris canonici*, it was basic
for Roman Catholic canon law until the promulgation of the *Codex
iuris canonici* (1917).
15 Cf. the use in the Lombard's *Sententiae* and elsewhere of *distinctio* as the
name of a chapter or section; the term refers primarily to the technique
of reconciling *contrarietates* (cf. W. Ullmann, *The Development of Papal
Government in the Middle Ages*, 371).
16 1172–1180.

which led him to support Becket against Henry II and Alexander III against Barbarossa, in the interests (at least, as he believed) of the universal law of reason and revelation against arbitrary force.

III

When we turn to the theological history of the period, we find at its head a second Anselm—Anselm of Laon.[17] Important figures of later generations pay glowing compliments to his learning and judgment, and even the criticisms of Abailard cannot obscure his historical importance.[18] A pupil of his great namesake, Anselm was the teacher of William of Champeaux and of Abailard, and through them of the Victorines and Peter Lombard. Whatever his failures in logical acumen, he was a meeting point of the exegetical tradition of earlier theology and the new techniques worked out by canonists and dialecticians. The development of the *quaestio*[19] by Anselm and his school played an important role in the progress of scholastic theology, and some of the originality commonly credited to Abailard's *Sic et non* should be transferred to the account of the theologians of Laon.

It is not easy, however, to determine the exact contribution of Anselm and the other scholastics of Laon. Despite the extensive researches of recent years, the work of the master cannot be isolated with much assurance, and even the school as a whole has still to be dealt with adequately. Nonetheless, we can say that Laon had a good deal to do with the development of the *quaestio* as the unit of scholastic exposition, that its collections of *sententiae*, whatever their defects of system, must occupy a place of honor in the genealogy of the later *summae*, and that the *glossa ordinaria*,[20] which provided "the working tool required

17 D. 1117.
18 Rupert of Deutz (*De volunt. dei*, i, *PL*, 170, 437) calls him "illustrious teacher" and "morning star of Laon." Guibert of Nogent (*Comm. in Gen., prooem., PL*, 156, 19) says that the brothers Anselm and Radulphus are "two luminaries brighter than stars." Cf. Wibald of Stavelot, *Epist.* 147 (*PL*, 189, 1250); John of Salisbury, *Epist.* 211 (*PL*, 199, 235). For Abailard's criticisms, cf. *Hist. calamit.*, 2 f. (*PL*, 178, 122 f.).
19 There are enough examples of the *genre* in this volume to give some idea of the development. The basic plan includes the raising of the question by the use of opposing authorities, the resolution of the question, and replies to the initial objections.
20 Both the *glossa marginalis* (or longer notes written in the margin of the text), long erroneously attributed to Walafrid Strabo (d. 849), and the *glossa interlinearis*.

for the theologian's reflection on the Biblical datum, whose first interpretation was furnished by the Fathers,"[21] was produced in large part at Laon—and at least as far as the *glossa* on the Psalms and the Pauline Epistles is concerned, by Anselm himself.[22] This last work is the most durable contribution of Laon to medieval theology.[23]

IV

The greatest of Anselm's pupils, Peter Abailard, has already been referred to. The outlines of his life, from his birth in 1079 at Le Pallet, in Brittany, through his scholastic triumphs and ecclesiastical conflicts and his tragic relationship with Heloise, to his death in 1142 in the affectionate care of Cluniac monks, are well known; indeed, we know Abailard better than most medieval personalities, and both his attractive and his tiresome qualities are generally acknowledged. His theological work has been less uniformly assessed, thanks in part to the condemnations aimed at his writings during his lifetime and in part to the ill-informed enthusiasm with which some modern historians have hailed him as a "morning star of the Enlightenment." It now seems established, however, that, despite his limitations, he is the great example between Anselm of Canterbury and the thirteenth century of a brilliant systematic theologian, capable of handling both traditional material and philosophical techniques with great skill, and also that his improvements in theological codification made him an important influence in later scholasticism.

Nonetheless, a certain ambiguity remains in Abailard's position as a theologian. It is clear enough that his "rationalism" is a dream shared by his obscurantist critics and his "liberal" admirers.[24] There can be no doubt of the ultimate priority of the Christian revelation in his intellectual loyalties; indeed, it has even been plausibly alleged that his approach to the use of reason in Christian thought is essentially that of Anselm of Canterbury.[25] At the same time, he manifests an intransigent confidence in his own reason which is lacking in

---

[21] Cf. C. Spicq, *Esquisse d'une histoire de l'exégèse latine*, 112.
[22] On the text, cf. Bibliography, below.
[23] Cf. C. Spicq, *op. cit.*, 113.
[24] Cf. J. G. Sikes, *Peter Abailard*, Ch. II.
[25] Cf. A. Dufourcq, "Saint Anselme: son temps, son rôle," *Revue de philos.*, 15 (1909), 602.

Anselm, and his dialectical skill is not balanced by profound metaphysical insights like the latter's. Moreover, his nominalistic tendencies were responsible for a subjectivism, and a failure to appreciate the "ontological" dimension of human experience, which distorted his theology of the atonement and made his interpretation of the moral life very one-sided. Over against this, however, we should set the genuine faith and piety expressed in Abailard's liturgical poetry, in which traditional themes are used with characteristic originality.[26]

V

When we turn to the school of St. Victor, the general picture is rather different. It is not that Hugh and his brethren are unaware of the problems of theological scholarship, or of the potentialities of the dialectical method, despite certain strongly antiphilosophical tendencies in their midst.[27] Their approach is, however, less narrowly dialectical than that of many of their contemporaries. Hugh's *De sacramentis* is an excellent example:

"Very sober in his patristic proofs, though completely impregnated with Augustine and the soundest tradition, the author appeals above all to the arguments of the Bible; he mingles with these remarkably bold conclusions, which disclose to us a powerful understanding and, by the literary development of the thought, remind us of the grand method of Anselm. This rarity of citations . . . is characteristic of an author who recommends the reading of the Fathers, notably of St. Gregory. But Hugh goes beyond the words—he assimilates the ideas of the ecclesiastical writers; too often the *sententiaires* are satisfied with their expressions. No harshness or dryness in the exposition; theses, proofs, difficulties, and replies follow one another or are intermingled, often with a kind of vivacity or with a lively and animated air, worthy of a dialogue."[28]

In the Victorine theology, moreover, there is evidence of a sense (often lacking in Abailard) of the mystery of God in creation and redemption. The very title of Hugh's great work suggests the whole school's awareness of the symbolic and quasi-sacramental character of God's world. In Richard we

---

26 Cf. J. de Ghellinck, *L'Essor de la littérature latine au XIIe siècle*, II, 293–295.
27 E.g., in Walter of St. Victor, *Contra quatuor labyrinthos Franciae*, ed. P. Glorieux, *Archives d'hist. doctr. et litt. du moyen âge*, 19 (1953), 187–335.
28 J. de Ghellinck, *Le Mouvement théologique du XIIe siècle*, 194.

find, combined with a rigorously rational demonstration of the plurality of persons in God, and a fresh awareness of the importance of the literal sense of Scripture, an "Anselmian" awareness of the primacy of faith, and a recognition of the sacramental significance of the outward events of the Biblical history—all illuminated and warmed by an Augustinian *mystique* of the soul's return to God. And then, in the same setting, we come upon the exquisite liturgical and devotional poetry of that gracious spirit, Adam of St. Victor. It is not too much to say that, taken as a whole, St. Victor offers one of the most engaging pictures that medieval intellectual life can show.

The abbey of Augustinian Canons at St. Victor was founded about 1110 by William of Champeaux, who through his withdrawal from the schools to this retreat created a rare combination of cloistered devotion and academic scholarship. The German Hugh arrived there about 1118, and taught from 1125 or so until his death in 1141, leaving behind him the name of a "second Augustine." In the course of his teaching he produced treatises on education and the liberal arts, Biblical commentaries, and—in his *On the Sacraments of the Christian Faith* —the first great *summa* of theology. The Scot Richard arrived some time before 1155, becoming subprior in 1159 and prior in 1162. Among his works, *On the Trinity* and *On Ezekiel's Vision* stand out—the first, as an important monograph in speculative theology; the second, as a pedestrian but historically influential essay in literal exegesis. Of the other distinguished Victorines, we can refer now only to Andrew, probably a pupil of Hugh and a greater exegete than Richard,[29] who died as Abbot of Wigmore in Herefordshire, and to Adam,[30] the master of liturgical poetry.[31]

VI

Despite the brilliance of his predecessors and contemporaries, the first prize in the twelfth century theological contest was won by the relatively unimaginative "Master of the Sentences," Peter Lombard. Coming to Paris from Italy between 1135 and 1139, he at first made his home with the Victorines, probably

---

[29] Andrew's work is still unpublished, but cf. extensive quotations in B. Smalley, *The Study of the Bible in the Middle Ages*.

[30] D. 1192.

[31] His specialty was the typically medieval "sequence"; for a full account of this form cf. *The New Oxford History of Music*, II: *Early Medieval Music up to 1300* (ed. A. Hughes, Oxford University Press, London, 1954), 128–174.

listened to Abailard's lectures, and certainly read his writings, as well as the barely completed *Decretum* of his compatriot, Gratian. By 1142, his commentary on the Pauline Epistles was making a name for him, in France and elsewhere. About 1148–1150, he visited the Roman curia, where he became acquainted with the *De fide orthodoxa* of the great "Schoolman" of the Greek Church, John of Damascus, just translated into Latin by Burgundio of Pisa.[32] Back in France by 1152, he became bishop of Paris in 1159, dying there in July, 1160. In the years immediately after his return to France, he completed his *Libri sententiarum*, the major theological textbook (after the Bible itself) of the later Middle Ages.

After Abailard and Hugh, the Lombard may well seem dull. "In his work there is little or hardly any metaphysics, the philosophical data are fragmentary or badly assimilated, there are frequent (and often intentional) cases of indecision in thought. But the exposition which he presents is rich in content, for the period, and assembles its materials in a relatively brief and convenient organic whole. Unlike other texts in the absence of long-drawn-out digressions, Peter Lombard's work goes foward accurately, is clear in its plan, alert to dialectical discussions, careful in noting all opinions, sufficiently impersonal to give free play to comment by other teachers, and rigorously orthodox from one end to the other (with the exception of one Christological proposition and several points of detail). The second of the two last advantages was bound to procure the almost immediate success of the book—since sound teaching was wanted in the schools—while the first was sure to guarantee its prolonged survival, thanks to the numerous commentators who were to take it as the basis of their own lectures."[33] With its incorporation of so many of the basic ideas of Hugh, of Abailard, of the *Summa sententiarum*,[34] of Ivo and Gratian, and its compact form, Peter Lombard's textbook could hardly have been bettered in its day. Whatever its defects, it was destined by its very limitations as well as its virtues to be the "positive" sourcebook on which the more creative "scholastic" theologians could build. It is not surprising, then, that we have manuscript evidence for the existence of *glossae super sententias* as early as 1160–1165; that the major theological works of such great teachers as Bonaventure, Albert the Great, Duns Scotus, and William Ockham, should take the form of *commentaria super*

---

[32] Cf. J. de Ghellinck, *op. cit.*, 374–385. [33] *Ibid.*, 228 f.
[34] Cf. *ibid.*, 197–201.

sententias, produced in the course of their teaching; that the first comprehensive work of the Thomist school should rather awkwardly follow the plan of the *Sentences*[35]; that the much more profound but much more difficult *Summa theologiae* of Aquinas should become the basis of teaching only in the sixteenth century; and that even in the sixteenth century the *Sentences* should find such diverse commentators as Martin Luther[36] and Dominic Soto.[37] Even in the Middle Ages, textbook writing was good business!

VII

In a sense, twelfth century theology reached its climax in Peter Lombard's *Sentences*. There was, however, to be a further period of reflection—marked by few great names, but important for the assimilation of the work of the preceding decades—before the decisive Aristotelian revival and the formulation of the thirteenth century syntheses. Within this period, as a matter of fact, certain names do deserve notice—among them, Petrus Comestor,[38] called *magister historiarum* on account of his successful *Historia scholastica*[39]; Petrus Cantor,[40] apparently the first theologian to give Biblical references by chapter and (in the *Psalms* and *Lamentations*) verse[41]; Peter of Poitiers,[42] one of the principal early commentators on the Lombard; Praepositinus of Cremona,[43] chancellor of the University of Paris, and an important Scholastic theologian; and Stephen Langton,[44] professor of theology and then chancellor at Paris, who became archbishop of Canterbury and a cardinal. Of these, Langton may serve to illustrate the scholarship of this period.

We are more likely, I suspect, to think of Langton as a hero of the opposition to King John of England than as a great theologian, but his reputation for statesmanship should not be allowed to obscure his importance as one of the greatest of medieval exegetes and an expert theologian. As long as most

---

[35] Viz., the *Defensiones* of John Capreolus (d. 1444); cf. P. Mandonnet, art. "Capréolus," *DTC*, 2, 1694.

[36] Cf. P. Vignaux, *Luther, commentateur des Sentences* (Vrin, Paris, 1935).

[37] Cf. C. J. Callan, art. "Soto, Dominic," *CE*, 14, 152 f.

[38] "Peter the Eater" (of books); d. 1179.

[39] A survey of Biblical history from Genesis to Acts (*PL*, 198, 1053–1722).

[40] D. 1197.

[41] Cf. A. M. Landgraf, "Die Schriftzitate in der Scholastik um die Wende des 12. zum 13. Jahrhundert," *Biblica*, 18 (1937), 74–94.

[42] D. 1205.   [43] D. c. 1210.   [44] D. 1228.

of his writings remain unprinted, a full account of his ideas and methods can hardly be expected. We may note, however, that his independence of mind, in relation both to Augustinian theology and to the traditional "spiritual" exegesis, shows the effects of the free discussions of the twelfth century, and that his "glosses," covering the whole Bible, are important for the development of "literal" exegesis, carefully distinguished from other approaches to Scripture. He is, incidentally, to be credited with the familiar chapter divisions of the Biblical text, and with the sequence of books—historical books (except *Maccabees*), Hagiographa, prophets—still followed in editions of the Vulgate.[45] It should be added that—whether *Veni, sancte spiritus* is his or not—he had a well-deserved reputation as a liturgical poet.

VIII

The problems of twelfth century theology arose from the interaction of Augustinian theology and the spiritual tradition of the monasteries with the forces released by the new intellectual and cultural developments. In part they were problems of method, posed by the emergence of *quaestiones* in the midst of the traditional *lectio divina*,[46] and the consequent separation of the theological *disputatio* from Biblical exegesis and of the "spiritual understanding" from both. The issues involved came fully into the open, however, only in the thirteenth century discussions of theology as a "science," and the twelfth century theologians are more interesting when they are actually dealing with specific problems with the help of their developed techniques.

The Augustinian heritage of the period can be seen in the discussion of the Trinity in terms of *caritas*, as by Richard of St. Victor, and in the influence now and later of Augustine's *De trinitate*, as well as in the dominant theology of original sin. While the Augustinian view of the latter, which was taken as identifying the essence of original sin with concupiscence, had

---

[45] Cf. S. Berger, *Histoire de la Vulgate pendant les premiers siècles du moyen âge* (Nancy, 1893), 304.

[46] Cf. B. Smalley, *op. cit.*, 26–36. The *lectio* is not the exclusive source of the *quaestio*; cf. A. M. Landgraf, "Quelques collections de 'Quaestiones' de la seconde moitié du XIIe siècle," *Recherches de théol. anc. et méd.*, 7 (1935), 122–126.

been radically challenged by Anselm of Canterbury, it continued, with significant but rare exceptions, to dominate the schools.[47] Though Abailard's criticism of the use of the term "sin" to describe anything but a deliberate personal act seems to have encouraged a more careful discrimination of the ultimate consequences of original sin from those of actual sin, it was too obviously rooted in his individualism and subjectivism to gain general assent. While Langton was feeling his way to a more adequate definition of original sin, his formula of the *macula animae* was too indefinite to serve as a rallying point. Thus, though the time was coming when mediating formulae would be produced, and the Anselmian emphasis on the loss of original justice would predominate over preoccupation with concupiscence (now relegated to the status of a "material" element of original sin), the twelfth century by and large remained loyally "Augustinian" in this area.

In the field of Christology, a problem was raised by the application of dialectic to the patristic and conciliar formulae, namely, the question of the metaphysical status of the humanity taken by the Word. In the second and human "nativity" of the Son, of which Anselm speaks,[48] exactly what is begotten? Since both Augustine and Anselm had spoken of the *assumptus homo*, without really confronting the dialectical question of the concreteness of the noun, some teachers sought to affirm the individuality of Christ's manhood in terms of a theory of two *supposita*[49] in his person—a view only saved from Nestorianism by logical inconsequence. Abailard, on the contrary, while not intending to minimize the physical reality of the elements of Christ's human nature, questioned the concreteness of that nature as an entity united to the Word. According to his "Christological nihilism," Christ as man is not anything[50]; the Son simply clothes his divine person in the elements of human nature. Peter Lombard, while he apparently favors the Abailardian view, records (under the influence of John Damascene) the third view, which was to predominate in the schools, to the effect that the human nature taken by the Word is concrete as united to his person, and in that sense is "something,"[51] but not an independent *suppositum* or person.[52]

As for the doctrine of the atonement, while Anselm's assump-

47 Cf. the texts from the school of Laon and from Hugh of St. Victor in this volume.
48 Cf. *Cur deus homo*, II, 9.   49 I.e., concrete, individual substances.
50 *Non est aliquid*.   51 *Aliquid*.
52 Cf. *Initiation théologique*, IV (Les Editions du Cerf, Paris, 1954), 49–55.

tions reappear in Hugh of St. Victor, Peter Lombard does little more than reproduce the pre-Anselmian symbols. The only original contribution of twelfth century theology is made by Abailard, who stresses the significance of the cross as manifestation of divine love, but is prevented by his subjectivism from understanding Christ's death as God's saving act, intrinsically efficacious for all men. His emphasis has appealed to many who have been repelled by hardened forms of Anselm's doctrine or have sought to express man's relation to God in terms of "personal"[53] relationships. Abailard's doctrine was, however, condemned in his own day, and theologians turned to the Anselmian doctrine, modified in its "rationalism" but untouched in its main lines.

For sacramental theology, the twelfth century was a crucial period. For example, while the dogma of transubstantiation was not defined until the Fourth Lateran Council of 1215, the term itself came into common use in the preceding century,[54] in the aftermath of the Berengarian controversy. The same period witnessed the fixing of the list of the seven sacraments for the Latin Church, partly at least as a result of the establishment by the theologians of a more precise definition of a sacrament.[55] Thanks above all to Gratian and Peter Lombard, the status which confirmation was to enjoy in the later Middle Ages and in the post-Reformation Roman and Anglican Churches was determined; whether this radically reduced the status of confirmation (thus anticipating the Protestant Reformation) or belittled baptism by defining the sacramental nature of confirmation is a subject of contemporary debate.[56] The sacramental meaning of penance, which by this time had taken the shape familiar in Western Catholicism, was clarified, and the way paved for the classical discussion of the relation of the sacrament of penance to the virtue of penitence, presented by Aquinas.[57] The relation of the "minor orders" of functionaries to the sacramental orders was discussed, and Peter Lombard, following a strong medieval tradition, defined the major orders in such a way as to deny the distinction of order between bishop and

[53] I.e., psychological.
[54] Cf. J. Pohle and A. Preuss, *Dogmatic Theology*, IX: *The Sacraments*, II (Herder, St. Louis, 1946), 111.
[55] Cf. P. Pourrat, *Theology of the Sacraments* (4th ed., Herder, St. Louis, 1930), 258 f.; 268–277.
[56] Cf. G. Dix, *The Theology of Confirmation in Relation to Baptism* (Dacre Press, Westminster, 1953), 27–30.
[57] *Sum. theol.*, IIIa, qq. 84–85.

presbyter. Whether this preserved the fundamental tradition of the Church against episcopal usurpations[58] or revealed the corrupting influence of papalism and a distorted sacerdotalism[59] is another controversial point; at any rate, the enduring influence of medieval "presbyterianism" cannot be altogether ignored.

On the philosophical side, one of the more important debates of the twelfth century had to do with the principles of moral action. In the area of objective standards, the doctrine of natural law, inherited from classical ethics and jurisprudence by way of such intermediaries as Augustine and Isidore, was developed under the influence of Roman and canon lawyers, and related to the Christian dogmas of creation and redemption. On the side of the moral subject, the virtues, natural and supernatural, moral and theological, were analyzed, and their place in the moral life discussed. Abailard's subjectivism led him to an exclusive emphasis on "intention" as the criterion of the moral act, while others, like Langton, made more of other circumstances, such as grace and the "infused virtues," as conditions of genuine goodness. It cannot be claimed that the twelfth century produced anything like a coherent *summa ethica*; here as elsewhere, however, it provided valuable material for the syntheses of Aquinas, Scotus, and others.

BIBLIOGRAPHY

GENERAL WORKS

The most interesting introduction to the culture of the period is C. H. Haskins, *The Renaissance of the Twelfth Century* (Harvard University Press, Cambridge, 1927). Other useful books are: G. Paré, A. Brunet, and P. Tremblay, *La Renaissance du XII*e *siècle* (Vrin, Paris, 1933); J. de Ghellinck, *L'Essor de la littérature latine au XII*e *siècle*, 2 vols. (Desclée, Paris, 1946).

For the theology of the period, the standard introduction is J. de Ghellinck, *Le Mouvement théologique du XII*e *siècle* (2d ed., Desclée, Paris, 1948). R. L. Poole, *Illustrations of the History of Medieval Thought* (2d ed., London, 1920), is also useful.

[58] A view which to some extent reflects that of Jerome; cf. *Epist.* 146 (*CSEL*, 56, 310 ff.).

[59] The view of seventeenth century Anglicans, in opposition both to the Jesuits and to the Puritans; the problem is one illustration of the relevance of medieval studies to modern "ecumenical" discussions!

THE CANONISTS

The *Decretum* and *Panormia* of Ivo of Chartres will be found in *PL*, 161; his *Tripartita* has not been printed. For his letters, cf. *PL*, 162, and J. Leclercq (ed.), *Correspondance* ("Les Belles Lettres," Paris, 1949). The best (but still imperfect) edition of Gratian is in E. Richter and E. A. Friedberg (eds.), *Corpus Iuris Canonici*, 2 vols. (2d ed., Leipzig, 1879–1881), Vol. I. For translations, cf. J. W. Somerville, *Gratianus in Jurisprudence, with Translations* (Law Reporter Printing Company, Washington, 1934).

On Ivo, see the following: E. Amann and L. Guizard, art. "Yves de Chartres," *DTC*, 15, 3625–3640; A. Foucault, *Essai sur Ives de Chartres* (Chartres, 1883); P. Fournier, *Les Collections canoniques attribuées à Yves de Chartres* (Bibliothèque de l'Ecole de Chartres, Vols. 57–58, Paris, 1896–1897); J. de Ghellinck, art. "Ivo of Chartres," *CE*, 8, 257.

On Gratian and his commentators, see the following: S. Kuttner, *Reportorium der Kanonistik (1140–1234: Prodromus corporis glossarum* (Vatican Library, Vatican City, 1937–   ); J. de Ghellinck, art. "Gratien," *DTC*, 6, 1727–1751; A. Van Hove, art. "Corpus Juris Canonici," *CE*, 4, 391–394; A. Van Hove, art. "Gratian," *CE*, 6, 730; J. F. von Schulte (ed.), *Die Summa des Stephanus Tornacensis über das Decretum Gratiani* (Giessen, 1891).

See also: A. G. Cicognani, *Canon Law* (Dolphin Press, Philadelphia, 1934); M. Grabmann, *Mittelalterliches Geistesleben*, 2 vols. (Munich, 1926), Vol. I, 65–103 ("Das Naturrecht der Scholastik von Gratian bis Thomas von Aquin").

JOHN OF SALISBURY

John's works are in *PL*, 199; modern editions of individual works include *Policraticus* 2 vols. (ed. C. C. J. Webb, Oxford, 1909), and *Metalogicon* (ed. C. C. J. Webb, Clarendon Press, Oxford, 1929).

On the school of Chartres, cf. A. Clerval, *Les Ecoles de Chartres au moyen âge du Ve siècle au XVIe siècle* (Paris, 1895); R. L. Poole (ed. A. L. Poole), *Studies in Chronology and History* (Clarendon Press, Oxford, 1934), 223–247 ("The Masters of the Schools at Paris and Chartres in John of Salisbury's Time").

See also: M. Demimuid, *Jean de Salisbury* (Paris, 1873); H. Liebeschütz, *Mediaeval Humanism in the Life and Writings of*

John of Salisbury (Warburg Institute, London, 1950); C. Schaarschmidt, *Joannes Sarisberiensis nach Leben und Studien, Schriften und Philosophie* (Leipzig, 1862); C. C. J. Webb, *John of Salisbury* (Methuen, London, 1932).

THE SCHOOL OF LAON

A quite unreliable text (probably interpolated) of the *Glossa marginalis* will be found in *PL*, 113–114. For the *Glossa inter-linearis* such texts as the commentaries of Nicholas of Lyra (d. 1349; many early eds.) must be consulted. An extensive bibliography of *quaestiones* and *sententiae* of the school of Laon (edited piecemeal, for the most part, in various journals) will be found in Landgraf, *Einführung*, 55–60.

See also: F. P. Bliemetzrieder, *Anselms von Laon systematische Sentenzen, Beiträge*, XVIII/2–3 (1936); G. Lefèvre, *Anselmi Laudunensis et Radulfi fratris eius sententiae excerptae* (Evreux, 1895); J. de Ghellinck, "The Sentences of Anselm of Laon and Their Place in the Codification of Theology during the XIIth Century," *Irish Theological Quarterly*, 6 (1911), 427–441 (dated, in part); O. Lottin, "Aux origines de l'école théologique d'Anselme de Laon," *Recherches de théol. anc. et méd.*, 10 (1938), 101–122.

PETER ABAILARD

Abailard's collected works will be found in *PL*, 178, and in V. Cousin (ed.), *Petri Abaelardi Opera*, 2 vols. (Paris, 1849–1859); an adequate edition is still needed. Good texts of some works may be found in B. Geyer, *Peter Abaelards philosophische Shriften, Beiträge*, XXI/1–4 (1919–1933); H. Ostlender, *Peter Abaelards Theologia "Summi boni," Beiträge*, XXXV/2–3 (1939). The *Historia calamitatum* has been well edited by J. T. Muckle, *Mediaeval Studies*, 12 (1950), 163–213, and translated by the same writer, as *The Story of Abélard's Adversities* (Pontifical Institute of Mediaeval Studies, Toronto, 1954). J. R. McCallum has made rather unreliable translations of *Scito teipsum* (*Abailard's Ethics*, Blackwell, Oxford, 1935) and (incomplete) *Theologia christiana* (*Abélard's Christian Theology*, Blackwell, Oxford, 1948). There is a separate edition of Abailard's hymns by G. M. Dreves, *Petri Abaelardi Hymnarius Paraclitensis* (Paris, 1891).

The best introduction to Abailard's work is J. G. Sikes, *Peter Abailard* (University Press, Cambridge, 1932). An older but valuable study is C. de Rémusat, *Abélard, sa vie, sa philosophie et sa théologie*, 2 vols. (2d ed., Paris, 1855). R. B. Lloyd, *The Stricken Lute: An Account of the Life of Peter Abailard* (Lovat Dickson, London, 1932), is a popular biography, and H. Waddell, *Peter Abelard: A Novel* (Constable, London, 1933), a biographical novel. E. Gilson, *Heloise and Abelard* (Regnery, Chicago, 1951), gives real insight into Abailard's mind.

See also: J. Cottiaux, "La Conception de la théologie chez Abélard," *Rev. d'hist. ecclés.*, 28 (1932), 247–295; 533–551; 788–828; P. Delhaye, "L'Enseignement de la philosophie morale au XII⁰ siècle," *Med. Stud.*, 11 (1949), 77–99; H. Denifle, "Abälards Sentenzen und die Bearbeitungen seiner Theologia vor Mitte des XII Jahrhunderts," *Archiv für litt. Gesch.*, 1 (1885), 402–469; 584–624; S. M. Deutsch, *Peter Abälard: ein kritischer Theologe des zwölften Jahrhunderts* (Leipzig, 1883); G. Frascolla, *Pietro Abelardo*, 2 vols. (S.T.E.P., Pesaro, 1950–1951); E. Kaiser, *Pierre Abélard critique* (Freiburg i. Schw., 1901); H. Ligeard, "Le Rationalisme de Pierre Abélard," *Recherches de science rel.*, 2 (1911), 384–396; E. Portalié, art. "Abélard," *DTC*, 1, 36–55; J. Rivière, "Les 'Capitula' d'Abélard condamnés au Concile de Sens," *Recherches de théol. anc. et méd.*, 5 (1933), 5–22; J. Schiller, *Abaelards Ethik im Vergleich zur Ethik seiner Zeit* (Munich, 1906); E. Vacandard, *Abélard, sa lutte avec saint Bernard, sa doctrine, sa méthode* (Paris, 1881).

THE VICTORINES

Somewhat unsatisfactory texts of Hugh of St. Victor will be found in *PL*, 175–177, and of Richard in *PL*, 196. For Adam, cf. E. Misset and P. Aubry, *Les Proses d'Adam de Saint-Victor: texte et musique* (Paris, 1900), and D. S. Wrangham, *The Liturgical Poetry of Adam of St. Victor* (text and tr.), 3 vols. (London, 1881). For a critical text of a fundamental work of Hugh, cf. C. H. Buttimer (ed.), *Hugonis de sancto Victore Didascalion, de studio legendi* (Catholic University of America, Washington, 1939). R. J. Deferrari (ed.) *Hugh of Saint Victor on the Sacraments of the Christian Faith* (Mediaeval Academy of America, Cambridge, 1951), is a very literal version, with certain debatable renderings.

Two pioneer studies of Hugh are: B. Hauréau, *Les Oeuvres de Hugues de Saint-Victor: essai critique* (Paris, 1886); A. Mignon, *Les Origines de la scolastique et Hugues de Saint-Victor*, 2 vols. (Paris, 1895). A survey of Richard's ideas will be found in C. Ottaviano, "Riccardo di San Vittore, la vita, le opere, il pensiero," *Mem. della R. Accad. dei Lincei*, 4 (Rome, 1933), 411–541.

See also: G. Grassi-Bertazzi, *La filosofia di Hugo da San Vittore* (Rome, 1912); J. Kleinz, *The Theory of Knowledge of Hugh of St. Victor* (Catholic University of America, Washington, 1944); H. Ostler, *Die Psychologie des Hugo von St. Victor*, *Beiträge*, VI/1 (1906); F. Vernet, art. "Hugues de Saint-Victor," *DTC*, 7, 240–308; H. Weisweiler, "Die Arbeitsmethode Hugos von St. Victor," *Scholastik*, 20–24 (1949), 59–87; 232–267; G. Dumeige, *Richard de Saint-Victor et l'idée chrétienne de l'amour* (Presses universitaires de France, Paris, 1952); J. Ebner, *Die Erkenntnislehre Richards von St. Victor*, *Beiträge*, XIX/4 (1917); A. E. Ethier, *Le De Trinitate de Richard de Saint-Victor* (Vrin, Paris, 1939); G. Fritz, art. "Richard de Saint-Victor," *DTC*, 13, 2676–2695; M. Lenglart, *La Théorie de la contemplation mystique dans l'oeuvre de Richard de Saint-Victor* (Alcan, Paris, 1935).

PETER LOMBARD

The collected works of the Lombard will be found in *PL*, 191–192. See also the critical edition of the *Libri quatuor sententiarum* 2 vols. (2d ed., Quaracchi, 1916).

For a general introduction to Peter Lombard's work, see two articles by J. de Ghellinck, "Pierre Lombard" (*DTC*, 12, 1941–2019), and "Peter Lombard" (*CE*, 11, 768 f.). The former concludes with a full bibliography.

See also: J. N. Espenberger, *Die Philosophie des Petrus Lombardus*, *Beiträge*, III/5 (1901); J. Kögel, *Petrus Lombardus in seiner Stellung zur Philosophie des Mittelalters* (Greifswald, 1897); J. Schupp, *Die Gnadenlehre des Petrus Lombardus* (Herder, Freiburg i.B., 1932).

STEPHEN LANGTON

The bulk of Langton's work has still to be published. Some excerpts are included in G. Lacombe and B. Smalley, *Studies on the Commentaries of Cardinal Stephen Langton* (reprint from *Archives d'hist. doct. et litt. du moyen âge*, 5 [1930]). See also A. M. Landgraf (ed.), *Der Sentenzenkommentar des Kardinals Stephan Langton*, *Beiträge*, XXXVII/1 (1952).

The only extensive introduction is the too brief work of F. M. Powicke, *Stephen Langton* (Clarendon Press, Oxford, 1928). See also his "Bibliographical Note on Recent Work upon Stephen Langton," *Eng. Hist. Rev.*, 48 (1933), 554–557. There is a good deal of important material in B. Smalley, *The Study of the Bible in the Middle Ages, passim.*

The translations of twelfth century material have been made from the following texts:

Ivo of Chartres	*PL*, 161, 47–49.
Gratian	ed. Friedberg, I, 1–3
John of Salisbury	ed. C. C. J. Webb, I, 234–247
Anselm of Laon	Lottin, *Psychologie et morale*, IV, 3:1, pp. 20 f.
School of Laon	Lottin, pp. 40–42
The Gloss	*PL*, 114, 545–550.
Peter Abailard	ed. Cousin, II, 202–209; 613–620; *Oxford Book of Medieval Latin Verse*, pp. 92 f.
Hugh of Saint Victor	*PL*, 176, 305–318
Richard of Saint Victor	*PL*, 196, 327–330; 527 f.; 891–893; 915–917
Adam of Saint Victor	*PL*, 196, 1527–1529
Peter Lombard	ed. Quaracchi, II, 593–597; 745–752; 785–787; 819; 892 f.; 901 f.
Stephen Langton	Lottin, pp. 102 f.; 354; 356; 358 f.; *Oxford Book*, pp. 136 f.

Ivo of Chartres: Decretum

THE TEXT

THE PROLOGUE (OPENING PARAGRAPHS)

I have labored long and painstakingly to unite in one work a selection of ecclesiastical rules, gathered partly from the epistles of Roman pontiffs, partly from the acts of councils held by Catholic bishops, partly from the treatises of orthodox Fathers, partly from the legislation of Catholic kings. My idea is that he who cannot have at hand the writings from which they are selected may at least find here things that will prove effective for the advancement of his own case. Therefore, beginning from the foundation of the Christian religion, that is, from faith, we have assembled the matters that pertain to the sacraments of the Church, those that pertain to the establishing or correcting of morals, and those that relate to the conclusion or determination of any business, all organized under general titles,[1] so that a searcher will not have to work through the whole volume, but need only note the general title appropriate to his own question and run through the chapters placed under it without intermixture. In this connection, we have thought it fitting to forewarn the prudent reader, so that if perhaps he does not fully understand the things he is reading, or even thinks that they are incompatible, he will not immediately find fault, but will carefully apply his mind to determining what is said according to severity, what according to moderation, what according to judgment, what according to mercy. The psalmist did not suppose that these were at variance among them-

---

[1] The *Decretum* is divided into seventeen parts in all, dealing with such varied subjects as: "Faith and the sacrament of faith, that is, baptism" (I), "The sacrament of the body and blood of the Lord" (II), "The primacy of the Roman Church" (V), "The behavior of clerics" (VI), "Lawful marriages" (VIII), "Magicians, etc." (XI), "Penance, etc." (XV).

selves, when he said: "Mercy and judgment I will sing to thee,
O Lord,"[2] and elsewhere: "All the ways of the Lord are mercy,
and truth."[3] For the principal intention of all ecclesiastical
discipline is this: either to destroy every construction which
erects itself against the knowledge of Christ[4] or to construct
God's building,[5] which stands firm by the truth of faith and
honesty of morals—or else, if this has been contaminated, to
cleanse it by remedies of penance. The mistress of this building
is charity, which, looking to the salvation of our neighbors,
directs that what each wishes to have meted out to himself *by*
others shall be done *to* others. Therefore, any ecclesiastical
teacher whatever who so interprets or organizes ecclesiastical
rules as to relate all that he teaches or expounds to the reign of
charity neither sins nor errs since, always bearing in mind the
salvation of his neighbors, he endeavors to attain to the due end
by sacred regulations. For this reason blessed Augustine says,
in dealing with ecclesiastical discipline: "Have charity, and do
whatever you will. If you correct, correct with charity; if you
spare, spare with charity."[6] But in these matters the highest
diligence is to be exercised, and the eye of the heart is to be
purified, since both in punishing and in sparing genuine charity
avails for the healing of diseases. Then no one seeks his own,[7]
in the manner of venal physicians, or incurs the prophetic
reproof: "They put to death the souls that were not dying, and
gave life to the souls that were not alive."[8] For the procedure
of bodily medicine aims either at dispelling diseases or at
healing wounds, or at preserving health or even increasing it,
nor does a physician seem to be contradicting himself when he
sometimes applies biting remedies, sometimes relaxing ones, to
the sick man, according to the character or seriousness of the
disease, and sometimes cuts a man with the knife when he
cannot help him with a poultice, or, conversely, helps a man

---

[2] Ps. 100:1 (P.B.V., 101:1).
[3] Ps. 24:10 (P.B.V., 25:9).
[4] Cf. II Cor. 10:5.
[5] Cf. I Cor. 3:9.
[6] I have not been able to find a text exactly like this in Augustine. The first
sentence, however, reflects the famous *Dilige, et quod vis fac* (*In epist. Ioan.
ad Parthos*, VII, 8 [*PL*, 35, 2033]), while statements on charity and
discipline can be found in a number of places in his writings. Cf. *De doctr.
christ.*, I, 22:21 (*PL*, 34, 27); *Sermo* 83, 7:8 (*PL*, 38, 518 f.); *De grat. et lib.
arb.*, 17, 34 (*PL*, 44, 902).
[7] Cf. I Cor. 13:5.
[8] Ezek. 13:19 (not quoted according to the Vulgate).

with a poultice when he does not dare to cut him with the knife. Similarly, spiritual physicians, namely, the doctors of Holy Church, do not differ with themselves or with one another, when they forbid the unlawful, command the necessary, exhort to the highest things, or are kind in venial matters; when they impose severe rules of penance in proportion to the hardness of heart of offenders, in order to correct them or to warn others; or when, seeing the devotion of those who grieve and wish to rise again, and considering their frailty, they place over these vessels[9] as a protection the pardon which they convey. For those who are gentle have an eye to the removal of worse diseases, and those who forbid unlawful things seek to deter men from death, while those who command necessary things desire to preserve health, and those who use persuasion seek to increase health. If he is aware of all this, the careful reader will understand that the sacred oracles really present one countenance, when he considers the distinctive meanings of admonition, of precept, of prohibition, of remission, and sees that these do not contradict each other or contain any inner inconsistencies, but rather dispense the remedies of health to all for their guidance. We must, however, determine a little more fully what weight these particular things have, and to whom they are appropriate, and decide which rules may and which may not be relaxed, and when or under what circumstances relaxation is possible.

Now the first admonition to be considered does not threaten punishment to a man who does not accept it, but promises a reward to those who assent to it. The Lord says in the Gospel: "If thou wilt be perfect, go sell what thou hast, and give to the poor, and thou shalt have treasure in heaven."[10] Observe that this statement of the Gospel locates perfection in man's will, and thus does not compel or threaten any more than the statement which commends eunuchs who have castrated themselves for the sake of the Kingdom of Heaven, and concludes: "He that can take it, let him take it."[11] But nevertheless, when anyone has bound himself to perfection by a vow, or has attained to a rank to which no one ought to attain without the virtue of continence,[12] that which before his promotion was

9 Cf. Rom. 9:22 f.
10 Matt. 19:21.
11 Matt. 19:12.
12 The reference is, of course, to clerical celibacy, the enforcement of which was such a conspicuous feature of the reform movement of this period.

voluntary now becomes necessary, and if it is not maintained a
penalty can be imposed. It is for this reason that the Lord also
says: "No man putting his hand to the plow, and looking back,
is fit for the kingdom of God."[13] For before his advancement he
could have been lower without being worse, but after his
advancement he is lower and worse. This much for admonition.

But mildness, as we see it, brings a remedy, and not a reward,
for the man who has not chosen better things; if anyone,
however, turns aside from this, he deserves the sentence of
death.[14] We know, for instance, that marriage is permitted to
the human race, for the avoidance of fornication,[15] and that
(by the witness of the same apostle) one who violates marriage
merits eternal punishment. For he says: "Fornicators and
adulterers God will judge."[16] Now this status of marriage—as
we said before about admonition—constrains no one except him
who has bound himself to it in the first place. For it is voluntary,
not necessary. Otherwise, anyone who did not marry a wife
would be a transgressor. But after a man has bound himself,
let him listen to the apostle saying: "Art thou bound to a wife?
Seek not to be loosed."[17] The same apostle also, when he was
speaking of marriage, did not say that if a woman marries she
deserves a reward, but he merely said, "She does not sin, if
she marries."[18] So also, if anyone encourages someone else to
undertake daily fasts, he does indeed persuade the man who
accepts the suggestion and perseveres in it to do a thing
deserving of reward. Now he who does not accept this does not
become better than he was; nevertheless, although he remains
inferior to the man who performs it, he is not made worse than
he was. But if he lapses from a vow that he has made, he becomes
lower and worse than he was before. In other words, if he keeps
himself within the limits of sobriety and a frugal table, he does
not attain to the supreme rewards, but if he falls into revelings
and drunkenness,[19] he is regarded as having done a thing
deserving of reproof and shame. Thus while those two conditions,[20] the one higher and the other lower, were a matter of
free choice before a vow was made, once the vow has been

13 Luke 9:62.
14 I.e., of eternal death.
15 Cf. I Cor. 7:1 f.
16 Heb. 13:4.
17 I Cor. 7:27.
18 I Cor. 7:28 (loosely quoted).
19 Cf. Gal. 5:21.
20 I.e., celibacy and marriage, or the ascetic and the nonascetic life.

made they become a matter of necessity, and have their own restrictions and regulations. As has already been said, if these are observed they obtain a remedy for some, and a reward for others, but the failure to observe them merits eternal punishment. In such matters, therefore, there should be deliberation before they are undertaken, but perseverance once they have been undertaken.[21]

---

[21] Cf. Anselm's use of the theory of "precepts and counsels" to illustrate God's freedom in our redemption (*Cur deus homo*, II, 5). For a careful statement of the traditional view of precepts and counsels, assumed here, cf. Thomas Aquinas, *Sum. theol.*, IIa–IIae, 184, 3.

Gratian: The Concord of Discordant Canons (Decretum)

THE TEXT

DISTINCTION I

LAW AND LAWS

Gratian: The human race is ruled by two things: natural law[1] and usages.[2] The law of nature is that which is contained in the Law and the Gospel, by which each man is ordered to do to another what he wishes to be done to himself, and by which he is forbidden to inflict on another what he does not wish to be done to himself. Wherefore Christ says in the Gospel: "All things therefore whatsoever you would that men should do to you, do you also to them: for this is the law and the prophets."[3]

For this reason Isidore says, in the fifth book of the *Etymologies*:

C. I. *Divine laws are settled by nature, human laws by usages.*

"All laws are either divine or human. The divine are established by nature, the human by usages; the latter, therefore, vary, since different things seem good to different nations. §1. Equity[4] is divine law[5]; right[6] is human law.[7] To pass through another's field is a matter of equity, not of right."[8]

G. By the words of this authority we are clearly given to understand in what divine and human law differ among themselves, since the name of divine or natural law stands for everything that pertains to equity,[9] while by the name of human law[10] we understand customs drawn up by law and

---

1 *Ius.* Where there is any ambiguity, the word rendered as "law" (whether *ius* or *lex*) is indicated; it may perhaps be said that *ius* stands more for legal principle, *lex* for legal enactment.
2 *Mores*—rendered as "usages," to distinguish from *consuetudo* ("custom").
3 Matt. 7:12.
4 *Fas.*   5 *Lex.*   6 *Ius.*   7 *Lex.*
8 Isidore of Seville, *Etymologiae*, V, 2 (*PL*, 82, 198). Gratian adds *agrum* (field).
9 *Fas.*   10 *Lex.*

handed down. §1. Now right[11] is a general term, containing many species under it.

Wherefore Isidore says in the same book:

C. II. *Right is the genus, law is its species.*

"Right is a general term, but law[12] is a species of right. Now *ius* is so-called because it is just. But all right consists of laws[13] and usages."[14]

C. III. *What law is.*

"A law[15] is a written ordinance."[16]

C. IV. *What usage is.*

"Now usage is long-continued custom, derived to a certain extent from usages."[17]

C. V. *What custom is.*

"Custom, however, is a certain right established by usages, which is taken for law[18] when law is lacking. §1. Nor does it matter whether it depends on Scripture or on reason, since reason recommends law[19] also. §2. Moreover, if law corresponds to reason, law will be all that corresponds to reason—all, at least, that is consistent with religion, or is consistent with discipline, or is beneficial for salvation. §3. Now it is called *consuetudo*, because it is in common use."[20]

G. Thus when it is said that "it does not matter whether it depends on Scripture or on reason," it is evident that custom has in part been collected in writings, in part preserved only in the usages of those who practice it. What is collected in writings is called ordinance or law,[21] while what is not collected in writings is called by the general name of custom.

1. There is also another division of law,[22] as Isidore attests in the same book when he says this:

C. VI. *What the species of law are.*

"Law is either natural law, or civil law, or the law of nations."[23]

C. VII. *What natural law is.*

"Natural law[24] is common to all nations, in that it is held everywhere by instinct of nature, not by some ordinance. It has to do with such things as the union of man and woman; the succession and education of children; the common possession

---

[11] *Ius.*   [12] *Lex.*   [13] *Leges.*
[14] Isidore, *op. cit.*, V, 3 (*PL*, 82, 199).   [15] *Lex.*
[16] Isidore, *loc. cit.*
[17] Isidore, *loc. cit.*, and II, 10 (*PL*, 82, 130).   [18] *Lex.*   [19] *Lex.*
[20] Isidore, as in n. 17, above.   [21] *Ius.*   [22] *Ius.*
[23] Isidore, *op. cit.*, V, 4 (*PL*, 82, 199).   [24] *Ius.*

of all things and the freedom, one and the same, of all; or the acquisition of those things which are taken possession of in heaven, on earth, and in the sea; also, with the return of a thing put in one's charge or of money entrusted to one, and the repelling of violence by force. §1. For this, or something very like it, is never regarded as unjust, but is looked on as natural and equitable."[25]

C. VIII. *What civil law is.*

"Civil law[26] is what each people or city establishes as its own law in divine or human matters."[27]

C. IX. *What the law of nations is.*

"The law[28] of nations has to do with the occupation of habitations, with building, fortification, wars, captivities, servitudes, reprisals, treaties of peace, truces, scrupulousness in not doing violence to ambassadors, prohibition of marriages between aliens. §1. This is called the law of nations, because almost all nations make use of this law."[29]

C. X. *What military law is.*

"Military law[30] has to do with the formalities of waging war; the obligations of making a treaty; advance against the enemy on signal, and combat; or withdrawal, again on signal; the discipline of military degradation, if a soldier deserts his post; the manner of military service; the order of ranks; the conferring of honors, as when wreaths or chains are granted; the distribution of booty, its just division according to the status and the exertions of different persons, and the commander's share."[31]

C. XI. *What public law is.*

"Public law[32] has to do with sacred things and with priests and magistrates."[33]

C. XII. *What the law of Roman citizens is.*

"The law[34] of the *Quirites*[35] pertains properly to the Romans, and none save the *Quirites* (that is, the Romans) maintain it.

---

25 Isidore, *loc. cit.*
26 *Ius.*
27 Isidore, *op. cit.*, V, 5 (*PL*, 82; 199).
28 *Ius.*
29 Isidore, *op. cit.*, V, 6 (*PL*, 82, 199 f.).
30 *Ius.*
31 Isidore, *op. cit.*, V, 7 (*PL*, 82, 200).
32 *Ius.*
33 Isidore, *op. cit.*, V, 8 (*PL*, 82, 200).
34 *Ius.*
35 Cf. O. Seyffert, rev. and ed. H. Nettleship and J. E. Sandys, *A Dictionary of Classical Antiquities* (London, 1891), 535: "The name of the oldest inhabitants of Rome. . . . Afterward it became the name of the Roman people . . . in home affairs, while *Romani* was used in connection with foreign affairs. *Quirites* was also used to indicate peaceable citizens, or civilians, as opposed to soldiers (*milites*)."

§1. This law deals with legitimate inheritances, the entering upon inheritances, wardships, the acquisition of things by long possession. These laws are met with among no other people, but are peculiar to the Romans, and are appointed for them alone."[36]

[36] Isidore, *op. cit.*, V, 9 (*PL*, 82, 200).

John of Salisbury: The Policraticus
(An Excerpt from the Fourth Book)

THE TEXT

PROLOGUE

The expression of the truth is unquestionably a difficult undertaking, and it is very frequently spoiled by the assault of the darkness of error or by the carelessness of the one who tries to express it. For when things are unknown, who rightly ponders what is true? However, the knowledge of things, in so far as it does not direct the ways of the disdainful, sharpens the stings of justice for the punishment of the transgressor. The first step, therefore, in philosophizing is to discuss the genera and the properties of things,[1] so that one may prudently learn what is true in individual things, and the second step is that each should faithfully follow whatever truth has shone upon him. Now this paved route of those who philosophize is open only to the man who cries out from the realm of falsehood into the liberty[2] by which those whom the truth has delivered are made free[3] and, serving the Spirit,[4] withdraw their necks from the yoke of wickedness and injustice. For "where the Spirit of" God "is, there is liberty,"[5] while the fear which is servile and consents to vices banishes the Holy Spirit. Moreover, it is the Spirit who speaks righteousness[6] in the sight of princes and feels no shame,[7] and who sets the poor in spirit[8] above, or at

---

[1] On "genus" and "property," cf. Aristotle, *Topica*, I, 5–6 (101^b36–103^a5); summary in W. D. Ross, *Aristotle* (3d ed., Methuen, London, 1937), 57.
[2] Cf. Rom. 8:20 f.
[3] Cf. John 8:32.
[4] Cf. Rom. 7:6.
[5] II Cor. 3:17.
[6] Cf. Ps. 51:5 (A.V. 52:3).
[7] Cf. Ps. 118:46 (P.B.V., 119:46).
[8] Cf. Matt. 5:3.

least on a level with, kings,[9] and teaches those whom he makes to cleave to him to speak and do the truth.[10] But he who will not hear or speak the truth is a stranger to the Spirit of truth.[11] But no more of this. Now let us hear in what respect a tyrant differs from a prince.

CHAPTER I

THE DIFFERENCE BETWEEN A PRINCE AND A TYRANT, AND WHAT A PRINCE IS

This, then, is the sole (or at least the greatest) difference between a tyrant and a prince, that the latter conforms to the law, and rules the people, whose servant he believes himself to be, by its judgment. Also, when he performs the duties of the commonwealth and undergoes its burdens, he claims for himself the first place by privilege of law, and is set before others in so far as universal burdens hang over the prince, while individuals are bound to individual concerns. On this account, the power over all his subjects is rightly conferred on him, so that, in seeking and accomplishing the welfare of each and all, he may be self-sufficient and the state of the human commonwealth may be best disposed, while one is the member of another.[12] In this, indeed, we follow nature, the best guide for living,[13] which arranged all the senses of its microcosm[14]—that is, its little world, man—in the head, and subjected all the members to the latter so that they all are rightly moved, as long as they follow the decision of a sound head. Therefore, the princely crown is exalted and shines with privileges as many and as great as it has believed to be necessary for itself. And this is done rightly, because nothing is more beneficial for the people than for the prince's necessity to be met—when his will is not opposed to justice, to be sure. Therefore (as many define him)

9 Cf. Luke 1:52.
10 Cf. John 16:13; I John 1:6.
11 Cf. John 14:17; 15:26; 16:13; I John 4:6.
12 Cf. Rom. 12:5.
13 Cf. Cicero, *De amicitia*, 5, 19 (Loeb Classical Library ed., *Cicero: De senectute, De amicitia, De divinatione* [Heinemann, London, 1938], 128).
14 The word *microcosmus* appears in Isidore of Seville, *Orig.*, III, 23 (*PL*, 82, 169); it does not seem to have been used (except as two words: *mikros kosmos*) by the ancient Greeks (cf. C. C. J. Webb's edition of the *Policraticus*, I, 235n.). The term had been used by John of Salisbury's teacher, Bernard of Chartres (on Bernard, cf. Gilson, *History*, 140; 619 f.).

the prince is the public ruler and a kind of image of the divine Majesty on earth.[15] Beyond doubt, it is shown that something great in the way of divine power indwells princes, when men submit their necks to their nods and very often fearlessly yield their necks to be smitten, and each for whom he is a matter of dread fears him by divine instigation. I do not think that this could happen, save by the act of the divine pleasure. For all power is from the Lord God,[16] and it has been with him always, and is with him eternally. Therefore, what the prince can do comes from God in such a way that the power does not depart from the Lord, but he exercises it by a hand that is subject to him, and that follows in all things the instruction of his clemency or justice. Thus "he that resisteth the power resisteth the ordinance of God,"[17] with whom rests the authority to confer it and (when he wills) to take it away or lessen it. For when a mighty one decides to rage against his subjects, this involves not just himself but also the divine dispensation, by which those who are subject to it are punished or vexed for God's good pleasure. So, for instance, during the depredations of the Huns, Attila was asked, by the devout bishop of a certain city, who he was, and replied, "I am Attila, the scourge of God." It is written that, when the bishop had reverenced the divine Majesty in him, he said, "Welcome to the servant of God," and, repeating, "Blessed is he that cometh in the name of the Lord,"[18] opened the doors of the church and admitted the persecutor, and through him attained to the palm of martyrdom.[19] For he did not dare to shut out the scourge of God, knowing as he did that it is the beloved son that is scourged,[20] and that the very power of the scourge comes from the Lord alone.[21] If, then, the power is to be reverenced in this way by the good, even when it brings misfortune to the elect, who will not reverence it? After all, it was instituted by the Lord "for the punishment of evildoers, and for the praise of the good,"[22] and it serves the laws with the readiest devotion. For,

15 On this definition of the *princeps*, cf. Vegetius, *Epitome rei militaris*, II, 5 f. (ed. C. Lang [2d ed., Leipzig, 1885], 38 f.).
16 Cf. Rom. 13:1.
17 Rom. 13:2.
18 Matt. 21:9.
19 Who was the bishop? A similar story is told of Lupus of Troyes (d. 478), but he was not martyred (cf. *Acta Sanctorum*, July, Vol. 7, 78; 82).
20 Cf. Heb. 12:6.
21 Cf. Deut. 32:27; Isa. 10:5–15.
22 Cf. I Peter 2:14

as the emperor says,[23] it is a statement worthy of the majesty of the ruler that the prince should acknowledge that he is bound by laws, because the authority of the prince depends on the authority of the law,[24] and it is certainly a greater thing for the realm when sovereignty is set under the laws, so that the prince understands that nothing is permitted to him if it is at variance with justice and equity.

CHAPTER II

What Law Is, and that the Prince, Although He Is Released from the Obligations of Law, Is Still the Bondservant of Law and Equity, and Bears a Public Character, and Sheds Blood Blamelessly

Princes should not think that anything is taken away from them in all this, unless they believe that the statutes of their own justice are to be preferred to the justice of God, whose justice is justice forever, and his law equity.[25] Besides, as legal experts affirm,[26] equity is the fitness of things, which makes everything equal by reason and desires equal laws for unequal things; it is equitable toward all and assigns to each what belongs to him.[27] But law is its interpreter, in so far as the will of equity and justice has been made known to it. Therefore, Chrysippus claimed that law has power over all things human and divine, and on that account is superior to all goods and evils and is the chief and guide of things and men alike. Papinian, a really great expert in the law, and Demosthenes, the powerful orator, seem to uphold the law and to subject the obedience of all men to it, inasmuch as in truth all law is the device and gift of God, the doctrine of wise men, the corrector of inclinations to excess, the settlement of the state, and the banishment of all crime, so that all who are engaged in the whole world of political affairs must live according to

23 Cf. *Codex Iustinianus*, I, 14:4, in *Corpus Iuris Civilis*, II (ed. P. Krueger, Berlin, 1888), 68.
24 *Ius*.
25 Cf. Ps. 118:142 (P.B.V., 119:142).
26 This definition was current in the Middle Ages, and was cited by Azo, the famous Bolognese legal expert of the thirteenth century (cf. *Policraticus*, ed. C. C. J. Webb, I, 237n.).
27 Cf. *Institutiones Iustiniani*, I, 1:1, ed. P. Krueger, *Corpus Iur. Civ.*, I (Berlin, 1889), 1.

it.[28] Thus all are closely bound by the necessity of maintaining the law, unless there may perhaps be someone to whom license seems to have been conceded for wickedness. Nevertheless, the prince is said to be released from legal obligations,[29] not because evil actions are allowed him, but because he should be one who cherishes equity, not from fear of punishment but from love of justice, and in everything puts others' advantage before his personal desires. But who will speak of the desires of the prince in connection with public business, since in this area he is permitted to desire nothing for himself save what law or equity suggests or the nature of the common welfare determines? For in these things his will ought to have the effect of a judgment, and it is quite right that what pleases him in such matters should have the force of law,[30] in so far as his sentence is not in disagreement with the intention of equity. "Let my judgment," the psalmist says, "come forth from thy countenance; let thine eyes behold the thing that is equitable,"[31] for an uncorrupt judge is he whose sentence is the image of equity, because of assiduous contemplation. The prince, then, is the servant of the public welfare and the bondservant of equity, and in that sense plays a public role, because he both avenges the injuries and losses of all and punishes all crimes with impartial justice.[32] Moreover, his rod and staff, applied with wise moderation, bring the agreements and the errors of all into the way of equity, so that the spirit rightly gives thanks to the princely power, when it says, "Thy rod and thy staff, they have comforted me."[33] It is true also that his shield is strong,[34] but it is the shield of the weak and it effectively intercepts the darts aimed at the innocent by the malicious. His function also is of the utmost benefit to those who have the least power, and is most strongly opposed to those who desire to do harm. Therefore,

---

28 On the last two sentences, cf. *Digesta Iustiniani* (=*Pandects*), I, 3:1 f., ed. T. Mommsen, *Corpus Iur. Civ.*, I, 5 (separate pagination for *Digesta*). For Eng. trans. of this and other texts, cf. C. H. Monro, *The Digest of Justinian*, 2 vols. (Cambridge, 1904–1909).

29 Cf. *Digesta*, I, 3:31 (*Corp. Iur. Civ.*, I, 6).

30 Cf. *Digesta*, I, 4:1 (*Corp. Iur. Civ.*, I, 7).

31 Ps. 16:2 (P.B.V., 17:2), quoted almost exactly.

32 Cf. the "Prayer for the Whole State of Christ's Church," in the *Book of Common Prayer*: "That they may truly and indifferently minister justice, to the punishment of wickedness and vice, and to the maintenance of thy true religion, and virtue."

33 Ps. 22:4 (P.B.V., 23:4).

34 II Kings 1:21 (A.V., II Sam. 1:21).

"he beareth not the sword in vain,"[35] when he sheds blood by it, but blamelessly, so that he is not a man of blood, but often kills men without thereby incurring the name or the guilt of a homicide. For if the great Augustine is to be believed, David was called a "man of blood,"[36] not because of his wars but on account of Uriah.[37] And it is nowhere written that Samuel was a man of blood or a homicide, even though he slew Agag, the very rich king of Amalek.[38] In fact, the princely sword is the "sword of the dove,"[39] which strives without animosity, smites without fury, and, when it goes into combat, conceives no bitterness whatsoever. For, just as the law proceeds against crimes without any hatred of persons, so the prince also punishes offenders most rightly, not by any impulse of anger but by the decision of a mild law. For though the prince may seem to have his own "lictors,"[40] we should believe that in fact he is his only (or his foremost) lictor, but that it is lawful for him to smite by the hand of a substitute. For if we consult the Stoics, who diligently search out the origins of names, we shall learn that he is called a "lictor"—as it were, a "striker of the law"—inasmuch as it pertains to his office to smite him who, in the law's judgment, is to be smitten.[41] On this account also, when the guilty were threatened with the sword, it used to be said in ancient days to the officials by whose hand the judge punished evildoers, "Comply with the decision of the law," or "Fulfill the law," so that the mildness of the words might in fact modify the sadness of the event.

[35] Rom. 13:4.
[36] Cf. II Kings 16:7 f. (A.V., II Sam. 16:7 f.); I Chron. 22:8.
[37] Cf. II Kings, ch. 11 (A.V., II Sam., ch. 11). The closest parallel I can find in Augustine is his statement that "men of blood" are those who hate their brethren (*Enarr. in Ps.* 138, 26 (*PL*, 37, 1801).
[38] Cf. I Kings 15:32 f. (A.V., I Sam. 15:32 f.)
[39] Jer. 46:16.
[40] On "lictors," cf. W. Smith, *Smaller Classical Dictionary* (ed. E. H. Blakeney, Everyman's Library, Dent, London, 1934), 308: "*Lictors*, attendants who carried the *fasces* (rods bound in bundle form, and containing an ax in the middle) before a Roman magistrate."
[41] *Lictor* is really derived, not from *legis ictor*, but from *ligare* (to bind together).

CHAPTER III

THAT THE PRINCE IS THE SERVANT OF PRIESTS AND BENEATH
THEM, AND WHAT IT MEANS TO CARRY OUT THE PRINCELY
OFFICE FAITHFULLY

The prince, therefore, receives this sword from the hand of
the Church, even though, to be sure, the latter does not possess
the sword of blood.[42] Nevertheless, she does possess it as well,
but makes use of it by the hand of the prince, to whom she has
conceded the power of keeping bodies under restraint, although
she has retained authority in spiritual matters for her pontiffs.[43]
Thus the prince is in fact the servant of the priesthood, and
exercises that part of the sacred duties which seems unworthy
of the hands of the priesthood. For while every duty imposed
by the sacred laws is a matter of religion and piety, the function
of punishing crimes, which seems to constitute a kind of image
of the hangman's office, is lower than others. It was on account
of this inferiority that Constantine, the most faithful emperor of
the Romans, when he had convoked the council of priests at
Nicaea,[44] did not dare to take the first place or mingle with the
assemblies of the presbyters, but occupied the lowest seat.[45]
Indeed, he reverenced the conclusions which he heard approved
by them as if he supposed that they proceeded from the judgment of the divine Majesty.[46] As for the written accusations,
stating the offenses of the priests, which they had drawn up
against one another and presented to the emperor, he received
them and put them away, still unopened, in his bosom.[47]

[42] Cf. *Policraticus*, VI, 8 (ed. Webb, II, 22 f.).
[43] In liturgical and other usage, *pontifex* is applied to all bishops, and not
simply to the pope (cf. "pontifical mass"). The symbol of the "sword"
(cf. Matt. 26:52; John 18:10) and of the "two swords" (cf. Luke 22:38),
seems to have been first applied to the authority of the Church by
Bernard of Clairvaux in 1149 (*Epist.* 256 [*PL*, 182, 463–465]; cf. *De
consider.*, IV, 3 [col. 776]). The *Policraticus* was written perhaps ten years
later. On the history of the idea, cf. H. X. Arquillière, "Origines de la
théorie des deux glaives," in *Studi Gregoriani*, I (Abbazia di San Paolo,
Rome, 1947), 501–521; P. Lecler, "L'argument des deux glaives,"
Recherches de science religieuse, 21 (1931), 293–399; 22 (1932), 151–177,
281–303.
[44] I.e., the first Council of Nicaea (A.D. 325).
[45] Cf. Cassiodorus, *Hist. tripart.*, II, 5 (*PL*, 69, 924).
[46] Cf. *ibid.*, II, 14 (col. 934).
[47] Cf. *ibid.*, II, 2 (col. 922); Rufinus, *Hist. eccles.*, I, 2 (*PL*, 21, 468); Gregory
the Great, *Epist.* 5, 40 (*PL*, 77, 766); Gratian, *Decret.*, II, 11, q. 1, c. 41
(ed. E. A. Friedberg, *Corpus Iuris Canonici*, I [Leipzig, 1879], 638).

Moreover, when he had recalled the council to charity and concord, he said that it was unlawful for him (as a man, and as one who was subject to the judgment of priests) to consider the cases of the gods, who can be judged by God alone. And he committed the books which he had received to the fire, without looking at them, because he was afraid to disclose the crimes or vices of the Fathers, lest he bring on himself the curse of Ham, the rejected son, who failed to cover what he should have respected in his father.[48] For the same reason, he is said (in the writings of Nicholas, the Roman Pontiff) to have stated: "Truly, if with my own eyes I had seen a priest of God, or anyone who had been clothed in the monastic habit, committing sin, I should have spread out my cloak and covered him, lest he be seen by anyone."[49] Theodosius also, the great emperor, when he was suspended from the use of the regalia and the badges of sovereignty by the bishop of Milan, because of a crime that was real enough, but not quite that serious, patiently and solemnly did the penance imposed on him for homicide.[50] Certainly, to appeal to the testimony of the doctor of the Gentiles, he who blesses is greater than he who is blessed,[51] and he who possesses the authority to confer a dignity surpasses in the privilege of honor him on whom the dignity itself is conferred. Besides, according to the very nature of law, it pertains to the same person to will and not to will, and it is he who has the right to confer who also has the right to take away.[52] Did not Samuel bring sentence of deposition against Saul on account of his disobedience, and substitute the lowly son of Jesse for him in the highest place in the kingdom?[53] But if he who is set up as prince has faithfully performed the function he received, he is to be shown great honor and great reverence, in proportion to the superiority of the head over all the members of the body. Now he performs his task faithfully when, mindful of his rank, he remembers that he bears in himself the totality of his subjects, and knows that he owes his own life not to himself but to others, and as it were distributes it among them with due charity. He owes his entire self, then, to God, most of

---

[48] Cf. Gen. 9:22 ff.
[49] Cf. Nicholas I, *Epist.* 86 (*PL,* 119, 944); Gratian, *Decret.*, I, dist. 96, c. 8 (p. 339).
[50] Cf. Ambrose, *De obitu Theodos.*, 24 (*PL,* 16, 1396); Paulinus, *Vita S. Ambrosii*, 24 (*PL,* 14, 35).
[51] Cf. Heb. 7:7.
[52] Cf. *Digesta Iustin.*, L, 17:3 (*Corp. Iur. Civ.*, I, 868).
[53] Cf. I Kings 15:26 to 16:13 (A.V., I Sam. 15:26 to 16:13).

himself to his fatherland, much to his kinsfolk and neighbors, and least (but still something) to strangers. He is debtor, then, to the wise and the unwise, to the small and the great.[54] In fact, this concern is common to all who are set over others,[55] both to those who bear the care of spiritual things and to those who exercise worldly jurisdiction. On this account we read of Melchizedek, who is the first king and priest referred to in Scripture—not to mention, for the present, the mystery by which he prefigures Christ, who was born in heaven without a mother and on earth without a father[56]—we read, I say, that he had neither father nor mother. It is not that he lacked either, but that flesh and blood do not by their nature bring forth kingship and priesthood, since in the creation of either respect of parents should not carry weight without regard for meritorious virtue, but the wholesome desires of faithful subjects should have priority. Thus, when anyone reaches the pinnacle of either kingship or priesthood, he should forget the affection of the flesh and do only what the welfare of his subjects demands. Let him be, therefore, the father and husband of his subjects, or, if he knows a more tender affection, let him practice it; let him strive to be loved more than he is feared, and let him show himself to them in such a light that out of sheer devotion they may put his life before their own and reckon his safety to be a kind of public life. Then everything will go well with him, and if need be a few guards will prevail by their obedience against countless enemies. For "love is strong as death,"[57] and a wedge which the cords of love hold together is not easily broken.[58]

When the Dorians were about to fight with the Athenians, they consulted oracles about the outcome of the battle. "The reply was that they would win unless they killed the king of the Athenians. When the war began, care for the king was the first order given to the soldiers. At that time Codrus was king of the Athenians. When he learned of the response of the god and the orders of the enemy, he changed his kingly garments and, bearing fagots on his neck, entered the enemy's camp. There in a crowd of his opponents he was slain by a soldier, whom he had struck with his sickle. When the king's body was recognized,

<hr />

54 Cf. Rom. 1:14.
55 Lit., *praelati* (i.e., those set before others, or "prelates").
56 Cf. Heb. 7:1–3.
57 S. of Sol. 8:6.
58 Cf. Eccl. 4:12.

the Dorians withdrew without a battle. And in this way the Athenians were delivered from war by the virtue of their chief, who offered himself to death for the preservation of the fatherland."[59]

Again, Lycurgus in his kingdom established decrees which set the people in obedience to their chiefs and the chiefs to the justice of their commanders.[60] "He abolished the use of gold and silver and the source of all crimes."[61] He gave to the senate the care of the laws, and to the people the power of electing the senate.[62] He decreed that a maiden "should be married without a dowry, so that wives and not money should be chosen. He intended that the greatest honor should correspond closely . . . with the age of the old—nor in fact does old age have a more honored place anywhere on earth."[63] Finally, "in order to give eternity to his laws, he bound the citizens by an oath not to change anything in his laws before he returned. . . . Then he set out for Crete, and lived there as a perpetual exile, and when he was dying he ordered his bones to be thrown into the sea, lest, if they were taken home, the Spartans might think that they were released from the obligation of their oath and might abrogate his laws."[64]

I use these examples more freely, because I find that the apostle Paul made use of them when he preached to the Athenians.[65] The illustrious preacher strove to impress "Jesus Christ, and him crucified"[66] on their minds in such a way that he might teach them, by the example of the Gentiles, that the deliverance of many had come about through the shame of the cross. But he also convinced them that these things came about only by the blood of the just and of those who carried on the magistracy of the people. Besides, no one could be found who was sufficient for the deliverance of all—namely, of Jews and Gentiles—save him to whom the Gentiles were given for an inheritance and for whose possession the whole earth was fore-

---

[59] Justinus, *Hist. Philip.*, II, 6:16–21 (Delphin Classics ed., London, 1822, I, 83 f.); quotation practically verbatim.
[60] *Ibid.*, III, 2:9 (p. 106).
[61] *Ibid.*, III, 2:12 (p. 106; reads "*as* the source").
[62] Cf. *ibid.*, III, 3:2 (p. 106).
[63] Cf. *ibid.*, III, 3:7–9 (p. 107).
[64] *Ibid.*, III, 11 f. (pp. 107 f.).
[65] Cf. *Acta Pauli*, in M. R. James, *The Apocryphal New Testament* (Oxford, 1926), 299; *Acta* of Dionysius the Areopagite, in *Acta Sanctorum*, October, Vol 4, 704; Richard of St. Victor, *De verbo incarn.*, 13 (*PL*, 196, 1007).
[66] I Cor. 2:2. For the description of Saint Paul as *praedicator egregius*, cf. Gregory the Great, *Epist.* 5, 40 (*PL*, 77, 767).

ordained.[67] Now he affirmed that this could only be the Son of Almighty God, since apart from God no one has subdued all nations and lands. Therefore, while he preached the shame of the cross, so that little by little the folly of the Gentiles should be made void, he gradually lifted up the word of faith and the language of his preaching to the word of God and the wisdom of God and even to the very throne of the divine Majesty, and, lest the power of the gospel should become worthless through the weakness of the flesh, because of the stumbling block of the Jews and the folly of the Gentiles,[68] he expounded the works of the Crucified, which were also supported by the testimony of public opinion, since it was agreed by all that God alone could do these things. But because public opinion often tells many lies on both sides, he assisted opinion itself, because his disciples did greater things,[69] as, for instance, when the sick were healed from any sickness whatever by the shadow of a disciple.[70] But why many things? He overthrew the subtleties of Aristotle, the acuteness of Chrysippus, and the snares of all the philosophers,[71] when he rose from the dead.

It is in everyone's mouth that the Decii, Roman commanders, devoted themselves for their armies.[72] Julius Caesar also said: "A commander who does not try to be esteemed by his soldiers does not know how to arm a soldier, does not know that the humanity of a general in an army tells against the enemy."[73] Caesar never said to his soldiers, "Go thither," but always said, "Come," for he used to say that labor shared with the commander seems less to soldiers. Moreover, according to the same author, bodily pleasure is to be avoided, for he used to say that men's bodies are wounded by swords in war, by pleasures in peace. For the conqueror of the nations had thought that pleasure could most easily be overcome by flight, because he who had subdued the nations was tied up in the coils of Venus by a shameless woman.[74]

---

67 Cf. Ps. 2:8.
68 Cf. I Cor. 1:23.
69 Cf. John 14:12.
70 Cf. Acts 5:15.
71 Cf. Jerome, *Epist.* 57, 12 (*CSEL*, 54, 526).
72 Cf. Augustine, *De civ. dei*, IV, 20 (*CSEL*, 40/1, 187).
73 Cf. Caecilius Balbus, *De nugis philosophorum* (ed. E. Wölfflin, Basel, 1855), 32.
74 *Scil.*, Cleopatra.

CHAPTER IV

THAT IT IS CERTAIN, BY THE AUTHORITY OF DIVINE LAW, THAT THE PRINCE IS SUBJECT TO THE LAW OF JUSTICE

But why do I appeal to examples borrowed from the Gentiles, even though they are so numerous, when anyone can be urged more suitably by laws than by examples to do what must be done? But lest you suppose that the prince himself is wholly free from laws, listen to the law which the "great king over all the earth,"[75] who is "terrible" and "who taketh away the spirit of princes,"[76] imposes on princes. "When thou art come," he says,[77] "into the land, which the Lord God will give thee, and possessest it, and shalt say: 'I will set a king over me, as all nations have that are round about'; thou shalt set him whom the Lord thy God shall choose out of the number of thy brethren. Thou mayest not make a man of another nation king, that is not thy brother. And when he is made king, he shall not multiply horses to himself, nor lead back the people into Egypt, being lifted up with the number of his horsemen, especially since the Lord hath commanded you to return no more the same way. He shall not have many wives, that may take possession of his mind,[78] nor immense sums of gold and silver. But after he is raised to the throne of his kingdom, he shall copy out to himself the Deuteronomy[79] of this law in a volume, taking the copy of the priests of the Levitical tribe, and he shall have it with him, and shall read it all the days of his life, that he may learn to fear the Lord his God, and keep his words and ceremonies, that are commanded in the law. And that his heart be not lifted up with pride over his brethren, nor decline to the right or to the left, that he and his son[80] may reign a long time over Israel." I ask, is he bound by no law, whom that law restrains? Certainly this is a divine law, and cannot be relaxed with impunity. If they are prudent, each of its words is thunder in the ears of princes. I say nothing of the election and the form required in the creation of a prince; consider with me for a little while the rule of living which is prescribed for him. When, it reads, he who professes himself to be the brother of the whole people by religious worship and

---

[75] Ps. 46:3 (P.B.V., 47:2).   [76] Ps. 75:12 f. (P.B.V., 76:11 f.)
[77] Deut. 17:14–20.   [78] Vulgate, "allure."
[79] So the Vulgate, transliterated from LXX.
[80] Vulgate, "sons."

charitable affection is set up, he shall not multiply horses to himself, since a large number of these would make him oppressive to his subjects. Now to multiply horses means to gather together more horses than necessity requires, for the sake of vainglory or some other fault. For "much" and "little", if we follow the chief of the Peripatetics,[81] refer to the decrease or excess of legitimate quantity in particular genera of things. Will he, then, be permitted to multiply dogs or birds of prey or savage beasts or any natural monsters whatever, when he is told that the number of horses—which are necessary for warfare and the requirements of the whole of life—must be of a legitimate quantity? There was no need for mention to be made in the law of actors and mimes, jesters and prostitutes, procurers and human monsters of this kind (which a prince ought to exterminate, and not to foster); indeed, the law does not simply exclude all these abominations from the prince's court, but also turns them out of the people of God. By the term "horses" we are to understand the necessary use of a complete household and all its equipment; whatever amount of this a concern for necessity or utility demands is legitimate. The useful and the virtuous[82] must, however, be equated, and government be chosen by the virtuous. For already in ancient times it was the view of the philosophers[83] that no opinion was more pernicious than the opinion of those who separate the useful from the virtuous, and that the truest and most beneficial judgment was that the virtuous and the useful are altogether convertible. Plato, as the histories of the Gentiles relate,[84] when he had seen Dionysius, the tyrant of Sicily, surrounded by his bodyguards, said, "What great evil have you done, that you need so many to guard you?" This certainly is unnecessary for a prince, who so attaches the affections of all to himself by his

---

81 The closest approximation to this statement in a work accessible to John of Salisbury is found in Aristotle, *Categ.*, 6 (5ᵇ15–29). It seems certain enough that he could not have read *Metaphysica*, X, 6 (1056ᵇ17–19).

82 On the useful (*utile*) and the virtuous (*honestum*), cf. R. J. Deferrari and M. I. Barry, *A Lexicon of St. Thomas Aquinas* (Catholic University of America, Washington, 1948), 120: "*Bonum honestum*, that good which is fitting, or decent, or strictly in accordance with the nature which seeks it for itself, not as a means to some further good, as opposed to *bonum utile*." The distinction, as John indicates, is classical: cf. Quintilian, *De instit.*, III, 8:13.

83 Cf. Cicero, *De offic.*, III, 3:11 (Loeb Classical Library ed. [Heinemann, London, 1928], 314 ff.).

84 Cf. Caecilius Balbus, *De nugis philos.*, 32.

services that any subject will risk his head for him when dangers threaten, since at the urging of nature the members are wont to risk themselves for the head, and "skin for skin and all that a man hath he will" lay down "for his life."[85]

The text [of Deuteronomy] goes on: "Nor lead back the people into Egypt, being lifted up with the number of his horsemen."[86] For everyone who is set in a high place is to exercise the greatest diligence, lest he corrupt his inferiors by his example and his misuse of things, and by way of pride or luxury lead back the people to the darkness of confusion. For it often happens that subjects imitate the vices of their superiors, because the people strive to be conformed to the magistrate, and each and every one readily desires that in which he sees that another is distinguished. There is a celebrated passage of the distinguished poet, in which he states the thoughts and words of Theodosius the Great:

"If you order and decree anything to be held in common,
First submit to what is ordered; then the people becomes
More observant of the right, nor does it refuse to accept it,
When it sees the lawgiver himself obey it. The nation
Is ordered by the king's example, nor can ordinances
Affect human inclinations as does the life of a ruler.
The inconstant multitude always changes with the prince."[87]

Now the means of individuals are far from equal to the resources of all. Each man dips into his own coffers, but the ruler draws on the public chest or treasury; if this by any chance fails, recourse is had to the means of individuals. But it is necessary for each private person to be satisfied with his own. If these prove to have been reduced, he who just now desired the ruler's renown is ashamed of the obscurity of his own disorder, mean as he is in his poverty. On this account thrift in the use of public goods was imposed by decree on the rulers of the Spartans, even though it is permissible by common right to make use of an inheritance or of something acquired by good fortune.

---

[85] Job. 2:4.   [86] Deut. 17:16.
[87] Claudian, De IV° cons. Honorii, 11. 296–302 (Loeb Classical Library ed. [London, 1922], I, 308).

Anselm of Laon: A Fragment on Original Sin

THE TEXT

If, as the apostle declares, many sons were to be brought to glory[1] this had to come about by the propagation of the human race. From the beginning, therefore, the good Creator made men so that they should in truth be good fathers of the flesh, while he himself was the good Creator of spirits.[2] While man retained the natural power of generation, he turned this quality of goodness into corruption by his sin, and thus could beget nothing but corruption from the corrupt mass.[3] Look, we see that the flesh itself is entirely corrupted from the fault of men. But when man, while he retained the natural power of generation, lost the quality of goodness, God the Creator both retained his own natural power of propagating souls and did not change his quality of goodness by which he made good men.

---

[1] Cf. Heb. 2:10.

[2] On the general acceptance of the "creationist" as opposed to the "traducianist" doctrine of the soul's origin, see O. Lottin, *Psychologie et morale aux XIIe et XIIIe siècles*, Vol. I, Pt. 3:1 (Abbaye du Mont César, Louvain, 1954), 57: "If the child's soul was derived from the soul of its parents, and thus from Adam's soul, the question would involve no difficulty: sin, an affair of the soul, would be transmitted directly from soul to soul. However, in spite of this advantage, the traducianist solution met with lively opposition in the bosom of the school [of Laon]: the soul of each child is created by God." Cf. the fragment from the MS, Brit. Mus. Arundel 360, fol. 62 recto, given by Lottin in *Recherches de théologie ancienne et médiévale*, 11 (1939), 256: "There have been four opinions concerning the soul: that other souls were propagated from the soul of the first man; that they are newly made for individuals; that they exist somewhere, and either are divinely sent or else freely fall into bodies. The fifth opinion had to do with the soul's nature. But it is certain that God makes individual souls for individuals."

[3] On the *corrupta massa*, cf. p. 106, n.13, above.

So, then, it is by man's fault, and not by God's, that the un-corrupt thing is profaned by its connection with a corrupt thing. If God were to withdraw souls from this connection—however corrupt it may be—he would cut us off from the law of his bounty concerning the propagation and salvation of the human race.

Ask yourself, however, whether souls can be affected by this connection. In fact, the unlimited goodness of God prescribed for itself a certain immutable law with respect to the salvation of men. According to this, he created rational spirits and set them in bodies, so that, by ruling the body and subjecting it to itself in obedience to God, the soul itself might in due time be made blessed with the body in God. Furthermore, such a union brings with it a great kinship between the two, so that, just as the body derives its life from the soul, the soul derives from the body the power of sense by which it can become incarnate. Thus one thing is wonderfully made from the two[4] and the soul naturally possesses such a great love for the body that it is frightened beyond measure at the thought of separa-tion from it. For this is the cause of bodily affliction[5]; this rightly exists with the body of condemnation, not only in adults but also in infants. And, to put it briefly, if anyone considers these two things—God's loving-kindness, which it was not right to bring to an end, in propagating the human race, and the fact that it was proper for the soul to possess the power of sense—he will find it easy to solve this question, which bothers so many people.

---

[4] Note the care with which the author seeks to do justice to the "duality" of soul and body, without falling into an unchristian "dualism."
[5] Reading *afflictionis*, with Brit. Mus. Arundel 360, fol. 62 recto.

The School of Anselm of Laon: A Question on Original Sin

THE TEXT

The next question has to do with the child who is born of ancestors who were purified in baptism from original sin and are all holy,[1] and who dies unbaptized before he comes to years of discretion.[2] Does he justly contract original sin, and is he justly punished for it?

Some usually answer the question in this way. Although his parents are clean from original sin and are holy people, nevertheless their son is involved in original sin. Augustine proves the point by these comparisons, in *On the Baptism of Young Children,* Book III[3]: "In the way in which the foreskin, after being removed by circumcision, remains in those who are begotten by the circumcised, and in the way in which the chaff, which is winnowed off so carefully by human labor, remains in the fruit which springs from the winnowed wheat—in this way the sin, which is cleansed by baptism, remains in those whom the baptized beget." Again, Augustine says, in *On Marriage and Concupiscence,* Book I[4]: "Just as a wild olive grows out of the seed of the wild olive, and at the same time nothing but a wild olive springs from the seed of the true olive, despite the very great difference between the wild olive and the olive, so what is born in the flesh, either of a sinner or of a just man, is in either

---

[1] Cf. I Cor. 7:14.
[2] Literally, "time of discretion," i.e., the age at which the child learns to distinguish (*discernere*) between good and evil (conventionally fixed at seven years).
[3] Augustine, *De pecc. mer.,* III, 8:16 (*CSEL,* 60, 142).
[4] Augustine, *De nupt. et concup.,* I, 19:21 (*CSEL,* 42, 234). The whole work is important for the understanding of the medieval discussion of original sin. There is an English translation in *Nicene and Post-Nicene Fathers,* 1st ser., Vol. V (New York, 1887), 257–308.

case a sinner . . . He is no sinner in act, when he is begotten, and is still new from his birth, but in guilt he is old. Made a man by his Creator, he is a captive of the deceiver, and needs a redeemer."

According to this answer, the little boy mentioned above is bound by original sin. But this was not in doubt. The question at issue, which is still unsolved, is this: By what justice is he bound by original sin, when his parents were clean from it? But Augustine, in the reply given above, solves this other problem presented to him by the Pelagians: If baptism cleanses from the ancient offense, those who are born of two baptized persons should be free from this sin, for such persons could not transmit to posterity what they did not possess at all.

Others want to solve the problem in this way. The parents in question were born spiritually, and by this generation they are clean from sin and just.[5] They were also begotten carnally, and by this generation they were conceived in sin.[6] Now they do not beget carnal sons by reason of spiritual generation, but by the movement of concupiscence which is in the flesh which they possess by carnal generation. Thus, although they are clean from sin by spiritual generation, and do not beget sinful sons by the latter, nevertheless they beget sons in sin by carnal generation. See Augustine, On Baptism, Book II[7]: "In vain some of them argue in this way: If a sinner has begotten a sinner, a just man likewise ought to have begotten a just man— as if anyone begat carnally because he was just, and not because he is moved in his members by concupiscence. For he begets because he still retains the old man, not because he has been advanced to newness among the children of God." And a little further on[8]: "In so far as they are children of God, they do not beget carnally, because it is of the Spirit, and not of the flesh that they themselves are begotten."

But the same question still remains, namely, on what ground pure and holy parents, by carnal generation, bring sin and condemnation on their children.

Consequently, the following reply is given. Although those parents are holy, they beget children in the sin of concupiscence, as David testifies,[9] and therefore a child begotten by them contracts original sin, and is to be punished for that sin.

---

[5] Cf. John 3:5 f.; I Cor. 6:11.   [6] Cf. Ps. 50:7 (P.B.V., 51:5).
[7] Augustine, De pecc. mer., II, 9:11 (CSEL, 60, 82); quotation abbreviated by the author.
[8] Ibid.   [9] Cf. Ps. 50:7 (P.B.V., 51:5).

This solution also can be countered in this way. They do beget in the sin of pleasure, but it is forgiven them, and they are purified from it by marriage, which God ordained,[10] and by the good of marriage.[11] Thus their son should not contract from them the sin of concupiscence, or original sin, from which they have been cleansed. See Augustine, *On Genesis as to the Letter*, Book IX[12]: "Therefore the weakness of both sexes, inclined though it is to fall into foulness, is duly rescued by the honorable state of marriage, so that what could be a duty for the whole is a remedy for the sick. Nor does it follow, because incontinence is an evil, that marriage, even when it unites the incontinent, is not a good; rather, ... because of this good, that evil is venial."

But still, in the judgment of the saints,[13] those who are brought forth in carnal concupiscence contract original sin, and so the reason for this view should be examined. The whole man—that is, both the flesh which is separated from the mass, and the mass from which it is divided—is possessed by the heat of dishonor before the separation of the seed. Moreover, the separation takes place in that impure heat, and when the separation has taken place the sin (that is, that impure action) is consummated. Now that sin, which was common to the separated part and to the parents from whom it was divided, is forgiven the parents because of marriage and the good of marriage which is in them. It is not pardoned, however, on account of the good of marriage, in the case of the particle which goes to produce another person, because that good is not to be found in it, nor is it pardoned by means of another remedy before baptism. Thus that particle possesses the sin of concupiscence, and by its means acquires and reaches original sin. See Augustine, in the *Enchiridion*[14]: "Having sinned, he was banished from that place." See also his statement in the book *On Marriage and Concupiscence*, addressed to Valerius, the chief of the soldiers[15]: "Because of this concupiscence of the flesh, what is born ..."

---

10 Cf. Mark 10:6–9.
11 On the "natural good of marriage," cf. Augustine, *De nupt. et concup.*, I, 4:5 (*CSEL*, 42, 215): "The union of male and female for the purpose of procreation."
12 Augustine, *De Gen. ad lit.*, IX, 7 (*CSEL*, 28, 275).
13 On the *sancti*, cf. p. 159, n. 34, above.
14 Augustine, *Enchir.*, 8:26 (*PL*, 40, 245). This and the following quotation are not given in full in Lottin's text, from which this translation is made.
15 Augustine, *De nupt. et concup.*, I, 18:21 (*CSEL*, 42, 233).

But an objection can be stated once more. The little piece of flesh which was separated either has always been animated, or was at one time inanimate. Now at any time when it is inanimate, it does not have sin, but it does not have sin when the soul is joined to it, because the latter was created pure, nor is the union of soul and flesh a sin, since it is God's work. Therefore, any little child, no matter who, seems to be wholly without sin.

The solution is this: the dead body of a murderer does not commit murder when it is dead, but because it perpetrated it while it was alive, even in its inanimate state it is bound by the guilt of murder, since it deserves to be punished for it, and will be punished when it is restored to the soul. When he is alive, too, a man is called a murderer, not because he is committing the act, but because he has committed it. In the same way, we should understand that inanimate flesh is not sinful in act, but that nevertheless it is bound by the guilt of sin and is said to have sin, because when it was animated[16] it performed the act for which it deserves to be punished and not to possess glory.

16 I.e., in the parents.

The School of Anselm of Laon: The Gloss on I Corinthians, Chapter 15

THE TEXT

"By which also you are saved."[1] If you keep that gospel, that is, the resurrection of the dead, on the ground on which I established it for you, namely, because of the resurrection of Christ. "Unless you have believed in vain." This means, if you do not hold to the resurrection of the dead. The faith which is not received in the hope of resurrection is to no purpose.[2]

"He rose again the third day."[3] And this I said according to the Scriptures. For Hosea says[4]: "He will revive us after two days, and on the third day we shall rise again in his sight." If, though dead and buried, he rose again, do not doubt that those who are dead and buried rise again.

"He was seen by Cephas."[5] Before the other *men* to whom, as we read in the gospel, he appeared; otherwise this would be contrary to the statement that he appeared first to the women.[6]

---

[1] I Cor. 15:2.
[2] Cf. Hervaeus of Bourg-Dieu, *in loc.* (*PL*, 181, 972); Peter Lombard, *in loc.* (*PL*, 191, 1674). On the role of Hervaeus in medieval exegesis, cf. A. M. Landgraf, "Der Paulinenkommentar des Hervaeus von Bourg-Dieu," *Biblica*, 21 (1940), 113–132. On Lombard's "gloss," cf. Landgraf, *Einführung*, 93 f.
[3] I Cor. 15:4.
[4] Hos. 6:3(2). (Not quoted according to Vulg.) The first instance of the use of this text in Latin theology seems to be Tertullian, *Adv. Iud.*, 13 (*CSEL*, 70, 321). Cf. Ambrosiaster, *in loc.* (*PL*, 17, 275); Thomas Aquinas, *in loc.* (Parma edit., XIII, 278).
[5] I Cor. 15:5.
[6] Cf. Pseudo-Primasius, *in loc.* (*PL*, 68, 543); Atto of Vercelli, *in loc.* (*PL*, 134, 396). The commentary of "Pseudo-Primasius" is really a reworking of Pelagius by a pupil of Cassiodorus; cf. E. Dekkers and A. Gaar, *Clavis patrum latinorum* (Abbey of St. Peter, Steenbrugge, 1951), 157.

"One born out of due time."[7] He is called "one born out of due time" because he was born out of lawful time, that is, before (or even after) he ought,[8] and later, being reborn, he received the apostolate, Christ having already been taken up.[9] Or I am "one born out of due time" because I am certainly the last in time and calling, if not in worthiness, labor, and preaching. In fact, he says this on account of humility, and proves it by saying, "I am not worthy."[10] Why, then, is he an apostle? "But by the grace of God."[11] At first, by grace alone, since only demerits went before his calling. But afterward, merits begin through grace.

"More abundantly."[12] This was realized more fully, because he lived by the work of his hands, and yet did not do less for the gospel.[13] And lest we should think that the will is able to do anything without God's grace, he adds, "Not I, but the grace," etc.

"And so you have believed."[14] He chides them because, although this faith was manifest to all the churches, they still departed from it.[15]

"And if Christ."[16] Up to now he has been showing that Christ is risen. Now, by his resurrection, he proves the resurrection of the dead. There were false apostles who denied that Christ had truly suffered, or been buried, or had risen again, or had even come in the flesh.[17]

"And we are found."[18] These and other things are brought in, so that the Corinthians may be ashamed of following the error of false apostles. These absurd things, which he also condemns, follow from their error. Therefore, lest they remain

---

[7] I Cor. 15:8.
[8] Cf. Haymo of Auxerre (not Haymo of Halberstadt), *in loc.* (*PL*, 117, 594).
[9] Cf. Ambrosiaster, *in loc.* (*PL*, 17, 276); Rabanus Maurus, *in loc.* (*PL*, 112, 138); Pseudo-Bruno the Carthusian, *in loc.* (*PL*, 153, 205). On the "Pseudo-Bruno," cf. Landgraf, *Einführung*, 53 f.; A. M. Landgraf, "Untersuchungen zu den Paulinenkommentaren des 12. Jahrhunderts," *Recherches de théologie ancienne et médiévale*, 8 (1936), 253–281); 345–368. He is perhaps to be identified with Anselm's brother, Radulphus of Laon.
[10] I Cor. 15:9.
[11] I Cor. 15:10.
[12] *Ibid.*
[13] Cf. Haymo, *in loc.* (*PL*, 117, 595).
[14] I Cor. 15:11.
[15] Cf. Rabanus, *in loc.* (*PL*, 112, 141); Hervaeus, *in loc.* (*PL*, 181, 976).
[16] I Cor. 15:14.
[17] Cf. Peter Lombard, *in loc.* (*PL*, 191, 1676 f.).
[18] I Cor. 15:15.

in this error, he says, "We are found," etc. "Against God." It is probably a greater (rather than a lesser) enormity to commend falsehood in God than to disparage his truth.[19]

"And if Christ be not," etc.[20] If Christ is not risen, Christ is held in death, and if in death, then in sin also, since sin is the cause of death. And if he is held in sin, he has not been able to remit your sins. And so you are still in your sins, which you believed had been remitted to you, and therefore your faith is vain.[21]

"For by a man."[22] Here are the beginnings, man and man, a man for life and a man for death. But the latter is just a man, while the former is God and man.

"And as."[23] By "as" is signified the likeness and cause, because as the corruption of Adam leads to death, so the Spirit of Christ leads to life.

"But everyone."[24] He expounds the order as a matter of certainty—both the times when it has happened, and the times when it is to happen, that the dead should rise again.[25] "Then who are," or (according to another reading), "Then they who are of Christ, in his coming"; that is to say, they shall rise. Thus those who believe in Christ, and are less worthy than he, will rise later in time and with a lesser dignity. And he explains "who are of Christ," when he adds, "Who have believed in his coming."

"Afterwards the end."[26] He states this in order to commend the resurrection. When the latter is accomplished, the end of the world and the consummation of all things will come about.[27] "When he shall have brought to nought." As long as the world endures, angels are set over angels, demons over demons, men over men, for the benefit of the living, or even for their deception.[28] But when men are gathered, all rule will cease among angels and men, so that there will be no discord between rulers and subjects.[29] Then all will know that none of these earthly or heavenly powers possessed anything of themselves,[30] but that all was from Him from whom are all things.[31]

"For he must reign."[32] The sense is: His reign must be manifested until at length all his enemies acknowledge that he

19 Cf. Hervaeus, in loc. (PL, 181, 977).
20 I Cor. 15:17.
21 Cf. Hervaeus, loc. cit.
22 I Cor. 15:21.
23 I Cor. 15:22.
24 I Cor. 15:23.
25 Cf. Ambrosiaster, in loc. (PL, 17, 278).
26 I Cor. 15:24.
27 Cf. Peter Lombard, in loc. (PL, 191, 1678).
28 Ibid. (col. 1679).
29 Cf. Haymo, in loc. (PL, 117, 597).
30 Cf. Rom. 13:1.
31 Cf. Ambrosiaster, in loc. (PL, 17, 280).
32 I Cor. 15:25.

reigns.[33] By saying, "Until," he excludes a greater manifestation, not a fuller continuation of his reign. Thus it appears elsewhere: "So are our eyes unto the Lord our God, until he have mercy."[34] The point is, not that they then turn away, but that they seek nothing more.

"Now the last."[35] Among other things, it is obvious that Christ has the power of raising men up, when the apostle adds, "The enemy death shall be destroyed last." Christ reigns now, and he shall reign then, but death will be destroyed last of all, that is, after all things, because men shall no longer be dissolved, as heretics think.[36] "Last of all," because there will be nothing that destroys after this mortal puts on immortality. "Enemy," to which we are hostile (or perhaps which is hostile to us). Another commendation of the resurrection.

"He is excepted, who put all things under him."[37] Since he has no source, he can on no account be subject to anything, for he is the beginning of all things.

"That God may be all in all."[38] Since every creature confesses that Christ is its head, and the head of Christ is God,[39] not only will there be one God in all things, that is, in the confession of all, but every creature will also confess that it is he from whom all things come.[40] "That God may be." He is the end whom the apostle affirmed many times in his argument above; afterward he explains piecemeal what the consummation is to be. "All" that can be desired. "In all" his members, because he who gave virtue will be the reward of virtue, since God will be the source of their satisfaction.[41]

"For the dead."[42] That is, for the remission of sins. Or else, for making themselves dead in the likeness of Christ's death; but why shall they do it, when they are not going to have life[43]? "If not at all." So that Christ is not risen; then why are they baptized, although sins are not remitted if Christ is not risen?

"For your glory."[44] Or, "By your glory." Here the apostle swears, so that we should know that it is not sinful to swear to the truth. This does not mean, however, that we are to swear in doubtful matters, and it is safer not to swear than to perjure oneself because one is accustomed to swearing. For to swear

[33] Cf. Peter Lombard, *in loc.* (*PL*, 191, 1680).
[34] Ps. 122:2 (P.B.V., 123:2).
[36] Cf. Hervaeus, *in loc.* (*PL*, 181, 982).
[38] I Cor. 15:28.
[40] Cf. Ambrosiaster, *in loc.* (*PL*, 17, 280).
[41] Cf. Peter Lombard, *in loc.* (*PL*, 191, 1681).
[43] Cf. Lanfranc, *in loc.* (*PL*, 150, 210).

[35] I Cor. 15:26.
[37] I Cor. 15:27.
[39] Cf. I Cor. 11:3.
[42] I Cor. 15:29.
[44] I Cor. 15:31.

to falsehood is a very grave sin. Yet swearing is not against the commandment, when it is not a matter of evil in him who swears, but of help for the incredulous or weak, who otherwise would not believe.

"If according to man."[45] That is, in fighting (namely, disputing) I acted rationally, because it is proper to man to believe that man does not die like a beast.[46] "Let us eat and drink, for tomorrow we shall die." He says this for the sake of those who, like cattle, are concerned only for the body, as if there were nothing to come after death, and who ask: "Who comes from there? I have not heard the voice of anyone coming from there." To these he says: You fool, would you believe it, if your father rose? The Lord of all is risen, and you do not believe. He willed to die and to rise up, that we all might believe one man, lest we be deceived by many. You would believe your father, who is going to die again, and you do not believe Him who is now immortal, who in fact has testimony in heaven,[47] testimony on earth,[48] testimony from angels,[49] testimony from the lower regions.[50]

"Be not seduced,"[51] by an impostor, for these look for a wound from medicine, and endeavor to twist a rope from the Scriptures, so that with it they may lay a deadly snare.[52] "Corrupt good manners." "Here he called good the trifling ones who are easily deceived."[53]

"Awake."[54] Do not wish for that, but awake from the body, and so you will be "just." And then he says, "Sin not" by consenting to them, because they do not know God.

"But some man will say."[55] So far, he has been proving the resurrection of the dead by reasoning; now he proves from the nature of things that it can be done. It is as if he said: It is proved by these reasons, but nevertheless some depraved person could speak as if the resurrection of the dead were impossible for nature. And if they rise, "with what manner of body?" They ask this as if they meant: It cannot be different from its present state of passibility and mortality. The apostle

---

[45] I Cor. 15:32.
[46] Cf. Pseudo-Bruno, *in loc. (PL,* 153, 209); Peter Lombard, *in loc. (PL,* 191, 1683).
[47] Cf. John 5:36 f.   [48] Cf. I John 5:5 ff.
[49] Cf. I Tim. 3:16; Luke 2:9–14.
[50] Cf. Eph. 4:9.   [51] I Cor. 15:33.
[52] Cf. Peter Lombard, *in loc. (PL,* 191, 1684).
[53] Theodoret, *in loc. (PG,* 82, 361).
[54] I Cor. 15:34.   [55] I Cor. 15:35.

replies, "Senseless man."[56] He calls him "senseless" because he does not pay attention to what he sees every day in the grain.

"Senseless man, that which thou sowest." So the dead will be able to live, and that in a better body, just as what you sow rises in a better state.[57]

"But God giveth it."[58] Therefore, just as bare grain is sown, and by God's command rises again, clothed in some way, and greatly increased, so by God's power the dead will be able to live, and to rise again with a better body.[59] "To every seed." So also he will reshape our former bodies, as Job says: "Whom I myself shall see, . . . and not another."[60] But there will be a difference in glory and nobility, even though they are of the same nature. For not all flesh is of the same nobility, although it is made of the same elements,[61] and this is what he is saying.

"The same flesh."[62] All flesh is body, but the converse does not hold; in the case of wood, for instance.[63]

"Celestial."[64] The bodies of those who rise again are heavenly; before they die, they are earthly, because they come from Adam. And because Christ is heavenly, they are called heavenly bodies, rather than flesh, on his account. But on account of Adam, because he is earthly, they are called earthly bodies.[65]

"For star differeth from star." etc.[66] "In my Father's house there are many mansions,"[67] although the same penny, namely, eternal life, is for all.[68] For the beatitude which the just receive is one, but the quality of their recompense is unequal.[69] But even though those who rise again are unequal in glory,

---

[56] I Cor. 15:36.
[57] Cf. Atto, *in loc.* (*PL*, 134, 404); Hervaeus, *in loc.* (*PL*, 181, 987).
[58] I Cor. 15:38.
[59] Cf. Peter Lombard, *in loc.* (*PL*, 191, 1685).
[60] Job 19:27.
[61] Cf. Hervaeus, *in loc.* (*PL*, 181, 987); Peter Lombard, *in loc.* (*PL*, 191, 1685 f.).
[62] I Cor. 15:39.
[63] Cf. Peter Lombard, *in loc.* (*PL*, 191, 1686).
[64] I Cor. 15:40.
[65] Cf. Ambrosiaster, *in loc.* (*PL*, 17, 283); Rabanus, *in loc.* (*PL*, 112, 151).
[66] I Cor. 15:41.
[67] John 14:2.
[68] Cf. Peter Lombard, *in loc.* (*PL*, 191, 1686); note the allusion to Matt. 20:1–16.
[69] Cf. Hervaeus, *in loc.* (*PL*, 181, 988).

God is all in all, because "God is charity,"[70] and charity brings about the common sharing of what individuals possess by all.

"It is sown."[71] That is to say, though a man is in a state of corruption from his conception until his dissolution, and afterward crawls with worms, nevertheless he will rise in incorruption.[72]

"A natural body."[73] That is to say, it derives nothing from the soul, beyond the fact that it is endued with sensation by it (as in the case of animals). "It shall rise a spiritual body," by being transformed into the nature of spirit, that is, by having certain spiritual qualities, since it will be quick and light and will not need food.[74] When he said that the body is to pass over into incorruption, he referred to corruption, so that the greater dignity of the resurrection might be shown. "If there be a natural body." It will, in truth, rise a spiritual body, since, if it now exists, it is natural. This implies that it certainly exists. At some time, it will be spiritual. For as we are animal because our fleshly father was made a living soul, in the resurrection we shall be spiritual, because in his resurrection our spiritual Father was made a quickening spirit.

"Man."[75] In some way these two men, the first and the second, are the whole human race, which is born of the first and reborn of the second. Christ is called "Adam," because he is of the same matter, and the "last Adam" because he is not to be succeeded by another man as head or founder of the human body.

"Yet that was not."[76] He has said that our bodies are to be spiritual, but lest anyone should doubt that the animal can be made spiritual, he proves it by the comparison with Christ, who, as he says, was made a quickening spirit. But in him "that was not first which is spiritual, but that which is natural; afterward the spiritual." The same thing will be able to take place in us.

"The first man."[77] The first man was in fact made a living soul, because, formed as he was of the dust, he was animal and passible by nature. "The second man," who is from heaven, because the divine nature has been united to human nature, will on that account be "heavenly," that is spiritual, in the resurrection, while, because the first father was "earthly," all

---

[70] I John 4:8.
[72] Cf. Hervaeus, in loc. (PL, 181, 988).
[74] Cf. Pseudo-Bruno, in loc. (PL, 153, 211).
[76] I Cor. 15:46.

[71] I Cor. 15:42.
[73] I Cor. 15:44.
[75] I Cor. 15:45.
[77] I Cor. 15:47.

are such. "Heavenly." Christ is said to be heavenly because he was conceived and born, not in human fashion, but by the divine will.[78]

"Now this I say."[79] The Jews believed in a resurrection to come, but it was to resemble our present life, so that they would marry and beget children. For this reason, some of them could not answer the Sadducees' question about the woman with seven husbands,[80] because the Sadducees were thinking of the resurrection in carnal terms. The apostle, however, removes this difficulty when he goes on to say, "That flesh." By "flesh and blood," he means the belly and sensual desire, or, in other words, the "works of the flesh,"[81] which will not be found there.[82] "Neither shall corruption possess incorruption." Lest you should think that his statement referred to the substance of flesh, he explained it further. He said, then, that flesh will not possess the Kingdom of God, because the corruption of mortality, to which the name of flesh is here given, will not possess incorruptibility.[83]

"We shall all indeed."[84] Or (according to Jerome, who asserts, in writing to Marcella, that those who are found alive will not die) all the dead shall rise again, and not all who are found alive shall be changed, but only the saints.[85]

"At the last."[86] That is to say, at the last sign that will be given these things may be fulfilled. This trumpet stands for the cry referred to in the text: "At midnight there was a cry made, Behold, the bridegroom cometh."[87] The word "trumpet" refers to some evident and striking sign,[88] which elsewhere is called "the voice of an archangel and . . . the trumpet of God."[89] In the Gospel it is called the voice which the dead who are in the

---

[78] Cf. John 1:13.
[79] I Cor. 15:50.
[80] Cf. Mark 12:18–25, and parallels.
[81] Gal. 5:19.
[82] Cf. Pseudo-Bruno, in loc. (PL, 153, 212).
[83] Cf. Lanfranc, in loc. (PL, 150, 213).
[84] I Cor. 15:51 (reading, with the Vulgate, "We shall all indeed rise again, but we shall not all be changed").
[85] Cf. Jerome, Epist. 59:3 (CSEL, 54, 543 f.); Pseudo-Primasius, in loc. (PL, 68, 552); Hervaeus, in loc. (PL, 181, 993).
[86] I Cor. 15:52.
[87] Matt. 25:6. Cf. Peter Lombard, in loc. (PL, 191, 1690).
[88] Cf. Hervaeus, loc. cit.
[89] I Thess. 4:15. Cf. Pseudo-Hugh of St. Victor, in loc. (PL, 175, 542). This commentary was written about 1160; cf. P. Glorieux, "Pour revaloriser Migne," Mélanges de science religieuse, 9 (1952), cahier supplémentaire, 67.

tombs shall hear, and when they hear it shall come forth.[90] "We shall be changed." He explains how this is to be done, or, indeed, what the change is like.

"Is swallowed up."[91] That is to say, it is destroyed in Christ's victory; or perhaps it means that it exceeded the limits of its conquests, when it attacked Christ[92]; or "death" may stand for the pleasure of sin consented to, which is conquered inasmuch as the servants of God will conquer the desires of their flesh.[93]

"O death, where is thy victory?"[94] These are words of the prophet[95] or of the apostle, rejoicing and taunting death, in the role of those who rise again, that the resurrection may appear more certain. He is saying: You have conquered in the dying, you are conquered in those who rise again.[96] The victory in which you had swallowed up the bodies of the dying was temporal, but that in which you were swallowed up in the bodies of those who rise again will endure eternally.

[90] Cf. John 5:28 f.
[91] I Cor. 15:54.
[92] Cf. Peter Lombard, in loc. (PL, 191, 1692).
[93] Cf. Rabanus, in loc. (PL, 112, 157).
[94] I Cor. 15:55.
[95] Cf. Hos. 13:14.
[96] Cf. Atto, in loc. (PL, 134, 408); Hervaeus, in loc. (PL, 181, 995).

Peter Abailard: Exposition of the Epistle to the Romans (An Excerpt from the Second Book)

THE TEXT

I

ON ROMANS 3:19–26

"Now we know . . ."[1] The apostle returns to his attack upon the Jews so that, as he has removed their boasting about circumcision, he may also remove it with respect to the law or external observances of any kind; for he fears, perchance, that he may appear to have commended the law too highly by his words, "First indeed because the words of God were committed to them."[2] So he first dismisses their boasting of the law by demonstrating that they have been censured rather than justified by the law.[3] Then he has marshaled evidences from the law—that is, from the Old Testament—through which he might build up a case that all are guilty, the Jews no less than the Gentiles.

But we know that the Jews are particularly censured by these evidences, for it is to them alone—though not about them only—that the law speaks, since it was to them alone that the law was given and charged. And this is what he says: "Now we know," etc., as if he were to declare: Although we have gathered out of the law very strong indictments of the Gentiles also, yet we know that the law was not spoken to them, for it had not been given to them, though it does concern them. "But to them only who are in the law."[4] That is, they are held chargeable to obey the law which they have received.

It should be noted that by the term "law" sometimes it is just the five books of Moses that are understood; at other times, the whole Old Testament, as in our present instance. So Saint Augustine, in the fifteenth book of his *On the Trinity*, says: "By the term 'law' sometimes all the oracles of God are referred

1 Rom. 3:19.   2 Rom. 3:2.
3 Cf. Rom. 2:13–25.   4 Cf. Rom. 3:19.

to, but at other times more accurately only the law which was given through Moses."5 "That" so "every mouth may be stopped."6 That the mouth may be restrained and quieted from any boasting of itself, and be opened only for the glorification of God, since we have learned, indeed, that even the very great glory of the particular people of God (which was theirs because of the law) is to be accounted as nothing—even though they thought themselves to be justified through the works of that law.

"And so [all the world may be] made subject."7 That is, let it humble itself before God, assuming that it has nothing of itself to boast about, since any supposed reason for self-gratulation has been removed even from those who appeared to be in high favor with God.

"Because by the works of the law"8—that is, by outward observances of the law to which that people gave studious attention, such as circumcision, sacrifices, keeping the Sabbath, and other symbolic ordinances of the same kind—"no flesh shall be justified in his sight"—that is, in God's sight. All such as fulfill the law merely according to the flesh and not according to the spirit will be accounted righteous in men's sight, perhaps—that is, according to human judgment which judges from outward and visible appearances—but not in God's.

"For by the law . . ."9 He relates two points to the two that have already been made: To the one where he says, "That every mouth may be stopped and all the world brought under the judgment of God," he links, "For through the law cometh the knowledge of sin." To that other utterance, "Because by the works of the law no flesh shall be justified before him," he joins the words, "But now without [the law the justice of God is made manifest]."10

So he connects his thoughts. It follows that men ought to be restrained from any self-gratulation by the law because through it they are rendered completely without excuse for their sins; by it their sins have become more recognizable rather than less—indeed, they have been increased—and farther on he is to declare the purpose of the law: "That sin . . . might become sinful above measure."11

---

5 Cf. Augustine, *De trin.*, XV, 18:30 (*PL*, 42, 1081).
6 Rom. 3:19.   7 *Ibid.*
8 Rom. 3:20.   9 *Ibid.*
10 Rom. 3:21.   11 Rom. 7:13.

"But now . . ."[12] I said that by particular works of the written law, that is, by those formal precepts of which natural law knows nothing, no one is justified in God's sight; but now, in this dispensation of grace, a righteousness[13] of God—something which God approves and by which we are justified in God's sight, namely love[14]—has been manifested, through the teaching of the gospel, of course, apart from the law with its external and particular requirements. Still, this is a "righteousness witnessed by the law and the prophets," who also enjoin it.

Upon what this righteousness depends he adds immediately by saying, "The justice of God."[15] He means the faith of Christ which we hold concerning him—either by believing him or by believing in him. And when he continued, "Them that believe," he did not specify anyone in particular, that it might be impartially extended over all.

By the faith which we hold concerning Christ love is increased in us, by virtue of the conviction that God in Christ has united our human nature to himself and, by suffering in that same nature, has demonstrated to us that perfection of love of which he himself says: "Greater love than this no man hath," etc.[16] So we, through his grace, are joined to him as closely as to our neighbor by an indissoluble bond of affection.[17] For this reason it is written further on: "Who then shall separate us from the love of God? Shall tribulation," etc.[18] And again, "For I am sure that neither death," etc.[19] A righteousness, I say, imparted to all the faithful in the higher part of their being—in the soul, where alone love[20] can exist—and not a matter of the display of outward works.

"For there is no distinction."[21] I said rightly over all without distinction—on the Gentiles assuredly as on the Jews—because there is no difference between them in this righteousness of God through faith in Christ, as there once was in connection with the works of the law. Just as all have sinned, so they are impartially justified by this manifestation of God's grace toward us. And this is what he says: "For all have sinned and do need the grace of God."[22] That is, they need, as a matter of obligation, to glorify the Lord.

---

12 Rom. 3:21.
13 *Iustitia*, as in the Vulgate.
14 *Caritas.*
15 Rom. 3:22.
16 John 15:13.
17 *Amor.*
18 Rom. 8:35; Vulgate: "love of Christ."
19 Rom. 8:38.
20 *Dilectio.*
21 Rom. 3:22.
22 Rom. 3:23; Vulgate reads "glory," not "grace."

"Being justified freely."[23] Freely, because they have been justified, not by any previous merits of their own, but by the grace of him—that is, God—who "first hath loved us."[24] What that grace really is—namely, a free and spiritual gift of God—he adds when he says, "Through our redemption accomplished by Christ whom God the Father set forth to be our propitiator,"[25] that is, our reconciler.

"In his blood." This means by his death; and since this propitiation is set forth and established by God, not for all but only for those who believe, he adds, "Through faith"; for this reconciliation affects them only who have believed it and hoped for it.

"To the showing of his justice"—that is, his love—which, as has been said, justifies us in his sight. In other words, to show forth his love to us, or to convince us how much we ought to love him who "spared not even his own Son"[26] for us.

"For the remission." That is to say that through this righteousness—which is love—we may gain remission of our sins, even as the Truth in person says concerning that blessed woman who was a sinner, "Many sins are forgiven her because she hath loved much."[27] I say that remission is granted, yes, even for past sins, "through the forbearance of God"[28]—because of the long-suffering of God, who does not summarily punish the guilty and condemn sinners, but waits a long time for them to return in penitence, and cease from sin, and so obtain forgiveness.

"For the showing . . ." First he had said simply for the showing of his righteousness; now he adds, "in this time" of grace—that is, of love[29] rather than of fear. And so when he speaks of his righteousness—that is, God's righteousness, in this time of grace, of course—he clearly intimates how he first understood this righteousness to be a love[30] which perfectly meets the needs of men of our time, which is the time of grace.

It is possible that the words, "Through the forbearance of God," should be taken with what follows, that is, with the clause, "For the showing of his justice in this time." So the sense may be that the Lord in this matter delayed or postponed his action in times past so that he might show forth his righteousness of which we have spoken—that is, his love—in this present

---

[23] Rom. 3:24 f.   [24] I John 4:19.
[25] The reading *propitiatorem* (rather than *propitiationem*) appears in the "Sixtine" Vulgate of 1590, but not in the "Clementine" editions.
[26] Rom. 8:32.   [27] Luke 7:47.
[28] Rom. 3:26.   [29] *Amor.*   [30] *Caritas.*

time. "That he himself may be just" in will, and "the justifier"
by his mighty act; that is, that he may both will to fulfill in
Christ what he had promised concerning our redemption or
justification, and as he has willed it, may complete it in deed.
"Of him who is of the faith of Jesus Christ." Namely, of him
who believes him to be Jesus, that is, Saviour, by virtue of what
Christ actually is—God and man.

II

A QUESTION

A most pressing problem obtrudes itself at this point, as to
what that redemption of ours through the death of Christ may
be, and in what way the apostle declares that we are justified
by his blood—we who appear to be worthy of still greater
punishment, seeing that we are the wicked servants who have
committed the very things for which our innocent Lord was
slain. And so it seems that we must first investigate why it was
necessary for God to take human nature upon him so that he
might redeem us by dying in the flesh;[31] and from what person
holding us captive, either justly or by fraud, he has redeemed
us; and by what standard of justice he has liberated us from the
dominion of that person who has given commands to which he
willingly submitted in order to set us free.[32]

Indeed, it is said that he has redeemed us from the dominion
of Satan; that it was Satan who (because the first man had
sinned and had yielded himself by voluntary obedience to him)
was exercising a total dominion over man; and that he would
always exercise the same unless a deliverer came. But since he
has delivered his elect only, when, either in this age or in the
age to come, did Satan or will Satan possess them more than
he does now? Did the devil torment that beggar who rested on
Abraham's bosom as he did Dives who is damned, although he
may have tortured him less? Or had he power even over
Abraham and the rest of the elect? When did that wicked
torturer have power over him who is described as being carried
by the angels into Abraham's bosom—concerning whom
Abraham himself pays testimony in the words, "But now he is
comforted and thou art tormented"?[33] Moreover, he declares
that a great gulf has been fixed between the elect and the
wicked so that the latter can never cross over to the former.

31 Cf. Anselm, *Cur deus homo*, I, i.   32 Cf. *ibid.*, I, 6.   33 Luke 16:25.

Still less may the devil, who is more evil than all, acquire any power in that place where no wicked person has a place or even entry.

And what right to possess mankind could the devil possibly have unless perhaps he had received man for purposes of torture through the express permission, or even the assignment, of the Lord? For if any slave wanted to forsake his lord and put himself under the authority of another master, would he be allowed to act in such a way that his lord could not lawfully seek him out and bring him back, if he wanted to? Who indeed doubts that, if a slave of any master seduces his fellow slave by subtle suggestions and makes him depart from obedience to his true master, the seducer is looked upon by the slave's master as much more guilty than the seduced? And how unjust it would be that he who seduced the other should deserve, as a result, to have any special right or authority over him! And even if such a fellow had previously had any right over him, would he not deserve to lose that right? It is written, forsooth, "He who abuses authority committed to him deserves to lose any special rights."[34] Where one slave was about to be set over the other and receive authority over him, it would never do for the more evil one who had absolutely no justification for preferment to be promoted; but it would be much more reasonable that the person who was seduced should possess a full claim for redress over the man who had caused the harm by his act of seduction. Furthermore, the devil could not grant that immortality which he promised man as a reward of transgression in the hope that in this way he might hold him fast by some sort of right.

And so from these reasonings it seems proved that the devil acquired no right against man whom he seduced simply by seducing him, except perhaps (as we said before) in so far as it was a case of the Lord's permitting it—by handing man over to the wretch who was to act as his jailer or torturer for punishment. For man had not sinned except against his own Lord, whose obedience he had forsaken. If, then, his Lord wanted to remit the sin, as was done to the Virgin Mary,[35] and as Christ also did for many others before he underwent his Passion—as it is reported of Mary Magdalene,[36] and as it is

---

[34] I have not been able to identify this quotation.
[35] This does not necessarily imply (but may seem rather to exclude) the immaculate conception of Mary.
[36] Cf. Luke 7:47; according to the tradition of the Western Church, Abailard identifies the sinful woman with Mary Magdalene.

recorded that the Lord said to the paralytic, "Be of good heart, son, thy sins are forgiven thee"[37]—if, I say, the Lord was willing to pardon sinful man apart from his Passion, and to say to his tormentor, "Do not punish him any further," how could the tormentor justly continue to torment him? For, as has been shown, he had received no absolute right of torture, but only such as came from express permission of the Lord.

So, if the Lord should cease to grant this permission, no right whatever would be left to the tormentor, and, if he should complain or murmur against the Lord, it would be quite appropriate for the Lord to reply, "Is thine eye evil because I am good?"[38] The Lord inflicted no loss upon the devil when, from sinning humanity,[39] he took upon himself pure flesh, and manhood free from all sin. Indeed, as man, he did not by his own merits ensure that he should be conceived, be born, and continue throughout his life without sin, but received this through the grace of the Lord upholding him. If, by the same grace, he wished to forgive sins to other men, could he not have delivered them from punishment? Assuredly, once the sins for which they were undergoing punishment have been forgiven, there appears to remain no reason why they should be any longer punished for them. Could not he, who showed such loving-kindness to man that he united him to his very self, extend to him a lesser boon by forgiving his sins?

So what compulsion, or reason, or need was there—seeing that by its very appearing alone the divine pity could deliver man from Satan—what need was there, I say, that the Son of God, for our redemption, should take upon him our flesh and endure such numerous fastings, insults, scourgings and spittings, and finally that most bitter and disgraceful death upon the cross, enduring even the cross of punishment with the wicked? In what way does the apostle declare that we are justified or reconciled to God through the death of his Son,[40] when God ought to have been the more angered against man, inasmuch as men acted more criminally by crucifying his Son than they ever did by transgressing his first command in paradise through the tasting of a single apple? For the more men's sins were multiplied, the more just it would have been for God to be angry with men. And if that sin of Adam was so great that it could be expiated only by the death of Christ, what expiation will avail for that act of murder committed against Christ, and for the

---

[37] Matt. 9:2.
[39] De massa peccatrice; cf. p. 106, n. 13.

[38] Matt. 20:15.
[40] Cf. Rom. 5:10.

many great crimes committed against him or his followers? How did the death of his innocent Son so please God the Father that through it he should be reconciled to us—to us who by our sinful acts have done the very things for which our innocent Lord was put to death? Had not this very great sin been committed, could he not have pardoned the former much lighter sin? Had not evil deeds been multiplied, could he not have done such a good thing for man?

In what manner have we been made more righteous through the death of the Son of God than we were before, so that we ought to be delivered from punishment? And to whom was the price of blood paid for our redemption but to him in whose power we were—that is, to God himself, who (as we have said) handed us over to his torturer? For it is not the torturers but the masters of those who are held captive who arrange or receive such ransoms. Again, how did he release these captives for a price if he himself exacted or settled the price for release of the same? Indeed, how cruel and wicked it seems that anyone should demand the blood of an innocent person as the price for anything, or that it should in any way please him that an innocent man should be slain—still less that God should consider the death of his Son so agreeable that by it he should be reconciled to the whole world!

These, and like queries, appear to us to pose a considerable problem concerning our redemption or justification through the death of our Lord Jesus Christ.

III

SOLUTION

Now it seems to us that we have been justified by the blood of Christ and reconciled to God in this way: through this unique act of grace manifested to us—in that his Son has taken upon himself our nature and preserved therein in teaching us by word and example even unto death—he has more fully bound us to himself by love; with the result that our hearts should be enkindled by such a gift of divine grace, and true charity should not now shrink from enduring anything for him.

And we do not doubt that the ancient Fathers, waiting in faith for this same gift, were aroused to very great love of God in the same way as men of this dispensation of grace, since it is written: "And they that went before and they that followed

cried, saying: 'Hosanna to the Son of David,' " etc.[41] Yet everyone becomes more righteous—by which we mean a greater
lover of the Lord—after the Passion of Christ than before,
since a realized gift inspires greater love than one which is only
hoped for. Wherefore, our redemption through Christ's
suffering is that deeper affection[42] in us which not only frees us
from slavery to sin, but also wins for us the true liberty of sons
of God,[43] so that we do all things out of love rather than fear—
love to him who has shown us such grace that no greater can
be found, as he himself asserts, saying, "Greater love than this
no man hath, that a man lay down his life for his friends."[44] Of
this love the Lord says elsewhere, "I am come to cast fire on the
earth, and what will I, but that it blaze forth?"[45] So does he
bear witness that he came for the express purpose of spreading
this true liberty of love amongst men.

The apostle, closely examining this great fact, exclaims
further on: "Because the charity of God is poured forth in our
hearts, by the Holy Ghost, who is given to us. For why did
Christ . . ."[46] And a few verses later, "God commendeth his
charity toward us; because when as yet . . ."[47] But these
utterances we shall expound more fully when we come to them.
Now, as befits brevity of exposition, let the foregoing suffice as
a summary of our understanding of the manner of our redemption. But inasmuch as our explanations are wanting in complete-
ness, let us keep further elaboration for our treatise *Theology*.[48]

IV

ON ROMANS 3:27

"Where is then thy boasting?"[49] I have said that righteousness apart from the law is now manifested through the faith of
Christ unto all alike who believe. So where, O Jew, is now thy

---

[41] Mark 11:9; the words *filio David* do not appear here in the Vulgate, but
are imported from Matt. 21:9.
[42] *Dilectio.*
[43] Cf. Rom. 8:21.
[44] John 15:13.
[45] Luke 12:49; *ardeat* for Vulgate *accendatur.*
[46] Rom. 5:5 f.
[47] Rom. 5:8.
[48] This refers, not to the *Theologia christiana*, but to the *Introductio ad theo-
logiam*, whose third book (part of which is now lost) was written after the
Expositio ad Romanos; cf. J. G. Sikes, *Peter Abailard*, 259–267.
[49] Rom. 3:27.

glorying, that extraordinary boasting in which thou usest to indulge concerning the law and its outward observances? It has been excluded, that is, taken away from thee, and made void. "By what law?" Has it perhaps been excluded by a law of works, that is, of some external deeds? "No, but by the law of faith"—as we have said, faith in Jesus Christ, meaning the love which comes from faith in our salvation through Christ.

If anyone believes and loves before he is baptized—like Abraham, about whom it is written, "Abraham believed God and it was reputed to him unto justice,"[50] and Cornelius, whose alms were accepted by God while he was yet unbaptized,[51] and anyone who is truly penitent about past sins, as the publican who went down from the Temple justified[52]—I do not hesitate to call such a person righteous, or to say that the man who restores to anyone what belongs to him possesses justice.[53] Likewise, also, we consider Jeremiah and John to have been sanctified from the womb, because, being wondrously enlightened, they already knew the Lord and loved him, though it was still necessary for them to undergo circumcision, which in those days took the place of baptism.[54] Why, then, you will ask, was it necessary for such individuals later to be circumcized or baptized, seeing they were already justified beforehand—by the faith and love that was in them, of course—and would inevitably be saved if they died at that time?

Nobody, to be sure, who is damned can die in a state of righteousness, even if he possesses charity. On the other hand, no one can be saved apart from baptism or martyrdom, once the meaning and purpose of baptism has been taught him. Yet a person could die in a state of charity before baptism or martyrdom; if he should die at that moment, you will say, he would have to be both saved and damned. But we claim that everyone who now honestly and purely loves the Lord for his own sake is predestined to life, and will never be overtaken by death until the Lord shows him what is of obligation concerning the sacraments, and also gives him the ability to understand it.

Indeed, what is being argued here—that the man who was already righteous before baptism, by believing and loving God, was in such a condition that, should he then die, he ought to be both saved and damned—can also be argued with respect

---

50 Rom. 4:3; cf. Gen. 15:6.　　　51 Cf. Acts 10:31.
52 Cf. Luke 18:13 f.　　　53 Cf. p. 250, n. 27.
54 Cf. Hugh of St. Victor, De sacram., I, p. 12, c. 2 (PL, 176, 349 f.); Peter Lombard, Sententiae, I, d. 1, 7–10, below.

to anyone who sins grievously, although predestined to life, for example, David when he committed adultery.[55] For as that man who was righteous ought to be saved, so should any righteous person who is predestinated; as the unbaptized should be damned, so should that adulterer. So it was with David at one time of his life, when, if he had died, he ought to have been both damned and saved.

Again, if it was a fact that he was in no condition to die well, and never in a condition in which he *could* not die badly (as long as he had free power of choice), nonetheless it is not true to say in the case of anyone at all that he must die both badly and well. Nay, rather, there is no condition in which a man *must* die well or *must* die badly; but at the particular times in which a man can die well, he can also in those same times die badly. Yet in no instance is it true to say that a man can die both well and badly at the same time. So with respect to the man who possesses charity before baptism, and is consequently righteous, we are of the opinion that he would never find himself in such a state that he would have to be simultaneously saved and damned, if he died.

Undoubtedly anyone who possesses charity before baptism might be without charity at the moment of death, and so die and be damned only. It would also be possible for a man to die "in a state of baptism"[56] before he was yet baptized, and so be saved. But if you were to say that a man can at the same time both be possessed of charity and yet not be "in a state of baptism," I no more accept your argument than if you should say that anyone could die committing adultery and at the same time be predestinated. However, it behooves the man who is predestinated to live well so that he may be saved, just as he who is already righteous through faith and love ought to be baptized because of the definite command of the Lord about baptism, or even to ensure the very continuance of righteousness. For if the man who possesses charity before he is baptized should end his life before being baptized, he would by no means continue in that same charity, with the result that, deep within, he would despair of eternal blessedness, and would have a presentiment that at his death he would immediately be damned forever.

55 Cf. II Kings, ch. 11 (A.V. II Sam., ch. 11).
56 *Baptizatus*, a term that must be taken in both a technical and a broader sense (hence, "in a state of baptism") if the argument is to be intelligible (G.E.M.).

But just as, before baptism, we already call a person righteous by faith—that is, by election, although his sins have not yet been remitted in the font, that is, their penalty has not yet been entirely forgiven—so also, after baptism, we do not yet call infants and those who are not of years of discretion righteous, even though they have received remission of sins and are clean in God's sight. For they cannot yet be capable of charity or righteousness, or possess any merits. Nevertheless, if they die in this childish state, when they begin to leave the body and see the glory prepared for them by God's mercy, at that moment, along with discernment, the love of God is born in them.

Yet so that no Jew may bring a charge against us—or, more important still, against the apostle—that we also are justified by a law of works, that is, of external acts such as baptism,[57] let this be our sufficient refutation on the subject of our justification, and the justification of all people, that it consists in love even before sacraments are received, whether we are talking about our sacraments or theirs. For the prophet also says in this connection, "Whensoever a sinner shall mourn for his sins, he shall be saved."[58]

---

[57] Abailard's general outlook keeps him from understanding the full significance of the sacraments as means of grace.
[58] Cf. Ezek. 18:27.

Peter Abailard: Ethics or the Book Called "Know Thyself"

THE TEXT

CHAPTER IX

GOD AND MAN UNITED IN CHRIST ARE NOT SOMETHING BETTER THAN GOD ALONE

Now let us go back to the previous point, to the statement that good added to good produces something better than either of them is by itself. You must guard against being led to say that Christ, that is, God and man joined together in a person, is something better than the divinity of Christ or even his humanity —or, in other words, than God himself united to man, or man himself assumed by God.[1] Certainly, it is agreed that in Christ both the man who is assumed and the God who assumes him are good, and each substance can be understood only as good, just as in individual men both the corporeal and the incorporeal substance are good, though the goodness of the body has no bearing on the worth or merit of the soul. But in fact who will dare to prefer the whole which is called Christ— namely, God and man together—or any number of things at all, to God, as though anything could be better than he, who is both the highest good and the source from whom all things receive whatever good they possess? It is true that, in order to carry out something, some things seem to be so necessary that God cannot do it without them, as aids or even primordial causes. Nevertheless, whatever the greatness of things may be, nothing can be said to be better than God. For although a number of good things is established, so that goodness may be found in many things, it does not happen in consequence that goodness is greater, any more than the fact that many are filled with knowledge,[2] or that the number of sciences is increasing, necessitates an increase in each person's knowledge, so that it

[1] On the *homo assumptus*, cf. the introduction to "Theologians of the Twelfth Century."
[2] *Scientia*.

becomes greater than before. So also, since God is good in himself and creates countless things which neither exist nor are good save through him, goodness is found in many through him, so that the number of good things is greater; no goodness, however, can be preferred to or equated with his goodness. Goodness, it is true, exists in man, and goodness in God, and though the substances or natures in which goodness is to be found are diverse, there is nothing whose goodness can be preferred to or equated with the divine goodness; thus nothing is to be called better (that is, a greater good) than God, or even equally good.

CHAPTER X

A MULTITUDE OF GOODS IS NOT BETTER THAN ONE GOOD

But it does not seem that a plurality of goodnesses or of good things can be found in act plus intention. For when intention is called good and activity is called good—as springing from good intention—only the goodness of the intention is referred to, nor does the term "good" retain the same sense, so that we can speak of many "goods." For example, when we say that a man is simple and a saying simple, we do not on that account concede that there are many "simples," since the word "simple" is being applied in two different ways. Let no one, therefore, force us to admit, when good work is added to good intention, that good is superadded to good as if there were several goods, in proportion to which the reward ought to be increased; as has been stated, we cannot correctly say that these are many goods, when the term "good" cannot possibly be fittingly applied to them in the same way.

CHAPTER XI

A DEED IS GOOD BECAUSE OF GOOD INTENTION

We say, in fact, that an intention is good, that is, right in itself, but that an action is good, not because it acquires any kind of goodness in itself, but because it comes from a good intention. It follows from this that the same thing may be done by the same man at different times, and yet that the action may sometimes be called good, sometimes bad, because of a difference of intention, and thus its relation to good and evil seems to be altered. The same thing happens to the proposition,

"Socrates is seated," or rather to our understanding of its truth or falsity, because at one moment Socrates is sitting, at another he is standing. Now Aristotle says that this alteration with respect to truth and falsity happens in this way in these propositions, not because they themselves, when they are changed with respect to truth and falsehood, undergo anything by a change of themselves, but because the subject-matter, namely, Socrates, is moved in himself—that is, changes from sitting to standing, or conversely.[3]

CHAPTER XII

ON WHAT GROUNDS AN INTENTION IS CALLED GOOD

There are those, however, who think that an intention is good or right, whenever someone believes that he is acting well, and that what he is doing is pleasing to God. This was the case with those who persecuted the martyrs, to whom the truth refers in the Gospel: "The hour cometh, that whosoever killeth you will think that he doeth a service to God."[4] The apostle expresses sympathy with the ignorance of such people, when he says: "I bear them witness, that they have a zeal of God, but not according to knowledge."[5] That is to say, they do these things, which they believe to be pleasing to God, with great fervor and longing, but because they are deceived in this zeal or eagerness of mind their intention is erroneous, nor is the eye of their heart single, so as to see clearly—that is, to preserve itself from error. Thus the Lord, when he distinguished deeds according to a right or not-right intention, carefully called the mind's eye (or intention) "single" and, as it were, pure from uncleanness, so that it could see clearly, or on the contrary he called it "darksome," when he said, "If thine eye be single, thy whole body shall be lightsome."[6] This means that if your intention is right, the whole mass of deeds springing from it, which can be seen in the manner of corporeal things, will be worthy of light (that is, good), and contrariwise. Thus intention is not to be called good simply because it seems good, but because it really is what it is thought to be—as, for example, when it believes that what it is aiming at is pleasing to God, and in addition is not deceived

---

[3] Cf. Aristotle, De interpret., 12 (21ᵇ10–15).
[4] John 16:2.
[5] Rom. 10:2.
[6] Matt. 6:22.

at all in its judgment. Otherwise the very infidels would have good works, just as we do, since they, no less then we ourselves, believe that they are saved—or, if you will, please God—by their works.

CHAPTER XIII

Sin Is Only That Which Is Done Against Conscience

If anyone asks, nonetheless, whether those who persecuted the martyrs or Christ sinned in that which they believed to be pleasing to God, or whether they could let pass without sin that which they thought should in no wise be let pass, certainly, in terms of our previous description of sin as contempt of God, or consent to that to which one believes that consent should not be given, we cannot say that they sinned in this, or that ignorance of anything, or even unbelief itself (in which no one can be saved), is sin. For those who do not know Christ, and on that account reject the Christian faith, because they believe that it is contrary to God, can hardly be said to show contempt of God in what they do for God's sake, and for that reason think that they do well—especially since the apostle says, "If our heart do not reprehend us, we have confidence before God,"[7] as if he were to say, Where we do not violate our own conscience, it is in vain that we fear being found guilty of sin before God. Yet if the ignorance of such men is not to be imputed for sin in any way, how is it that the Lord himself prays for those who crucify him, saying: "Father, forgive them, for they know not what they do"[8]? Or how is it that Stephen, taught by this example, entreats for those who are stoning him, saying, "Lord, lay not this sin to their charge"[9]? For it does not seem that forgiveness should be granted, if no sin has gone before, nor does forgiveness normally mean anything but the remission of the penalty deserved by sin. Besides, Stephen clearly calls what sprang from ignorance "sin."

CHAPTER XIV

In How Many Ways the Term "Sin" Is Used

But to reply to the objections more fully, one should know that the term "sin" is used in different ways. Properly, however, sin means actual contempt for God or consent to evil, as

[7] I John 3:21.   [8] Luke 23:34.   [9] Acts 7:60.

we mentioned above.[10] From this little children are exempt, as well as the naturally simple-minded. Since these have no merits, because they lack reason, nothing can be imputed to them for sin, and they are saved by the sacraments alone. A victim offered for sin is also called "sin," as when the apostle speaks of Jesus Christ as having been "made sin."[11] The penalty of sin is also called "sin" or a "curse,"[12] as when we say that sin is forgiven, meaning that the penalty is remitted, and that the Lord Jesus "bore our sins,"[13] meaning that he endured the penalty for our sins, or the penalties springing from them. But when we say that young children have "original sin," or that we all, as the apostle says, sinned in Adam,[14] this amounts to saying that our punishment or the sentence of our condemnation takes its rise from his sin.[15] The actual works of sin, also, or whatever we do not rightly know or will, we sometimes call "sins." For what does it mean for anyone to have committed sin, except that he has put his sin into effect? Nor is this strange, since conversely we refer to sins themselves[16] as deeds, as in the statement of Athanasius, when he says: "They shall give account for their own deeds. And they that have done good will go into life eternal, they that have done evil into eternal fire."[17] For what does "for their own deeds" mean? Does it mean that judgment will only be returned for the intentions that were carried out in action, so that he who has more deeds to point to will receive a greater recompense? Does it mean that he who was unable to put his intention into effect will be exempt from condemnation, like the devil who did not obtain in effect what he had anticipated in desire?[18] It cannot mean this. "For their own deeds," then, refers to their consent to the things which they decided to carry out, that is, to the sins which with the Lord are reckoned as deeds done, since he punishes them as we punish deeds.

Now when Stephen speaks of the "sin" which the Jews were committing against him in ignorance, he means by "sin" the very penalty which he was suffering on account of the sin of our first parents (just as the term is applied to other penalties from the same source), or else he is referring to their unjust action in

---

10 Cf. Ch. III (Cousin, II, 596 ff.).

11 II Cor. 5:21.   12 Cf. Gal. 3:13.

13 I Peter 2:24.   14 Cf. Rom. 5:12.

15 Note Abailard's refusal to describe original sin as "sin," in any proper sense.

6 I.e., intentions.   17 From *Quicumque vult.*   18 I.e., equality with God.

stoning him. He asked indeed that it should not be charged to
them, or, in other words, that they should not be punished
bodily on its account. For here God often punishes some persons
corporally, when no fault of theirs requires it, and yet not
without cause—as, for instance, when he sends afflictions to the
just with a view to their purification or testing, or when he
permits some to be afflicted, so that afterward they may be
delivered and he may be glorified for the benefit he has conferred. This happened in the case of the blind man, of whom he
himself said: "Neither hath this man sinned, nor his parents;
but that the works of God should be made manifest in him."[19]
Who will deny, either, that innocent children are sometimes
imperiled or afflicted along with wicked parents, by the fault of
the latter—as in the case of the men of Sodom[20] and of a good
many other peoples—so that greater terror may be inspired in
the wicked by the wider extension of punishment? It was
because he had carefully noted this that blessed Stephen
prayed that "sin" (that is to say, the punishment he was
enduring at the hands of the Jews, or that which they were
wrongly doing) should not be charged to them, or, in other
words, that they should not be punished physically because of it.

The Lord was also of this mind, when he said, "Father,
forgive them,"[21] meaning, Do not avenge, even by physical
punishment, this that they are doing against me. Such revenge
could, in fact, have reasonably been taken, even if no fault of
theirs had gone before, so that others who saw it, or even they
themselves, might learn from the punishment that they had not
acted rightly in this matter. But it was fitting for the Lord, by
this example of his own prayer, to encourage us supremely to
foster the virtue of patience and display the highest love, so
that he should display to us in deed what he himself had taught
us by word of mouth—namely, to pray also for our enemies.[22]
Therefore, when he said, "Forgive," this did not refer to any
previous fault or contempt of God which they had in this
matter, but had to do with the reasonableness of imposing a
penalty, which, as we have said, could follow with good cause,
even without any previous fault. This happened to the prophet
who was sent against Samaria and by eating did what the Lord
had forbidden. Since he did not presume to do anything in
contempt of God, but was deceived by another prophet, he
incurred death in his innocence, not so much from any guilty

[19] John 9:3.   [20] Cf. Gen., ch. 19.
[21] Luke 23:34.   [22] Cf. Matt. 5:44.

fault as from the actual doing of the deed.[23] God indeed, as blessed Gregory recalls, sometimes changes his sentence, but never his purpose.[24] That is to say, he often determines that what for some reason he had planned to command or to threaten shall not be carried out. But his purpose remains fixed, or, in other words, what in his own resolution he plans to do never lacks efficacy. He did not, we know, adhere to what he had enjoined on Abraham concerning the sacrifice of his son,[25] or to his threat against the Ninevites,[26] and thus, as we have said, he changed his sentence. So the aforesaid prophet, whom he had forbidden to take food on his journey, believed that his sentence had been changed, and indeed that he would certainly be in the wrong if he did not listen to the other prophet, who claimed that he had been sent by the Lord for the very purpose of refreshing his weariness with food. He did this, therefore, without blame, since he was resolved to avoid blame. Nor did sudden death harm him, when it delivered him from the tribulations of this present life, while it was a profitable warning to many, since they saw a just man thus punished without fault, and observed the fulfillment in him of that which is elsewhere addressed to the Lord: "Thou, O God, forasmuch as thou art just, orderest all things justly, since him also who deserveth not to be punished thou dost condemn."[27] This means: Thou dost condemn, not to eternal but to bodily death. For some, such as children, are saved without merits, and attain to eternal life by grace alone. Similarly, it is not absurd that some should endure bodily penalties which they have not deserved; this is certainly the case with young children who die without the grace of baptism, and are condemned to bodily as well as to eternal death. Many innocent persons, moreover, suffer affliction. What is strange, then, in the fact that those who crucified the Lord could reasonably incur temporal punishment by that unjust action, as we have said, even though ignorance excuses them from blame? It was for this reason that he said, "Forgive them"—in other words, Do not bring upon them the penalty which, as we have said, they could not unreasonably incur.

Moreover, if what they did through ignorance, or even the

23 Cf. III Kings 13:24 (A.V., I Kings 13:24).
24 Cf. Gregory the Great, *Moral. in Iob*, XVI, 37:46 (*PL*, 75, 1144).
25 Cf. Gen., ch. 22.
26 Cf. Jonah, ch. 4.
27 Cf. Wisdom of Solomon 12:15, which actually says the opposite.

ignorance itself, is not properly called "sin" (that is, contempt of God), this applies to unbelief as well, even though the latter necessarily shuts off the entrance to eternal life from adults who have the use of reason. In fact, it is enough for eternal damnation not to believe the gospel, to be ignorant of Christ, not to receive the sacraments of the Church, even though this is done not so much by malice as by ignorance. Concerning such persons the truth also says: "He that doth not believe is already judged,"[28] while the apostle declares, "He who knows not shall not be known."[29] But when we say that we sin unwittingly—that is, that we do something which is not fitting—by "sin" we mean, not contempt, but the action. For the philosophers also equate sinning with doing or saying something in an unfitting way, even though there is nothing here that seems to have any bearing on an offense against God. Thus Aristotle, when he spoke of the faulty attribution of relations (in *Ad aliquid*[30]), said: "But sometimes the relation will not seem to be reciprocal, unless it is attributed appropriately to that which is mentioned. For if he sins[31] in making the attribution, as in speaking of the 'wing of a bird,' the connection is not reciprocal, as if one might speak of the 'bird of a wing.' " If, therefore, in this way we describe as "sin" everything that we do badly, or that we possess contrary to our salvation, then we shall certainly call "sins" both unbelief and ignorance of the things that must necessarily be believed for salvation, even though no contempt for God is in evidence. I think, nevertheless, that sin, properly speaking, is that which can never happen without blame. But ignorance of God, or unbelief, or actual deeds which are not done rightly, can occur without blame. For suppose that someone does not believe the gospel of Christ, because the proclamation has not reached him, as the text of the apostle indicates: "How shall they believe him, of whom they have not heard? And how shall they hear without a preacher?"[32] In that case, what blame can be attributed to him because he does not believe? Cornelius did not believe in Christ until Peter had been sent to him and had instructed him concerning this. Moreover, even though he previously knew and loved God by natural law, and so merited to be heard for his prayer, and to have his alms accepted by God, nevertheless, if by any chance

---

[28] John 3:18.   [29] I Cor. 14:38.
[30] The title refers to the beginning of the chapter in the not very literal translation Abailard was using; the reference is to *Categ.*, 7 ($6^b36–7^a4$).
[31] *Peccet.*   [32] Rom. 10:14.

he had departed from this light before he believed in Christ, we should not dare to make him any promise of life, however great his good works seemed. Nor should we number him with the faithful, but rather with unbelievers, no matter how great the zeal for salvation which had possessed him.[33] Indeed, many of God's judgments are an abyss. Sometimes he draws those who resist, or at least are less concerned for their salvation, and repels those who present themselves, or at least are more ready to believe—all by the deepest counsel of his dispensation. For thus he rejected him who offered himself: "Master, I will follow thee whithersoever thou shalt go."[34] But when another excused himself on the ground of the solicitude he felt for his father, he did not tolerate this dutiful excuse of his, even for an hour.[35] Again, in rebuking the stubbornness of cities, he said: "Woe to thee, Chorazin, woe to thee, Bethsaida, for if in Tyre and Sidon had been wrought the miracles that have been wrought in you, they had long ago done penance in sackcloth and ashes."[36] You see, he tendered them not only his own preaching, but also a display of miracles, even though he already knew that they were not going to be believed. But as for the other cities of the Gentiles, though he was aware that they were ready to receive the faith, he did not deem them worthy of a visit from himself. And yet, when some of their citizens perished, deprived of the word of preaching—even though they were prepared to accept it—how can we blame them for that, when we see that it did not happen by any negligence of theirs? Nevertheless, we say that this their unbelief, in which they died, was enough to condemn them, although the cause of this blindness in which the Lord abandoned them is less clear to us.[37] Perhaps if anyone finds the cause in their sin, committed without guilt, it will be permitted, since he finds it absurd that they should be condemned without any sin at all.

Nonetheless, as we have often indicated, we think that the term "sin" can properly be applied to guilty negligence alone, and that this cannot exist in anyone, of any age whatever, without his deserving to be condemned. But I do not see how not believing in Christ, which is certainly a matter of unbelief, ought to be imputed as a fault to young children, or to those to whom belief in Christ has not been proclaimed. Nor do I

---

[33] Cf. Acts 10:1 f.   [34] Matt. 8:19.
[35] Cf. Matt. 8:21 f.   [36] Matt. 11:21.
[37] Note the authentically Augustinian attitude.

see how blame attaches to anything that is done by invincible ignorance, when we have not even been able to foresee it—for instance, if someone kills a man with an arrow because he does not see him in a wood, while he intends to shoot at wild beasts or birds. Nonetheless we say that he sins, but through ignorance, just as we sometimes admit that we sin, not only in consent but also in thought. But in this case we do not use the term properly, as equivalent to fault, but apply it loosely to that which it is not at all fitting for us to do, whether it is done by error or by negligence, or in any other unfitting way. This, then, is what it means to sin by ignorance: not to bear any blame, but to do what does not befit us—to sin in thought, that is, by willing what it is not at all fitting for us to will, or in speech or in act, that is, by saying or doing what should not be said or done, even if all these things happen to us involuntarily and by our ignorance. Thus we may also say that those who persecuted Christ or his people, whom they thought they ought to persecute, sinned in act. Nevertheless, they would have sinned more grievously if they had spared them against their own conscience.

Peter Abailard: Hymn for Saturday Vespers

THE TEXT

O what their joy and their glory must be,
Those endless Sabbaths[1] the blessed ones see!
Crown for the valiant; to weary ones rest;
God shall be all, and in all ever blest.[2]

What are the Monarch, his court, and his throne?[3]
What are the peace and the joy that they own?
Tell us, ye blest ones, that in it have share,
If what ye feel ye can fully declare.

Truly "Jerusalem" name we that shore,[4]
"Vision of peace," that brings joy evermore!
Wish and fulfillment can severed be ne'er,
Nor the thing prayed for come short of the prayer.

We, where no trouble distraction can bring,
Safely the anthems of Sion shall sing;[5]
While for thy grace, Lord, their voices of praise
Thy blessed people shall evermore raise.[6]

There dawns no Sabbath, no Sabbath is o'er,
Those Sabbathkeepers have one and no more;[7]
One and unending is that triumph song
Which to the angels and us shall belong.

[1] In the Latin liturgical books, *sabbatum* means Saturday, not Sunday!
[2] Cf. I Cor. 15:28.
[3] Note the characteristically medieval court symbolism: *rex, curia, palatium.*
[4] Cf. Gal. 4:26, and the noble old hymn "Urbs beata Hierusalem" (*Oxford Book of Medieval Latin Verse*, 36).
[5] Cf. Ps. 136:3 f. (P.B.V., 137:3 f.).
[6] In the original, there is a play on *gratia* (grace) and *gratias* (thanks).
[7] Cf. Heb. 4:9.

Now in the meanwhile, with hearts raised on high,
We for that country must yearn and must sigh,
Seeking Jerusalem, dear native land,
Through our long exile on Babylon's strand.[8]

Low before Him with our praises we fall,
Of whom, and in whom, and through whom are all;
Of whom, the Father; and through whom, the Son;
In whom, the Spirit, with these ever One.[9]

[8] Note the echoes of Augustine, *De civ. dei.*
[9] Common doxology for Abailard's hymns in this meter.

Hugh of Saint Victor: On the Sacraments of the Christian Faith (Book One, Part Eight: On the Restoration of Man)

THE TEXT

CHAPTER I

ON THE FACT THAT THREE THINGS MUST BE CONSIDERED REGARDING THE RESTORATION OF MAN

Man's first sin was pride,[1] which was followed by a threefold penalty. One of these, which is a penalty and nothing else besides, is the mortality of the body.[2] The other two, which are both penalties and sins, are, first, the concupiscence of the flesh,[3] and, second, the ignorance of the mind.[4] Since, therefore, man was struck by a penalty such as would not cleanse his guilt but rather increase it, he would have descended through temporal punishment to eternal punishment, had he not afterward been set free through grace. His judgment, however, was deferred, lest he should be found liable to condemnation if he were to be judged immediately. And since the mercy of God had foreordained him to salvation, it assigned to man a place of repentance and correction in this time of waiting and delay. This it did, in order that it might meanwhile, through its grace, make him capable of being judged by itself for salvation, not merely out of pity, but also with justice.[5]

Three things, therefore, take first place in our consideration of man's restoration—the time, the place, and the remedy. The time is the present life from the beginning of the world

---

[1] Cf. Ecclus. 10:15 (A.V., 10:13); Augustine, *De gen. ad. lit.*, XI, 18 f. (*CSEL*, 28/1, 350–352); *De civ. dei*, XIV, 13:1 (*CSEL*, 40/2, 31 f.); *De mus.*, VI, 13:40 (*PL*, 32, 1184 f.); *Enarr. in Ps.* 18, 1 (*PL*, 36, 156); *Tr. in Ioan.* 25, 15 f. (*PL*, 35, 1603 f.).

[2] Cf. Rom. 5:12; Augustine, *Op. imperf. c. Iulian.*, II, 186 (*PL*, 45, 1222).

[3] Cf. Augustine, *C. Iulian. pelag.*, V, 3:8 (*PL*, 44, 786 f.); *De nupt. et concup.*, I, 23:25 (*CSEL*, 42, 237); *De spir. et. lit.*, 33, 59 (*CSEL*, 60, 218); *De cont.*, 8, 21 (*CSEL*, 41, 165 f.).

[4] Cf. Rom. 1:21; Augustine, *Epist.* 194, 6:27 (*CSEL*, 57, 196 f.).

[5] In this volume *iustitia* is sometimes translated "justice," sometimes "righteousness," according to the context.

until the end of the age. The place is this world. The remedy consists in three things: faith, the sacraments, and good works. The time is long, in order that man may not be caught unprepared. The place is difficult, in order that the transgressor may be chastised. The remedy is efficacious, in order that the one who is sick may be healed.

CHAPTER II

ON THE FIVE PLACES

There are five places: one in which there is only good and the supreme good, and one in which there is only evil and the supreme evil; two others after these, one which is below the highest, wherein there is only good but not the supreme good, the other which is above the lowest, wherein there is only evil but not the supreme evil; one in the middle, wherein is both good and evil, and neither the supreme good nor the supreme evil. In heaven there is only good and the supreme good; in hell there is only evil and the supreme evil. In paradise there is only good, but not the highest good; in the purgatorial fire there is only evil, but not the supreme evil. In the world there is good and evil, but neither supreme good nor supreme evil. Paradise is the place of beginners who advance to that which is better, and accordingly in that place there had to be good only, because creation must not have been begun from evil. This good could not, however, be the highest good, for if it had been there, there would have been no progress for those who had been placed there. Heaven is the place of those who are confirmed in good and who through discipline have attained to the highest degree of progress. One good only, the supreme good, is placed in it. Hell is the place of those who are confirmed in evil and who have irrecoverably forsaken discipline, and accordingly evil only and the supreme evil is placed there. The purgatorial fire is the place of those who were less fully corrected in the first correction and who are to be perfected in the second. Therefore it had to have evil only, that it might be worse than the former place where both evil and good exist together. The world is the place of those who err and must be restored, and therefore both good and evil are disposed in it simultaneously, in order that men on the one hand might receive consolation through the good, and on the other hand might receive correction through the evil. Yet neither the supreme good nor the supreme evil are there, in order that there might be a place where those who persist in evil might regress, and where those who depart from evil might progress.

Accordingly, heaven is in the highest place; after heaven, paradise; after paradise, the world; after the world, the purgatorial fire; and after purgatory, hell. Therefore, the devil, who had fallen from the highest place, was thrust down into the lowest, because he was not to be restored.[6] Man, however, since he did not fall from the highest place, was not placed in the lowest,[7] but in the middle, that he might have a place where he could ascend through the merit of righteousness or descend through the guilt of sin.

CHAPTER III

How Man Was Disposed to Repentance

Accordingly, since a time of repentance had been granted, man was set in this world in a place of repentance, so that he might correct evil things and recover good things. The purpose of this was that, when man, after he has been corrected, comes at last to the judgment, he might receive, not the penalty for sin, but the glory prepared for him as a reward for righteousness. It remains, then, that while there is time he should seek advice and ask for help for his correction and liberation. But as man is found to be sufficient of himself for neither, it is necessary that God, who by his grace delays the judgment, should by the same grace meanwhile supply advice for the escape and after the advice bestow help. So, then, it is fitting that he should, for the time being, lay aside the role of the judge, and first take on himself the role of an adviser, and afterward that of a helper. He must act in such a way, at least, as at first to leave man entirely to himself, so that man himself may both experience his own ignorance and understand that he needs advice, and thereafter may feel his weakness and recognize that he needs help.

For such a reason, therefore, man was left entirely to himself in the time of the natural law.[8] Afterward, in the time of the written law, advice was given him when he recognized his ignorance.[9] Finally, in the time of grace, help was bestowed on

---

6 Cf. Augustine, *Ad. Oros. c. priscill. et origen.*, 4 f. (*PL*, 42, 671 f.).
7 Cf. Augustine, *De nupt. et concup.*, I, 23:26 (*CSEL*, 42, 238 f.).
8 Cf. Augustine, *Epist.* 157, 3:15 (*CSEL*, 44, 462 ff.).
9 Cf. Augustine, *Enarr. in Ps.* 57, 1 (*PL*, 36, 673 f.); 118, 25:4 (*PL*, 37, 1574).

him when he admitted his weakness.[10] The advice consisted in the reckoning of satisfaction, the help in the effecting of redemption.

Consequently, that we may be able to know more clearly the reckoning of the satisfaction which man must repay the Creator for his sin,[11] it is necessary first of all that we should, for a little while, consider man's case more attentively. This case, actually, is prepared to be pleaded between three parties: God, man, and the devil.

CHAPTER IV

On Man's Case Against God and the Devil

Accordingly, these three appear in the case: man, God, and the devil. The devil is convicted of having done injury to God, because he has both abducted his servant, man, by fraud and held him by violence.[12] Man is likewise convicted of having done injury to God, since he has both despised his commandment and, by placing himself under the ownership of another, deprived him of his service. Likewise, the devil is convicted of having done injury to man, since he has both deceived him by promising him good things beforehand and harmed him by bringing evils upon him afterward. The devil, therefore, unjustly holds man, but man is justly held, since the devil never deserved to oppress man as one subject to himself, but man deserved through his sin to be surrendered to oppression by him. For even though man did not know that what the devil promised was false, yet he was not ignorant of the fact that, even if it were true, he ought not to desire anything against the will of the Creator. Accordingly, as far as his sin is concerned, man is justly subject to the devil, but this subjection is unjust, as far as the deceit of the devil is concerned.

Were man, then, to have such an advocate that by his power the devil could be brought into court, man would justly speak against his dominion, since the devil had no just case for making a lawful claim on man. But no such advocate could be found save God alone. However, God was unwilling to take up man's case, because he was still angry at man for his sin.[13] It was

---

10 Cf. Augustine, *Enarr. in Ps.* 83, 10 (*PL*, 37, 1065); *Epist.*, 145, 3 (*CSEL*, 44, 268 f.).
11 Note the "Anselmian" formulation of the problem.
12 Cf. the treatment of the "devil's rights" by Anselm and Abailard.
13 Cf. Augustine, *Sermo* 302, 22:20 (*PL*, 38, 1593).

necessary, therefore, that man should first placate God, and thereafter, with God as his advocate, begin his suit against the devil. But he was not able to placate God in a reasonable manner except by making restitution for the loss which he had caused and making satisfaction for his contempt. Man, however, had nothing which could fittingly compensate God for the loss inflicted, for if he were to give anything of the irrational creation, in return for the rational creature which had been taken away, it would be too little.[14] But neither could he repay a man for man, for he had taken away a righteous and innocent one and found no one save a sinner.[15] Consequently man found nothing whereby he might placate God for himself, since, whether he were to give his possessions or himself, the repayment would not be worthy.

Therefore, when God saw that man was not able by his own strength to escape from the yoke of his condemnation, he had pity on him. First, he freely came to his help out of sheer mercy, that he might thereafter deliver him through justice. In other words, since man of himself had not the means of escaping justice, God of his mercy bestowed justice upon him. For the deliverance of man would not have been perfectly reasonable unless it were made just on both sides; that is, that as God with justice could seek out man, so man too might escape with justice. Man, however, could never have this justice unless God were to bestow it on him through his mercy. In order, therefore, that God might be placated by man, God freely gave to man that which he was in duty bound to repay to God. He accordingly gave to man a Man whom he could repay in man's stead, one who was not merely equal to the first man but superior to him, so that a worthy repayment might be made. Therefore, in order that in man's stead a Man greater than man might be repaid, God became Man for man. As Man he gave himself to man, so that he might receive himself from man.[16] God, the Son of God, became incarnate, and the God-Man Christ was given to men, as Isaiah says: "A boy is given to us," etc.[17] The fact, therefore, that Christ was given to man, was God's mercy. That Christ was repaid by man was man's justice. For in the Nativity of Christ, God was justly placated toward man, since for man there was found a Man who was

---

14 Cf. Anselm *Cur deus homo*, I, 20 ff.
15 Cf. *ibid.*, I, 24.
16 Cf. *ibid.*, II, 6 f.
17 Isa. 9:6, reading *puer* instead of *filius* (Vulgate).

not merely equal to man, but, as has been said, was superior to him. Therefore, in the Nativity of Christ the angels proclaimed peace to the world, saying, "Glory to God in the highest, and on earth peace to men of good will."[18]

It was, however, still left to man, that as he had placated wrath by restoring the loss, so likewise, for the sake of making satisfaction for his contempt, he must become worthy of escaping the penalty. But this could not happen fittingly unless he were willingly and obediently to take upon himself the penalty which he did not owe, in order that he might become worthy to be delivered from the penalty which he had deserved through his disobedience. Sinful man, however, could not pay this penalty, because he, on account of the guilt of the first contempt, could not bear whatever penalty he took upon himself as anything but his just deserts. Therefore, in order that man might justly escape the penalty that was his due, it was necessary that a man who owed no penalty should take upon himself the penalty for man. Accordingly, Christ by being born paid man's debt to the Father, and by dying expiated man's guilt, so that, when he himself bore on man's behalf the death which he did not owe, man because of him might justly escape the death which he owed. Thus the devil would now find no occasion for calumny, since the devil himself was not to have dominion over man, and man was worthy to be set free.

So the same One both maintained our judgment and our cause, as it is written, "For thou hast maintained my judgment and my cause."[19] He has maintained our cause because he paid the debt to the Father on our behalf, and by his death expiated our guilt. He has maintained our judgment because, when he descended into hell and broke the gates of death, he set free the captives who were being held there. Accordingly, the judgment of the devil against God was executed from the very beginning of the world; the judgment of man against the devil was executed in the Passion of Christ; the judgment of man against God is delayed till the end of the world. For this reason man, if he is willing first of all to be reconciled to God through Christ, will thenceforth await his judgment without fear of condemnation.

18 Luke 2:14.
19 Ps. 9:5 (P.B.V., 9:4).

CHAPTER V

ON THE DISTINCTION OF THE JUDGMENTS

There are four judgments: according to foreknowledge, according to cause, according to works, according to recompense. It was according to foreknowledge that we were judged before we existed. It is according to cause that we are judged from the time that we begin to exist, when we are good or evil. It is according to works that we are judged when we show outwardly in deeds what our inward character is like. It is according to recompense that we shall be judged, when we shall know by receiving the reward of our deeds what God from eternity has foreseen our character to be.

Of these four judgments, two are hidden,[20] namely, judgment according to foreknowledge and judgment according to cause, and accordingly in these a human judgment is not included. Two are manifest, namely, judgment according to works and judgment according to recompense. In the case of one of these, namely, judgment according to works, the power to judge in the present is given to men by God. But in the case of the other, namely, judgment according to recompense, judgment will be given, not by men, but by God in the presence of men. Judgment according to foreknowledge is hidden and unchangeable, judgment according to cause is hidden and changeable, judgment according to works is manifest and changeable, judgment according to recompense is manifest and unchangeable. Judgment according to works is, after a fashion, an image and a sacrament of judgment according to recompense, since the one manifests cause and hints at foreknowledge, while the other will manifest cause and confirm foreknowledge.

It ought likewise to be considered that judgment is made in one way when the sentence is determined, in another way when it is made known. Indeed, in determining the sentence of every judgment, the Father, the Son, and the Holy Ghost judge together. In making known the sentence, however, the Son alone judges. In his divinity he, together with the Father and the Holy Ghost, is able to determine the sentence of every judgment, but in his humanity he alone has received the power to make known the sentence of every judgment.[21] Wherefore his

20 Cf. Augustine, *Enarr. in Ps.* 9, 1 (*PL*, 36, 117).
21 Cf. John 5:27; Augustine, *De civ. dei*, XX, 30:4 (*CSEL*, 40/2, 509 ff.); *Tr. in Ioan.* 21, 13 (*PL*, 35, 1571 f.).

humanity, which has not power to determine the sentence, said, in relation to the determination of the sentence, "I judge not any man."[22] Yet, because it has authority to make known the terms of that which has been determined, it adds, "As I hear, so I judge."[23] For what it hears within, when the sentence is determined, it judges outwardly when it is made known.

Having thus briefly set forth these things concerning the distinction of the judgments, let us return to the main order of our discourse.

CHAPTER VI

WHY GOD BECAME MAN

Thus God became man in order that he might set free man whom he had made, so that man's Creator and Redeemer might be one and the same. Thus the Son was sent in order that he might show his assent to the Father's adoption of men.[24] Wisdom came that it might overcome malice, so that the enemy, who had overcome by cunning, might be overcome by prudence.

CHAPTER VII

WHAT CHRIST'S PASSION HAD TO DO WITH US

From our nature he took a victim for our nature, that the whole burnt offering to be offered up for us might come from that which is ours.[25] This he did in order that the redemption might have to do with us, by this very fact that the offering was taken from that which is ours. We are truly made partakers of this redemption if we through faith are united to the Redeemer himself, who through the flesh entered into fellowship with us. Human nature, in fact, had become wholly corrupted through sin, and had become wholly liable to condemnation because of sin.[26] Accordingly there would not have been injustice, had it been wholly condemned.[27] But grace came and chose some· from the mass of mankind through mercy for salvation, while it left others for condemnation through justice.[28] Those whom it

---

[22] John 8:15.   [23] John 5:30.

[24] Cf. Heb. 2:10–18; Gal. 4:4 f.; Rom. 8:29.

[25] Cf. Augustine, *De civ. dei*, X, 6 (*CSEL*, 40/1, 456); Fulgentius of Ruspe, *Epist.* 14, 37 (*PL*, 65, 425); Gregory, *Moralia*, XVII, 30:46 (*PL*, 76, 32).

[26] Cf. Augustine, *De pecc. mer.*, II, 10:15 (*CSEL*, 60, 86 f.).

[27] Cf. Augustine, *De nat. et grat.*, 5, 5 (*CSEL*, 60, 236).

[28] Cf. Augustine, *De pecc. orig.*, 29, 34 (*CSEL*, 42, 193 f.); *Enarr. in Ps.* 118, 28:1 (*PL*, 37, 1583); *Epist.* 186, 4:12 (*CSEL*, 57, 54 f.).

saved through mercy it did not save without justice, for it was in its power to be able to do this justly. Yet had it not saved them it would have acted justly, because in terms of their own merit if it had acted thus it would not have been unjust.

CHAPTER VIII

OF THE JUSTICE OF POWER AND OF EQUITY

For there is one kind of justice which arises from the obligation of the doer, and another kind which arises from the merit of him who is the object of the action. Justice arising from the obligation of the doer is of power, justice arising from the merit of him who is the object of the action is of equity. By the justice of power there is permitted to the doer of an action, without injustice, whatever is due to his power, if he so wishes. By the justice of equity there is recompensed to the object of an action, even though he be unwilling, that which is due to his merit. Accordingly, when God punishes the sinner, he acts justly, since it is due to his power that he can do this if he wishes. And he who suffers the penalty is justly punished, since according to his merit there is recompensed to him that which is owed to his merit. Thus in that case there is the just power by which God acts justly and is just, and the fair retribution by which the sinner justly suffers; by which, however, he is not just but his penalty is just.

When, on the other hand, God justifies the sinner, he acts justly, and he is just by the justice of the power whereby this is permitted him.[29] But he who is justified is just by the justice which he receives, but not by the fact that he receives it contrary to his merit. Yet he is not unjust, since he himself does not do what he receives, but merely passively receives it. He who does it is just because he does it, and by virtue of the justice whereby he does it. And he who receives it is just by the justice which he receives, yet not because he receives it, since he, having no justice of his own, receives justice through grace alone.

CHAPTER IX

ON PASSIVE AND ON COMPELLING JUSTICE

It must likewise be known that there is one kind of justice which is passive, and another kind which is compelling. By

---

[29] Cf. Augustine, *Tr. in Ioan.*, 26, 1 (*PL*, 35, 1606 f.); Anselm, *Proslogion*, 9.

virtue of passive justice an act is just if it is done, but it is not unjust if the act is not done. By virtue of compelling justice an act is done justly in the sense that if it were not done, this would be unjust. Wherefore passive justice is subject to dispensation, while active justice is subject to necessity. God, therefore, when he takes some from the mass of mankind to salvation, makes use of the justice of power due to himself; but when he leaves some to perdition he makes use of the justice of permitted equity. In the one case he acts according to that which is due to him; in the other, he acts according to our merit.

Were he, however, to abandon those whom he now takes to salvation, there would be no injustice, since they would receive the justice of equity according to their merits. Were he, on the other hand, to take those whom he now abandons, there would likewise be no injustice, since in their salvation he would make use of the justice of power. Accordingly, both in the case of those who are saved and of those who are condemned, it is passive justice by virtue of which that which is done is just in such a manner that even if it were done otherwise it would not be unjust. For even those who are justly condemned according to their merits could justly be saved through God's grace, had God willed it. Again, those who through God's grace are justly saved could be justly condemned if God had been unwilling to save them.[30] So, then, in either case, whatever he willed was just. Even had he willed otherwise it would not have been unjust, since his will has such power that, whatever he wills, it is permitted to him to do it without injustice.

CHAPTER X

THAT GOD COULD HAVE REDEEMED MAN IN AN OTHER MANNER, HAD HE WILLED IT

Because of this, we are right in declaring that God would have been able to achieve the redemption of mankind in a quite different manner, had he so willed. It was, however, more appropriate to our weakness that God should become man, and that he, by taking man's mortality on himself for the sake of man, should transform man for the hope of his immortality. In this way man might have hope of ascending to the good things of Him who has descended, as he sees, to bear his evils, and the humanity which has been glorified in God might be an

30 Cf. Augustine, *Epist.* 194, 2:5 (*CSEL*, 57, 179 f.).

example of glorification to men.[31] Thus, in the fact that he suffered they might see what they must repay him, and in the fact that he is glorified they might consider what they must expect from him. In this way he himself can be the way by his example, and the life by his reward.[32]

CHAPTER XI

THE REASON FOR WHICH THE SACRAMENTS WERE INSTITUTED

After the first parent of mankind came into this world, when he was driven out of paradise because of the sin of disobedience, the devil, having previously seduced him by fraud, from now on exercised the right of tyranny over him and possessed him by violence. But God's providence, which disposed him to salvation, tempered the rigor of justice through mercy. Thus, though he allowed man to be oppressed by the devil for a time, yet he prepared for him a remedy out of the very penalty itself, lest he should be oppressed by the devil forever. So, then, from the very beginning of the world he set before man the sacraments of his salvation, whereby he might seal him with the expectation of future sanctification,[33] so that whoever received them with right faith and firm hope, because of obedience to divine institution, might attain to a share in freedom, even though he had been placed under the yoke of bondage.[34] Accordingly, he set forth his edict, informing and teaching man that whoever should choose to await him as a saviour and deliverer would have to prove his desire for the same election by the reception of his sacraments. The devil too set forth his sacraments whereby he might bind his own to himself, in order that the more plainly he severed them from those who rejected his rule, the more securely he might possess them.

Wherefore, as some received the sacraments of the devil and others the sacraments of Christ, mankind soon began to be divided into opposing factions, and two families were made, the one of Christ, the other of the devil.[35] For what shall I

---

[31] Cf. II Cor. 8:9; fifth century hymn, *Aeterne rex altissime* (Eng. tr., *The English Hymnal*, No. 141).
[32] Cf. John 14:6.
[33] Cf. Augustine, *De spir. et lit.*, 21, 36 (*CSEL*, 60, 189); *C. Faust. manich.*, XIX, 12 f.; 17 (*CSEL*, 25, 510 f.; 514 ff.).
[34] Cf. Gal. 5:1; I Tim. 6:1.
[35] On this theme, cf. Augustine, *De civ. dei*, together with the work of Hugh's contemporary, Otto of Freising, *De duab. civ.* (Eng. tr. C. C. Mierow, *The Two Cities*. Columbia University Press, New York, 1928).

call the incarnate Word but a king, who entered the world, through the manhood which he took upon himself, to wage war with the devil and drive him out as a tyrant and as one who by violence rules over that which is not his own? And what shall I call those earlier saints who were elected from the beginning before the incarnation of the Word but excellent soldiers, who in battle go before their king who is coming after them, strengthened and armored as if by weapons of a sort[36] by the very sacraments by which they were then sanctified? What likewise shall I call those who follow, who have been elected from the incarnation up to the end, but other soldiers, who with one accord and with eagerness follow, not another leader, but their very king himself as he goes before them, and who, though they are new soldiers armed with new weapons, are armed by the same king and take up the fight against the same foe? Accordingly, whether they go before him or follow him, they bear the sacraments of the one king, they fight under the one king, they vanquish the same tyrant, some of them going before him who was to come, others following him as he goes before them.[37]

Consequently, it is clear that from the beginning there were Christians, though not in name, yet in fact. For there are three ages through which the span of the present world runs: the first, the age of the natural law; the second, the age of the written law; the third, the age of grace.[38] The first age is from Adam till Moses; the second, from Moses till Christ; the third, from Christ till the end of the world. Likewise there are three kinds of men: the men of the natural law, the men of the written law, and the men of grace. Those men may be called men of the natural law who order their lives by natural reason alone. Or, rather, those may be called men of the natural law who walk according to the concupiscence in which they were born. The men of the written law are those who are taught to live well by outward precepts. The men of grace are those who by the inspiration of the Holy Ghost are not only enlightened that they may recognize the good which must be done, but also are inflamed thereby to love it and are strengthened thereby to perform it. To make our distinction clearer—the men of the natural law are openly evil, the men of the written law are

36 Cf. Eph. 6:10–17.
37 Cf. Abailard, *In ep. ad Rom.*, above.
38 Cf. Augustine, *De trin.*, IV, 4:7 (*PL*, 42, 892 f.); *Enarr. in Ps.* 103, 3:5 (*PL*, 37, 1362); *De div. quaest. LXXXIII*, 61, 7 (*PL*, 40, 52).

fictitiously good, the men of grace are truly good.[39] Those who are fictitiously good are covered, those who are openly evil are uncovered. These are signified by Gog and Magog,[40] which are interpreted as "covered" and "uncovered."[41] They are foretold as being about to come to persecute God's people, because these two kinds of people always persecute those who are truly good. In the first kind of men are numbered the pagans; in the second kind, the Jews; in the third kind, the Christians.

These three kinds of men have never been lacking since the beginning. Yet the age of the natural law belongs to those who are openly evil, for at that time they were most numerous and most eminent. The age of the written law belongs to those who are fictitiously good, since at that time men serving in fear made their works pure, but not their minds. The age of grace belongs to those who are truly good, who now, even though they are not more numerous, are more eminent, and by God's grace are preferred in public even by those who are contrary to them in their lives. Know, then, that at no time, whatever, from the beginning of the world till its end, there either was or is a truly good man save him who is justified by grace, and that no one could ever have obtained grace except through Christ.[42] Consequently you must recognize that all, whether they came before him or come after him, have been saved by the one remedy of sanctification. Look, therefore, on the camp of our king and the array of his army, as they shine with spiritual arms! How great is the multitude that encompass him as he goes forth, the multitude both of those who go before him and of those who follow after him!

CHAPTER XII

On the Time of the Institution of the Sacraments

It is believed that the time of the institution of the sacraments began from the moment when our first parent, on being driven into the exile of this mortal life from the joys of paradise by the merit of disobedience, was held in subjection to the first corruption, with all his posterity up to the end. For from the

---

[39] Cf. Augustine, *Sermo*, 152, 11 (*PL*, 38, 825).
[40] Cf. Ezek. 38:2; 39:1, 6; Rev. 20:7.
[41] Cf. Augustine, *De civ. dei*, XX, 10 (*CSEL*, 40/2, 454 f.).
[42] Cf. Augustine, *De pecc mer.*, I, 10:11; 14:18 (*CSEL*, 60, 12; 18); *De nat. et grat.*, 9, 10 (*CSEL*, 60, 238 f.).

moment that man, when he had fallen from the state of the first incorruption, began to be sick in body through mortality and sick in soul through iniquity, God straightway prepared a remedy in his sacraments for restoring man. These he set forth for man's healing at different times and places, as the reason and the cause demanded. Some were before the law, some under the law, others under grace. Though they are different in appearance, yet they have one effect and produce the one health.

If anyone, then, asks the time of the institution of the sacraments, let him know that the time for a remedy lasts as long as there is sickness. Accordingly, the present life, which runs from the beginning of the world till the end through mortality, is the time of sickness and the time for a remedy. In it and because of it the sacraments were instituted. Some of them were instituted from its beginning and ran their course in their time and were effective for restoring health, in so far as it had been granted them and in so far as it was to be granted through them. These sacraments ceased when their time had been completed, and others succeeded in their place to produce the same health.[43] Again, after these others were added (as it were, last of all), which were not to be succeeded by others. These were like perfect medicines which would consume the sickness itself and fully restore perfect health. And all these things were done according to the judgment and dispensation of the physician, who saw the sickness itself and knew what kind of remedies were to be applied to it at various times.

Furthermore, we find that one sacrament was instituted even before the sin of man. For we read that matrimony was ordained even before man sinned, in the place where, by the witness of Scripture, woman is mentioned as being made "a help" for man, associated with him.[44] Yet this was not instituted at that time for a remedy, but for a duty, since there was no sickness in man to be healed, but there was a virtue to be practiced. Wherefore, of the three causes of the institution of the sacraments, we find here but two, namely, instruction and practice. For where there was no pride humiliation was not necessary, but there was reason, which needed to be taught with a view to greater knowledge, and there was virtue, which needed to be advanced to greater perfection.

43 Cf. Augustine, *De vera relig.*, 17, 34 (*PL*, 34, 136); *Tr. adv. Iud.*, 3, 4 (*PL*, 42, 53).
44 Cf. Gen. 2:18–25; Mark 10:5–9.

Thus this sacrament is found with a unique law as well as a unique institution. And order seems to demand that before we proceed in our discussion to the things which must be said concerning the remaining sacraments we preface them with a few special remarks concerning this sacrament, with respect to the things that will be seen to pertain to its first institution, and that we leave for the following discourse the things which pertain to its second institution. For this sacrament has a two-fold institution, the one before sin for duty, the other after sin for a remedy. It ought, then, to be treated in a special manner according to the institution which is special to it, so that in the discourse that follows it may be treated with the other sacraments according to that institution which it has in common with them.

CHAPTER XIII

On the Institution of Matrimony Before Sin

The sacrament of matrimony alone, of all the sacraments which were instituted for man's remedy, is said in Scripture to have been instituted before man's sin. It was not instituted because of sin, but for a sacrament and a duty only—for a sacrament for the sake of instruction, for a duty for the sake of practice. For there were these two elements in matrimony— the state of matrimony itself and the duty of matrimony— either of which was a sacrament. Matrimony consisted in the consent of the bond of fellowship, the duty of matrimony con- sisted in the union of the flesh. Matrimony was the sacrament of a certain spiritual fellowship between God and the soul through love, and in this fellowship the soul is the bride and God is the bridegroom.[45] The duty of matrimony was the sacrament of a fellowship between Christ and the Church, which was to come about through the flesh which he was to take upon himself, and in this fellowship Christ was to be the bridegroom and the Church was to be the bride.[46] In both cases he who was the bridegroom was the greater, and his love was drawn through kindness to the inferior. In both cases she who was the bride was inferior, since she was not sufficient to herself and was unable to stand by herself. Accordingly, it was more by necessity that her love was turned to him who was greater than herself. He who was greater conferred a benefit

[45] Cf. Augustine, C. Faust. manich., XXII, 38 (CSEL, 25, 631 f.).
[46] Cf. Eph. 5:22–33; Augustine, Tr. in Ioan., 8, 4 (PL, 35, 1452).

by loving, she who was inferior accepted a benefit by loving. The sacrament, therefore, of this fellowship which consists on either side of mutual love, was formed when matrimony was instituted as the sacrament of the one fellowship, while in the matrimony of the other fellowship the sacrament was to be found in the duty of matrimony.

For this reason, human nature was distinguished by a two-fold quality, so that it appeared stronger in the man, but weaker and needing another's help in the woman.[47] And the two were joined in one by one love and one fellowship, so that they were in one love, and through the one love remained in one fellowship. The man, indeed, was joined therein that he might be the image of God in this sacrament, and be inclined toward love by kindness. The woman, on the other hand, was joined therein that she might express the form of the rational soul and be moved to love rather by necessity and, as it were, by the consideration of some advantage. But they were joined in such a manner that from both sides love was voluntary, for if it were not voluntary, it could be neither true love nor the sacrament of true love.

Again, that another sacrament might be formed in this fellowship, God commanded that the male and the female should be joined in one flesh, so that as they were already one through love, they also became one in the duty of matrimony through one intercourse of the flesh. It was so ordained that it might be shown that He, who in his divinity already was joined to the soul through love, afterward through the taking of flesh was joined to his Church. Furthermore, lest the matrimonial fellowship between the male and the female should be profitless, there was added after the sacrament of matrimony a duty to be fulfilled in the intercourse of the flesh, so that, as they were joined in matrimony, they might be exercised for virtue through obedience, and might be fruitful through the generation of offspring.[48] In this duty it was given to the male, as he was the greater, to engender from his own that which was to be propagated, while to the woman it was given to conceive and to give birth. Thus it might be shown in the same similitude that in that invisible fellowship the rational soul could in no wise bear fruit unless it first conceived the seed of virtue from God.

There was yet another element in human nature which was

[47] Cf. I Peter 3:7.
[48] Cf. Gen. 1:27 f.; *De pecc. orig.*, 35, 40 (*CSEL*, 42, 198 f.).

to be shown through the fellowship of marriage. Man, in fact, is so constituted that a certain element should be supreme in him, and that there should be nothing higher than that in man. After it another element is under it and subject to it, and then another element last of all is set in the lowest place and subjected to the other two. Reason, in fact, was set in the highest place, intent solely upon divine and unseen things and conforming itself to the divine will.[49] After this there is a certain other reason which looks upon bodily and visible things, and, subjected as it was to the higher reason and informed by it,[50] it had dominion over sensation, which was subjected to it and set in the third and lowest place.[51] So, then, these three principles were found in man: wisdom, prudence, and sensation. Wisdom is the reason which considers divine things, prudence the reason which considers human things, while sensation is the affection or desire for earthly things. The first of these, reason, ruled only and was not ruled by another. The last of these, sensation, was merely ruled and did not rule. The intermediate principle, reason, at once was ruled by the higher and ruled the lower.

According to this likeness three living creatures were brought forth: one a rational being which bore rule, a second irrational being which was made subject to it, and the third, likewise a rational being, which while ruled by the higher being yet bore rule over the lower, in company with the higher. Accordingly, man was the image of wisdom, woman was the form of prudence, while the beast was the likeness of sensation and appetite. Because of this the serpent beguiled the woman by advocating

---

[49] Cf. Augustine, *De mus.*, VI, 10:25 (*PL*, 32, 1177); *De lib. arb.*, II, 6:13 (*PL*, 32, 1248).

[50] This distinction between *ratio superior* and *ratio inferior* finds its *locus classicus* in Augustine, *De trin.*, XII, 3:3 (*PL*, 42, 999). The two parts of man's reason are not separate or diverse powers, but are distinguished only in terms of function; reason is *superior* as it considers eternal things, and *inferior* as it considers temporal things (*ibid.*, XII, 4:4, *PL*, 42, 1000). The higher reason is the basis of *sapientia*, knowledge of eternal things, while lower reason is the basis of *scientia*, knowledge of temporal things (*ibid.*, XIV, 1:3, *PL*, 42, 1037). It is in the higher reason that we find the image of God (*ibid.*, XII, 7:10, *PL*, 42, 1005). The same distinction between the two functions of reason is made by Bonaventure (*II Sent.*, d. 24, p.1, q.2, a.2, concl., *Opera omnia*, II, 564), Thomas Aquinas (*Sum. theol.*, Ia, q.79, a.9), and Matthew of Aquasparta (*Quaest. de cognit.*, 2, *Quaest. disp.*, I, 255). (R.D.C.)

[51] Cf. Augustine, *Quaest. de Num.*, 59 (*CSEL*, 28, 366 f.); *De vera relig.*, 29, 53 (*PL*, 34, 145).

sin, and the woman, having been beguiled, inclined the man to consent. This happened because the appetite of sense first suggests the delight of sin to the prudence of the flesh; and thereafter the prudence of the flesh, having been beguiled by the delight of sin, draws reason to consent in iniquity. For these and like reasons human nature was divided into separate parts, so that in one part it might be stronger, while in the other it is shown to be weaker, and so that in it there might be found a principle which rules and another that is ruled.

Further, there was added outwardly in the flesh a distinction in the senses, which, while not necessary in matrimony as far as the virtue of the sacrament is concerned, yet was necessary because without it the function of generation could not be fulfilled. Accordingly matrimony and the duty of matrimony were instituted before sin, and both were instituted for a sacrament, so that matrimony might be hallowed by the pure love of the mind, and also that the duty of matrimony might be fulfilled without pollution of the flesh. Now, however, since human flesh was corrupted through man's sin, it is true that after sin the intercourse of the flesh cannot take place without carnal concupiscence.[52] But perhaps someone may be moved to ask why, after sin, man cannot fulfill this very important function without sin. To him who diligently considers the matter a plain reason occurs. As long as the rational spirit was subject to its Creator it found no contradiction in its flesh, and the members of the body were subject to the dominion of the soul, so that they never moved apart from it or toward something else contrary to it. But after the spirit through pride was puffed up against its Creator, it deservedly lost the right of its former dominion over its lower self, so that the members of the body, to avenge the injury done to the Creator, contradicted its rule, since they were not to be subject to this except through the Creator.[53] Since, however, human life could not possibly subsist if the rational spirit were to have no power over the members of the body, God in part exercised his vengeance through justice and in part tempered it with mercy, so that he might at the same time punish sin and cherish nature. Hence, so that disobedience might be clearly revealed, he removed one member in the human body from the power of the soul, namely, the one through which offspring was to be engendered in the

[52] Cf. Augustine, *Epist.* 187, 9:31 (*CSEL*, 57, 108 f.).
[53] Cf. Augustine, *De civ. dei*, XXII, 23 (*CSEL*, 40/2, 640 f.); *Sermo* 151, 5 (*PL*, 38, 817); *C. Iulian. pelag.*, V, 16:66 (*PL*, 44, 820).

flesh. In this way all who should be begotten through that member might know that they were "children of disobedience,"[54] and from their origin might recognize their own nature and the nature of those of whom they were begotten. Since, then, the sign of disobedience was placed in this member through which human propagation had to pass, it is plainly shown to all who pass through it that they are begotten with the sin of disobedience.[55] For, as it were, by the very inscription which is written on the gate through which they pass they realize whence they come and whither they go.

Accordingly, because of this the remaining members of the body, which follow the government of reason, can function without sin, but this member does not function without sin, since concupiscence reigns in it particularly, because it does not follow the command of the will. For this member fails to follow the government of the will to such a degree that, just as it sometimes does not move when the soul wills, so it often moves even when the soul does not will it. Hence carnal intercourse ought not to have been practiced by man from the time that it could not be practiced without shameful concupiscence and the lust of the flesh. For man himself made this unlawful for himself from the time that he made himself incapable of fulfilling it lawfully. But since the weakness of human flesh would flow out more shamefully into all kinds of concupiscence if it were not lawfully contained in some part, that which at first was instituted solely for a duty was afterward granted for a remedy.[56] It follows that, as long as it is permitted in order that a greater evil may be avoided, the very evil of weakness which belongs to it is excused through marital chastity.

Concerning the first institution of matrimony, then, the things which have been said in this place will suffice.

54 Cf. Eph. 2:2; 5:6; Col. 3:6 (not Vulgate rendering).
55 Cf. Augustine, *De nupt. et concup.*, II, 7:17 (*CSEL*, 42, 269 f.); *C. Iulian. pelag.*, V, 4:34 (*PL*, 44, 804 f.); *Op. imperf. c. Iulian.*, I, 48; II, 31; IV, 50 f.; 55 (*PL*, 45, 1070 f.; 1155; 1368 f.; 1372).
56 Cf. Augustine, *De Gen. ad lit.*, III, 21 (*CSEL*, 28/2, 88); *De civ. dei*, XXII, 24 (*CSEL*, 40/2, 642 ff.); *De lib. arb.*, III, 20:55 (*PL*, 32, 1297); *Sermo* 51, 13:22 (*PL*, 38, 345); *Sermo* 278, 9 (*PL*, 38, 1272).

Richard of Saint Victor: Mystical Comments on the Psalms

THE TEXT

ON PSALM EIGHTY-FOUR

"Justice and peace have kissed."[1] One kind of peace exists before repentance, when the spirit submits to the flesh. Another kind of peace appears after penance has been done,[2] when the flesh is subdued to the spirit. For there is peace when the flesh desires and the spirit gives its assent. There is also peace, however, when the spirit commands and the flesh submits. Of the spirit at peace with the flesh it is said: "Now are the things that are to thy peace, but the days shall come, and they shall straiten thee on every side, and beat thee flat to the ground."[3] And again: "Peace, peace, and there is no peace,"[4] because that which is not true peace should not be called peace. Of the flesh at peace with the spirit it is said: "And peace, which surpasseth understanding, keep your hearts and minds."[5] Between the first peace and the last discord is born, war is waged, hatred is pursued, because "the flesh lusteth against the spirit, and the spirit against the flesh,"[6] when the body is being chastised and reduced to servitude. But when the warfare is accomplished, and the victory achieved, peace is arranged, discord quieted, and the transition made from one peace to the other, from the carnal to the spiritual, from the false to the true, from the evil to the good. In the first peace, the flesh dominates and the spirit serves. In the second peace the spirit

---

[1] Ps. 84:11 (P.B.V., 85:10).
[2] Note the ambiguity of *poenitentia*, as signifying both the inward virtue of "penitence" and the outward action of "penance"; cf. Thomas Aquinas, *Sum. theol.*, IIIa, qq. 84, 85.
[3] Luke 19:42–44, rather loosely quoted.
[4] Cf. Jer. 8:11.
[5] Phil. 4:7.
[6] Gal. 5:17.

reigns and the flesh submits. The first peace lies in the "region of unlikeness,"[7] where concupiscence reigns. The second peace is found in the land of promise, where justice holds sway. The passing over is indeed difficult, for it is not given to pass over from nation to nation, or from one kingdom to another people, save by "a strong hand and a stretched out arm."[8] What does it mean to pass from nation to nation, save to pass from the longings[9] of the flesh to the longings of the spirit? What does it mean to pass from kingdom to kingdom, save to pass from the kingdom of iniquity to the kingdom of charity? Distinguish, therefore, these three times: the first, when concupiscence is fulfilled; the second, when penance is accomplished; and the third, when justice is loved. Thus, as long as the flesh longs, while the spirit gives assent, there is peace, it is true, but not good peace, because it is not just, and therefore justice is displeased. Because it abominates peace of this sort, justice withdraws, and while peace does remain, it remains alone. But at length, after concupiscence has been fulfilled, it happens that the heart is stung to penitence and converted to justice, and these spring up. Then, suddenly, on the one hand the longings of the spirit are violently kindled, and on the other the longings of the flesh. The spirit indeed longs, but the flesh contradicts it. Peace is put to flight, justice returns, a mighty battle is begun. Nor does the spirit rest until it takes its kingdom in its own flesh by right, and sentences the latter to perpetual servitude. Thus the flesh serves, but first unwillingly and afterward voluntarily. Peace is established again, and a pure conscience, and this time peace comes in such a way that justice does not withdraw. Nor do they merely suffer each other now; rather, they embrace more lovingly, and link themselves by a kiss of charity, as it is written: "Justice and peace have kissed." First, therefore, there is peace, but peace alone, in the time when concupiscence is experienced. Secondly, however, there is justice, and justice alone, in the time when penance is accomplished. But last of all there are peace and justice together, in the time of the cleansed conscience.

[7] On the *regio dissimilitudinis*, cf. E. Gilson, *The Mystical Theology of St. Bernard* (Sheed and Ward, London, 1940), 45, 115 f., 205. The phrase goes back to Augustine, *Conf.*, VII, 10:16 (*CSEL*, 33, 157).
[8] Deut. 5:15.
[9] *Concupiscentias*; note the neutral sense of the term.

Richard of Saint Victor: On Ezekiel's Vision (*The First Part of the Prologue*)

THE TEXT

A LITERAL EXPLANATION OF THE ANIMALS AND WHEELS

There are many for whom the divine Scriptures become sweeter, when they are able to perceive in them some fitting meaning according to the letter. And then, as it seems to them, the structure of the spiritual understanding is more firmly established, when it is properly founded on the solidity of the historical sense. For who could lay any foundation, or firmly establish it, on the void and empty alone? For since the mystical senses are drawn out and formed from the harmonious likeness of those things that are put forward in the letter, how can the latter furnish us for spiritual understanding, at least as far as those places are concerned where it is in opposition to itself, or else proclaims nothing that is not trifling? Thus people of this sort are often scandalized, rather than edified, when they come upon places like this in the Scriptures. The ancient Fathers, on the contrary, readily accepted the fact when they ran into places of this kind in the Scriptures, which could not stand according to the letter. For from these they compelled certain persons who accepted Holy Scripture, and yet mocked at the allegorical senses—they compelled them, I say, from these absurd passages of the letter—to flee to the spiritual interpretation, since they did not dare to deny that nothing that the Holy Spirit has written, even in the greatest possible absurdity of the letter, is useless. For this reason, I think, it happened that, in dealing with certain more obscure texts, the ancient Fathers silently passed over the exposition of the letter, or at least treated it rather more negligently, although if they had set about it more thoroughly they could undoubtedly have done it more perfectly than any modern scholar.[1] But I do not mean

[1] Note the description of Richard's contemporaries as *moderni*.

to pass over, in silence, the fact that certain people, as though on account of reverence for the Fathers, do not want to attempt the things which the latter neglected, lest they seem to presume in going beyond their forefathers. But having a veil for their idleness of this kind, they settle down in a stupefied leisure, and deride, mock, and blow upon the industry shown by others in the search for and discovery of the truth. But "he that dwelleth in heaven shall laugh at them, and the Lord shall deride them."[2] Let us, however, take up with all avidity the things investigated by the Fathers, and let us diligently and with all alacrity search after the things neglected by them, and let us display publicly with all liberality the things that we have found and know to be correct. Then that which was written may be fulfilled: "Many shall pass over, and knowledge shall be manifold."[3] For instance, blessed Gregory expounded that marvelous vision of the celestial animals, which Ezekiel saw, according to the mystical interpretation.[4] But how it can stand according to the letter he does not say; in fact, he says of the second vision that it cannot stand according to the letter.[5] And this indeed is true, but only according to the acceptation which he himself assigned to it there, for if we wish to examine the same letter in terms of another presentation, perhaps we shall manage to draw out from it a fitting interpretation, even according to the historical sense. Certainly the same man says, in the same exposition of Ezekiel, that for the most part something is expressed obscurely in the sacred utterance so that, by God's marvelous dispensation, it may be expounded in many ways.[6] The manifold exposition, therefore, of sacred Scripture should never be spurned, in so far as it seems to agree with reason or to serve our welfare. In so far, then, as each has received grace for this, let no one hesitate to seek with all diligence for the things which the sagacity of the Fathers either passed over out of industry or else could not unfold, wrapped up as they were in occupation with more necessary things. Thus I shall readily say what seems good to me concerning this prophetic vision, for perhaps this our exposition, whatever it is like—even if it cannot satisfy another's skill—will by good fortune be able to

2 Ps. 2:4.
3 Dan. 12:4.
4 Cf. Gregory the Great, Homil. in Ezech. (PL, 76, 785–1072). Bk. I, hom. 2–7 (cols. 795–853), cover the same ground as Richard's prologue.
5 The closest parallel I have found to this is in Gregory, Homil. in Ezech., I, 6:17 (PL, 76, 835).
6 Gregory, op. cit., I, 6:1 (PL, 76, 829).

assist the diligence of others to this end, and to give some help to the business of research.

Now he says of the living creatures: "There was the likeness of a man in them."[7] In fact, as far as pertains to the letter, this was, on the one hand, the likeness of a man, and on the other hand it was not, as what follows indicates. On the one hand it was, since they had the face and hands of a man, and, again, on the other hand it was not, since they had wings and feet like a calf and several faces; on this account he adds with respect to them: "Every one had four faces, and every one four wings."[8] If heavenly living creatures have four faces and corresponding parts, then, contrary to the nature of terrestrial animals, they are able to see in every direction at the same moment. And "their feet were straight feet."[9] They had to have straight feet, so that they could step in every direction without any turning of the body, as is gathered from what follows. "And the sole of their foot was like the sole of a calf's foot."[10] These living creatures are described as having a calf's sole so that we may understand that they are protected naturally, and not, as in the case of men, by the result of industry. But for them to be able to step in the same way in every direction it was necessary for the shape of their feet to exceed calf likeness in some part. Moreover, when it is said that there were "sparks" in them, or, rather, coming from them, as if of "glowing brass,"[11] it is shown that they had fiery faces which scattered burning sparks. "And they had faces and wings on the four sides."[12] Certainly if, as was said above, they had four faces, and if, as is said here, that had these on four sides, it must be that on each side, as far as the letter is concerned, they had only one. Moreover, they had four wings, so that in whatever direction they were turned, they could fly equally well in any direction.

7 Ezek. 1:5.   8 Ezek. 1:6.   9 Ezek. 1:7.
10 Ibid.   11 Ibid.   12 Ezek. 1:8.

Richard of Saint Victor: On the Trinity

THE TEXT

SELECTIONS FROM BOOK ONE

CHAPTER I

WE ACQUIRE THE KNOWLEDGE OF THINGS IN A THREEFOLD WAY: BY EXPERIENCE, BY REASONING, BY BELIEF

If we wish to ascend with keen minds to the knowledge of sublime realities, the price of achievement is first to know in what ways we usually have knowledge of things. Now, if I am not deceived, we acquire knowledge of things in a threefold way. For we judge some things by experience, we infer other things by reasoning, we possess certainty of other things still by believing. And, in fact, we acquire knowledge of temporal things by experience itself. But we rise to the knowledge of eternal things, sometimes by reasoning, sometimes by believing. For certain of the things we are commanded to believe seem not only above reason, but even against human reason, unless they are investigated by deep and most subtle searching, or, rather, are manifested by divine revelation. Thus, in our knowledge or our affirmation of these things we are accustomed to rest more upon faith than upon reasoning, more upon authority than upon argumentation, according to the text of the prophet: "Unless you believe, you will not understand."[1] But something else in these words seems to require careful attention. The understanding of these things is put before us by this authority as a thing to be conditionally, but not categorically, denied, when it is said, "Unless you believe, you will not understand." Therefore, those who possess trained minds must not despair of reaching the understanding of such things. At the same time, let them feel themselves firm in faith, and of proved constancy in the affirmation of their faith through all things.

[1] Isa. 7:9; cf. p. 73, n. 22.

CHAPTER II

NOTHING IS HELD MORE FIRMLY THAN THAT WHICH IS APPREHENDED WITH CONSTANT FAITH

But in all this one thing is above measure wonderful, namely, that as many of us as are truly faithful hold nothing more surely, nothing more constantly, than what we apprehend by faith. For these things were revealed to the fathers from heaven, and divinely confirmed by so many great and marvelous portents that it seems to be a kind of madness to harbor even the slightest doubt in these matters. Thus countless miracles and other things which can only be done by divine power lead to faith of this sort and do not permit us to doubt. Thus we use, for the attestation and even the confirmation of these truths, signs in place of arguments, and portents instead of experiments. Would that the Jews would pay attention! Would that the pagans would take notice! When we are able with such great security of conscience in this respect to approach the divine judgment, shall we not be able to speak with all confidence to God: O Lord, if it is error, we have been deceived by thyself, for these things have been confirmed in us by such great signs and wonders—such indeed as could only be done by thee? Certainly they have been delivered to us by men of the highest sanctity; moreover, since they have been proved by the highest and most authentic attestation, thyself "working withal, and confirming the word with signs that followed,"[2] it follows assuredly that those who are perfectly faithful are more ready to die for the faith than to deny the faith. For beyond doubt nothing is held more firmly than that which is apprehended by constant faith.

CHAPTER III

THIS WORK HAS TO DO WITH WHAT WE ARE COMMANDED TO BELIEVE CONCERNING ETERNAL THINGS

Thus we must indeed enter by faith into the knowledge of those things of which it is rightly said to us, "If you do not believe, you will not understand."[3] Nevertheless, we must not halt as soon as we reach the entrance itself, but must always be hastening to the more inward and deeper things of under-

---

[2] Mark 16:20.   [3] Cf. n. 1.

standing, and must press on with all zeal and the greatest diligence, so that by daily increases we may be able to advance to the knowledge of the things we hold by faith.[4] It is in the full knowledge and perfect understanding of these that eternal life is obtained. Truly, the highest benefit lies in the acquisition of these things, the highest enjoyment in the contemplation of them. These are the highest riches, these the everlasting pleasures; in the taste of these is the ultimate sweetness, in the enjoyment of these is infinite delight. Thus in this work we have undertaken to deal with those things which we are commanded to believe by the rule of Catholic faith—not about anything at all, but about eternal things. For we do not intend, in this work, to do anything about the sacraments[5] of our redemption which are done in time, and which we are commanded to believe and do believe. For there is one method of treating these matters, and another way of dealing with eternal things.

CHAPTER IV

THE MODE OF PROCEDURE IN THIS WORK: NOT SO MUCH TO BRING FORWARD AUTHORITIES AS TO PRESS ON TO REASONING

In so far, therefore, as God grants it to us, it will be our intention in this work to adduce reasons which are necessary, and not merely probable, for the things we believe,[6] and to season the lessons of our faith by the explanation and interpretation of the truth. For I believe without any doubt that not only probable but also necessary arguments are available for the explanations of such things as exist necessarily, even though it may happen that at present they hide from our industry. In the case of all things which began to be in time, by the good pleasure of the Creator it is possible for them to exist and it is possible for them not to exist, and it follows, by the same token, that their existence is not so much inferred by reasoning as proved by experience. But things that are eternal simply cannot not-exist; just as they never have not-been, so they certainly shall never not-be, or, rather, they always are what they are, nor can they be another thing or exist in another

---

[4] Cf. Anselm, *Epist. de incarn. verbi*, above.
[5] *Sacramentum* has here its general sense of a sacred mystery, rather than the more precise sense of an ordained, visible means of grace; cf. the usage of Hugh of St. Victor in *De sacramentis christianae fidei*.
[6] Cf. the argument of Anselm's *Cur deus homo*.

way.[7] Now it seems altogether impossible for any necessary thing not to exist, and to lack a necessary reason, but it is not for any soul to elicit reasons of this kind from the deep and obscure bosom of nature, and as it were to draw them out publicly, having brought them from some inmost secret place of wisdom. Many are less worthy of this, many less fitted for this, many less eager for this, and we rarely or hardly ever think of what we ought always, if it were possible, to hold before our eyes. With what sort of zeal, I ask, and with what great longing ought we to take pains over this matter, to marvel at this spectacle on which depends the highest blessedness of all who are to be saved! Now I believe that I have done something, if only it has been given to me to give to zealous minds even a little help in this matter, and by my zeal to incite lukewarm minds to such zeal.

CHAPTER V

A Brief Preview of What Is Dealt with in the Following Pages

I have often read that there is no God but one; that he is eternal, uncreated, infinite; that he is almighty and the Lord of all; that everything that exists is from him; that he is everywhere, and everywhere whole, not divided into parts. I have read concerning my God that he is one and three, one in substance but three in persons; all these things I have read, but I do not remember having read by what all these are proved.[8] I have read that in the true divinity there is but one substance; that in the unity of substance there are several persons, each distinguished from each of the others by his particular property;[9] that there is a person who is of himself, not of any other;[10] that there is a person who is of one alone, but not of himself;[11] that there is a person who is of two persons together, but not from one alone.[12] I hear daily concerning the

---

7 Cf. Anselm, *Proslogion*, 22, and *passim*.
8 All the doctrinal statements in this chapter are derived from the *Quicumque vult.*
9 On the *proprietates personales* of the persons of the Trinity (i.e., the ground of the distinction of person from person), cf. Thomas Aquinas, *Sum. theol.*, I a, q.40.
10 I.e., the Father, who is *ingenitus* (unbegotten).
11 I.e., the Son, begotten of the Father alone, before all ages.
12 I.e., the Holy Spirit, understood as proceeding from Father and Son.

three that there are not three eternals, but one eternal; that there are not three uncreated nor three infinites, but one uncreated and one infinite. I hear concerning the three that there are not three almighties, but one almighty; I hear nonetheless that there are not three Gods, but one God; not three Lords, but one Lord. I find that the Father is not made, nor begotten; that the Son is not made, but begotten; that the Spirit is not made, nor begotten, but proceeding. All these things I often hear or read, but I do not recall having read how all these are proved; authorities[13] abound in all these matters, but arguments do not equal them; experiences are lacking in connection with all these things, and arguments are rare. I think, then, that (as I have already said above) I shall have achieved something if in the study of this sort of question I can give at least a little help to studious minds, even though it may not be given me to satisfy them.

SELECTIONS FROM BOOK THREE

CHAPTER I

HITHERTO WE HAVE BEEN DEALING WITH THE UNITY OF THE DIVINE SUBSTANCE; NOW WE ARE TO ASK IN SOME WAY WHAT WE SHOULD THINK CONCERNING THE PLURALITY OF DIVINE PERSONS

In what has been said up to the present about the unity or attributes of the divine substance we have carried out the discussion as it seemed best to us. But in the remainder of the work we have planned to inquire what we ought to think concerning the plurality or the properties of the divine persons. The first question which we apparently must discuss is this:

13 *Auctoritates.* The evolution and various meanings of the term *auctoritas,* and its role in medieval scholarship, are outlined by M. D. Chenu, *Introduction à l'étude de saint Thomas d'Aquin* (Institut d'études médiévales, Montreal, 1950), 109–113. The term refers initially to the quality in virtue of which a man is considered worthy of consideration or belief; secondly, it means the person who possesses this quality; finally, it comes to mean the writings of such a person, or the specific text invoked in support of a particular argument. It constitutes a kind of argument from tradition, an attempt to establish a consensus of witnesses to the truth of a position. On the methods used in effecting a reconciliation of discordant authorities, from Isidore of Seville to Abailard, cf. J. de Ghellinck, *Le Mouvement théologique du XIIᵉ siècle,* 482 ff. (R.D.C.).

Is there, in that true and simple divinity, a true plurality, and does that number of persons (as we believe) amount to three? Secondly, we must ask how unity of substance can be combined with plurality of persons. But, in the third place, it will be necessary to inquire whether, according to the teachings of our faith, there is one Person alone who is of himself, while each of the others proceeds from another, and any other things which need to be investigated in this connection. Finally, if it is given to us to demonstrate these things from reason, it will be necessary to carry our inquiry to this point: Whether in those two persons who proceed otherwise than from themselves there are diverse modes of procession,[14] and which mode is proper to each, and what follows with respect to the properties and concerning the names of each of them. Now in the matters that remain to be investigated, it is necessary to apply much greater diligence and press forward more ardently, inasmuch as less can be found in the writings of the Fathers from which we can demonstrate these things—demonstrate them, I say, not by testimonies drawn from the Scriptures, but by the attestation of reason. Now let him who will laugh at my plan of inquiry, and him who will jeer—and fairly enough. For, to own the truth, knowledge does not actually lift me up, so much as the ardor of a burning mind stimulates me to hazard the attempt. What if it is not given to me to arrive at the goal of my endeavor? What if I fail in my running? I shall rejoice nonetheless in seeking the face of my Lord,[15] if I have always run, labored, sweated, according to my powers. And if I should happen to fail before reaching the too great things I seek, because of the great length, the difficulty, and the hardness of the way, I shall have done something if in fact I can say truthfully, I have done what I could, I have sought and I have not found him, I have called and he has not answered me. And look, that ass of Balaam's, which delayed its rider on his journey,[16] urges and incites me—by what means I know not—to run the way I have begun. I also hear her speaking and saying to me: He who could make me able to speak will doubtless be able to give the same gift to you as well. But now let us press on with all diligence to what we have planned.

14 I.e., *generatio* and *spiratio*; cf. Thomas Aquinas, *Sum. theol.*, Ia, q.30, a.2.
15 Cf. Ps. 26:8 (P.B.V., 27:9); Anselm, *Proslogion*, 1.
16 Cf. Num. 22:22–35.

CHAPTER II

How, Beginning from the Attribute of Charity, It Is Proved by the Fullness of Goodness that Plurality of Persons Cannot Be Lacking in the True Divinity

From the above we have learned that complete goodness, in all its fullness and perfection, is to be found in that highest and universally perfect good. But where the fullness of goodness exists, true and supreme charity cannot be lacking. For nothing is better than charity, nothing more perfect than charity.[17] Now no one is properly said to have charity because of his private and particular love[18] of himself. For charity to exist, then, it is necessary for love to tend to another; where plurality of persons is lacking, therefore, there simply cannot be charity. But perhaps you will say: Even though there were only one person in that true divinity, nonetheless he could in fact have charity toward his creation; rather, he would have it. He could not, however, have the highest charity toward a created person. But it is impossible that charity should be inordinate in the goodness of that highest wisdom. A divine person, then, could not have the highest charity toward a person who was not worthy of the highest love.[19] But for charity to be supreme and supremely perfect, it must be so great that it could not be greater, it must be such that it could not be better. But as long as anyone loves no one but himself, that private love which he has toward himself demonstrates that he has yet to reach the highest level of charity. A divine person, however, would certainly not have anything that he could fittingly love as himself, if he did not have a wholly deserving person to love. But no person could be wholly deserving of the love of a divine person if he were not God. Therefore, in order for the fullness of charity to have its place in that true divinity, it is necessary for any divine person not to lack a wholly worthy person, and by the same token not to lack divine fellowship. Observe, then, how easily reason proves that plurality of persons cannot be lacking in the true divinity. Certainly, God alone is supremely good. God alone,

---

[17] Cf. I Cor. 13:13.
[18] *Amor*; this chapter is an outstanding example of what A. Nygren calls the "caritas-synthesis" (cf. *Agape and Eros*, 2d Engl. ed., rev. [S.P.C.K., London, 1953]).
[19] *Dilectio*.

therefore, is to be supremely loved. A divine person, therefore, could not display the highest love[20] toward a person who lacked divinity. But the fullness of divinity could not have existed without the fullness of goodness. But the fullness of goodness could not have existed without the fullness of charity, nor the fullness of charity without the plurality of divine persons.

[20] *Dilectio.*

Adam of Saint Victor: Sequence for a Saint's Day

THE TEXT

Joy and triumph everlasting
    Hath the heavenly Church on high;
For that pure immortal gladness
    All our feast-days mourn and sigh:
Yet in death's dark desert wild
Doth the mother aid her child,[1]
Guards celestial thence attend us,
Stand in combat to defend us.

Here the world's perpetual warfare
    Holds from heaven the soul apart;
Legioned foes in shadowy terror
    Vex the Sabbath of the heart.[2]
O how happy that estate
Where delight doth not abate;
For that home the spirit yearneth,
Where none languisheth nor mourneth.

There the body hath no torment,
    There the mind is free from care,[3]
There is every heart rejoicing,
    Every heart is loving there.
Angels in that city dwell;
Them their king delighteth well:
Still they joy and weary never,
More and more desiring ever.

---

[1] On the somewhat unusual description of the church triumphant as the "mother," and the church militant as the "daughter," cf. J. Julian, *A Dictionary of Hymnology* (rev. ed., London, 1915), 1103.
[2] On the "Sabbath rest" as the goal of the Christian, cf. Abailard's hymn, *O quanta qualia*, above.   [3] Cf. Rev. 21:4.

There the seers and fathers holy,
   There the prophets glorified,
All their doubts and darkness ended,
   In the Light of light abide.
There the saints, whose memories old
We in faithful hymns uphold,
Have forgot their bitter story
In the joy of Jesu's glory.

There from lowliness exalted
   Dwelleth Mary, Queen of grace,
Ever with her presence pleading
   'Gainst the sin of Adam's race.
To that glory of the blest,
By their prayers and faith confest,
Us, us too, when death hath freed us,
Christ of his good mercy lead us.

—*From* The Yattendon Hymnal, *edited by Robert Bridges, by permission of The Clarendon Press, Oxford.*

Peter Lombard: The Four Books of Sentences

THE TEXT

BOOK III, DISTINCTION X

CHAPTER I

WHETHER CHRIST, AS MAN, IS A PERSON OR A SOMETHING

It is often asked by certain people, whether Christ, as man, is a person, or whether he is a something.[1]

The arguments on both sides of the question agree. For that he is a person they proclaim for these reasons. If, as man, he is a something, he is either a person, or a substance, or something else. But he is not something else; therefore he is a person or a substance. But if he is a substance, he is either rational or irrational. But he is not an irrational substance; therefore he is rational. If, as man, he is a rational substance, then he is a person, because that is the definition of a person: "A rational substance of an individual nature."[2] If, therefore, as man, he is a something, he also, as man, is a person.

But conversely, if, as man, he is a person, either he is the third person in the Trinity, or another person. But he is not another person; therefore he is the third person in the Trinity. But if, as man, he is the third person in the Trinity, then he is God.

Because of these incongruities and others, some say that Christ as man is not a person nor a something, unless, by chance, "as" expresses a unity of person. For "as" has many senses[3]: sometimes it expresses a condition or property of divine nature, or human nature; sometimes the unity of a person;

---

[1] The opinion that Christ, as man, is not a something was condemned as heretical by Alexander III in 1177. Cf. J. de Ghellinck, *Le Mouvement théologique de XIIᵉ siècle*, 252 ff.

[2] Cf. Boethius, *Lib. de pers. et duab. nat.*, 3 (*PL*, 64, 1343): "A person is an individual substance of a rational nature"; a good many of Peter's patristic quotations are inexact.

[3] "As" seems the best rendering of *secundum* in this context.

sometimes it refers to a habit; sometimes to a cause. Let the reader attend to the point of this distinction carefully and store it in his memory, lest its sense be confused, when the word occurs with respect to Christ.

The conclusion in the argument above, that if Christ, as man, is a rational substance, then he is a person, does not follow. For only the soul of Christ is a rational substance, not his person, for the latter does not act through itself but rather when joined to another thing. That description of a person, however, is not given for those three persons.

But now they endeavor to prove in another way that Christ, as man, is a person, because Christ, as man, "was predestinated the son of God"[4]; but that is what he was predestined to be. Therefore if he was predestined, as man, to be the son of God, then, as man, he is the son of God.

To which it can be said that Christ is that which he was predestined to be; for he was predestined to be the son of God, and he truly is the son of God. But, as man, he was predestined to be the son of God, because he had this predestination through grace, as man. However, he is not the son of God as man, unless perhaps "as" expresses a unity of person. Then the sense would be: he, who is man, is the son of God. Thus he, a human being, is the son of God, through the grace which he has. But if a cause is signified, it is false; for it is not by the fact that he is man that he is the Son of God.[5]

CHAPTER II

Whether Christ, as Man, Is an Adopted Son

If it is asked whether Christ is an adopted son, as man, or in some other way, we reply that Christ is not an adopted son in any way, but only a natural Son. For he is a Son by nature, not by the grace of adoption.

He is not called Son by nature as he is called God by nature; for he is not Son from that by which he is God, since he is Son by the property of nativity, while he is God by the nature of divinity. However the term nature, or Son of nature, is used because he is a Son naturally, having the same nature as he who begot.

4 Rom. 1:4; cf. Abailard, *Sic et non*, 69 (*PL*, 178, 1441).
5 On the distinction made in this answer, cf. the *Glossa* on Rom. 1:4, as given by Nicholas of Lyra.

Moreover he is not an adopted son, because he did not first exist and then become adopted as son, as we are spoken of as adopted sons in that when we were born we were "sons of wrath" but have been made "sons of God" through grace.[6] There never was a time when Christ was not a son and therefore he is not an adopted son.

But against this one can argue thus: If Christ is the son of man, that is of a virgin, it is either by grace or by nature, or by both. If this is so by nature, then it is either by divine nature or by human nature; but not by divine nature, therefore either by human nature or else he is not by nature the son of man. If it is not by nature, then by grace alone; and indeed, if by human nature, not thereby less through grace. If, therefore, he is the son of the virgin by grace, he seems to be an adopted son, so that the same man is a natural Son of the Father and an adopted son of the virgin.

To this it can be said that Christ is the son of the virgin by nature, or naturally, or naturally and by grace. He is not, however, the adopted son of the virgin, since it is not through adoption, but through union, that he is called the son of the virgin. For he is called son of the virgin in that in the virgin he received a man into the unity of a person; and this was by ᵥgrace, not by nature.

Thus Augustine in On John says: "That the Only-begotten is equal to the Father is not from grace but from nature. However that a man was assumed into the unity of person of the only-begotten, is from grace, not from nature."[7] Christ, therefore, is the adopted son neither of God nor of man, but the Son of God naturally and the son of man naturally and by grace.

Augustine shows that he is the son of man naturally in the book To Peter on the Faith: "He, namely God, who is naturally the only-begotten Son of God the Father, was made the son of man naturally."[8]

Moreover, that he is not an adopted son, and yet is son by grace, is proved by the following testimonies.

Jerome, in On the Epistle to the Ephesians, says: "It is written about Christ Jesus, that he was always with the Father, and that the paternal will never, as it were, preceded him"[9]; "and

---

[6] Cf. Eph. 2:3; Abailard, Sic et non, 67 (PL, 178, 1437).
[7] Augustine, Tr. in Ioan. 74, 3 (PL, 35, 1828).
[8] Cap. 2, 14 (PL, 40, 757); this work was actually written by Fulgentius of Ruspe.
[9] Cap. 1, 5 (PL, 26, 478).

he was son by nature, we by adoption. He never was not a son; we, before we were, were predestined, and then we received the Spirit of adoption, because we believed in the Son of God."[10]

Hilary too, in Book III of *On the Trinity*, says: "The Lord saying, 'Glorify thy Son,' is witness that he is Son not only by name, but also by property. We are sons of God, but not like this Son. For he is true Son, in the strict sense, by origin, not by adoption; by truth, not by name; by nativity, not by creation."[11]

Augustine, in *On John*, also says: "We are sons by grace, not by nature; the Only-begotten is by nature, not by grace. Does this also refer to the man in the Son himself? Yes, certainly."[12]

Ambrose too, in Book I of *On the Trinity*, says: "Christ is Son, not through adoption but through nature. We are called sons through adoption, but he is Son through the truth of nature."[13]

These statements make it evident that Christ is not a Son by the grace of adoption. That is the grace understood when Augustine asserts that he is not Son by grace; for by the grace, not of adoption, but rather of union, the Son of God is the son of man, and conversely.

CHAPTER III

WHETHER THE PERSON OR THE NATURE WAS PREDESTINED

Next, if the question is asked whether that predestination, which the apostle mentions, is with reference to the person or to the nature, it can be answered definitely. The person of the Son, which always was, was predestined so far as the man assumed is concerned; so that that very person, namely, a human being, would be the Son of God. The human nature was predestined to be personally united to the Word of the Father.[14]

---

10 *Ibid.*
11 Hilary, *De trin.*, III, 11 (*PL*, 10, 82); cf. John 17:5.
12 Augustine, *Tr. in Ioan.* 82, 4 (*PL*, 35, 1844).
13 Cf. Ambrose, *De fide.* I, 19:126 (*PL*, 16, 580).
14 Cf. Abailard, *Sic et non*, 69 (*PL*, 178, 1441).

BOOK IV, DISTINCTION I

CHAPTER I

On the Sacraments

The Samaritan, approaching the wounded man, used the bands of the sacraments to heal him,[15] since God instituted the remedies of sacraments against the wounds of original and actual sin.

Four things to be considered first present themselves in this connection[16]: What is a sacrament? Why was it instituted? Of what things does it consist and is it made up? What is the difference between the sacraments of the old and of the new law?

CHAPTERS II–IV

What Is a Sacrament?

(Chapter II) "A sacrament is a sign of a sacred thing."[17] However a sacrament is also called a sacred secret just as it is called a sacrament of the deity,[18] so that a sacrament both signifies something sacred and is something sacred signified; but now it is a question of a sacrament as a sign.

Again, "A sacrament is the visible form of an invisible grace."[19]

(Chapter III) "A sign is something beyond the appearance, which it presses on the senses, for it makes something else enter thought."[20]

(Chapter IV) "Some signs are natural, such as smoke signifying fire; others are given";[21] and of those which are

---

15 Cf. Luke 10:30.
16 Cf. *Sum. sent.*, 4, 1 (*PL*, 176, 117); Hugh of St. Victor, *De sacram.*, I, p. 9, 1 (*PL*, 176, 317).
17 Cf. Augustine, *De civ. dei*, X, 5 (*CSEL*, 40/1, 452); *C. advers. leg. et prophet.*, 9, 34 (*PL*, 42, 658). Cf. n. 16 above.
18 On *sacramentum*, *secretum*, and *mysterium* in the formative period of the Latin theological vocabulary, cf. J. de Ghellinck, *et. al.*, *Pour l'histoire du mot 'sacramentum*,' I (Louvain, 1924). (E.R.F.)
19 Augustine, *Quaest. in Pent.*, III, 84 (*PL*, 34, 712). Cf. *Sum. sent.*, *loc. cit.*, Abailard, *Introd.*, I, 2 (*PL*, 178, 984).
20 Augustine, *De doct. christ.*, II, 1:1 (*PL*, 34, 35).
21 *Ibid.*, 1:2.

given, certain ones are sacraments, certain ones are not, for every sacrament is a sign, but not conversely.

A sacrament bears a likeness of that thing whose sign it is. "For if sacraments did not have a likeness of the things whose sacraments they are, they would properly not be called sacraments."[22] For that is properly called a sacrament which is a sign of the grace of God and a form of invisible grace, so that it bears its image and exists as its cause.[23] Sacraments were instituted, therefore, for the sake, not only of signifying, but also of sanctifying.[24]

For those which were instituted for the sake of signifying only are signs only and not sacraments; just as were the carnal sacrifices and ceremonial observances of the old law,[25] which were never able to make the offerers righteous; because, as the apostle says, "the blood of goats and of oxen, and the ashes of an heifer being sprinkled, sanctify such as are defiled, to the cleansing of the flesh,"[26] not of the soul; for that defilement was the touching of a dead man.

Thus Augustine says: "I know of no other iniquity which the law cleanses except contact with a dead man. He who had touched one 'was unclean seven days'; but he was purified according to the law on the third day and on the seventh, and was clean,"[27] so that he might enter the Temple.

Those legal means also cleansed meanwhile from bodily leprosy; but never was anyone justified by the works of the law, as the apostle says,[28] even if they were done in faith and love. Why? Because God imposed them for servitude, not for justification, and that they might be a figure of Him who was to come,[29] wishing them to be offered to him rather than to idols. These things, therefore, were signs, but nevertheless sacraments also, even though they are often referred to less properly in the Scriptures, because they were signs of a sacred thing which they certainly did not perform. The apostle calls those things "works of the law"[30] which were instituted only for the sake of signifying or as a burden.

[22] Augustine, *Epist.* 98, 9 (*CSEL*, 44, 531); cf. *Sum. sent.*, *loc. cit.*
[23] Cf. *Sum. sent.*, *loc. cit.*
[24] Cf. *ibid.*
[25] Cf. Lev. 16:15.
[26] Heb. 9:13.
[27] Augustine, *Quaest. in Pent.*, IV, 33 (*PL*, 34, 735); cf. Num. 19:11.
[28] Cf. Rom. 3:20; Gal. 2:16.
[29] Cf. Rom. 5:14.
[30] Rom. 5:14; cf. Acts 15:10.

CHAPTER V

WHY THE SACRAMENTS WERE INSTITUTED

"The sacraments were instituted for a threefold cause: as a means of increasing humility, as a means of instruction, and as a spur to activity.

"As a means of increasing humility indeed, so that man submits himself, out of reverence for God's command, to sensible things which by nature are beneath him. By this humility and obedience he is more pleasing and meritorious to the God by whose command he seeks salvation in things lower than himself, although not from them, but through them from God.

"They were also instituted as a means of instruction so that, through that which is perceived from without in a visible form, the mind may be instructed to understand the invisible virtue which is inward; for man, who before sin saw God without a medium, is so dulled through sin that he does not know how to grasp divine things unless he is stirred by human things.

"Similarly they were instituted as a means of spurring into activity, for since man cannot be unoccupied, a useful and healthy spur is provided for him in the sacraments, by means of which he turns away from empty and harmful occupation."[31] For he whom practice makes free to attend to goodness is not easily captured by the tempter. Thus Jerome warns, "Always be earnestly engaged in some work, so that the devil may find you occupied."[32] "Of activity, moreover, there are three kinds; one pertains to the building up of the soul, another to the nourishment of the body, the other to the overturning of each."[33]

Since, therefore, God could give grace to man without the sacraments, to which he has not bound his power,[34] he has instituted sacraments for the aforesaid reasons.

"Moreover, there are two constituents of a sacrament, namely, words and things: words such as the invocation of the Trinity; things such as water, oil, and the like."

---

[31] Hugh, *De sacram.*, I, p. 9, 3 (*PL*, 176, 319 ff.), abbreviated at some points; cf. *Sum. sent., loc. cit.*

[32] Cf. Jerome, *Epist.* 125, 11 (*CSEL*, 56, 129 f.).

[33] *Sum. sent.*, 4, 1 (*PL*, 176, 118).

[34] Not in the sense that God does not always act in the sacraments, but in the sense that he may act outside them. (E.R.F.)

CHAPTER VI

On the Difference Between the Old and New Sacraments

Now there remains to be seen the difference between the old sacraments and the new, so that we may call sacraments what in former times used to signify sacred things, such as sacrifices and oblations and the like.

Augustine, indeed, briefly indicated the difference between these, when he said, "While the former only promised and signified, the latter give salvation."[35]

CHAPTER VII

On Circumcision

Nevertheless there was among them a certain sacrament, namely, circumcision, conferring the same remedy against sin which baptism now does.

Thus Augustine says[36]: "From the time that circumcision was instituted among the people of God it was a 'seal of the righteousness of faith'[37] and availed for old and young for the purging of original and former sin; just as baptism began to avail for the restoration of man from the time when it was instituted."

Again Bede says: "Circumcision in the law effected the same means of healthful cure against the wound of original sin which baptism customarily effects in the time of revealed grace, with the exception that they were not able yet to enter the doorway of the Kingdom of Heaven. However, after death, consoled in the bosom of Abraham in blessed rest, they waited with joyful hope for the beginning of celestial peace."[38]

In these words it is clearly conveyed that through circumcision, from the time of its institution, the remission of original and actual sin for young and old was offered by God, just as now it is given in baptism.

---

[35] Augustine, *Enarr. in Ps.* 73, 2 (*PL*, 36, 931).
[36] *De nupt. et concup.*, II, 11:24 (*CSEL*, 42, 276 f.). Everything in Chs. VII–X was taken by the Lombard from *Sum. sent.*, 4, 1 (*PL*, 176, 119); cf. Ivo of Chartres, *Decret.*, p. 1, 50, and *Panorm.*, I, 11 (*PL*, 161, 80; 1049); Abailard, *Sic et non* (*PL*, 178, 1504); Gratian, *Decret.* C. *Ex. quo* (6), De consecr., dist. 4 (Friedberg, I, 1363).
[37] Rom. 4:11.
[38] Bede, *Hom.* 10, *in circumcis. domini* (*PL*, 94, 54.)

CHAPTER VIII

WHAT REMEDY THOSE WHO WERE BEFORE CIRCUMCISION HAD

Moreover, a question is asked about men who lived before the circumcision, and about women who lived before and after, namely, what remedy they had against sin.

Some say that sacrifices and oblations availed for them for the remission of sin. But it is better to say that those who sprang from Abraham were justified through circumcision. Women, indeed, were justified through faith and good works, either their own, if they were adults, or those of their parents if they were children. Those children who were before the circumcision were justified in the faith of their parents, while parents were justified by the virtue of sacrifices, that is, by what they understood spiritually in those sacrifices.

From this Gregory concludes: "What the water of baptism has the power to do among us was done among the ancients in various ways: for children by faith alone, for adults by the virtue of sacrifice, and for those who sprang from the descendants of Abraham by the mystery of circumcision."[39]

CHAPTER IX

ON THE INSTITUTION AND CAUSE OF CIRCUMCISION

Here it must be said how circumcision was instituted; and why; and why it was changed through baptism.

Abraham first received the command of circumcision as a test of obedience;[40] nor was circumcision commanded to him alone, but also to his seed, that is, to all the Hebrews. It used to be done according to the law on the eighth day, with a stone knife, in the flesh of the foreskin.

Circumcision was given for many reasons; for example, so that through obedience to the commandment Abraham might please God, whom Adam had displeased through transgression. It was also given as a sign of the great faith of Abraham, who believed that he would have a son in whom the blessing of all

---

[39] Gregory the Great, *Moral. in Iob*, IV, 3 (*PL*, 75, 635); cf. *Sum. sent., loc. cit.*; Abailard, *loc. cit.*; Ivo, *Decret., loc. cit.*, and *Panorm.*, I, 10 (*PL*, 161, 1049); Gratian, *Decret.*, C. *Quod autem*, De consecr., dist. 4 (Friedberg, I, 1362).

[40] Cf. Gen. 17:10 f.; Josh. 5:2, which is also discussed below. This whole chapter comes from the *Glossa* on Rom. 4:10, Gen. 17:10, and John 7:22.

would be brought about. Then, too, it was given that by this sign that people might be distinguished from the rest of the nations.

Circumcision was therefore ordered to be done in the flesh of the foreskin, because it was instituted as a remedy for original sin, which we derive from our parents through the concupiscence which dominates more especially in that part. And since the first man experienced the guilt of disobedience in that part, it was fitting that he receive the sign of obedience there.

It was done on the eighth day, with a stone knife,[41] because at the common resurrection, which is to happen at the eighth age, all corruption will be cut away from the elect through the Rock Christ, and through the resurrection of Christ, brought about on the eighth day, the soul of each one who believes in him will be circumcised from sins. "Therefore there are two things in that sacrament."[42]

Furthermore, circumcision was changed through baptism, for the sacrament of baptism is more complete and perfect because it bears a fuller grace. For in the former, sins are put away only, but neither grace assisting to good works nor the possession of virtues nor their increase is offered, while in baptism not only are sins abolished, but also assisting grace is conferred and virtues are increased. Whence it is called "water of refreshment,"[43] which waters arid places and endues those places already fruitful with fuller abundance. Any man, however just he may be through faith and love which he possessed before, when he comes to baptism receives there more abundant grace; but this is not so in circumcision. Hence it was only a sign to one already justified through the faith of Abraham; it conferred nothing upon him inwardly.

CHAPTER X

On Infants Dead Before the Eighth Day on Which Circumcision Was Performed

If a question is asked about young children who died before the eighth day, before which circumcision was not performed, according to the law, namely, whether they were

---

41 In the original, there is a play on "stone knife" (*petrino cultro*) and "rock Christ" (*petram Christum*).

42 *Sum. sent., loc. cit.,* cf. Augustine, *Tr. in Ioan.,* 30, 5 (*PL,* 35, 1634).

43 Ps. 22:2 (P.B.V., 23:2).

saved or not, the same response can be given which is given about children dead before baptism: it is certain that they perish.[44]

Thus Bede says: "He who now proclaims through the Gospel in an awesome way and yet for our salvation: 'Unless a man be born again of water and the Holy Ghost, he cannot enter into the kingdom of God'[45] proclaims of old through the law: 'The male whose flesh of his foreskin shall not be circumcised, that soul shall be destroyed out of his people: because he hath broken my covenant.'[46] Perhaps, however, under the law, with the approaching necessity of death, they used to circumcise boys before the eighth day without incurring sin, just as is now done in the Church about baptism."[47]

BOOK IV, DISTINCTION II

CHAPTER I

ON THE SACRAMENTS OF THE NEW LAW

Now let us approach the sacraments of the new law, which are: baptism, confirmation, the bread of blessing, that is, the eucharist, penance, extreme unction, orders, marriage. Of these some provide a remedy against sin and confer assisting grace, such as baptism; others are only a remedy, such as marriage; others strengthen us with grace and power, such as the eucharist and orders.

If it is asked why the sacraments were not instituted soon after the fall of man, since righteousness and salvation are in them,[48] we say that the sacraments of grace were not to be given before the coming of Christ, who brought grace, for they receive power from his death and Passion. Christ did not wish to come before man was convinced that neither the natural nor the written law could support him.

---

[44] On the history of the problem of unbaptized children and their fate, and the emergence of views milder than that expressed here, cf. P. Gumpel, "Unbaptized Infants: May They Be Saved?" *Downside Review*, 72, No. 230 (November, 1954). (E.R.F.)

[45] John 3:5.

[46] Gen. 17:14.

[47] Bede, *loc. cit.* and *Comm. in Luc.* 2 (*PL*, 92, 337).

[48] Cf. *Sum. sent.*, 4, 1 (*PL*, 176, 118).

"Marriage, however, was certainly not instituted before sin as a remedy, but as a sacrament and a duty";[49] after sin, indeed, it was a remedy against the corrupting effect of carnal concupiscence, with which we shall deal in its place.[50]

BOOK IV, DISTINCTION VII

CHAPTER I

ON THE SACRAMENT OF CONFIRMATION

Now something must be added about the sacrament of confirmation, about the power of which a question is customarily raised.

For the form is plain, namely, the words[51] which the bishop says when he signs the baptized on the forehead with sacred chrism.

CHAPTER II

THAT IT CAN BE GIVEN ONLY BY THE HIGHEST PRIESTS

This sacrament[52] cannot be performed by others than the highest priests, neither does one read that in the time of the apostles it was performed by others than the apostles themselves, nor can it or ought it to be performed by others than those who hold their places. For if it is attempted otherwise, it is held null and void and will not be reckoned among the sacraments of the Church. Presbyters are permitted to touch the baptized on the breast, but not to sign the forehead with chrism.[53]

49 Hugh, *De sacram.*, I, p. 8, 12 f.; II, p. 11, 1; 3 (*PL*, 176, 314; 480 f.); cf. Gen. 2:24 (see also pp. 312–318, above).

50 Cf. IV, dist. 26 (Quaracchi ed., II, 912 ff.).

51 I.e., "I sign thee with the sign of the cross and I confirm thee with holy chrism, in the name of the Father and of the Son and of the Holy Spirit."

52 For this chapter, cf. *Sum. sent.*, 6, 1 (*PL*, 176, 137); Ivo, *Decret.*, p. 1, 257; 297; *Panorm.*, I, 115 (*PL*, 161, 120; 131; 1069); Gratian, *Decret.*, C. *Manusquoque* (4), De consecr., dist. 5 (Friedberg, I, 1413).

53 For last words, cf. Ivo, *Decret.*, p. 1, 263 and *Panorm.*, I, 116 (*PL*, 161, 121; 1070); Gratian, *Decret.*, C. *Presbyteris* (119), De consecr., dist. 4 (Friedberg, I, 1398).

CHAPTER III

What Is the Power of This Sacrament?

The power of this sacrament is a gift of the same Holy Spirit for strengthening who was given in baptism for remission of sins.[54]

Hence Rabanus says: "The Spirit is given to the baptized person by the highest priest through the imposition of a hand, so that he may be strengthened through the Spirit to declare to others what he attained to in baptism."[55]

Again: "All the faithful ought to receive the Holy Spirit through the imposition of the hand of bishops after baptism, so that they may be full Christians."[56]

Gregory, however, wrote to bishop Januarius to this effect: "It has come to our notice that certain presbyters have been scandalized because we have prohibited presbyters from touching those who have been baptized with chrism; and indeed, in so doing, we have acted according to the ancient use of our Church. But if there be some, where there are no bishops present, who are rendered at all unhappy by this custom, we concede that presbyters ought to anoint the baptized on the forehead with chrism."[57] "But it is thought that that was conceded once only to check a cause of offense."[58]

CHAPTER IV

Whether This Sacrament Is Nobler than Baptism

"Know, that each is a great sacrament, but one is to be held with greater veneration, as is said by the greater authorities."[59]

He, indeed, says that the sacrament of confirmation is

---

[54] Cf. introduction to "Theologians of the Twelfth Century."

[55] Rabanus Maurus, *De instit. cleric.*, I, 30 (*PL*, 107, 314).

[56] Ivo, *Decret.*, p. 1, 260; 296; *Panorm.*, I, 113 (*PL*, 161, 121; 131; 1069); Gratian, *Decret.*, C. *Omnes fideles* (1), De consecr., dist. 5 (Friedberg, I, 1413).

[57] *Regist.*, IV, indict. 12, epist. 26 (*PL*, 77, 696); cf. Gratian, *Decret.*, C. *Pervenit* (1), dist. 95 (Friedberg, I, 331).

[58] Gratian, *Decret.*, on C. *Presbyteros* (2), *ibid.* (Friedberg, I, 332).

[59] Ivo, *Panorm.*, I, 114 (*PL*, 161, 1069); Gratian, *Decret.*, C. *De his vero* (3), De consecr., dist. 5 (Friedberg, I, 1413). Cf. Hugh, *De sacram.*, II, p. 7, 4 (*PL*, 176, 461).

greater. This, perhaps, is not on account of the greater virtue or benefit which it confers, but because it is given by nobler ministers and is performed on a nobler part of the body, that is, on the forehead; or perhaps because it offers a greater increase of virtues, while baptism avails rather for remission.

This is what Rabanus seems to mean when he says that, "in the unction of baptism the Holy Spirit descends to consecrate a dwelling for God; in that of confirmation the sevenfold grace of the same Spirit, with all the plenitude of sanctity and power, comes into a man."[60]

This sacrament, like baptism, ought to be given only by the fasting to the fasting, unless necessity demands otherwise.[61]

CHAPTER V

WHETHER IT CAN BE REPEATED

Like baptism or orders, it ought not to be repeated.[62] For injury is not to be done to any sacrament, and this is believed to be done when that which is not to be repeated is repeated.

For about baptism and orders, which ought not to be repeated, Augustine plainly says: "Each is a sacrament and is given by a certain consecration: the one when one is baptized; the other when one is ordained. And therefore in the Catholic Church neither can be repeated,"[63] because injury must not be done to either. This undoubtedly must also be held about confirmation. As to the others, whether they can be repeated, or ought to be repeated, we shall consider further on.[64]

---

[60] Rabanus, *loc. cit.*; cf. Ivo, *Panorm.*, I, 118 (*PL*, 161, 1070), and Gratian, *Decret.*, C. *Novissime* (5), *ibid.* (Friedberg, I, 1414).

[61] On fasting, cf. Ivo, *Decret.*, p. 1, 254, and *Panorm.*, I, 119 (*PL*, 161, 120; 1071); Gratian, *Decret.*, C. *Ut ieiuni* (6) and *Ut episcopi* (7), *ibid.* (Friedberg, I, 1414); Hugh, *De sacram.*, II, p. 7, 5 (*PL*, 176, 462).

[62] The principle involved here is that of the impossibility of repeating sacraments which confer "character"; on this traditional idea, cf. P. Pourrat, *Theology of the Sacraments*, Ch. IV. (E.R.F.)

[63] Augustine, *C. Epist. Parm.*, II, 13:28 (*PL*, 43, 70); cf. Ivo, *Decret.*, p. 2, 97, and *Panorm.*, III, 77 (*PL*, 161, 185; 1147); Gratian, *Decret.*, C. *Quod quidam* (97), c.1, q.1, §1 (Friedberg, I, 393).

[64] Cf. IV, dist. 23, 4 (II, 890 ff.).

BOOK IV, DISTINCTION XIV

CHAPTER I

ABOUT PENANCE AND WHY IT IS CALLED PENANCE

After these matters something must be said about penance. Penance is a necessity for those who are far away, that they may draw near.

For it is, as Jerome says, "a second plank after a shipwreck,"[65] because if anyone, by sinning, should corrupt the vesture of innocence received in baptism, it can be repaired by the remedy of penance.[66] The first plank is baptism, whereby the old man is put off and the new man put on; the second, penance, by which we raise ourselves again after a fall, while the old garment is put away again and the new garment, which was lost, is resumed. The erring can be renewed after baptism through penance, but not through baptism; a man may do penance often, but he may not be baptized often.

Baptism is a sacrament only, but penance is said to be both a sacrament and a virtue of the mind.[67] For there is an internal penitence and an external penance: the external is the sacrament, the internal is a virtue of the mind. Each of these is a cause of health and of justification.

As to whether all external penance is a sacrament, or, if not all, what is to be understood by this name, we shall investigate in the sequel.[68]

The preaching of John started from penance, when he said, "Do penance: for the kingdom of heaven is at hand."[69] "Moreover the herald taught what the Truth afterward preached; for he began his sermon[70] with penance."[71]

---

[65] Jerome, *Epist.* 130, 9 (*CSEL*, 56, 189); on this and the following points, cf. *Sum. sent.*, 6, 10 (*PL*, 176, 146).

[66] Cf. Eph. 4:22, 24.

[67] Note the ambiguity of *poenitentia*, as equivalent both to "penitence" and to "penance"; this has encouraged the misuse of certain texts (such as Matt. 3:2) in support of an exaggerated emphasis on external works of "penance" in Latin Christianity. (E.R.F.)

[68] IV, dist. 22, 2 (II, 888 f.).

[69] Matt. 3:2.

[70] Cf. Matt. 4:17.

[71] Cf. *Glossa ordinaria, ad loc.* (*PL*, 114, 87).

BOOK IV, DISTINCTION XXIV

CHAPTERS I–III

ON HOW MANY ECCLESIASTICAL ORDERS THERE ARE

Let us now enter upon the consideration of sacred orders.[72]

There are seven degrees or orders of spiritual functions, as is plainly handed down by the writings of the holy Fathers and is shown by the example of our head, namely, Jesus Christ. He exhibited the functions of all in himself and left to his body, which is the Church, the same orders to be observed.

(Chapter II) Moreover, there are seven on account of the sevenfold grace of the Holy Spirit, and those who are not partakers of the Spirit approach ecclesiastical orders unworthily. As to those in whose minds the sevenfold grace of the Holy Spirit is diffused, when they come to the ecclesiastical orders, they are believed to receive fuller grace in the very act of advancing through the spiritual grades.

(Chapter III) "Such men are to be chosen as clergy for spiritual ministration as can worthily handle the Lord's sacraments. For it is better for the priesthood of the Lord to have few ministers, who are able to carry out the work of God worthily, than to have many useless ones, who bring a grave burden on the ordainers."[73] The men who ought to be ministers of Christ are those who are adorned by the sevenfold grace of the Holy Spirit and whose doctrine and spirituality[74] are transfused by grace into others, lest sordid lives crush with their feet the heavenly pearls of spiritual words and divine offices.[75]

In the sacrament of the sevenfold Spirit there are seven ecclesiastical degrees, namely, doorkeeper, lector, exorcist, acolyte, subdeacon, deacon, priest; all, however, are called clerics, that is, those chosen by lot.[76]

---

[72] A good deal of the material of this distinction comes from Hugh, *De sacram.*, II, p. 3 (*PL*, 176, 421 ff.).

[73] Gratian, *Decret.*, Can. *Tales ad ministerium* (4), dist. 23 (Friedberg, I, 81).

[74] *Forma conversionis*; cf. E. Gilson, *The Mystical Theology of St. Bernard*, 43; 135. (E.R.F.)

[75] Cf. Matt. 7:6.

[76] Cf. Acts 1:26 (lot = *klēros*).

CHAPTER XII

On Presbyters

Although all spiritual states are sacred, the canons well conclude that only two are so called, namely, the diaconate and the presbyterate;[77] for "it is written that the primitive Church had these alone,"[78] and about these alone have we the command of the apostle.[79] "The apostles ordained bishops and presbyters in each city.[80] We read also of Levites ordained by the apostles, of whom blessed Stephen was the greatest.[81] The Church appointed subdeacons and acolytes for itself as time went on."[82]

CHAPTER XIII

What Is Called an Order?

If it is asked what that which is called an order is, it can definitely be said that it is a certain sign, that is, a sacred something, by which spiritual power and office are handed to the ordinand. Therefore a spiritual character in which there is an increase of power is called an order or grade.[83]

And these orders are called sacraments because in receiving them a sacred thing, grace, which the things that are there done figure, is conferred.

CHAPTERS XIV–XVI

On Names of Dignity or Offices

There are certain other names, not of orders, but of dignities and offices. "Bishop" is both the name of a dignity and of an office.

(Chapter XV) "The word episcopacy is used because he who is made a bishop superintends, bearing the care of those

---

77 Cf. introduction to "Theologians of the Twelfth Century."
78 Gratian, *Decret.*, Can. *Nullus in episcopum* (4), dist. 60 (Friedberg, I, 227).
79 Cf. I Tim. 3:2.
80 Cf. Acts 14:23.
81 Cf. Acts 6:5.
82 Gratian, *Decret.*, dist. 21, in princip. (Friedberg, I, 66).
83 This is the basis of the equating of episcopate and presbyterate *as orders*; priesthood in both grades is marked by the power of consecrating the sacrament of the altar. (E.R.F.)

below him. For the Greek *skopein* Latin uses *intendere*; moreover *episkopoi* in Greek is interpreted as *speculatores* in Latin;[84] for one who is placed first in the church is called a *speculator*, because he oversees and watches over the habits and life of the people placed below him."[85]

(Chapter XVI) "The bishop is the chief of priests, as it were the path of those who follow. He is also called the highest priest; for he makes priests and deacons, and distributes all ecclesiastical orders."

[84] Isidore is simply developing the original meaning of the title "bishop."
[85] Isidore of Seville, *Etymol.*, VII, 12:11 (*PL*, 82, 291); Gratian, *Decret.*, C. *Cleros*, §7 (Friedberg, I, 68). The next chapter comes from the same source.

Stephen Langton: A Question on Original Sin

THE TEXT

We have original sin, which we contracted from Adam. Now this is either a stain of the soul,[1] which is effaced in baptism, or an inclination to sin, which is in the soul.

If it is an inclination—in other words, what we also call a foment[2] and a weakness of nature—that inclination remains in the soul even after baptism; what, then, does baptism accomplish, or what does it efface? If you say that it effaces nothing, but brings it about that what formerly was sin, namely, the inclination, is no longer sin after baptism. But when it was sin, it was from the devil, while now that it is not sin, it is from God, since it is a punishment, and every punishment comes from God, and thus something which was from the devil alone is now from God alone.

But if you say that this inclination or foment is not original sin, but that the latter is a certain stain of the soul, which is linked to the inclination, and that this stain is effaced in baptism, how is Augustine's statement true when he says that original sin passes away as to guilt, but remains in act?[3]

Most people answer this question by saying that original sin is the very inclination to sin, which is called a foment, and that it is accidental to it to be original sin.

But on the contrary: If it is accidental to the foment to be original sin, or indeed to be sin, then when it is said that the foment is sin, this term "sin" connotes, or even links to the foment, something accidental which is effaced in baptism. That accident, therefore, rather than the foment, should be

---

[1] *Macula animae.*   [2] *Fomes.*
[3] Cf. Augustine, *Retract.*, I, 14:3 (*CSEL*, 36, 73); *De nupt. et concup.*, I, 25:28 (*CSEL*, 42, 240).

called original sin, since the latter can never coexist with grace.[4]

Perhaps you will say that it is accidental to the foment to be sin, because it is accidental to it to be imputed for condemnation.

On the contrary: It is imputed for condemnation either by reason of itself alone or of its own essence, or else by reason of an accident.[5] If it is imputed by reason of an accident, then the latter will be original sin. If it is imputed by reason of its essence alone, then it remains as great as before after baptism.

Again, it is absurd to say that that which of itself and by itself makes a man worthy of eternal punishment can coexist with charity. (I say both of itself and by itself, because of venial sin to which mortal sin is linked.[6])

Thus, in answer to the present question, we say without prejudice that original sin is not the foment or inclination to sin, but is a certain stain of the soul linked with the inclination to sin, and that this stain is effaced in baptism.

To understand this more fully, observe that the flesh of Adam was corrupted by the eating of the apple, and that this applies also to all flesh which descends from him by way of concupiscence.[7] For this reason, when the flesh of a child is begotten from the heat of lust in the commingling of the two seeds, it has a certain filthiness or corruption by which it is filthy and corrupt in itself and is apt to corrupt something else, just as an eel contains in itself the cause of fever. But when the soul is infused into a filthy and corrupt body on the forty-sixth day from the conception of the seeds,[8] from the corrupt and filthy vessel into which it is infused it contracts an inclination to sin, which is called the foment. This is accompanied by a certain stain, which is called original sin; this stain is contracted from the aforesaid filthiness, and is effaced in baptism.

But since that stain is linked to the inclination to sin, and is

---

[4] Thus Langton repudiates in advance Luther's formula, *simul iustus et peccator*.

[5] Note the "realistic" interpretation of imputation, as grounded in some real quality of the subject.

[6] Langton is trying to make plain the traditional distinction between "mortal" sin, as that which alienates from the love of God, and "venial" sin. Cf. Thomas Aquinas, *Sum. theol.*, Ia–IIae, q.72, a.5.

[7] Note that a certain role is still played by concupiscence, as the medium of the transmission of original sin.

[8] Note the precise theory of the time of the infusion of the human soul, and the definite temporal gap between conception and animation.

contracted along with it, what pertains to the inclination is attributed to the stain, and conversely. And sometimes the inclination is even called original sin, just as sometimes the stain linked to ignorance is referred to as ignorance and ignorance is referred to as sin, even though ignorance is not itself sin, but a stain linked to ignorance is.

Therefore, when Augustine says that original sin passes away as to guilt but remains in act,[9] it must also be understood in this way. Original sin itself, in fact, passes away both in act and in guilt, since it is completely effaced in baptism. Nonetheless, Augustine says that it remains in act, because of the inclination to sin, which does remain.

[9] Cf. n. 3, above.

Stephen Langton: Fragments on the Morality of Human Acts

I

ON THE TEXT, "A GOOD MAN OUT OF A GOOD TREASURE BRINGETH FORTH GOOD THINGS"

On the passage in the Gospel of Luke: "A good man out of the good treasure of his heart bringeth forth good things,"[1] the interlinear *Glossa*[2] says: "As much as you intend, that much you do." From this authority three questions emerge. The first concerns the will where opinion is contrary to the truth, as in the case of someone who decides to commit fornication because he believes that what is really a mortal sin is venial. The second has to do with the will which does not attain to its preconceived end, as in the case of someone who kills a man, when he intended to kill a wild beast. The third is this: Are the will and the act the same sin or different sins? That they are different is proved in this way.

II

ON WILL AND INTENTION

(i)

After this, the question is raised whether intention is the same thing as will.[3]

This seems to be the case, since it is the same movement to will to feed a poor man and to will to feed a poor man for God's

---

[1] Luke 6:45, partly assimilated to Matt. 12:35.

[2] The *Glossa interlinearis*, like the *Glossa marginalis*, is associated with the name and school of Anselm of Laon. Its incidental notes were actually written between the lines of the Biblical text.

[3] Cf. O. Lottin, *Psychologie et morale aux XIIᵉ et XIIIᵉ siècles*, IV, 3:1, pp. 355 f.: "A preliminary question presents itself: What meaning must be given to the term *intentio* in the classical axiom? Theologians had been attempting an answer since Peter Lombard, but without success. Stephen Langton will have no greater success. Sometimes the term *intentio* includes

sake; therefore, will and intention are the same thing. On the contrary: The intention embraces the end and the will; therefore, they are not the same thing. We affirm that this word "intention" is equivocal. For "intention" refers to a quality[4] of the mind, which springs from the will and the end. But "intention" also refers to the end, and in this sense it is not the same thing as will. Sometimes, however, "intention" refers to the movement, and in this sense it is the same thing as will.

(ii)

The question: Whether intention and will are the same sin.

For the affirmative: Every sin lies in a movement, and the movement of intention is the movement of the will; therefore a sin of intention is a sin of will.

On the contrary: Intention and will are different things, and the will can remain fixed, while the intention is altered, and none the less sin will be committed in intention; therefore, intention and will are different sins.

I reply. If intention refers to a quality, they are different sins; if to a movement, they are the same. For intention refers to turning toward a thing.

(iii)

Suppose that a man does a certain thing which belongs to the genus of good things, and intends to do a greater good than he actually does. Perhaps he is directed to give alms, but he himself believes that fasting is a greater good, and therefore fasts. In that case, he does as much good as he intends to do.[5] But observe that this quantity of intention relates to the quantity of remission of penalty, not to the quantity of merit, for the quantity of merit is not reckoned according to intention, but according to the quantity of charity, while the quantity of remission of penalty is reckoned according to the quantity of the thing or opinion.

On the contrary: He who intends to commit a greater evil than the one he actually commits sins more. Now God is more

---

at the same time both *voluntas* and *finis*, denoting this vital movement of the will toward an end—a meaning already given by the Lombard; sometimes it denotes the end, and in this sense intention differs from will; sometimes it denotes the movement of the latter, and in this sense intention and will are identical."

[4] *Qualitas*—quality or condition.

[5] Cf. the maxim from the *Glossa*, already quoted.

inclined to reward than to condemn; therefore, if this man intends to do a greater good than he actually does, he gains greater merit.

I reply. This does not hold. For good actions have virtues underlying them, but evil actions do not have vices underlying them, for because someone is good he also does good, but not conversely. Now the quantity of good is measured by the quantity of charity possessed previously, or indeed at that moment, but the circumstances of an evil action—contempt and suchlike—determine the quantity of evil. Since, therefore, in evil the quantity of guilt is reckoned according to intention and contempt and other circumstances like these, while in good the quantity of merit is reckoned according to the quantity of charity which really precedes the act, we are dealing with two different situations.

III

On Will and Deed

Suppose that two catechumens are in a state of equal charity. One of them has, in fact, the opportunity of receiving baptism, and actually receives it, while the other does not. For the affirmative: He who wants to be baptized, but does not have the opportunity, does as much as he intends, because the will is reckoned to him for the deed. But this man intends as much as the other; therefore, he does as much as the other.[6]

On the contrary: In him who is baptized grace is increased by the virtue of baptism; in the other it is not. And thus the former attains to a greater good than he who is not baptized. Therefore, the will is not reckoned to the latter for the deed.

I reply. That authority of Matthew is quite irrelevant.[7] For the statement, "You do as great a good as you intend," is not to be construed as meaning that intention or will alone has the same force as the deed, since this is not the case in the remission of a penalty. Rather, the sense is this: God regards, not the deed, but the intention of the doer.[8]

On the contrary: God's recompense is based, not on the amount given, but on the amount from which it is given, as in

---

[6] Cf. Abailard's discussion of baptism, in the excerpt from *In ep. ad Rom.*, above.

[7] Cf. the *Glossa*, as above.

[8] Cf. Matt. 5:27 f.

the case of Zacchaeus[9] or of the widow[10] or of Cain and Abel.[11] Therefore, that authority has to do with the meriting of eternal life, not with the remission of punishment.

I reply to the objection in this way. The will to be baptized avails as much for the man who does not have the opportunity as the will plus the fact of baptism for the other, if you add, "In the same state of charity." For all works done in the same state of charity are equally meritorious, and yet to be baptized is nonetheless effectual for him who is baptized, because on the occasion of baptism charity grows in him.

This same explanation can be applied to the case of one person only. To be baptized avails as much for him as to will to be baptized, and conversely—and so on, as above.

9 Cf. Luke 19:1–10.
10 Cf. Mark 12:42.
11 Cf. Gen. 4:1–7.

Stephen Langton: *The Golden Sequence*

THE TEXT

Come, thou Holy Paraclete[1]
And from thy celestial seat
   Send thy light and brilliancy:[2]
Father of the poor,[3] draw near,
Giver of all gifts,[4] be here:
   Come, the soul's true radiancy.

Come, of comforters the best,
Of the soul the sweetest guest,[5]
   Come in toil refreshingly[6]:
Thou in labor rest most sweet,[7]
Thou art shelter from the heat,[8]
   Comfort in adversity.[9]

O thou Light,[10] most pure and blest,
Shine within the inmost breast
   Of thy faithful company[11]:
Where thou art not, man hath nought,
Every holy deed and thought
   Comes from thy divinity.[12]

---

[1] *Spiritus; Consolator* appears in l. 7.
[2] Cf. Ps. 42:3 (P.B.V., 43:3).   [3] Cf. Job 29:16.
[4] Cf. James 1:17.   [5] Cf. John 14:23 ff.
[6] *Dulce refrigerium*; cf. Augustine, *De agone christ.*, 9, 10 (*CSEL*, 41, 112 f.).
[7] Cf. Matt. 11:28.   [8] Cf. Isa. 25:4.
[9] Cf. II Cor. 7:4.   [10] Cf. I John 1:5.
[11] Cf. the antiphon, *Veni, sancte spiritus, reple tuorum corda fidelium* (11th century or earlier), given in the *Missale Romanum* as part of the gradual for Pentecost.
[12] Cf. Gal. 5:16 ff.

What is soilèd, make thou pure,[13]
What is wounded, work its cure,[14]
　What is parchèd, fructify;[15]
What is rigid, gently bend,
What is frozen, warmly tend,
　Strengthen what goes erringly.

Fill thy faithful, who confide
In thy power to guard and guide,
　With thy sevenfold mystery[16]:
Here thy grace and virtue send,
Grant salvation in the end,
　And in heaven felicity.

—Attributed to Stephen Langton

[13] Cf. Ps. 50:12 (P.B.V., 51:10); Titus 3:5.
[14] Cf. Jer. 30:17.
[15] Cf. Isa. 44:3 f.
[16] *Sacrum septenarium.* The reference is to the "gifts of the Holy Spirit," listed in Isa. 11:2. The Hebrew text enumerates six spiritual gifts, but LXX and Vulgate insert *eusebeia* or *pietas* before the reference to the "fear of the Lord"; cf. the principal prayer of the Anglican rite of confirmation. The gifts of the Spirit played a part in the elaborated medieval doctrine of the supernatural virtues, etc.; cf. Thomas Aquinas, *Sum. theol.*, Ia–IIae, q. 68.

THE THIRTEENTH CENTURY
AND AFTER

The Thirteenth Century and After: Certain Tendencies

THE THIRTEENTH CENTURY IS AT ONCE A splendid and a tragic era in the history of Western Christendom. This ambiguity is nowhere better illustrated than in its intellectual activities, which were at once the supreme achievement and the beginning of the decline of the medieval experiment. On the one hand, the endeavors of the twelfth century to link the traditional Augustinian theology with the world of secular knowledge were fulfilled in the work of Bonaventure and Aquinas and their contemporaries. Within the setting of the great universities, whose expansion was an expressive symbol of the intellectual advances of the age, earlier studies in literature and logic were crowned by the effective recovery of the body of knowledge represented by the works of Aristotle, and this comprehensive interpretation of the world stimulated a fuller investigation of theological and philosophical issues than any earlier age had witnessed. And yet, on the other hand, while some of the greatest scholars sought to make full use of the newly gained intellectual treasures, others were more profoundly impressed by the radical threat to Christian faith implied in Greek naturalism and determinism, and great rifts began to weaken the structure of the medieval syntheses.

A brief recapitulation of the background of thirteenth century thought will be sufficient here. The sources of the Aristotelian renaissance, which so effectively challenged the thirteenth century mind,[1] are to be found in part in the earlier and more limited intellectual renewal of the twelfth century, in

[1] The importance of new knowledge of the Greek Fathers should also be noted; cf. M. D. Chenu, *Introduction à l'étude de saint Thomas d'Aquin* (Vrin, Paris, 1950), 44; C. Dawson, *Medieval Essays*, 99–102.

part in fresh contacts with the Islamic[2] and Byzantine[3] worlds, which offered inexhaustible resources to scholars now technically equipped to deal with them. In all this, particular attention should be paid to the "Arab" writers, who, while their influence should not be emphasized to the exclusion of other important factors, were most effective in impressing the significance of Aristotle on the schools of Western Christendom. For several centuries of Islamic history the writings and ideas of Aristotle, transmitted by way of Byzantium and Syria, had exercised a preponderant influence on a vital tradition of philosophical and scientific thought, and the development of Latin scholasticism was conditioned by this tradition. Indeed, Islamic and Jewish philosophers were studied with such care that the influence of their divergent and often highly eclectic versions of Aristotle can be traced in the diversity of schools in later medieval Europe.[4]

In attempting to classify the various responses of the Latin Christian mind to the new knowledge, we must not try to impose too simple or doctrinaire a formula on the almost unmanageable data. We can, however, point to three main types of theological and philosophical reaction to the new situation. In assessing them, it will be equally important to note the universal influence of Aristotle and to recognize the diversity and independence of the positions taken up in relation to his teaching.

The most straightforward response was a literalist Aristotelianism, which, however delicate the nuances of its relation to Christian theology may have been, took the world-view of Aristotle, carefully interpreted by Averroes, as the utterance of essential human reason.[5] In any analysis of the more integrally

---

[2] Spain (especially Toledo) and Sicily were notable centers of Islamic influence.

[3] Note, for example, the translations of Aristotle's Greek text by William of Moerbeke (1215–1286), Latin Archbishop of Corinth.

[4] On the influence of Avicenna (Ibn Sina, 980–1037), cf. E. Gilson, "Pourquoi saint Thomas a critiqué saint Augustin," *Archives d'hist. doct. et litt. du moyen âge*, 1 (1926), 5–127; M. A. Goichon, *La Philosophie d'Avicenne et son influence en Europe médiévale* (2d ed., Adrien-Maisonneuve, Paris, 1951). On Avicebron (Ibn Gabirol, c. 1021–1058), cf. G. Théry, "L'Augustinisme médiéval et le problème de la forme substantielle," *Acta hebdomadae augustinianae-thomisticae* (Turin-Rome, 1931), 140–200. On Maimonides (Moses ben Maimon, 1135–1204), cf. various authors, *Moses ben Maimon, sein Leben, seine Werke und sein Einfluss*, 2 vols. (Leipzig, 1908–1914).

[5] On Averroes (Ibn Roschd, *Commentator*, 1126–1198) and Averroism, cf. F. C. Copleston, *History of Philosophy*, Vol. II: *Augustine to Scotus*, 187; 197–200; 435–441.

Christian treatments of Aristotle, the presence of this kind of "modernism," with its deep involvement in a naturalistic philosophy, must be taken into account. Indeed, it may well be that "Averroism" did more than any other doctrine to undermine the Scholastic attempt at synthesis, by impugning both the rationality of theology and the potential orthodoxy of reason. Even if it is rash to question the Christian intentions of Siger of Brabant, the greatest figure commonly associated with Latin Averroism, or to ascribe to him or to his disciples the attempt to accommodate philosophy to theology by means of a doctrine of the "double truth," their viewpoint did imply the inevitability of a great divorce between faith and reason, grace and nature.[6]

The effect of the Averroist threat can be seen in a second response, peculiarly characteristic of the Franciscan tradition in the thirteenth century, but dominant in the theological world as a whole during much of that period.[7] This response was, of course, diversified in so far as the content of a given theologian's teaching depended in part on his interpretation of Aristotle and on the non-Aristotelian influences which happened to prevail in his mind. The common characteristic of this whole school, however, was the effort to exploit Aristotle and other philosophers in the interests of a sophisticated presentation of Augustinian theology and philosophy. Since in many respects this is the Anselmian and Victorine tradition expanded, its power need not surprise us.

Nonetheless, an indelible impression was eventually made on Western theology by a third viewpoint, represented in rather different ways by Albert the Great and Thomas Aquinas. This outlook is marked at once by a greater openness than any "Augustinian" had shown toward the new philosophical ideas, and by an independence in the face of the Aristotelian material, in particular, which differs sharply from the Averroist attitude. Within this common framework, however, certain contrasts appear. In Albert, we meet an eclecticism which is prepared to try to incorporate very diverse elements, including a strong interest in empirical science, but which ultimately fails to solve

[6] For different views of Siger of Brabant, cf. P. Mandonnet, *Siger de Brabant et l'averroïsme latin au XIIIe siècle*, 2 vols. (2d. ed., Louvain, 1908–1911); F. Van Steenberghen, *Aristote en Occident: les origines de l'aristotélisme parisien* (Institut supérieur de philosophie, Louvain, 1946). Cf. also the list of important studies by A. Maurer and others in Gilson, *History*, 718 f.
[7] Cf. Gilson, *History*, 327–361.

the problem of assimilating Aristotelian, as contrasted with Neoplatonic, material.[8] (Albert is well described as attempting to "co-ordinate a Platonizing spiritualism with the Aristotelian experimentalism."[9]) In Aquinas, on the other hand, we meet a unique attempt to transcend both Aristotle and Augustine as philosophical auxiliaries of theology, while making judicious use of the insights of both.[10]

When we try to estimate the theological significance of these fundamental attitudes, it is fairly clear that the Averroist position actually represents the Greek challenge to Christianity, translated into medieval Latin, or at best a desperate effort to hold Greek naturalism and Christian faith together, without really resolving the great debate of the thirteenth century. As for the viewpoint for which Thomas Aquinas spoke most effectively, while in the long run it became the most influential attitude in Western Catholicism, and in its own time was probably the most creative outlook, intellectually and culturally, it was hardly the typical answer of the thirteenth century to its most urgent problems. For these reasons—and also because the Thomist position is extensively treated in Volume XI of this series—we shall devote the space available here to the more conservative, or "Augustinian" viewpoint, which deserves attention on both historical and theological grounds, as thoroughly characteristic of its age and as a significant formulation of the issues of faith and reason. This concentration may be especially useful because the "triumph of St. Thomas Aquinas"[11] has dazzled many casual observers into overlooking the importance of the "Franciscan" alternative in the thirteenth century and later.[12]

II

The renewed Augustinianism of the thirteenth century had a strong affinity with the spiritual outlook of the Franciscan

[8] On Albert (1206–1280), cf. *Le Bienheureux Albert le Grand* (*Revue thomiste*, 36 [1931]); *Studia Albertina* (*Beiträge*, Supplementband 4 [Münster, 1952]).
[9] M. D. Chenu, *op. cit.*, 38.
[10] Cf. V. J. Bourke, *Thomistic Bibliography* (St. Louis University Press, 1945); P. Mandonnet and J. Destrez, *Bibliographie thomiste* (Paris, 1921); M. D. Chenu, *op. cit.*; E. Gilson, *Le Thomisme* (5th ed., Vrin, Paris, 1948).
[11] The famous symbolic painting by Francesco Traini in St. Catherine's, Pisa, is reproduced by A. Walz, *St. Thomas Aquinas: A Biographical Study* (Newman Press, Westminster, Md., 1951), frontispiece.
[12] *Franciscan Studies*, published quarterly at St. Bonaventure, N.Y., is one impressive witness to the continuing vitality of this tradition.

order,[13] and the succession of Minorite teachers from Alexander of Hales to Matthew of Aquasparta includes most of the great names of the school. Nonetheless, this type of thought was not the preserve of the Franciscans. Its background includes two great academic figures, William of Auvergne[14] and Robert Grosseteste[15] (representing Paris and Oxford respectively), who began the assimilation to Augustinianism of the Neoplatonic and Aristotelian ideas current among the Arabs. (This enterprise is typified by their amalgamation of the doctrine of the illumination of the mind by the creative Word with the Aristotelian theory of the "active intellect," in their interpretation of intellectual knowledge.[16]) Grosseteste, moreover, as the stanch friend of the English Franciscans, played a large part in the formation of the Oxford Franciscan school, in which, in particular, his scientific interest was continued by such men as Roger Bacon.[17]

The Franciscan school proper begins with the rather tentative efforts of Alexander of Hales and the more coherent work of John of La Rochelle.[18] The latter is noteworthy for his orderly presentation of many great Franciscan themes, as well as for his incorporation of important Aristotelian concepts into the Augustinian framework.[19] The great constructive mind, however, of the first Franciscan school is Bonaventure, one of

[13] Cf. E. Gilson, *La Philosophie de saint Bonaventure* (2d. ed., Vrin, Paris, 1943), 59–75; 379–396; A. C. Pegis, "St. Bonaventure, St. Francis and Philosophy," *Med. Studies*, 15 (1953), 1–13.

[14] C. 1180–1249. Cf. M. Baumgartner, *Die Erkenntnislehre des Wilhelm von Auvergne* (*Beiträge*, 2/1, Münster, 1895); A. Masnovo, *Da Guglielmo d'Auvergne a San Tommaso d'Aquino*, 3 vols. (2d. ed., Vita e Pensiero, Milan, 1945–1946).

[15] 1175–1253. Cf. D. A. Callus (ed.), *Robert Grosseteste, Scholar and Bishop: Essays in Commemoration of the Seventh Centenary of His Death* (Clarendon Press, Oxford, 1953); A. C. Crombie, *Robert Grosseteste and the Origins of Experimental Science. 1100–1700* (Clarendon Press, Oxford, 1953); L. E. Lynch, "The Doctrine of Divine Ideas and Illumination in Robert Grosseteste," *Med. Studies*, 3 (1941), 161–173; J. T. Muckle, "Robert Grosseteste's Use of Greek Sources in His Hexameron," *Medievalia et Humanistica*, 3 (1945), 33–48; G. B. Phelan, "An Unedited Text of Robert Grosseteste on the Subject-Matter of Theology," *Revue néo-scol. de phil.*, 36 (1934), 172–179.

[16] Cf. Gilson, *History*, 258; 264.

[17] C. 1220–c. 1300. Cf. R. Carton, *La Synthèse doctrinale de Roger Bacon* (Paris, 1924); E. Lutz, *Roger Bacon's Contribution to Knowledge* (Wagner, New York, 1936).

[18] Cf. Gilson, *History*, 327–331.

[19] Cf. D. H. Salman, "Jean de la Rochelle et les débuts de l'averroïsme latin," *Archives d'hist. doct. et litt. du moyen âge*, 16 (1947–1948), 133–144.

the finest of medieval thinkers,[20] with whom should be associated John Pecham[21] and Matthew of Aquasparta,[22] distinguished theologians in their own right, but faithful exponents of his fundamental ideas. In their collective work, certain doctrines may be found which constitute the typical structure of Franciscan thought. For example, they assert the "active potentiality" of matter, in terms of Augustine's doctrine of *rationes seminales*, or implanted forms, in order to avoid a naturalistic exaggeration of the creative efficacy of secondary causes.[23] They assert the plurality of "substantial forms" in man, in order to minimize the involvement of the human spirit, with its divine resemblance and supernatural vocation, in the physical world order.[24] They identify substance and faculties in the human soul, in order to manifest the essential character of the soul as an image of the Trinity in unity.[25] They insist on the dependence of human intelligence on divine illumination in every act of certain knowledge, and, whatever precise construction they may put on this doctrine, are thus led to undertake the closest interweaving of natural knowledge and faith.[26] They assert the primacy of the will in human personality, and of love in human life, against the challenge of Greek intellectualism to human liberty and Christian piety, and as a result stress the "practical" nature of theology, as ordered to affective contemplation rather than to intellectual perfection.[27] All these ideas express a fundamental antipathy to Aristotelian naturalism and a concern for divine freedom and creativity, for creaturely dependence and responsibility.[28]

The passage from Bonaventure in this volume gives vivid expression to the Franciscan sense of the intimate relation of the human spirit to the divine, and of its radical dependence on the latter, even if at the same time it shows the difficulty—which was eventually to contribute to the first great crisis within the

[20] Cf. Gilson, *History*, 327–331.   [21] D. 1292. Cf. *ibid.*, 359 f.
[22] Cf. *ibid.*, 341.   [23] Cf. *ibid.*, 339; 687, n. 24.
[24] Cf. E. Gilson, *La Philosophie de saint Bonaventure*, 254–273; A. C. Pegis, *St. Thomas and the Problem of the Soul in the Thirteenth Century* (St. Michael's College, Toronto, 1934).
[25] Cf. *ibid.*, 165–191.
[26] Cf. *ibid.*, 304–324. This is one of the most authentically Augustinian ideas in the whole complex; strangely enough, however, it was not stated (even though implied) by as good an Augustinian as Anselm.
[27] Cf. L. Amoros, "La teología como ciencia practica en los tiempos que preceden a Escoto," *Archives d'hist. doct. et litt. du moyen âge*, 9 (1934), 261–303.
[28] Cf. Gilson, *History*, 340; 348; 407.

Franciscan school—of speaking of illumination in such a way as to maintain this unique relation of the human mind to God without confusing it either with God's universal sustaining activity in nature or with his gracious self-revelation.[29] As for Matthew of Aquasparta, who is an important figure in the Augustinian-Aristotelian controversies of the late thirteenth century, several of the issues involved in these controversies (with regard, for instance, to the intellect's knowledge of singulars, and the soul's knowledge of itself) are reflected in the text presented here. The special interest of this *Quaestio*, however, lies in Matthew's defense of the traditional Augustinian position concerning faith and reason. Although he is willing to make limited use of the Aristotelian terminology and theory of abstraction, he resists his opponents' attempt to develop a clear delimitation of the respective spheres of faith and reason, philosophy and theology, the natural and the supernatural. Contrary to the Aristotelians, he believes that reasons or proofs can be adduced in support of articles of faith without eliminating faith.[30] For him, reason is not even relatively autonomous, but can reach truth only in dependence on divine illumination, thought of as a special (rather than general) influence of God.

One school of historians has exaggerated the parallels between the Franciscan and the Thomist use of Aristotelian material,[31] with the inevitable implication that the Franciscan school produced an incomplete version of the synthesis achieved by Thomas Aquinas. In view of the declared attitude of Bonaventure and others,[32] to say nothing of their admitted genius and the general lucidity of their thought, such an interpretation is hard to defend. It is true that the Franciscans tried to take account of the new knowledge, and their effective presentation of solutions for the fresh problems of the thirteenth century helps to distinguish them from earlier Augustinians. Nonetheless, they were primarily interested in maintaining the older tradition, as the only effective defense against the acute

---

[29] Cf. M. C. d'Arcy, "The Philosophy of St. Augustine," in *A Monument to St. Augustine* (Sheed and Ward, London, 1930), 155–196; R. Jolivet, "La Doctrine augustinienne de l'illumination," in *Mélanges augustiniens* (Rivière, Paris, 1931), 52–172.

[30] Cf. Thomas Aquinas, *Sum. theol.*, IIa-IIae, 1, 4.

[31] Cf. F. Van Steenberghen, *Siger de Brabant d'après ses œuvres inédites*, II (Institut supérieur de philosophie, Louvain, 1942), 464.

[32] Cf. Bonaventure, *Sermo 4 de rebus theol.*, 18 f. (*Opera*, V, 572), on the *scientia* of Aristotle, the *sapientia* of Plato, and the union of both in Augustine. For Matthew, cf. p. 407, n. 26, below.

dangers of Averroism, and to this end they were prepared, if driven to it, to attack even the theological synthesis of an Aquinas, on the ground of its excessive generosity toward Aristotle. Thus, rather than construing the Franciscan synthesis as a preliminary essay in Thomism, we should recognize that it stands for a significantly different estimate of the intellectual situation of the thirteenth century, and that its typical theses are formulated in the light of that estimate. It was, in fact, this deliberate (if enlightened) conservatism that precipitated the condemnations of 1277, in which, as Gilson points out, we must see the beginning of the end of the medieval intellectual experiment.[33] Such historical hindsight, however, must not reduce our appreciation of the intellectual alertness and competence of the great Franciscans.

III

The condemnations of 1277 did not, of course, bring the intellectual debate of the thirteenth century to an abrupt end. On the contrary, numerous representatives of our main trends can be found in the following centuries. The Averroists, for example, were active as late as the seventeenth century, and formed the hard core of the rigid Aristotelian opposition to the rise of modern science.[34] A tendency of Thomist inspiration—though manifesting some uncertainty as to the authentic interpretation of "the Angelic Doctor"—began with Giles of Rome[35] and the early Dominican Thomists,[36] was a dominant factor in Counter-Reformation theology,[37] and survives as a vital force in contemporary Roman Catholic thought.[38] A line of "Albertist" thinkers, who developed certain distinctive lines of thought of Albert the Great, can be traced at least through the fourteenth century.[39] Finally, disciples of Bonaventure form an important group, which includes, in addition to Pecham and Matthew of Aquasparta, such persons as Eustachius of Arras,

---

[33] On the content and meaning of the condemnations, cf. Gilson, *History*, 402–410.

[34] Cf. *ibid.*, 522.

[35] D. 1316. Cf. E. Hocedez, "Gilles de Rome et saint Thomas," in *Mélanges Mandonnet* (Vrin, Paris, 1930), I, 385–409; P. W. Nash, "Giles of Rome, Auditor and Critic of St. Thomas," *Modern Schoolman*, 28 (1950), 1–20.

[36] Cf. M. Grabmann, *Mittelalterliches Geistesleben*, I, 332–431; II, 512–613.

[37] Cf. F. C. Copleston, *History of Philosophy*, Vol. III: *Ockham to Suarez*, 335–352.

[38] Cf. A. Doolan, *The Revival of Thomism* (Clonmore and Reynolds, Dublin, 1951).

[39] Cf. Gilson, *History*, 431–437.

Walter of Bruges, Bartholomew of Bologna, and Roger Marston.[40]

This continuous Franciscan tradition is a most significant force in later medieval theology. The Franciscan mind, still alive to the problems of the period, in due course produced a newer Augustinianism, devoted to the same concerns, but conscious of the more compelling criticisms advanced by Thomists and others. The most influential promoters of the Augustinian reconstruction are Richard of Middleton[41] and Henry of Ghent,[42] while the greatest master of this later school is John Duns Scotus, one of the most powerful and subtle minds of the Middle Ages.

Although on some issues Scotus stands between the older Franciscan school and the Thomist position,[43] and repudiates some of the more obscure or debatable aspects of the Bonaventurian tradition—for example, the doctrine of illumination—he is dominated by fundamental Augustinian motives. Thus he is still concerned with the maintenance of the divine transcendence and liberty, and of the primacy of the will in human personality, against attempts to subject both to a naturalistic system.[44] While his own tendency to separate reason and faith is often exaggerated—partly, at least, under the influence of texts falsely ascribed to him—it is not unfair to say that, given his historical circumstances, this emphasis on the emancipation of God and man alike from rational necessities helped to weaken the link between revealed truth and philosophical principle.[45] To this process, moreover, his rigorous criticism of the claims of metaphysical speculation gave a certain impetus,[46] so that his philosophical treatment of the question of God has considerable historical importance.

Scotus' proof of God's existence is governed by his idea of metaphysics as the science of being at its ultimate degree of abstraction, where the notion becomes "univocal" (or applicable to everything in the same sense). Within being as thus understood we can discern two primary modes, the finite and

---

40 Cf. *ibid.*, 340–344.
41 Or "de Mediavilla"; cf. *ibid.*, 347–349.
42 D. 1293; not a Franciscan, but fundamental for understanding of the school. Cf. *ibid.*, 447–454; J. Paulus, *Henri de Gand: Essai sur les tendances de sa métaphysique* (Vrin, Paris, 1938).
43 Here he reflects Richard of Middleton; cf. E. Hocedez, *Richard de Middleton, sa vie, ses œuvres, sa doctrine* (Louvain, 1925), 386.
44 Cf. E. Gilson, *Jean Duns Scot* (Vrin, Paris, 1952), 643–647.
45 Cf. Gilson, *History*, 460.   46 Cf. *ibid.*, 463 f.

the infinite, and the supreme task of metaphysics is to prove the
existence of infinite being, over against finite beings. This
proof begins with the demonstration of a "first" being, and concludes by showing that this being is infinite. Once this is
accomplished—*a posteriori*, since in Scotus' metaphysic of being
no *a priori* argument from the notion of God is possible—a
modus vivendi is established between philosophy and theology,
since the liberty of divine action implied in the theological
doctrines of creation and redemption is safeguarded by the
proof of God as infinite being. By the same token, however, the
range of necessary demonstration in philosophy is radically
reduced, because of the emphasis on divine freedom—this
despite the fact that in theology Scotus is prepared to assert
such doctrines as the immaculate conception of the blessed
Virgin Mary, with the help of Anselmian *rationes necessariae*—
and consequently the ground common to revelation and reason
is narrowed.[47]

IV

The intellectual fecundity of the Franciscans was far from
exhausted in the work of Bonaventure and Scotus and their
disciples. On the contrary, the Franciscan tradition produced a
third main type of doctrine, which, constituted as it was of a
blend of authentic Augustinian preoccupations with principles
essentially destructive of the great scholastic syntheses, forms a
span in the bridge between the Middle Ages and the modern
world.[48] William Ockham's work was, of course, only one
factor in the crisis of medieval thought and culture, manifested
on the intellectual side in the widespread triumph of the *via
moderna* over Thomists, Scotists, and others, whose doctrines
were lumped together under the label of the *via antiqua*.[49] The
sources of the intellectual chaos of the early fourteenth century
include the dissolution of Thomism and Scotism from within
by the circulation of an "improved Aristotelianism"[50]—easily
confused, as later history has shown, with the Thomism of
Aquinas[51]—and the critical work of such authors as the Domin-

---

[47] For a full exposition, cf. E. Gilson, *Jean Duns Scot*, 11–215. The divine
freedom does not extend to the principle of contradiction or to the
essences of creatable beings; cf. Gilson, *History*, 460 f.
[48] Cf. *ibid.*, 498 f.
[49] Cf. *ibid.*, 471–489. It seems clear that the name is "William Ockham,"
not "of Ockham"; cf. P. Böhner, *The Tractatus de Successivis attributed to
William Ockham* (Franciscan Institute, St. Bonaventure, N.Y., 1944), 4 f.
[50] Cf. Gilson, *History*, 471 f.   [51] Cf. *ibid.*

ican Durandus of Saint-Pourçain[52] and the Franciscan Peter Aureolus.[53] It remains true, nevertheless, that the "nominalism" of which Ockham is the classical exponent was the most explosive force of all.

Theological and philosophical criticism are interestingly correlated in the Ockhamist doctrine. For example, it reveals the influence of the Augustinian theological reaction of the fourteenth century, represented at Oxford by Thomas Bradwardine[54] and others, which reformulated the older Augustinian opposition to Aristotelianism. Ockham, indeed, came under Augustinian fire because of his "Pelagianizing" tendencies,[55] but themes derived from the earlier Franciscan tradition dominated his theology. The latter is complicated, however, by a strong philosophical influence, historically opposed to Augustinianism, criticized by the Augustinians, itself critical of traditional Augustinianism, and yet sometimes tentatively related to the latter—for instance, in the teaching of Gregory of Rimini.[56] This philosophical nominalism[57] is often assumed, by those who forget that Ockham was, above all, a theologian,[58] to be the dominant factor in his development, but, while its importance cannot be disputed, that importance lies in its alliance with an extreme theological voluntarism, which it both fortifies and isolates from a philosophy of the natural order and natural reason.[59] It is the Augustinian critique of the latter that finds a full (if one-sided) expression in the Ockhamist emancipation of the divine will from any intelligible order of moral values, a liberation which pretty well completes the dissolution of the nexus between nature and supernature, reason and faith.[60] Moreover—and this is of great importance for the

[52] Cf. F. C. Copleston, op. cit., 25–28.　　[53] Cf. ibid., 29–39.
[54] D. 1349. Cf. P. Glorieux, art. "Thomas Bradwardine," DTC, 15, 765–773; G. Chaucer, Canterbury Tales, "The Nonne Preestes Tale," ll. 4420–4442.
[55] Cf. A. Gwynn, The English Austin Friars in the Time of Wyclif (Oxford University Press, London, 1940), 80.
[56] D. 1358. Cf. ibid., 57 f.; Gilson, History, 502 f.
[57] Cf. ibid., 499–520.
[58] Cf. R. Guelluy, Philosophie et théologie chez Guillaume d'Ockham (Vrin, Paris, 1947), 360; F. C. Copleston, op. cit., 47 f.
[59] Cf. R. Guelluy, op. cit., 221–258; 353; A. Lang, Die Wege der Glaubensbegründung bei den Scholastikern des 14. Jahrhunderts (Beiträge, 30/1–2, Münster, 1931).
[60] Cf. E. Bonke, "Doctrina nominalistica de fundamento ordinis moralis apud Gulielmum de Ockham et Gabriel Biel," Collectanea francisc., 104 (1944), 57–83.

climate of opinion within which late medieval theology had to work—Ockham's political writings, by giving support to strong contemporary tendencies, contributed to the dissolution of the social order of the Middle Ages.[61] While the judicious formulation of the issues in such a text as the *Octo quaestiones*, excerpted in this volume, may obscure the passion of Ockham's antipapal polemic, the destructive implications of the arguments brought against the papal claims can hardly be overlooked.

By their very nature, the forces that dissolved medieval civilization created the problems that succeeding generations had to face, and thus contributed more or less directly to the constitution of the modern world. Both the limitations and the freshly creative ideas of Renaissance and Reformation and Counter-Reformation (to say nothing of later developments) are related to common problems inherited from the Middle Ages. For example, the theological voluntarism of the Augustinians, strengthened by the nominalist critique of rational order, issued both in the majestic theology of Calvinism[62] and in the ominous doctrines of the apostles of royal "sovereignty."[63] As for philosophical influences, we may note how the Lutheran attempt to restate the Pauline gospel against nominalist "Pelagianism" was at once stimulated and hampered by the heritage of philosophical positivism, which drastically affected the presentation of the doctrine of grace.[64] Example could be piled upon example, because, for good or ill, much of the later history of the Western mind is the story of an attempt to make new correlations of diverse elements inherited from the medieval world.

[61] Cf. P. Böhner, "Ockham's Political Ideas," *Review of Politics*, 5 (1943), 462–487; G. de Lagarde, "Marsile de Padoue et Guillaume d'Ockham," *Revue des sciences rel.*, 17 (1937), 168–185; 428–454.

[62] Cf. C. Calvetti, *La filosofia di Giovanni Calvino* (Vita e Pensiero, Milan, 1955). It is noteworthy that Thomas Bradwardine's great work, *De causa dei contra Pelagium et de virtute causarum, ad suos Mertonenses*, was first printed (London, 1618) by order of the pro-Calvinist archbishop George Abbot of Canterbury.

[63] Cf. J. Maritain, *Man and the State* (University of Chicago Press, 1951), 28–53.

[64] Cf. P. Vignaux, "Sur Luther et Ockham," *Franziskanische Studien*, 32 (1950), 21–30. For an interesting and sympathetic discussion of the interaction of authentic theological concern with nominalist philosophical influences in Luther and others, cf. L. Bouyer, *Du protestantisme à l'église* (Editions du Cerf, Paris, 1954).

BIBLIOGRAPHY

GENERAL WORKS

Full treatments of this period will be found in the works listed in the General Bibliography. Some of the most important thinkers are discussed in D. E. Sharp, *Franciscan Philosophy at Oxford in the Thirteenth Century* (Oxford University Press, London, 1930). Useful discussions of some of the most urgent issues of the thirteenth century will be found in the following studies of one of its most prominent figures: D. L. Douie, *Archbishop Pecham* (Clarendon Press, Oxford, 1952); F. Ehrle, "John Peckham über den Kampf des Augustinismus und Aristotelismus im XIII Jahrhundert," *Zeitschrift für kathol. Theol.*, 13 (1889), 172–193; A. Teetaert, art. "Pecham, Jean," *DTC*, 12, 100–140.

See also E. Bettoni, *Il Problema della cognoscibilità di Dio nella scuola francescana* (Cedan, Padua, 1950); M. D. Chenu, art. "Kilwardby, Robert," *DTC*, 8, 2354–2356.

BONAVENTURE (1221–1274)

The standard critical edition of the *Opera omnia* of Bonaventure is the ten-volume Franciscan edition (Quaracchi, 1882–1902); see also another redaction of his *Collationes in Hexaemeron* (Quaracchi, 1934). English translations include a text from the commentary on the *Sentences* (in R. McKeon, *Selections from Medieval Philosophers*, II, 118–48), as well as the *Breviloquium* (tr. E. E. Nemmers, Herder, St. Louis, 1946).

The outstanding study of Bonaventure is E. Gilson, *La Philosophie de saint Bonaventure* (2d ed., Vrin, Paris, 1943; Eng. tr. from 1st ed., *The Philosophy of St. Bonaventure*, Sheed and Ward, London 1938).

The following may also be consulted: A. Baroni, *La scuola*

375

francescana guidata dal suo serafico dottore San Bonaventura, 3 vols. (Florence, 1886); F. Imle and J. Kaup, *Die Theologie des hl. Bonaventura* (Franziskus-Druckerei, Werle i. W., 1931); R. Lazzarini, *San Bonaventura filosofo e mistico del cristianesimo* (Bocca, Milan, 1946); G. Sestili, *La filosofia di San Bonaventura* (Marietti, Turin, 1928); E. Smeets, art. "Bonaventure," *DTC*, 2, 962–986.

A number of important problems are dealt with in the following: J. d'Albi, *Saint Bonaventure et les luttes doctrinales de 1267–1277* (Tamines, 1922); J. M. Bissen, *L'Exemplarisme divin selon saint Bonaventure* (Vrin, Paris, 1929); I. Hislop, "Introduction to St. Bonaventure's Theory of Knowledge," *Dominican Studies*, 2 (1949), 46–55; F. Imle, *Gott und Geist: Das Zusammenwirken des geschaffenen und des ungeschaffenen Geistes im höheren Erkenntnisakt nach Bonaventura* (Franziskus-Druckerei, Werle i. W., 1934); J. Krause, *Die Lehre des hl. Bonaventura über die Natur der Körperlichen und geistigen Wesen und ihr Verhältnis zum Thomismus* (Paderborn, 1888); E. Lutz, *Die Psychologie Bonaventuras* (*Beiträge*, 6/4–5, Münster 1909); B. A. Luyckx, *Die Erkenntnislehre Bonaventuras nach den Quellen dargestellt* (*Beiträge*, 23/3–4, Münster, 1923); B. Rosenmöller, *Die religiöse Erkenntnis nach Bonaventura* (*Beiträge*, 25/3–4, Münster, 1925).

MATTHEW OF AQUASPARTA (c. 1240–1302)

The only substantial printed text is *Quaestiones disputatae selectae*, 3 vols. (Quaracchi, 1903–1935). One of the *Quaestiones de fide et cognitione* (from Vol. I) is translated in R. McKeon, *Selections from Medieval Philosophers*, II, 240–302.

The most useful studies are M. Grabmann, *Die philosophische und theologische Erkenntnislehre des Kardinals Matthaeus ab Aquasparta* (Vienna, 1906), and E. Longpré, art. "Matthieu d'Aquasparta," *DTC*, 10, 375–389.

JOHN DUNS SCOTUS (1266–1308)

The only complete edition of the *Opera omnia* is that of Wadding (Lyons, 1639), reprinted in 26 vols. (Paris, 1891–1895), which includes several spurious or doubtful works. (Cf. Gilson, *History*, 763 f.) Partial critical editions include the beginning of the *Opus Oxoniense* in the Scotist Commission's edition, directed by C. Balić (Typis Polyglottis Vaticanis, 1950–), of which 2 vols. have now appeared; *Tractatus de primo principio* (ed. E. Roche, with Eng. tr., Franciscan Institute, St. Bonaventure, N.Y., 1949); *Ioannis Duns Scoti theologiae marianae elementa* (ed. C. Balić, Sebenico, 1933), containing selections from the commentaries on the *Sentences*. A passage from the *Opus Oxoniense* is translated in R. McKeon, *Selections from Medieval Philosophers*, II, 313–350.

The best studies are E. Gilson, *Jean Duns Scot: Introduction à ses positions fondamentales* (Vrin, Paris, 1952), and E. Longpré, *La Philosophie du bienheureux Duns Scot* (Paris, 1924). The following, while valuable, must be read with care because of their use of the spurious *De rerum principio*: C. R. S. Harris, *Duns Scotus*, 2 vols. (Clarendon Press, Oxford, 1927); B. Landry, *La Philosophie de Duns Scot* (Paris, 1922); P. Minges, *Joannis Duns Scoti doctrina philosophica et theologica*, 2 vols. (2d ed., Quaracchi, 1930).

The following should also be consulted: C. Balić, art. "Duns Scoto, Giovanni," *Enciclopedia cattolica*, 4, 1982–1990; E. Bettoni, "De argumentatione Doctoris Subtilis quoad existentiam Dei," *Antonianum*, 28 (1953), 39–58; J. Klein, *Die Charitaslehre des Johannes Duns Scotus* (Münster, 1926); J. Klein, *Der Gottesbegriff des Johannes Duns Scotus* (Paderborn, 1913); N. Micklem, *Reason and Revelation: A Question from Duns Scotus* (Nelson, Edinburgh, 1953); P. Minges, *Das Verhältnis zwischen Glauben und Wissen, Theologie und Philosophie, nach Duns Scotus* (Paderborn, 1908); R. Seeberg, *Die Theologie des Johannes Duns Scotus* (Leipzig, 1900); C. L. Shircel, *The Univocity of the Concept of Being in the Philosophy of John Duns Scotus* (Catholic University of America Press, Washington, 1942); A. M. Vellico, "De charactere scientifico theologiae apud Doctorem Subtilem," *Antonianum*, 16 (1941), 3–30.

WILLIAM OCKHAM (c. 1300–c. 1350)

There is no early or modern edition of Ockham's *Opera omnia*, but a critical edition in about 25 vols. is projected by the Franciscan Institute, St. Bonaventure, N.Y. A number of editions (including modern critical texts) of individual works are listed in Gilson, *History*, 783. Among the more important are *The Tractatus de Successivis attributed to William Ockham* (ed. P. Böhner, St. Bonaventure College, St. Bonaventure, N.Y., 1944), with a valuable biographical introduction; *Tractatus de praedestinatione et de praescientia dei et de futuris contingentibus* (ed. P. Böhner, St. Bonaventure, N.Y., 1945); *Guillelmi de Ockham opera politica*, Vol. I (ed. J. G. Sikes *et al.*, Manchester University

Press, 1940); *De sacramento altaris* (ed. T. B. Birch, with Eng. tr., Lutheran Literary Board, Burlington, Iowa, 1930). Other translations will be found in R. McKeon, *Selections from Medieval Philosophers*, II, 360–421, and S. C. Torney, *Ockham: Studies and Selections* (Open Court, LaSalle, Ill., 1938); Selections from a number of medieval political texts, including Ockham's *Dialogus*, are translated in E. Lewis, *Medieval Political Ideas*, 2 vols. (Knopf, New York, 1954).

The most valuable introductions to Ockham's general position will be found in R. Guelluy, *Philosophie et théologie chez Guillaume d'Ockham* (Vrin, Paris, 1947), and in two articles by P. Vignaux, "Nominalisme," *DTC*, 11, 717–784, and "Occam," *ibid.*, 864–904 (with E. Amann).

Other useful studies include the following: L. Baudry, *Guillaume d'Ockham, sa vie, ses oeuvres, ses idées sociales et politiques*, Vol. I (Vrin, Paris, 1950); P. Böhner, "The Realistic Conceptualism of William Ockham," *Traditio*, 4 (1946), 307–336; G. N. Buescher, *The Eucharistic Teaching of William Ockham* (Franciscan Institute, St. Bonaventure, N.Y., 1950); F. Federhofer, "Die Psychologie und die psychologischen Grundlagen der Erkenntnislehre des Wilhelm von Ockham," *Philos. Jahrbuch*, 39 (1926), 263–287; G. Giacon, *Guglielmo di Occam*, 2 vols. (Vita e Pensiero, Milan, 1941); F. Hochstetter, *Studien zur Metaphysik und Erkenntnislehre Wilhelms von Ockham* (Berlin, 1927); G. Martin, *Wilhelm von Ockham: Untersuchungen zur Ontologie der Ordnungen* (de Gruyter, Berlin, 1949); E. A. Moody, *The Logic of William of Ockham* (Sheed and Ward, London, 1935); S. U. Zuidema, *De philosophie van Occam in zijn Commentar op de Sententien*, 2 vols. (Schipper, Hilversum, 1936; texts in Vol. II).

Original Sources

The texts translated below will be found in the critical editions already listed, as follows:

Bonaventure	*Opera omnia*, V, 17–27
Matthew of Aquasparta	*Quaestiones disputatae*, I, 128–153
John Duns Scotus	*Opera omnia*, II, 128–148
William Ockham	*Opera politica*, I, 69–71; 82–84

Bonaventure: Disputed Questions Concerning Christ's Knowledge

THE TEXT

Question Four

WHETHER WHATEVER IS KNOWN BY US WITH CERTITUDE IS KNOWN IN THE ETERNAL REASONS THEMSELVES

I

Arguments for and Against the Thesis

IT IS PRESUPPOSED THAT THE ETERNAL REASONS ARE really indistinct in the divine art or knowledge.[1] The question is whether they are the grounds of knowing in all certain knowledge.[2] To ask this is to ask whether whatever is known by us with certitude is known in the eternal reasons themselves. And that this is so is evident from manifold authority.[3]

1. Augustine, *On the Teacher*[4]: "Referring to all the things which we understand, we consult, not the speaker who utters words, but the guardian truth within the mind itself. . . . Moreover, he who is consulted teaches; for he who is said to reside in the inner man is Christ, . . . the unchangeable excellence of God and his everlasting wisdom, which every rational soul does indeed consult."

2. Again, the same, *On the True Religion*[5]: "It is clear that there exists, above our mind, a norm[6] which is called truth. It is already incontestable that this immutable nature, which is above the human mind,[7] is God. . . . For this is that immutable truth, which is rightly called the norm of all the arts and the art of the almighty Artificer."

3. Again, Augustine, in the second book of *On Free Will*[8]: "That beauty of wisdom and truth . . . neither passes with

---

[1] Cf. q. 3 (Bonaventure, *Opera omnia*, V, 10–16).
[2] On *rationes*, cf. R. J. Deferrari, *Lexicon of St. Thomas Aquinas*, 937–942.
[3] The *auctoritates* (or classical texts) are followed by more fully argued "reasons."
[4] Augustine, *De magist.*, 11, 38 (*PL*, 32, 1216).
[5] Augustine, *De vera rel.*, 30:56 to 31:57 (*PL*, 34, 147);
[6] *Legem.*
[7] The original text reads: *anima rationalis.*
[8] Augustine, *De lib. arb.*, II, 14:38 (*PL*, 32, 1262).

time nor changes with locality. It is not interrupted by night or shut off by shadow, nor is it subject to the bodily senses. To all those turned to it from the whole world, who love it, it is near; to all it is everlasting; it is in no place, it is never lacking; it warns without, it teaches within. . . . No one judges it, and without it no one judges rightly; and thus it is manifest, without doubt, that it is greater than our minds, since by it alone each mind is made wise, and judges, not concerning it, but through it concerning other things." But if you say that it follows from this that we see *by* the reasons, but not *in* the truth or *in* the reasons, there is Augustine to the contrary, in the twelfth book of the *Confessions*[9]: "Suppose that both of us see that what you say is true, and both again see that what I say is true, where, I ask you, do we see it? In truth, I do not see it in you, or you in me, but both of us see it in the selfsame unchangeable Truth, which is above our minds."

4. Again, in the eighth book of *The City of God*, speaking of the philosophers, he says[10]: "Those whom we rightly prefer to all . . . declared that the light of our minds for learning all things was the very God himself, by whom all things were made."

5. Again, in the eighth book of *On the Trinity*, chapter three[11]: "When the mind so pleases us that we prefer it to every corporeal light, . . . it does not please us in itself, but in that art by which it was made. For, having been made, it is approved because of that source in which it is seen to have been when it was still to be made; now this is the truth and the simple good."

6. Again, in the ninth book of *On the Trinity*, chapter six[12]: "It is proved that we either accept . . . or reject, when we rightly approve or reject anything, by other rules which remain altogether unchangeable above our mind."

7. Again, in the same book, chapter seven[13]: "In that eternal truth, from which all temporal things are made, we behold by the sight of the mind the form according to which we exist, and in accordance with which we do anything by true and right reason, either in ourselves or in corporeal things."

8. Again, in the fourteenth book of *On the Trinity*, chapter

---

9 Augustine, *Conf.*, XII, 25:35 (*CSEL*, 33, 336).
10 Augustine, *De civ. dei*, VIII, 7 (*CSEL*, 40/1, 366).
11 Augustine, *De trin.*, VIII, 3:5 (*PL*, 42, 950).
12 *Ibid.*, IX, 6:10 (col. 966).
13 *Ibid.*, IX, 7:12 (col. 967).

fifteen[14]: "When the ungodly see the rules according to which each ought to live, where do they see them? Not in their own nature, since it is agreed that their minds are mutable, but these rules are unchangeable; nor in the character of their own mind, since these are rules of justice. Where does he discern that what he does not have is to be had? Where, then, are they written, unless it is in the book of that light which is called truth, from which every just law is copied?" ... If you say that he retracted this, see, on the contrary, Augustine, *Retractations*, book one[15]: "It is credible, that even those who are unskilled in certain disciplines may give true answers, when they can receive the eternal light of reason, where they perceive these immutable truths—not because they first knew them and then forgot them, as it seemed to Plato."[16] ... Again[17]: "The intellectual nature is linked not only to intelligible but even to immutable things, having been made in this order so that, when it moves to the things to which it is linked, or even to itself, it may give true answers concerning them, in so far as it sees them."

From these "authorities" of Augustine it is manifestly clear that all things are known[18] in the eternal reasons.

9. Again, Ambrose[19]: "By myself I see nothing save the empty, the fleeting, the perishable." Therefore, if I see something with certitude, I see it through something which is above me.

10. Again, Gregory,[20] on the text of John, ch. 14,[21] "He will teach you all things," says: "Unless the same Spirit is present to the heart of the hearer, the speech of the teacher is useless. Let no one, therefore, ascribe to the man who teaches what he understands from the teacher's mouth, because unless there is within us one who teaches, the tongue of the teacher labors outwardly for nothing."

11. Again, the same in the same place: "Behold, you all alike hear one voice of the speaker, but still you do not perceive alike the sense of the voice you hear. Since, therefore, the voice

[14] *Ibid.*, XIV, 15:21 (col. 1052); compressed.
[15] Augustine, *Retract.*, I, 4:8 (*CSEL*, 36, 24 f.).
[16] Cf. Plato, *Meno*, 81A ff.
[17] Augustine, *Retract.*, I, 7:2 (*CSEL*, 36, 35).
[18] *Sciuntur* (equivalent to *certitudinaliter cognoscuntur*).
[19] Fragment described by Migne (*PL*, 47, 1150) as the "last chapter of the *Soliloquies*" of Augustine.
[20] Gregory, *Homil. in evang.*, II, 30:3 (*PL*, 76, 1222).
[21] John 14:26.

is not different, why is the understanding of the voice in your heart different, unless it is that, while the speaker's voice admonishes all together, there is an inward master who teaches some in particular concerning the understanding of the voice?" But if our intellect were self-sufficient for understanding through the light of created truth, it would not need a teacher from above. Since, therefore, it does need one, it is evident, etc.

12. Again, Anselm, in the *Address*,[22] chapter fourteen: "How great is that light, from which shines every truth that gives light to the rational mind! How full is that truth, in which is to be found everything that is true, and outside which there is only nothingness and falsehood!" Therefore, if what is true is not seen, save where it is, nothing true is seen except in the eternal truth.

13. Again, Origen[23]: "Even if human nature had not sinned, it could not shine by its own powers." But understanding is a kind of shining, so that even if it had not sinned, it could not understand by its own powers. Therefore it needs a higher agent.

14. Again, the *Glossa*, on the verse of the psalm,[24] "Thy hands have made me and formed me; give me understanding"[25]: "God alone gives understanding; for it is through himself, who is light, that God enlightens pious minds."

15. Again, Isaac says,[26] in dealing with the text of the psalm[27] "In thy light we shall see light": "As that by which the sun can be seen goes out from the sun, and nevertheless that which displays the sun does not desert the sun, so with God light, which goes out from God, irradiates the mind, so that it may first see the very shining, apart from which it would not see at all, and may see other things in it." According to this, therefore, all things are seen in the divine light.

16. Again, the philosopher, in the sixth book of the *Ethics*, chapter three, according to the new translation[28]: "We all suppose that what we know cannot happen otherwise, but when things that may happen otherwise are outside our range of observation, whether they exist or not is hidden from us. Of

22 *Proslogion*.
23 *Homil. in prol. evang. Ioan.*, 1:3, attributed to Erigena (*PL*, 122, 290).
24 Ps. 118:73 (P.B.V., 119:73).
25 On this verse the *Glossa ordinaria* reproduces Augustine, *Enarr. in Ps.* 118, 18:4 (*PL*, 37, 1553); cf. Bonaventure, *Opera omnia*, III, 895.
26 Isaac Stella, *De anima* (*PL*, 194, 1888).
27 Ps. 35:10 (P.B.V., 36:9).
28 Aristotle, *Ethica Nicom.*, VI, 3 (1139b20–25).

necessity, then, the object of knowledge[29] is eternal, for all absolutely necessary beings are eternal, and things that are eternal are ungenerated and incorruptible." Therefore, there cannot be knowledge with any kind of certitude, where the nature[30] of eternal truth is not to be found. But this is only to be found in the eternal reasons; therefore, etc.

Again, the same thing is proved by reasoning, and first by reasons taken from the words of Augustine, but secondly by other reasons. For Augustine, in the second book of *On Free Will*,[31] in *On the True Religion*[32] and *On the Teacher*,[33] in *On Music*, VI,[34] and *On the Trinity*, VIII,[35] suggests reasons of this sort.

17. Everything unchangeable is higher than the changeable; but that by which it is known with certitude is unchangeable, because it is necessary truth. But our mind is changeable; therefore, that by which we know is above our minds. Now there is nothing above our minds save God and eternal truth; therefore divine truth and eternal reason is that by which knowledge exists.

18. Again, everything that is not subject to judgment is higher than that which is subject to judgment. But the norm by which we judge is not subject to judgment; therefore, that by which we know and judge is above our mind. But this can only be eternal truth and reason; therefore, etc.

19. Again, everything infallible is higher than the fallible. But the light and truth, by which we know with certitude, is infallible; therefore, since our mind is fallible, that light and truth is above our mind. But this is the eternal light and truth; therefore, etc.

20. Again, every light that ensures certitude is illimitable, since it shows itself to all and displays the knowable to them with the same certitude. But illimitable light cannot be created light, but can only be uncreated, since every created thing is limited and finite and is multiplied in different things; therefore, this light must necessarily be uncreated. But it is by this light that we know with certitude; therefore, etc.

21. Again, everything necessary is endless, since it cannot be

---

[29] *Scibile.*   [30] *Ratio.*
[31] Cf. *De lib. arb.*, II, 9:25 to 15:39 (*PL*, 32, 1253–1262).
[32] Cf. *De vera rel.*, 30:54 to 32:59 (*PL*, 34, 145–149).
[33] Cf. *De magist.*, 11, 38 (*PL*, 32, 1216).
[34] Cf. *De musica*, VI, 12:35 f. (*PL*, 32, 1182 f.).
[35] Cf. *De trin.*, VIII, 3:4 f.; 6:9 (*PL*, 42, 949 ff.).

otherwise, now or in the future, but that by which we know with certitude is necessary truth, and is, therefore, endless. But every such thing is above every created thing, since every creature must have proceeded from nonbeing to being, and, as far as lies in it, it can be turned again to nonbeing. Since, then, that by which we know excels every created truth, it is uncreated truth.

22. Again, every created thing is, in itself, comprehensible, but according to the philosopher[36] the laws of numbers, figures, and demonstrations, when they are increased to infinity, are incomprehensible to the human intellect. Therefore, when laws of this sort are seen by human intellect, they must necessarily be seen in something which exceeds everything created. But nothing of this sort can be found save God and eternal reason; therefore, etc.

23. Again, when a wicked man knows justice, he knows it either by its presence or by a likeness received from without, or by something which is above. But not by its presence, since it is not present to him; or through a species received from without, since it has no likeness that can be abstracted through sense;[37] therefore it is necessary for him to know it through something else, which is above his intellect. (The same reasoning holds for all the other spiritual things that he knows.) If, then, the wicked knows in the eternal reasons, this applies a fortiori to others. . . . If you say that he knows it through its effects, it can be objected against this[38] that, if something is not known in any way, what is effected by it is not known. For instance, if I do not know what man is, I never know what is done by man. If, therefore, we do not have knowledge of justice first of all, we shall never know that this or that is done by it. It remains, therefore, that it must be known in the eternal reason. The same argument can be used concerning any intelligible substantial form whatever, and thus to all knowledge with certitude.

24. Again, as God is cause of being, so he is principle of knowing and order of living.[39] But God is the cause of being in such a way that nothing can be effected by any cause, unless he himself moves that which acts, by himself and his own eternal

---

[36] Cf. Aristotle, *Phys.*, I, 4; III, 6 (187^{b}7–13; 207^{a}30–32); Augustine, *De lib. arb.*, II, 8:20 ff. (*PL*, 32, 1251–1253), and *De trin.*, XI, 8:12 ff. (*PL*, 42, 994–997).

[37] On species and abstraction, cf. Deferrari, *op. cit.*, 1041–1044.

[38] Cf. Augustine, *De trin.*, VIII, 6:9 (*PL*, 42, 953–956).

[39] Cf. Augustine, *De civ. dei*, VIII, 4 (*CSEL*, 40/1, 360).

power.[40] Therefore, nothing can be understood, unless he himself by his eternal truth immediately enlightens him who understands.

25. Again, no being that is defective, so far as lies in it, is known save through a perfect being.[41] But every created truth, as far as lies in its own power, is darkness and defect; therefore nothing enters the understanding save through that highest truth.

26. Again, nothing is known rightly and with certitude unless it is referred to the rule that cannot in any way be bent. Now this rule is nothing but that which is essentially rectitude itself, and this is nothing save eternal truth and reason. Nothing, therefore, is known with certitude, unless it is referred to the eternal rule.

27. Again, in the twofold division of the soul into "higher" and "lower,"[42] lower reason takes its rise from the higher, and not conversely. But reason is called higher in so far as it is turned toward the eternal laws, and lower in so far as it is concerned with temporal things, and therefore, primarily and naturally, the knowledge of eternal things is in the soul before that of temporal things. It is impossible, then, for anything to be known by it with certitude, unless it is aided by those eternal reasons.

All the reasons that I have just presented are drawn out of the words of Augustine in different volumes.

Moreover, other reasoning makes the same thing evident.

28. Knowledge of the same sensible thing cannot be possessed by different people together and at once, except through something common,[43] and similar reasoning applies to the knowledge of the same intelligible object. But some one truth, though in no way multiplied, can be understood by different people, just as it can be stated in a proposition; therefore, it is necessary that it should be understood through some one thing that is not multiplied in any way. But the one reality which is in no way multiplied in different things can only be God; therefore the principle of our knowledge of any given thing is the truth itself, which is God.

29. Again, intellect is related to the truth, as affectivity to the good, and everything true comes from the highest truth, as

[40] Cf. Bonaventure, *II Sent.*, d. 37, a.1, q.1 (*Opera omnia*, II, 861–864).
[41] Cf. Boethius, *De consolat.*, III, pr. 10 (*CSEL*, 67, 64).
[42] Cf. p. 316, n.50.
[43] Cf. Augustine, *De lib. arb.*, II, 7:15 ff. (*PL*, 32, 1249 f.).

every good comes from the highest goodness. But it is impossible for our affection to be drawn directly to a good, unless in some way it attains the highest goodness. Therefore, our intellect cannot have certain knowledge of something true, unless in some way it attains to the highest truth.[44]

30. Again, the true is only known through truth, and only by known truth, at that—and especially through the truth that is best known. Now this latter truth is that which cannot be thought of as nonexistent, and this is not created but uncreated truth.[45] Therefore, whatever is known with certitude is known in the eternal truth and reason.

31. Again, by nature the soul is turned toward the intelligible outside it, and toward the intelligible inside it, and toward the intelligible above it. Now turning toward the intelligible outside it is the least simple matter, while turning to the intelligible within it is simpler, and turning to the intelligible above it is the simplest of all, because the latter is closer to the soul than the soul is to itself. But the simpler something is, the greater priority it has;[46] therefore, the turning of the soul toward the truth itself that is closest to it is naturally prior to its turning toward itself or toward external truths. It is impossible, therefore, for it to know anything, unless it knows that highest truth first of all.

32. Again, every being in potentiality is reduced to act by means of something existing in act in that genus.[47] But our intellect is in potentiality, as intellect is in a boy; therefore, if it is to become intelligent in act, this can only come about through him who knows all things in actuality. But this describes the eternal wisdom alone; therefore, etc. . . . If you say that this is the active intellect,[48] then I raise this problem: either the active intellect already understood what it learns, or it did not; if not, then nothing could be made intelligent in act through it; but if it did, then either that which learns understands and is ignorant of the same thing at the same time, or else the active intellect is not something that belongs to the soul, but is above the soul. But God alone is above the soul; therefore, etc. . . . If you say, that the active intellect is called

---

[44] Cf. Augustine, *De trin.*, VIII, 3:4 (*PL*, 42, 949 f.); Anselm, *De verit.*, 10; 13.
[45] Cf. Anselm's argument in the *Proslogion*.
[46] Cf. Aristotle, *Metaph.*, X, 1 (1059^{b}34–36).
[47] Cf. *ibid.*, VIII, 8 (1049^{b}23–27).
[48] *Intellectus agens.*

"active," not because it understands in actuality, but because it causes understanding,[49] I say, on the contrary, that every intelligent thing is higher and better than the nonintelligent. If, then, the active intellect is not intelligent, it will never make itself or another intelligent in act, since it cannot produce something better and higher than itself; therefore, if it is made intelligent in act, this must be done through something above it. But this can only mean the eternal reason and truth; therefore, etc.

33. Again, suppose that all creatures are destroyed, and the rational spirit alone remains; there will remain with it the knowledge of disciplines, namely, of numbers and figures. But this cannot be on account of any true being they have in the spirit or in the universe; therefore, it must necessarily be on account of the being they have with the supreme Artificer.

34. Again, according to all the "saints,"[50] God is said to be the teacher of all knowledge, for one of these reasons: Either he co-operates in a general way with every intellect, as he does with other creatures also, or he infuses a gift of grace, or in knowing the intellect attains to him. If it is because he co-operates in a general way, then it would follow that he teaches the senses as he does the intellect, but this is absurd. If it is because he infuses a gift of grace, then every cognition will be gratuitous or infused, and thus none will be acquired or innate, but this is most absurd. It remains, then, that God is to be called our teacher because our intellect attains to him as to the light of our minds and the principle by which we know every truth.

But objections are brought against this, both from authority and from reason. The arguments from authority are as follows.

1. In the last chapter of First Timothy[51] it is said of God: "Who only hath immortality, and inhabiteth light inaccessible, whom no man hath seen, nor can see." But everything through or in which we know is accessible to the knower; therefore, that through or in which we know cannot be the light of eternal reason or truth.

2. Again, Augustine, *On the Trinity*, I[52]: "The sight of the human mind is too weak to be focused on so excellent a light, unless it is cleansed by the righteousness of faith." If, then, the

---

[49] Cf. Bonaventure, *II Sent.*, d.24, p.1, a.2, q.4 (*Opera omnia*, II, 567–571).
[50] Cf. p. 159, n. 34.
[51] I Tim. 6:16.
[52] Augustine, *De trin.*, I, 2:4 (*PL*, 42, 822), reading *emundetur* instead of *nutrita vegetetur*.

light of eternal truth were the principle of our knowing all truths, only the cleansed and holy soul would know the truth. But this is false; therefore the premise on which it depends is false also.

3. Again, *On the Trinity*, IX[53]: "As the mind itself, then, acquires the concepts of corporeal things through the bodily senses, so it acquires those of incorporeal things through itself." It seems, therefore, that in knowing it is not necessary for it to know whatever it does know through the eternal reasons.

4. Again Augustine, *On the Trinity*, XII[54]: "One should believe that the nature of the intellectual mind was so made that in the order of nature, according to the Creator's design, it sees everything related to intelligible things by means of a certain incorporeal light of its own genus, just as the eye of the flesh sees the things that surround it in this corporeal light." It seems, therefore, that if the created light of corporeal nature is adequate for the knowledge of the objects of sense, the created spiritual light is also sufficient (along with the cognitive power) for the knowledge of intelligible objects of the same genus.

5. Again, Gregory, in the *Morals*[55]: "When the mind is hung aloft in . . . contemplation, whatever it . . . perfectly sees is not God." But the principle of our knowing is perfectly perceived in knowledge with certitude; therefore, a principle[56] of this sort is not God or something in God. Therefore, etc.

6. Again, Dionysius, in the *Epistle to Gaius*[57]: "If anyone, seeing God, understands what he sees, he does not see God himself, but some one of those beings and objects of knowledge that exist, while God himself remains above understanding and substance.[58] When we know, therefore, in the present life, our mind does not attain to uncreated truth.

7. Again, the philosopher says, in *On the Soul*, III,[59] that "our intellect is exercised in connection with the continuous and with time."[60] But those eternal reasons are wholly beyond

---

[53] *Ibid.*, IX, 3:3 (col. 963).
[54] *Ibid.*, XII, 15:24; Gilson (*Introduction à l'étude de saint Augustin*, 107, n. 1) prefers to render *sui generis* as *d'un genre particulier*, because of the implications of the rendering suggested above. (R.D.C.)
[55] Gregory, *Moral. in Iob*, V, 36:66 (*PL*, 75, 716).
[56] *Ratio*.
[57] *Epist.* 1; translation close to that of Erigena (*PL*, 122, 1177).
[58] Erigena: "mind and essence."
[59] Hinted at in Aristotle, *De anima*, III, 6 (430a26–430b19); more clearly put in *De memor. et reminiscent.*, 1 (449b30–450a14).
[60] I.e., cannot act altogether apart from spatial continuity and temporal movement.

time; when we understand, therefore, our intellect does not attain to those reasons in any way.

8. Again, he says in the same place[61]: "Just as in every nature there is a factor by which it is productive of all things, and another factor by which it may become all things, so we must understand, with respect to the intellect, that there is an active intellect and a potential intellect.[62] But these are sufficient for perfect cognition; therefore, there is no need for the assistance of an eternal reason.

9. Again, experience teaches that "out of many sense-perceptions is produced one memory, out of many memories one experience, out of many experiences one universal, which is the foundation[63] of art and science,"[64] since, when we lose one of our senses, we lose the knowledge of the things that are related to that sense.[65] Therefore, in the wayfaring state, knowledge with certitude comes from below, while knowledge in the eternal reasons comes from above. As long, then, as we are in the state of wayfarers, knowledge by the light of the eternal reasons is not appropriate for us.

10. Again, imaginative knowledge does not need a higher light; rather, the force of the imaginative power alone is sufficient for us to imagine something. If the intellect, therefore, is more powerful than imagination, it will be more fully self-sufficient for knowing something with certitude, apart from any higher light.

11. Again, the senses can enjoy certain knowledge without any certitude that comes from an eternal reason. If the intellect, therefore, is more powerful than sense, it will be even more fully able to know and understand with certitude, apart from any such light.

12. Again, nothing more is required for complete knowledge than the knower and the abstract object of knowledge, together with the turning of the former toward the latter. But all this can come about through the power of our intellect without the eternal reason; therefore, etc.

13. Again, no power needs external assistance for anything that it can do freely. Now "we understand when we wish"[66];

61 *De anima*, III, 5 (430ª10–15), paraphrased.
62 *Intellectus agens et intellectus possibilis.*
63 *Principium.*
64 Cf. Aristotle, *Anal. post.*, II, 19 (100ª4–9).
65 Cf. *ibid.*, I, 18 (81ª38–40).
66 Cf. Aristotle, *De anima*, II, 5 (417ᵇ24).

therefore, in order to know something with certitude, we do not need the light of the eternal reasons.

14. Again, the principles of being and of knowing are the same.[67] Thus, if the proper and intrinsic principles of being of creatures themselves are only created, whatever is known is known through created reasons—and not, therefore, through eternal reasons and lights.

15. Again, to each knowable object there corresponds its proper principle of knowledge, in order that it may be known with certitude. But those principles of knowledge are not distinctly perceived by any wayfarer's intellect; nothing, therefore, has to be known properly and separately in them.

16. Again, suppose that whatever is known with certitude is known in an eternal reason. Since "that by reason of which something is known is itself better known,"[68] it will follow that those eternal reasons are better known to us. But this is obviously false, since they are more fully concealed from us than anything else.

17. Again, it is impossible to see anything in a mirror, unless we see the mirror itself. Therefore, if everything that is known with certitude is seen in those eternal reasons, it is necessary that the first light and the eternal reasons should be seen. But this is false and absurd, and therefore the premise is also false and absurd.

18. Again, if everything that is known with certitude is known in those eternal reasons, while those reasons are equally certain with respect to contingent and to necessary things, as well as with respect to future and to present things, then we should have certain knowledge of contingents as well as of necessary things, and of future as well as of present things. But this is false, and consequently the premise is false also.

19. Again, suppose that we know in the eternal reasons. Now the eternal reasons are the highest causes, while wisdom is the knowledge of the highest causes;[69] therefore, everyone who knows something with certitude is wise. But this is false; therefore, etc.

20. Again, if heavenly knowledge[70] is knowledge through the eternal reasons, in which the blessed see whatever they see, then, if all certain knowledge came through those eternal

---

[67] Cf. Aristotle, *Metaph.*, i, 1 (993[b]30).
[68] Cf. Aristotle, *Anal. post.*, I, 2 (72[a]30–34).
[69] Cf. Aristotle, *Metaph.*, I, 1 (981[b]25–982[a]1).
[70] Knowledge pertaining to the *patria*, contrasted with the *status viae*.

reasons, all those who knew with certitude would be blessed, and only the blessed would know with certitude. But this is false.

21. Again, if everything that is known is seen in the eternal reasons, then, since the mirror of the eternal reasons is an expression of will,[71] and whatever is known in such a mirror is known by revelation, it follows that whatever is known in this way is known in a prophetic manner or by revelation.

22. Again, if everything that is known is known in the eternal reasons, it is known either through a veil or without a veil. If it is known through a veil, then nothing is clearly known; if it is known without a veil, then all see God and the eternal exemplar[72] without any obscurity.[73] But this is false, as far as the wayfaring state is concerned;[74] therefore, etc.

Again, these objections are brought against Augustine's reasoning.

23. If every immutable truth is above the soul, and is, therefore, eternal and God, then, since the truth of every demonstrative principle is immutable,[75] every such truth will be God. Nothing, therefore, would be known except God.

24. Again, suppose that every immutable truth is the truth of the eternal art, while the latter is one and one only. Then all immutable truth will be one and one only. Now it is possible to obtain some immutable truth about any being whatsoever—as is obvious, since this is an immutable truth: If Socrates is running, Socrates is moving. According to this, therefore, all beings will be one.

25. Again, if everything that is God is to be adored with divine worship,[76] and the truth of every immutable principle is God, then every such truth should be adored. Therefore, the truth of the proposition, two and three are five, is to be adored.

26. Again, if every immutable truth is God, then everyone who clearly sees some immutable truth clearly sees God. But the demons and the damned clearly see some immutable truths; therefore, they clearly see God. Since this is to be blessed,[77] the damned are blessed. But nothing could be more

---

[71] *Voluntarium*; the point has to do with divine freedom in creation.
[72] The Logos.
[73] *Aenigmate*.
[74] Cf. I Cor. 13:12.
[75] Cf. Aristotle, *Anal. post.*, I, 4 (73ª21–24).
[76] *Latria*, in contrast to *dulia*.
[77] Cf. Matt. 5:8.

absurd than this; therefore, it is most absurd to say that every-thing that is known, if it is known with certitude, is known in the eternal reasons.

II

Conclusion

I reply. In order to understand the foregoing, we must note that, when it is said that everything that is known with certitude is known in the light of the eternal reasons, this can be inter-preted in three ways.

(a) The first interpretation states that the evidence of the eternal light accompanies knowledge with certitude as the whole and sole principle of knowledge. This interpretation is inaccurate, inasmuch as it allows for no knowledge of things except in the Word. But in that case knowledge on earth would not differ from knowledge in heaven, or knowledge in the Word from knowledge in the proper genus, or scientific knowledge from sapiential knowledge,[78] or knowledge of nature from knowledge of grace, or knowledge by reason from knowledge by revelation. Now since all these things are false, this interpre-tation certainly must not be maintained. For this is the opinion put forward by some—such as those of the first Academy[79]—to the effect that nothing is known with certitude save in the archetypal and intelligible world. But it was from this opinion, as Augustine says in *Against the Academics*, Book II,[80] that the error of those of the new Academy was born, namely, that nothing whatever can really be known,[81] since the intelligible world is concealed from human minds. And therefore, wishing to hold the first opinion together with their own position, they fell into manifest error, since "a little error in the beginning is a great one in the end."[82]

(b) The second interpretation states that the influence of the eternal reason necessarily accompanies knowledge with certi-tude, so that, in knowing, the knower does not attain to the eternal reason itself, but only to its influence. But this manner of speaking is certainly inadequate, according to the words of

---

[78] In the sense of the common medieval (and Aristotelian) distinction between "science" and "wisdom."
[79] I.e., the original Platonic doctrine.
[80] Cf. Augustine, *C. Acad.*, II, 5 ff.; 11 ff. (*PL*, 32, 924 ff.).
[81] This skepticism was grounded in the Platonic critique of sense-knowledge.
[82] Cf. Plato, *Cratylus*, 436D; Aristotle, *De caelo*, I, 5 (271^{b}9–10); Averroes, *ad loc.* (Venice ed., 1574, V, fol. 23 recto), a passage often quoted by Scholastics.

blessed Augustine, who showed by express statements and reasoning that in knowledge with certitude the mind has to be directed by immutable and eternal reasons—not as by a habit of its own mind,[83] but as by those things which are above it in the eternal truth. And, therefore, to say that our mind, in knowing, does not reach beyond the influence of uncreated light is to say that Augustine was deceived, since it is not easy in expounding him to make the "authorities" taken from him say this. But this is a highly absurd statement to make about such a great father and a most authoritative[84] doctor among all the expositors of Holy Scripture.

Moreover, that influence of light is either God's general influence upon all creatures or God's special influence by grace. But if it is his general influence, then we should no more call God the giver of wisdom than the giver of fertility to the earth, and it means no more to say that knowledge comes from him than that wealth does. On the other hand, if it is his special influence (of the same sort as grace), then on this assumption all knowledge is infused, and none is acquired or innate. But all these notions are absurd.

(c) This leaves us with the third interpretation, as a kind of mean between two extremes. Thus we shall say that, for knowledge with certitude, an eternal reason is necessarily required as regulative and motive principle—not, indeed, as the sole principle, or in its own complete clarity, but acting with the created reason, and seen by us "in part,"[85] in accordance with our wayfaring condition.

And this is what Augustine suggests in *On the Trinity*, XIV, chapter 15[86]: "Even the ungodly think of eternity, and rightly blame and rightly praise many things in the conduct of men." He says in addition that they do this by rules which are written "in the book of that light which is called truth." Moreover, the nobility of knowledge and the dignity of the knower necessarily require that our mind, when it knows with certitude, should in some way attain to those rules and immutable reasons.[87]

I say that the nobility of knowledge requires this, because certain knowledge cannot exist unless there is immutability on the part of the object of knowledge, and infallibility on the

---

[83] E.g., not by its own "scientific" knowledge alone.
[84] *Authenticus.*   [85] I Cor. 13:12.
[86] *De trin.*, XIV, 15:21 (*PL*, 42, 1052).
[87] Cf. Bonaventure, *Sermo* 1 for 22d Sunday after Pentecost (*Opera omnia*, IX, 441–444).

part of the knower. Now created truth is not immutable absolutely, but from its relation to what is above it; similarly, the light of the creature is not altogether infallible by its own power—since each was created and passed from nonbeing into being. If then, for full knowledge recourse is had to a wholly immutable and stable truth and to a wholly infallible light, in knowledge of this kind it is necessary to have recourse to the heavenly art, as to light and truth—light, I say, giving infallibility to the knower, and truth giving immutability to the object of knowledge. Therefore, since things have being in the mind, and in their proper genus, and in the eternal art, the truth of things is not sufficient for the soul itself to have certain knowledge—in so far as they have being in it or in their proper genus—because there is mutability on both sides. For certain knowledge, the soul must in some way attain to them as they are in the eternal art.

The same requirement is imposed by the dignity of the knower. The rational spirit has a reason divided into higher and lower; therefore, just as the lower part without the higher is not sufficient for the full deliberative judgment of reason in matters of action, so it is inadequate for the full judgment of reason in speculative matters.[88] But this higher part is that in which the image of God is to be found; it both cleaves to the eternal reasons and, by them, judges and defines with certitude whatever it defines—in both cases, because it is the image of God.

For the creature is related to God under the aspects of a vestige, an image, and a likeness.[89] In so far as it is a vestige, it is related to God as its principle; in so far as it is an image, it is related to God as its object; but in so far as it is a likeness, it is related to God as to a gift infused into it. And, therefore, every creature which proceeds from God is a vestige; every creature which knows God is an image; every creature (and that alone) in which God dwells is a likeness.[90] And according to these three degrees of relationship there are three degrees of the divine co-operation.

In the activity which proceeds from the creature in so far as it is a vestige, God co-operates as the creative principle. In the activity which proceeds from the creature in so far as it is a likeness—such as a meritorious work, pleasing to God—God

---

88 *Speculatio* means contemplation rather than conjecture in this context.
89 Cf. Bonaventure, *Breviloq.*, II, 12 (*Opera omnia*, V, 230).
90 Cf. Bonaventure, *I Sent.*, d. 3, p. 1, q. 2; *II Sent.*, d. 16, a. 2, q. 3 (*Opera omnia*, I, 73; II, 404–406).

co-operates in the manner of an infused gift. But in the activity which proceeds from the creature in so far as it is an image, God co-operates as a moving principle, and certain knowledge, which does not come from the lower reason apart from the higher, is an example of this kind of activity.

Since, then, certain knowledge belongs to the rational spirit, in so far as it is the image of God, it follows that in this knowledge the spirit attains to the eternal reasons. But since, as long as it is in the wayfaring state, it is not fully deiform, it does not attain to them clearly and fully and distinctly. Still, in so far as it approximates more or less closely to deiformity, it attains to them more or less closely, but it always does attain to them in some way, since the nature of the image can never be detached from the rational spirit.[91] Therefore, in the state of innocence, because it was the image unmarred by sin, even if it did not possess the full deiformity of glory, it attained to them "in part," but not "in a dark manner."[92] But in the state of fallen nature it lacks deiformity and suffers from deformity, and thus it attains to the eternal reasons both "in part" and "in a dark manner." But in the state of glory it lacks all deformity and possesses full deiformity, and thus it attains to them fully and clearly.

Again, since the soul is not an image with respect to its whole self, it attains the likeness of things, abstracted from a phantasm, as proper and distinct principles of knowledge, apart from which it is insufficient in itself to know the light of eternal reason, as long as it is in the wayfaring state—unless perhaps it may transcend this state in some special way, as is the case with those who are enraptured, and with the revelations of certain prophets.

It is to be granted, then, as reasoning shows and as the authoritative statements of Augustine expressly assert, that in all certain knowledge those principles of knowledge are attained by the knower. They are reached in one way, however, by the wayfarer, and in another by him who enjoys the vision of God;[93] in one way when we possess science, and in another when we possess wisdom; in one way by the prophet, and in another by the man who understands in the ordinary way. All this has already been made plain, and will be evident in the solutions offered for the objections.

[91] Bonaventure differs here from some later disciples of Augustine.
[92] I Cor. 13:12.
[93] *Comprehensor* (contrasted with *viator*).

III

Answers to the Objections

1. To the first objection, then, that God dwells in light inaccessible, we should reply that the text refers to access to that light in the fullness and splendor of its brightness. In this sense it is not approached by the creature's power, but only through the deiformity of glory.

2. To the objection that "the sight of the human mind is too weak to be focused on so excellent a light, etc.," we should reply that in order to know through the eternal reasons the mind does not need to be focused on them, except in so far as it may know in a sapiential way. For the man of wisdom attains to those reasons in one way, and the man of science in another; the man of science attains to them as things that move him, while the man of wisdom finds rest in them—and to this wisdom no one comes unless he first is "cleansed by the righteousness of faith."

3. In answer to the objection that the mind has knowledge by itself of incorporeal things, it should be said that, just as in the creature's works the Creator's co-operation must not be overlooked, so an uncreated principle of knowledge is not excluded from a created principle of knowledge, but on the contrary is included in the latter.

4. To the objection that the mind sees in a light of its own genus, it can be answered that, in a broad sense, every incorporeal light (created or uncreated) is called a light of its own genus. But even if we interpret this as a reference to a created light, this does not exclude the uncreated light, nor does it follow that we do not know in the eternal truth, but simply that we know in the light of created truth as well as in the eternal truth. Now this is indeed true, yet it does not contradict my opinion as stated.

5, 6. To the objections drawn from Gregory and Dionysius, we should reply that neither of them denies that "the true light, which enlighteneth every man that cometh into this world,"[94] is reached by our minds. They merely assert that in this life it is not yet fully seen.

7–9. In reply to the objections drawn from the philosopher, to the effect that we understand in relation to the continuous

[94] John 1:9.

and to time, and that we have a potential and an active intellect, as well as the objection which has to do with the experience of human knowledge, it is to be said that all this presupposes that the light and reason of created truth concurs with our intelligence. Nevertheless, as was said above, the light and reason of created truth are not excluded, because it is possible for the soul, in its lower part, to attain to the things that are below, while nevertheless the higher part attains to the things that are above.

10. To the objection concerning imaginative cognition, it is to be replied that the cases are not similar, because this cognition does not possess certitude, and therefore does not have recourse to the immutable.

11. In answer to the objection drawn from sense-perception, it should be said that the certitude of sense is not the same as that of understanding. For the certitude of sense stems from the binding of a power which functions by way of nature and has to do with a determinate object. Since, however, the intellect is a power that is free to understand all things, its certitude cannot come from such a source, and thus it is necessary for it to come from something that is not bound, but is free, without any possible defect of mutability or fallibility. Now the light and reason of eternal truth is like this; the intellect, therefore, has recourse to the latter as the fount of all certitude.

12. To the objection that nothing more is required for knowledge than the knower and the knowable, together with the turning of the former toward the latter, it is to be answered that this turning includes a judgment. Certain judgment, however, is realized only through a law that is itself certain and above judgment—according to Augustine's statement, in the book *On the True Religion*[95] and the book *On Free Will*,[96] to the effect that "no one judges of the truth, and without the truth no one judges rightly." Thus the eternal reason and truth is included in these conditions of knowledge.

13. In reply to the objection that we understand when we will, and in consequence need no external assistance, it is to be said that there are two kinds of external assistance: one which is always present, and another which is absent and distant. It is evident that this objection is conclusive with respect to the second kind of assistance, but not to the first, since, if corporeal light were always present in the eye, as spiritual light is always

[95] Cf. *De vera rel.*, 30 f.:56 f. (*PL*, 34, 146–148).
[96] Cf. *De lib. arb.*, II, 14 (*PL*, 32, 1261 f.).

present in the mind, we should see when we will, just as we understand when we will.

14. To the objection that the principles of being and of knowing are the same, we should reply that the intrinsic principles of being are not sufficient for full knowledge any more than they are for being, apart from that first extrinsic principle, which is God. Therefore, although those principles are in some way a principle of knowledge, they do not on that account exclude the primary ground of knowing from our knowledge, any more than they exclude creation in the case of the act of being.

15. To the objection that to each and every knowable object there corresponds its proper principle of knowledge, it is to be replied, that those reasons are not the whole ground of our knowing, because we do not see them with full distinctness in themselves, but along with them we require a created light of principles, and likenesses of known objects, from which, with respect to each and every thing that is known, we derive the proper principle of our knowledge of it.

16. In reply to the objection that "that by reason of which something is known is itself better known," it is to be said that, as is already evident, it is in conjunction with the truth of principles, and not by itself alone, that the eternal reason moves us to knowledge. (While this condition does not hold for the eternal reason specifically in itself, it applies generally in the wayfaring state.) Thus it does not follow that it is known to us in itself; rather, it is known to us as it shines forth in its principles and in its generality, and so, in a particular way, it is most certain to us, because our intellect simply cannot think that it does not exist, and this assuredly cannot be said of any created truth.

17. As far as the objection drawn from a mirror is concerned, this applies to the mirror whose nature it is to represent something properly and distinctly and, in addition to this, to constitute the term of our vision. This is evident in a material mirror, which represents a visible species distinctly and properly, and is the term of our vision. Now these conditions do apply to the eternal mirror as far as those who have the vision of God are concerned—as is evident from what was said before.[97]

18. In reply to the objection that these reasons are equally certain with respect to contingent and to necessary things, it is

---

[97] Cf. Aquinas, *Sum. theol.*, Ia, 84, 5.

to be said that this reasoning would be quite conclusive if these reasons were the total ground of our knowledge, and if an object were seen entirely in them. This is not the case, however, in the circumstances of our present condition, because along with the eternal reasons we need proper likenesses and principles of things, separately received, and we do not come across these in contingent things, but only in necessary things.[98]

19. To the objection that, if we have knowledge in these reasons, everyone who knows anything is wise, we should reply that this does not follow, because attaining to these reasons does not make anyone wise, unless he reposes in them and knows that he attains to them. (The latter, indeed, is characteristic of the wise man.) For the intellects of those who simply know attain to reasons of this sort as motive principles, while the intellects of the wise attain to them as principles which lead them to their repose.[99] And since there are few who attain to them in this way, there are few wise men, even though there are many who have knowledge; indeed, there are few who know that they attain to these reasons. What is more, there are few who want to believe this, because an intellect not yet raised to the contemplation of eternal things finds it difficult to grasp the truth that God is thus present and near to it, despite what Paul says in Acts, ch. 17, that he is "not far from every one of us."[1]

20. The reply to the objection drawn from heavenly knowledge is already obvious—namely, that there is a great difference between knowledge "in part" and "in a dark manner,"[2] on the one hand, and perfect and distinct knowledge, on the other. This point was touched on above.

21. To the objection that the mirror of the eternal reasons is an expression of will, etc., we should reply that, as the apostle says in Rom., ch. 1, "That which is known of God is manifest in them."[3] Although God is simple and one in form, nevertheless that eternal light and that exemplar represent certain things as it were outwardly and openly, and other things more deeply and hiddenly. The former are those things that are done according to the necessary rule of the divine art, while the latter are the things that are done according to the disposition of God's hidden will. Now what is called a "voluntary" mirror is so-called with respect to things that have their exemplar

[98] Cf. Aristotle, *Anal. post.*, I, 6 ($74^{b}5$-$75^{a}37$).
[99] *Reductivae et quietativae.*   [1] Acts 17:27
[2] I Cor. 13:12.   [3] Rom. 1:19.

in God in the second way, rather than in the first. In the eternal reasons, therefore, natural things are known by reason's natural power of judgment,[4] but supernatural and future things are known only by the gift of revelation from on high; thus this argument does not really affect the position previously stated.

22. To the objection drawn from the fact that whatever we know in them is known either through a veil or without a veil, it should be answered that the reason for our inability in the wayfaring state to know anything in the eternal reasons without a veil and without obscurity lies in the obscuring of the divine image.[5] It does not follow, however, that nothing is known with certitude or clarity, since the created principles, which in some sense are media of knowledge (though not apart from those reasons), can be seen by our mind clearly and without a veil. (Nevertheless, if it were said that nothing is fully known in this life, this would involve no great incongruity.)

23–26. To the objections against Augustine's reasoning, to the effect that, if the immutable truth is God, then the truth of a demonstrative principle would be God, and that all truths would be one, and that they would be objects of worship, and that the demons would see God—to all these we should reply that the immutable truth is spoken of in two ways: absolutely, and in relation to something higher. Now when it is said that immutable truth is above the mind, and is God, this refers to the absolutely changeless truth. But when it is said that the truth of a demonstrative principle, which refers to something created, is immutable, it is evident that it is immutable, not absolutely, but in relation to something above it, since every creature comes from nonbeing and can return to nonbeing. And if it is objected that this truth is absolutely certain to the soul itself by itself, it must be said that, although a demonstrative principle, in so far as it expresses something complex,[6] is created, nevertheless the truth signified by it can be signified in one of three ways: with respect to what it is in matter, or what it is in the soul, or what it is in the divine art—or, for that matter, in all these ways together. For truth in the external sign is the sign of truth in the soul, because "spoken words are

---

[4] On the *naturale iudicatorium* of reason, cf. Augustine, *De lib. arb.*, III, 20:56 (*PL*, 32, 1298), as quoted by Bonaventure, *II Sent.*, d. 39, a. 1, q. 2 (*Opera omnia*, II, 901 and n. 2).

[5] Cf. Bonaventure, *II Sent.*, d. 23, a. 2, q. 3 (II, 542–547).

[6] I.e., a judgment linking two terms; cf. Deferrari, *op. cit.*, 187.

symbols of experiences which are in the soul"[7]; but the soul in its own highest aspect is concerned with higher things, just as in its lower aspect it is concerned with these lower things, since it is a mean between created things and God, and thus truth in the soul is related to that twofold truth, as a mean to two extremes, so that from the lower it receives relative certitude,[8] while it receives absolute certitude from the higher. And thus, as Augustine's reasoning shows, if truth of this kind is absolutely immutable, it is above the soul. But the contrary reasoning is related to the truth—with which demonstration is properly concerned—which is immutable in relation to something above it. Now this truth is multiplied in diverse things; it is not adorable; it is perceptible by the demons and the damned. But the truth which is absolutely immutable can be clearly seen by those alone who can enter into the innermost silence of the mind, and to this no sinner attains, but he who is a supreme lover of eternity, and he alone.

[7] Aristotle, *De interpret.*, 1 (16a3).
[8] *Secundum quid*, contrasted with *simpliciter*.

Matthew of Aquasparta: Disputed Questions on Faith

THE TEXT

Question Five

IN THE FIFTH PLACE, IT IS ASKED WHETHER THOSE THINGS WHICH ARE OBJECTS OF FAITH CAN BE PROVED BY REASON

I

Arguments Against the Thesis

TO THIS QUESTION, IT IS FIRST ARGUED THAT those things which are objects of faith cannot be proved by reason.

1. The apostle[1] says: "Faith is the substance of things to be hoped for, the evidence of things that appear not." Gregory,[2] discussing this text, says: "Surely it is clear that faith is the evidence of things which cannot be apparent. When things are apparent, they are not objects of faith, but of perception." But the things proved by reason are apparent. Therefore, those things which are objects of faith cannot be proved by reason.

2. Again, Hugh, in Book I, *On the Sacraments*,[3] distinguishing the various degrees of knowledge or cognition, says that "some men are deniers, some are doubters, some are conjecturers, some are believers, and some are knowers." From this it is argued as follows: No two of the earlier members of this series can coincide, and therefore the final two cannot reasonably be considered equivalent. For instance, deniers and doubters, doubters and conjecturers, conjecturers (those holding opinions) and believers, cannot be in accord; therefore neither can believers and those who know by reason.

3. Again, Augustine, in his *Epistle to Paulina on the Vision of God (Epistle* 112),[4] says: "It is one thing to know something by way of the body, like the sun in the sky, or a mountain, or a tree, or a physical object on the earth, as you will; and another

---

[1] Heb. 11:1.
[2] Gregory the Great, *In evang.*, II, 26:8 (*PL*, 76, 1202A).
[3] Hugh of St. Victor, *De sacram.*, I, 10:2 (*PL*, 176, 303D).
[4] *Epist. ad Paul. de vis. dei (Epist.* 147) 1:6 (*CSEL*, 44, 280).

thing to see by an intuition of the mind something no less evident, like our will which we see within ourselves when we are willing, or our memory when we are remembering, or our intellect when we are thinking, or anything like these in the soul without the body. It is yet another thing, however, to believe what we see neither in the body nor in the mind, which is neither present nor recalled as having been present, as that Adam was created without parents, that Christ was born of the Virgin, suffered and rose from the dead," and things of this kind. And later[5] he says: "There is this distinction between seeing and believing: present things are seen, absent things are believed. Those things which are not before us are believed, things which are before us are seen." But things proved by reason and clearly discerned are present and before us, or else present to the view of the mind. Therefore, those things which are objects of faith cannot be proved by reason.

4. Again, Hugh, in Book I, *On the Sacraments*,[6] says: "Some things are from reason, some are according to reason, some are above reason, and some are contrary to reason. Things from reason are necessary, those according to reason are probable, those above reason are marvelous, and those contrary to reason are incredible. Certainly the two extremes are absolutely not receptive of faith. Things from reason are thoroughly known, and since they are known they cannot be believed. Likewise, things which are really contrary to reason cannot be believed with reason, since they are not susceptible to any reason, and reason will never assent to them. Therefore, only things according to reason and those above reason can receive faith. In the case of the former, faith is aided by reason, and reason is perfected by faith, because the things believed are according to reason. And if reason does not understand the truth of these things, still it does not contradict faith in them. On the other hand, in the case of things which are above reason, faith is not aided by any reason, because reason does not attain to the things which faith believes." From the first[7] we see that there cannot be faith in regard to objects of knowledge; from the third,[8] that there cannot be any reason in regard to objects of faith. Therefore, etc.

---

[5] Cf. *ibid.*, 2:7 (*CSEL*, 44, 280–281).
[6] *De sacram.*, I, 3:30 (*PL*, 176, 231D–232A).
[7] I.e., things from reason.
[8] I.e., things above reason.

5. Again, according to the philosopher,[9] "singulars cannot be demonstrated." Augustine agrees with this, when he says, in the *Book of 83 Questions*,[10] that "there are some things which are always believed and never known, like all the passing particulars of history." But faith is almost entirely concerned with singulars. Therefore, those things which are objects of faith cannot be proved by reason.

6. Again, the things in which we have faith are mainly contingent, like the creation of the world before it was created, the incarnation of Christ before it took place, and the future resurrection. But according to the philosopher,[11] "there is demonstrative knowledge only of things which are not capable of being otherwise than they are."

7. Again, "no science proves its proper principles, but they are postulated as self-evident."[12] To do otherwise would be to go on *in infinitum*, as is clear from this principle: "The whole is always greater than its part."[13] But articles of faith are, above all, principles of the highest science; therefore, in no way can they be proved by reason.

8. Again, all our reasoning is taken from sensible things,[14] or at least from created things. But according to Augustine, in Book XV, *On the Trinity*,[15] "every creature has fallen away from the divine, and no likeness is found which is not to a greater extent unlikeness."

9 Cf. Aristotle, *Anal. post.*, I, 18 (81b7–9); *De anima*, II, 5 (417b22); Bonaventure, *Collat. in Hexaem.*, 10 (*Opera omnia*, V, 277–288); *Brevil.*, Prolog., 5 (*Opera omnia*, V, 207).

10 *De div. quaest. lxxxiii*, q. 48 (*PL*, 40, 31).

11 Cf. *Ethica Nicom.*, VI, 3 (1139b19–23); *Anal. post.*, I, 4 (73a21–24).

12 Cf. Aristotle, *Anal. post.*, I, 9 (76a16–18); I, 3 (72b19). Proper principles (*propria principia*) are the basic truths or axioms of any science. They are not proved by reference to some prior principle, but are known through themselves (*per se nota*); the mind assents to them from an understanding of the terms alone.

13 Cf. Aristotle, *Problem.*, XVI, 7 (914b1–8).

14 Cf. Aristotle, *De anima*, III, 8 (432a3–8). Matthew does not discuss this proposition in his rebuttal to this argument. His views on the subject are well summarized in the following remarks of M. de Wulf (*History of Medieval Philosophy*, 3d Eng. ed., Longmans, London, 1938, Vol. II, p. 195): "Every idea of the corporeal comes from without through the channel of sense. Nevertheless, the sensible object does not act upon the soul. Rather, on the contrary, the soul forms, on the occasion of the organic impression, a corresponding sensation." This is not a theory of occasionalism; the form of the object perceived is the necessary *partial* cause of the knowledge of any sensible thing; cf. *infra*, note 65.

15 *De trin.*, XV, 20:39 (*PL*, 42, 1088); cf. Bonaventure, I *Sent.*, d. 13, dub. 8 (*Opera omnia*, I, 241).

Again, miracles, which are objects of faith, have neither a reason nor an example in nature; otherwise they would not be marvelous, as Augustine points out in his *Epistle to Volusianus*[16]: "If an example of this is required, it will not be surprising (he is speaking of the incarnation); if a reason is sought, it will not be remarkable. But in marvelous things, the entire explanation of the deed is the power of the doer." Therefore, etc.

9. Again, according to the philosopher, in Book II of the *Ethics*,[17] "virtue is concerned with difficulty," and the greater the difficulty, the greater the virtue. But faith is a virtue, and among the virtues it is of more virtue than reason. But things which have reason present no difficulty. Therefore, those things which are matters of faith cannot have reason.

10. Again, whatever can be proved by reason lies under the judgment of reason; for according to Augustine,[18] judgment is only of inferior things. But those things which are objects of faith are above reason, and above the judgment of reason. Therefore they cannot be proved by reason.

11. Again, the Damascene[19] says: "We receive, reverence, and learn everything which has been handed down to us, by the Law and the Prophets as well as by the apostles and evangelists, and require nothing beyond this." Therefore, in matters of faith, reason ought not to be required; but if it could be had, it ought to be required. Therefore, etc.

12. Again, the apostle[20] says: "Bringing into captivity every understanding unto the obedience of Christ." From this it is gathered that the things of faith transcend our intellect. Thence it is argued as follows: "No accident transcends or goes beyond its subject" (as Augustine says in Book IX, *On the Trinity*[21]). But reason is an accident of the intellect, and hence does not

---

[16] *Epist. ad Volus.* (*Epist.* 137), 2:8 (*CSEL*, 44, 107).

[17] *Ethica Nicom.*, II, 3 (1105ᵃ9).

[18] Cf. *De lib. arb.*, II, 14:38 (*PL*, 32, 1261–1262); *De vera relig.*, 31:58 (*PL*, 34, 147–148); Bonaventure, I *Sent.*, d. 3, q. 1, ad 4 (*Opera omnia*, I, 69); *Itin. mentis in deum*, II (*Opera omnia*, V, 302); *De scient. Christi*, q. 4 (*Opera omnia*, V, 17), and translation above.

[19] John of Damascus, *Expositio fidei orthodoxae* (cited by medieval authors as *De fide orthodoxa*) I (*PG*, 94, 791A). The *Exact Exposition of the Orthodox Faith*, the third part of John Damascene's major work, *The Source of Knowledge*, first appeared in Latin in the twelfth century, in two translations (one partial); cf. Gilson, *History*, p. 600.

[20] II Cor. 10:5.

[21] *De trin.*, IX, 4:5 (*PL*, 42, 963); cf Bonaventure, I *Sent.*, d. 3, pt. 2, a. 2, ad 4 (*Opera omnia*, I, 91).

transcend the intellect. Therefore, as the intellect cannot attain to the things of faith, neither can reason. Therefore, etc.

13. Again, things which are contrary to reason cannot be proved by reason. But many objects of faith are contrary to reason. Therefore, those things at least cannot be proved by reason. The proof of the minor premise appears in the sacrament of the altar, wherein the accidents remain without the subject. This is altogether contrary to reason, for it implies a contradiction. "The being of an accident is to inhere."[22] Therefore, if it does not inhere, it does not exist. Therefore, at once it is and is not. Therefore, etc.

14. Again, in things which are related as higher and lower, that which is proper to the higher according to its kind is not proper to the lower according to its kind. But faith and knowledge are related as higher and lower; for as Hugh says, in Book I, *On the Sacraments*,[23] "faith is a kind of certitude of mind above opinion and below knowledge." But, according to Augustine,[24] "it is proper to knowledge, in the nature of knowledge, to be recommended by reason." Hence, this is not proper to faith, in the nature of faith. Therefore, those things which are objects of faith cannot be recommended by reason.

15. Again, as hope is related to the obtaining of what is hoped for, so faith is related to the knowledge of what is believed. But nothing which is hoped for is already obtained. Therefore, nothing which is believed, while it is believed, is known or understood. Therefore, nothing which is believed can be proved by reason.

16. Again, faith has two aspects: certitude and obscurity. Hence it can be described as a kind of certitude in matters of divinity, with an enigma; so that by its certitude it accords with knowledge, and by its obscurity it accords with ignorance. But from that aspect which it has in common with knowledge, on account of the certitude, nothing believed is unknown; hence, from that aspect in which it accords with ignorance, nothing believed is known. Therefore, etc.

---

[22] Cf. Bede the Venerable, *Sententiae*, I, A (*PL*, 90, 968D) (not authentic, author unknown; cf. P. Glorieux, *Pour revaloriser Migne, Mélanges de science religieuse*, cahier supplémentaire, 1952, p. 51); Aristotle, *Metaph.* VII, 1 (1028ª18–25); *Topica*, I, 5 (102ᵇ4–14).

[23] *De sacram.*, I, 10:2 (*PL*, 176 330C); cf. Bonaventure, III *Sent.*, d. 23, a. 1, q. 1 (*Opera omnia*, III, 471).

[24] Cf. *Retract.*, I, 13:5 (*CSEL*, 36, 68).

II

On the Contrary

1. Augustine says, in Book XIV, *On the Trinity*[25]: "I do not attribute to this knowledge[26] everything that man can know in matters human, in which there is much useless vanity and harmful inquisitiveness; but only that which begets, nourishes, defends, and strengthens most wholesome faith which leads to true blessedness." But the nourishing and strengthening of faith is by reasons. Therefore, etc.

2. Again, Hugh, in Book I, *On the Sacraments*,[27] distinguishing three kinds of believers, says: "There are some men of faith who choose to believe by piety alone that which (whether it must be believed or not) they do not comprehend by reason. Others approve by reason what they believe by faith. Still others, by pure heart and clear conscience within, already begin to taste what they believe by faith. In the first case, piety alone makes the choice; in the second, reason joins its approval; in the third, purity of intelligence gains certitude."

3. Again, Augustine, *On the Usefulness of Believing*,[28] says: "What we believe we owe to authority; what we understand, to reason." But all objects of belief are objects of understanding, since the gift of understanding[29] is ordained to that end. Therefore all objects of belief can be proved by reason.

---

[25] *De trin.*, XIV, 1:3 (*PL*, 42, 1037).

[26] I.e., the knowledge called *scientia*. Earlier in the passage, Augustine distinguishes the knowledge of things human, which he calls "*scientia*," from the knowledge of things divine, which he calls "*sapientia*." Matthew states (*Q*. 2 *de cog.*, *resp.*; *Quaest. disp.*, I, 250 ff.) that whereas Plato and his followers provided only for *sapientia*, and Aristotle and his followers provided only for *scientia*, he prefers, like Augustine, to follow a middle way, making provision for both. Cf. *infra*, note 65.

[27] *De sacram.*, I, 10:4 (*PL*, 176, 332D).

[28] *De util. cred.*, 11:25 (*CSEL*, 25, 32).

[29] *Donum intellectus*, a term which Matthew uses very frequently in this Question, refers to the gift of understanding or insight, one of the seven-fold gifts of the Holy Spirit (cf. Isa. 11:2, 3), a habit (more or less permanent quality) of the intellect of the believer (cf. *infra*, ad 12), making possible the knowledge of supernatural truth. (Cf. Augustine, *Serm.* 347, *PL*, 39, 1524–1525; Gregory the Great, *Moral.*, II, 49:77, *PL*, 75, 592 f.; Aquinas, *Sum. theol.*, Ia–IIae, q. 68; Bonaventure, *Collat. de sept. donis spirit. sanct.*, 8, *Opera omnia*, V, 493–498). A discussion of "Dons du Saint-Esprit," with ample Scriptural, patristic and medieval references, by A. Gardeil, may be found in *DTC*, IV, 1728–1781.

4. Again, among all the things in which we have faith, the greatest, most excellent, and most difficult is the mystery of the Trinity. But the philosophers attained to this by reasons, when they were not illuminated by the ray of faith. Therefore, much more can all other objects of faith be proved by reason. The proof of the minor premise appears in Book X of Augustine's *City of God*,[30] where he says that "Porphyry the Platonist spoke of the Father, and the intellect of the Father, and a certain intermediary, meaning the Holy Spirit."

5. Again, the same author, in Book VII of the *Confessions*,[31] recounts that he found the Gospel of John in certain books of the Platonists; if not in the same words, at least with the same meaning: "That *in the beginning was the Word, and that the Word was with God, and that the Word was God; and that all things were made by him,* . . . that *was made*[32]; *in him was life, and the life was the light of men,* and that *the light shone in darkness,* as far as: *There was a man sent from God.*" But here the mystery of the Trinity is disclosed. Therefore, etc.

6. Again, no faculty is justly blamed for not reaching or tending toward its object if it lacks the means of doing so. Sight, for example. But the means in knowledge with intellectual certitude is either overwhelming demonstration, or else the clearness of the matter. But the intellect is blamed for failing to attain to knowledge of divinity; and therefore it does not lack the means of attaining to such knowledge. But it is agreed that this is not a case of the clearness of the matter. Therefore there can be necessary demonstration of these things.

7. Again, the philosopher, in the *Posterior Analytics*,[33] distinguishes demonstration *propter quid*, which is by the cause, and demonstration *quia*, which is by the effect. "A proper effect leads, moreover, to knowledge of the cause."[34] But the demons

---

30 *De civ. dei*, X, 23 (*CSEL*, 40, 1, 484). Augustine's statement is: "[Porphyry] speaks of God the Father, and of God the Son, whom he calls (in Greek) the intellect or mind of the Father. In regard to the Holy Spirit, however, he says nothing or nothing clearly, for I do not understand what other he speaks of as medium between these two."

31 *Confess.*, VII, 9:13 (*CSEL*, 33, 154). Augustine quotes Jn. 1:1–5.

32 In the text of Matthew, the words "*without him was nothing made,*" preceding "*that was made,*" are missing.

33 Cf. *Anal. post.*, I, 13 (78a21 ff.); II, 1 (89b21); Bonaventure, III *Sent.*, d. 24, a. 2, q. 3, n. 8 (*Opera omnia*, III, 521).

34 Cf. Aristotle, *Anal. post.*, II, 12 (95a24 ff.); Bonaventure, I *Sent.*, d. 3, pt. 1, q. 2, contra 2 (*Opera omnia*, I, 71–72). A proper effect (*effectus proprius*), as distinguished from *effectus alienus* or *extraneus*, is one that is proper or peculiar to its cause.

know that men are damned for the sin of unbelief; therefore they must know what should be believed. Unless they know and understand the things which should be believed by faith, they cannot know that these men are unbelievers. Therefore, etc.

8. Again, Augustine, in Book I, *On the Trinity*,[35] says: "In no other matter does one err more dangerously, nor more laboriously nor more fruitfully discover something, than when one inquires into the unity of the Trinity, the Father, Son, and Holy Spirit." Therefore, knowledge of the Trinity is necessary to salvation. But, according to the philosopher,[36] a lower nature is not lacking in necessary things: much less, therefore, a higher nature. Therefore, the human intellect can come to knowledge of the Trinity, of itself, without the habit of faith; and this can only be by natural reasons.

9. Again, "he who is capable in the greater matter is capable in the lesser."[37] But it is greater to love God for himself and above all things than it is to know that God is three and one, which is believable by faith. But it can be proved by reason that God is to be loved for himself and above all things; therefore it can also be proved by reason that God is three and one.

10. Again, what is not believed cannot be known: therefore what is believed must necessarily be known. But according to Augustine,[38] "knowledge is only by reason." Therefore, etc.

III

Conclusion

I answer. In regard to this question opinions differ. Some say that objects of faith can in no way be proved by reason so that one and the same person could at once believe something by faith and prove it by reason. Their argument is that what is believed is not seen (whence it is believed): what is known by reason, however, by the very fact that it is known, is seen. Therefore, as the same thing cannot be both seen and not seen by one and the same person, neither can it be believed by faith and known by reason.

[35] *De trin.*, I, 3:5 (*PL*, 42, 822).
[36] Cf. *De anima*, III, 9 (432^{b}21–24).
[37] Cf. *ibid.*, III, 4 (429^{b}3).
[38] Cf. *Retract.*, I, 13:5 (*CSEL*, 36, 68).

Without prejudice, this position does not seem to me probable, although it has been held by great men.[39] First, because if one and the same person cannot both believe and know one and the same truth, if he believed it first and later proved it by reason, reason would have destroyed faith, which is false. For when all the articles of faith were objects of understanding, by a gift of understanding or by reason (as Augustine[40] says), he could advance so far in this life that faith would be completely destroyed, which is altogether false. We see to the contrary, that however much anyone advances in understanding, so much the more he advances in faith.

Secondly, while it is certain that the philosophers have proved demonstratively that God is one (as is clear from Book VIII of the *Physics*[41]) and similarly that he is the Creator, it is also evident that the authority of Scripture revealed by God says this in Deuteronomy[42]: "The Lord thy God is one Lord"; and in the beginning of Genesis[43]: "In the beginning God created heaven and earth." I ask whether the understanding of a believer adheres to this truth more on account of reason or on account of authority. On account of authority, certainly, for on that account he would risk his life. Therefore, what he believes by faith and what he understands by reason remain together, and one does not exclude the other. Further, supposing that reason destroys faith, I propose that the person who first believed and afterward understood by reason forgets the reasons, which is possible. He will then be left without any knowledge, or else it must be that faith is bestowed upon him a second time, which does not seem likely. Otherwise, it must be that faith and reason remain together.

Thirdly, the claim that faith and understanding are totally incompatible (since, as Augustine says, *On the Usefulness of Believing*[44]: "What we believe we owe to authority, what we understand to reason") is altogether false. To the contrary, there is never understanding without faith, according to

---

[39] For instance, by Aquinas; cf. *Sum. theol.*, IIa–IIae, q. 1, a. 5: ". . . it is impossible that one and the same thing should be believed and seen by one and the same person. Hence it is equally impossible for one and the same thing to be an object of science and belief for the same person"; cf. Bonaventure, III *Sent.*, d. 24, a. 2, q. 3 (*Opera omnia*, III, 521 ff.).

[40] Cf. *De vera relig.*, 7:13 (*PL*, 34, 128–129); Bonaventure, III *Sent.*, d. 24, a. 3, q. 1 seq. (*Opera omnia*, III, 525 ff.).

[41] Cf. *Phys.*, VIII, 6 (259a–260a).

[42] Deut. 6:4.   [43] Gen. 1:1.

[44] *De util. cred.*, 11:25 (*CSEL*, 25, 32).

Isaiah, ch. 7[45]: "Unless you believe, you will not understand."

To the question raised, therefore, we must answer without prejudice that we can speak of objects of belief in two ways: either *with respect to the objects of belief themselves* or *with respect to our intellects*. If we speak *with respect to objects of belief themselves*, I say that all objects of belief have most certain reasons. First truth, which illuminates what is to be believed, cannot be without reason. Richard of Saint Victor, in Book I, *On the Trinity*,[46] says this: "I believe without doubt," he says, "that there are not only probable, but necessary arguments for any explanation of necessary things, although these as yet happen to lie hidden from our industry." And later[47] he says: "It seems altogether impossible for any necessary thing not to exist, or to be without necessary reason."

If, on the other hand, we speak of objects of belief, or of the things which are of faith, *with respect to our intellects*, I say that there are certain of them which are to faith like fundamentals or fundamental principles, like the *common properties of divinity*; such as God exists, God is one, God is simple, eternal, boundless (or infinite), immutable, all-powerful, all-wise, and all-good, and such like. These things certainly can be proved by necessary reason, through natural investigation by the intellect, of unbelievers as well as of believers, as both the philosophers have demonstrated (as we see from the philosopher's *Physics*, Book VIII,[48] and *Metaphysics*, Book II[49]), and the apostle[50] says: "The invisible things of God from the creation of the world are clearly seen, being understood by the things that are made, his eternal power also and divinity," since, as the Book of Wisdom[51] says, "by the greatness of the beauty and of the creature the creator of them may be seen, so as to be known thereby." Although such things are proved by demonstrative reason, they are none the less believed by faith, as the apostle[52] says: "He that cometh . . . must believe that he is," and as Augustine says, in Book XI of the *City of God*[53]: "Of all visible things, the world is the greatest; of invisible things, the greatest is God.

---

[45] Isa. 7:9. Cf. p. 73, n. 22, above.

[46] *De trin.*, I, 4 (*PL*, 196, 892C). "First truth" (*veritas prima*) refers to things pertaining to the Godhead; it is the formal aspect of the object of faith (cf. Aquinas, *Sum. theol.*, IIa–IIae, q. 1, a. 1; a. 6, ad 2).

[47] *Ibid.*   [48] Cf. *Phys.*, VIII, 10 (266ª10–267ᵇ27).

[49] Cf. *Metaph.*, II, 2 (994a–994b).   [50] Rom. 1:20.

[51] Wisdom of Solomon 13:5.   [52] Heb. 11:6.

[53] *De civ. dei*, XI, 4:1 (*CSEL*, 40, 1, 514).

But that the world exists, we see; that God exists, we believe."
So, in these matters, these two kinds of knowledge (by faith and
by demonstration) do not mutually exclude one another, as we
have seen partly, and will see more and more fully.

There are other objects of belief which pertain to the
special properties of divinity, like the mystery of the Trinity: that
the Father begets the Son, coequal to and consubstantial with
himself; that the Holy Spirit proceeds from the Father and the
Son, as the mutual and binding love between them, coequal to
them and consubstantial with them; and these three Persons
are one God. Although these things "have necessary reasons,"
as we have said, since "they have necessary and immutable
truth" (as Richard[54] says), still they cannot be proved by the
power of the intellect, since they exceed human understanding
and are altogether above reason. But the mind cleansed and
raised by faith comes by that to understanding (since, as
Augustine[55] says, "Faith opens a way for understanding"), and
by a superinfused gift of understanding it can attain to knowledge and proof of these things, from the divine arrangements
of things, and the vestiges found in created beings; and
especially from the nature of the image,[56] as Augustine and
Richard have proved. Thus Augustine[57] says, distinguishing
three kinds of objects of belief: "The third kind consists of
things which are first believed and afterwards understood. In
matters of divinity, there are things which cannot be understood
except by the *pure in heart*, when the precepts are kept which are
received with reference to the good life."

---

[54] *De trin.*, I, 4 (*PL*, 196, 892C).

[55] Cf. *De pecc. merit. et remiss.*, I, 21:29 (*CSEL*, 60, 27–28); *Epist.* 137,
4:15 (*CSEL*, 44, 117).

[56] *Ex ratione imaginis. Ratio=forma, idea, species*, etc. (Cf. G.E. Demers,
"Le divers sens du mot 'ratio' au moyen âge," in *Etudes d'histoire littéraire
et doctrinale du XIIIe siècle*, Première série, Paris et Ottawa, 1932, pp.
105 ff.). In the Augustinian tradition, the forms of all created things are
participations in, or imitations of, the divine Ideas, after which they are
modeled. Thus, in the contemplation of created things in the illumination
of the eternal reasons (*rationes aeternae*), the soul is led to knowledge of God.
This involves moral as well as intellectual illumination. In all creatures
there are vestiges (*vestigia*—footprints or traces) of God, in so far as they
participate in unity, truth, and goodness, and are dependent upon God
as cause; but "image" (*imago*) expresses a more formal likeness, the
intellectual soul of man in its threefold structure of memory, understanding, and will. It is the higher part of the soul (*ratio superior*, cf.
supra, p. 316, n. 50) which judges with certitude, and it is in this part
that the image of God is found.

[57] *De div. quaest. lxxxiii*, q. 48 (*PL*, 40, 31); cf. Matt. 5:8.

For this reason, the same doctor, in Book I, *On the Trinity*,[58] undertakes, "God helping, to give an account, which they demand, how the Trinity is the one and only and true God, and how the Father, Son, and Holy Spirit are rightly said, believed, and understood to be of one and the same substance or essence; that they may not be baffled as if by evasions, but may test the matter itself and find that that is the highest good which the most purified minds discern, and that this is why they are unable to understand it, because the eye of man's mind does not focus in so excellent a light, unless it is quickened, nourished by the righteousness of faith." Later on,[59] he says that this "may so serve these wordy arguers, more exalted than capable, that they may find something they cannot doubt." And Richard, in Book I, *On the Trinity*,[60] says that it is his purpose "to adduce, not probable, but true and necessary reasons for the things we have believed." Also, Anselm, at the beginning of Book I of *Why God Became Man*,[61] says: "As the right order requires that we should first believe the fundamentals of the Christian faith rather than presume to judge them by reason, so it seems to me negligence if, after we have been confirmed in faith, we do not study to understand what we believe."

There are other objects of belief, pertaining to the *divine works*: to the work of creation, as that the world was created; or to the work of redemption, as that Christ was incarnate, dead, and so on; still others to the work of judgment, like the resurrection of bodies, the everlasting glory of the saints, and the eternal punishment of the evil. Because such things wait upon the Will of God, and do not in themselves have necessary and immutable truth (since they are contingent), not even the intellect of the believer can prove them by necessary reason. It cannot be proved necessarily that the world was created, since it was not created of necessity; nor necessarily that Christ was incarnate, since he was not incarnate of necessity; nor can it be proved necessarily that the resurrection will take place, since it will not take place of necessity. These things are first believed by faith, and afterward a mind advancing to understanding with the aid of that gift can prove that they were not, or are not, impossible, and thus that they were, or are, appropriate.

---

[58] *De trin.*, I, 2:4 (*PL*, 42, 822). On the meaning of Augustine's phrase, "eye of the mind" (*acies mentis*), cf. Gilson, *Introduction à l'étude de saint Augustin*, 3ᵉ ed. (J. Vrin, Paris, 1949), p. 284, n. 1.
[59] *Ibid.*   [60] *De trin.*, I, 4 (*PL*, 196, 892C).
[61] *Cur deus homo*, I, 2 (Schmitt, II, 50).

And so Augustine (*On True Religion*[62]), having said that the works of the Father, Son, and Holy Spirit are indivisible, and how we find vestiges of the Trinity in every created thing, adds[63]: "When this has been grasped, it will be clear enough (as far as is possible for man) how all things are subject to their God and Lord by necessary, indefeasible, and just laws. Then we understand all those things which at first we believed only by following authority, partly so that we see them as most certain, partly so that we see that they were possible, and hence appropriate; and we become sorry for those who do not believe them, but have preferred to deride us who believe rather than to share our belief. For when the eternity of the Trinity and the mutability of the creature are known, the holy taking of manhood, the birth from the Virgin, and the death of the Son of God for us, his resurrection from the dead, his ascension into heaven and sitting at the right hand of the Father, the forgiveness of sins, the day of judgment, and the resurrection of bodies, are not merely believed, but also judged to relate to the mercy of the most high God, which he has shown to the human race."

This, however, is to be noted: although necessary reason cannot be given as to why the works of God were done, like why Christ was incarnate and why the world was created, yet something concerning Christ and the creation of the world can be proved by necessary reason, even by unbelievers: for instance, that the world was not created from eternity (since the nature[64] of creation excludes this), that Christ was not born of his mother from eternity, and so on.

So I say, in summary, that objects of faith, or those things in which we have faith, can be proved by reason, in the way we have outlined. For the understanding of this, an explanation can be undertaken:

The *first reason* is taken from the side of the *beliefs* which first truth prescribes for belief and assent. First truth, however, from which all reason flows and emanates, and, indeed, all illumination of reasoning is lighted,[65] can, as we have said, prescribe nothing without reason.

---

[62] *De vera relig.*, 7:13 (*PL*, 34, 128–129).
[63] *Ibid.*, 8:14 (*PL*, 34, 129).   [64] *Ratio.*
[65] We know and judge all things in the eternal reasons, in the light of first truth, from which the light of reason is kindled (cf. Augustine, *De trin.*, XII, 2:2, *PL*, 42, 999; *De vera relig.*, 31:57, *PL*, 34, 147; 39:72, *PL*, 34, 154; Bonaventure, *Itin. mentis in deum*, III, 3, *cum nota* 5, *Opera omnia*, V, 304). This light is not the object of our knowledge, but the moving principle (*ratio motiva*), exercising a regulating function in regard to our

The *second reason* is taken from the side of the *divine effects*. Upon every effect, according to Augustine (*City of God*, Book XI[66]), the divine wisdom has impressed its vestiges (in some cases more, in some less) which lead those who understand and are not blind to knowledge of things divine. This is especially true of the image found in rational creatures.

The *third reason* is taken from the side of *created things*, and especially the human intellect, which, by virtue of the fact that it is made in the image of God,[67] is destined by its nature for knowledge of God, although it cannot rise to this perfectly, because of the clouding of sin and the burden of the corruptible body.[68]

And the *fourth reason*, therefore, is taken from the side of the *infused gift*. As Augustine says in Book I, *On the Trinity*,[69] our intellect is cleansed by faith, that "it may see the ineffable ineffably." There is added to the intellect thus cleansed a gift of understanding, by which the mind is further elevated and illuminated, so that it comes to see by most certain reason (as we have seen above[70] on the authority of Augustine) those things which it believes but is not of itself able to understand.

Unbelievers, however, cannot come to know the Trinity through these vestiges which rational creatures reflect as in a glass, because without a heart purified by faith they cannot know even that it is a glass; and hence they cannot come to know through it the things which are visible there. Thus Augustine says, in Book XV, *On the Trinity*[71]: "Those who know their own mind, in whatever way it can be seen, and in it this Trinity, and yet do not believe nor understand that it is

---

knowledge of things. Hence Matthew says that it is not the *only*, nor the *whole*, reason of knowing; our knowledge is also dependent upon sense, memory, and experience (*Ratio cognoscendi materialis est ab exterioribus, unde ministrantur species rerum cognoscendarum*. . . . Q. 2 *de cog., Quaest. disp.*, I, 261). On Matthew's theory of knowledge, and the problems involved in the attempt to reconcile the doctrine of illumination with the Aristotelian theory of abstraction, see S. Belmond, "A l'école de saint Augustin," in *Etudes franciscaines*, 1921, pp. 7–25, and E. Gilson, "Sur quelques difficultés de l'illumination augustinienne," *Revue néo-scolastique de philosophie*, Feb., 1934 (Hommage à M. de Wulf), pp. 321–331).

66 Cf. *De civ. dei*, XI, 24 (*CSEL*, 40, 1, 547–548).
67 Cf. Gen. 9:6.
68 Cf. Wisdom of Solomon 11:15; Augustine, *De civ. dei*, XIX, 4 (*CSEL*, 40, 2, 375).
69 *De trin.*, I, 1:3 (*PL*, 42, 821).
70 Cf. *supra*, notes 40 and 62.
71 *De trin.*, XV, 24:44 (*PL*, 42, 1091); cf. I Tim. 1:5; I Cor. 13:12.

the image of God, do indeed see the glass, but so far do not see through it him who is to be seen there. Thus they do not know that what they see is a glass, that is, an image. If they knew this, perhaps they would realize that he whose glass this is should be sought through it, and somehow provisionally be seen, their hearts being purified by *unfeigned faith* so that·he who is now seen *through a glass* may be seen *face to face*."

But it still remains to be seen how, together with so much clarity of reason, the hiddenness of faith and the obscurity of belief can remain. This is manifestly and clearly seen when three things have been taken into consideration:

The *first* is *the greatness of the matters to be understood*, and *the deficiency of our power of understanding* because of the burden of the body and the cloudiness of the phantasms. Because of these things, the mind, however much it sees and understands, never so understands but that, if it does not actually fall into error, at least it can doubt; and therefore belief is necessary. However much it sees and understands, it never understands so fully but that something remains not understood, which must be believed. Thus Augustine says, in Book I of the *Soliloquies*[72]: "While the soul is still in this body, even if it sees very fully, that is, knows God, yet because the bodily senses still go their own way, if they are not actually able to lead into error, they can ·at least lead to a doubtful conclusion. Faith can be called that which resists these senses and believes that the soul's knowledge is true." In the XIXth Book of the *City of God*,[73] Augustine says that "the soul nevertheless has certain knowledge of matters which it apprehends by mind and reason, although this is very limited because of the burden of the flesh"; and he says in Book XV, *On the Trinity*[74]: "Faith seeks, understanding finds, as was spoken by the prophet: *Unless you will believe you will not understand.* Again, the understanding still seeks him whom it finds, for *God looked down upon the children of men, to see if there were any that did understand or did seek God.* For this reason, therefore, man ought to understand: that he may seek God." So the understanding finds, that faith may yet continually seek.

The *second* consideration is *the way of reasoning or demonstration.*

---

[72] *Solil.*, I, 7:4 (*PL*, 32, 876).
[73] *De civ. dei*, XIX, 18 (*CSEL*, 40, 2, 405).
[74] *De trin.*, XV, 2:2 (*PL*, 42, 1058); Augustine quotes Isa. 7:9 (LXX), and Ps. 13:2 (P.B.V., 14:3), or Ps. 52:3 (P.B.V., 53:3); cf. Augustine, *Enarr. in Ps.* 52:5 (*PL*, 36, 615–616).

According to the philosopher,[75] the way of demonstration is twofold: ostensive, or leading to the impossible.[76] The ostensive is twofold: the first way is through the cause a priori, the demonstration called *propter quid*. Objects of belief cannot be demonstrated in this way, because things divine have no external cause. The second way is a posteriori, through the effect and through signs, the demonstration called *quia*. Although this way provides knowledge, yet, since it does not explain the nature of the matter investigated with reference to its cause, and does not indicate its mode, it provides understanding in such a way that something as to mode and cause must still be believed.

The other way is demonstration *leading to the impossible*, and this way, although it convinces and forces the intellect to assent, yet does not disperse the obscurity. It does not show the proper cause of the matter, nor its mode, and does not prove the matter directly, and therefore faith is always necessary with this kind of demonstration. Thus Augustine says in his *Retractations*, Book I,[77] that "knowledge of truth is most meager in this life."

The *third* consideration is *the mutual relation and connection of beliefs*. Although the unity of the divine essence considered by itself, and the Trinity of Persons considered by itself, can both be proved by reason, it is altogether incomprehensible how unity can accord with Trinity. Similarly, it can be proved by reason that the world was created instantaneously from nothing, and, no less, that God is immutable; but as to how he created the world without any change and innovation in himself, the understanding necessarily hesitates unless faith believes. Thus Richard, in Book IV, *On the Trinity*,[78] after explaining very well how the unity of divine essence and also the Trinity of Persons are proved by necessary reasons, says: "And indeed, when each of these considerations and assertions is studied alone and in itself, nothing seems more believable or more true; but when we compare one with the other and study how

---

[75] Cf. *Anal. prior.*, I, 22 (40a4 ff.).

[76] An ostensive demonstration (*demonstratio ostensiva*) is a *direct* proof, which shows the matter in question to be true. Demonstration *propter quid* shows the truth of the matter deductively by reference to its proper cause or principle. Demonstration *quia* shows the truth of the matter, but does not prove it by reference to its proper principle, the adequate cause of its truth. Demonstration leading to the impossible (*demonstratio ducens ad impossibile*) is an *indirect* proof, equivalent to *reductio ad absurdum*.

[77] *Retract.*, I, 13:3 (*CSEL*, 36, 66).

[78] *De trin.*, IV, 1 (*PL*, 196, 930–931).

they can be reconciled, however manifold the arguments of reason, the matter soon comes into doubt, unless the stability of faith stands in the way."

I say, therefore, that in matters of divinity, knowledge by faith and knowledge by reason stand together so that one does not exclude the other. Only the knowledge of clear and immediate *vision* will eliminate faith, when "we shall see him as he is." This kind of knowledge is called "face to face," about which the apostle[79] says: "Now we see through a glass and in an enigma; then face to face."

When all these things have been seen, from here on the arguments can easily enough be refuted.

IV

Answers to the Rejected Arguments

Against the first argument, it must be said that there are two ways in which a thing may be apparent. The first is by *full*, clear, and *immediate* evidence, and of this kind of apparentness there cannot be faith. On the contrary, this altogether eliminates faith. The other way is by *partial* and *mediate* knowledge, and of this kind there can be faith, and, as we have said in the principal solution, it does not destroy faith. The apparentness of reasons, however, is not by full or immediate evidence; on the contrary, with this apparentness the obscurity and enigma of faith remain.[80]

To 2, it must be said that the comparison between the earlier and the final members of this series fails. To deny and to doubt, to doubt and to conjecture, to conjecture and to believe are opposed; but to believe and to understand by reason are not opposed. On the contrary, one is directed toward the other, as we have seen.

To 3, the answer is clear. I say that there is *clear and immediate sight*, and this alone destroys faith, as we have already said; but there is also *sight through the medium of reason*, and this does not destroy faith. This is Augustine's meaning. I see fully and immediately distinguish my will when I am willing, my memory when I am remembering, or my mind when I am thinking, and

---

[79] I Cor. 13:12.

[80] On the argument of this paragraph, cf. Bonaventure, III *Sent.*, d. 24, a. 2, q. 3 (*Opera omnia*, III, 522–524); see T. Heitz, *Essai historique sur les rapports entre la philosophie et la foi* (Paris, 1909), pp. 110 ff.

therefore I do not believe these things.[81] But things proved by reason are seen by some argument, and are present by a medium, and thus they are seen or are present in such a way that they can none the less be believed, for the reasons given above.

To 4, it must be said that Hugh in those words is referring to the distinction set forth in the principal solution. Some things are *from reason*, like fundamental principles and quasi pre-suppositions of faith,[82] which are self-evident, as that God exists, and things of this kind. I say *from reason*, not because they lie beneath reason, but because in these matters reason is capable of itself. Such things, in so far as they are of this kind, "do not receive faith." Thus Hugh's statement is to be understood per se and with reduplication. Other things are *according to reason*, like the special properties of divinity. While reason is not of itself capable in these matters, yet, illuminated by the ray of faith and elevated by the gift of understanding, even though it may not comprehend the truth of these things, it does not contradict our faith in them. On the contrary, faith is aided by reason and reason is perfected by faith. Still other things are *above reason*, like divine marvelous works, which reason does not understand. Since they are contingent, they cannot have necessary reason;

[81] Matthew holds, against the Aristotelians (cf. Aquinas, *Sum. theol.*, Ia, q. 87, aa. 1, 2), that "the soul knows itself and its habits by its essence and not only by its act" (Q. 5 *de cog.*, *Quaest. disp.*, I, 317). This is in accord with the Augustinian tradition: cf. Gilson, *Introduction à l'étude de saint Augustin*, pp. 61, 101, 321; *La Philosophie de saint Bonaventure*, 2ᵉ ed. (J. Vrin, Paris, 1943), p. 279.

[82] *Quasi praeambula*. According to Aquinas, demonstrative reason can be given for the *praeambula* of faith (*Sum. theol.*, IIa–IIae, q. 2, a. 10, ad 2) which are related to the doctrine of faith as nature is related to grace: "*Sicut autem sacrem doctrina fundatur super lumen fidei, ita philosophia super lumen naturale rationis: unde impossibile est quod ea quae sunt philosophiae, sint contraria eis quae sunt fidei, sed deficiunt ab eis. Continent tamen quasdam similitudines eorum, et quaedam ad ea praeambula, sicut natura praeambula est ad gratiam*": *Expos. super Boetium de trin.*, q. 2, a. 3, resp. (P. Mandonnet, ed., S. Thomae Aquinatis, *Opuscula omnia*, Sumptibus P. Lethielleux Biblio-polae Editoris, Paris, 1927, *Opusc.* XVI, [III, 51]). Although the *praeambula* are objects of scientific knowledge and are presupposed by the doctrine of faith, they are reckoned among the articles of faith because they are objects of faith for those who do not know them by demonstration (*Sum. theol.*, Ia, q. 1, a. 5, ad 3). Matthew uses the *quasi*, a scholastic device which "*permet de ne pas perdre le bénéfice d'un rapprochement abstraitment inexact*" (M. D. Chenu, *Introduction à l'étude de saint Thomas d'Aquin*, Montreal, Institut d'études médiévales, and Paris, J. Vrin, 1950, p. 102). On the sense in which Matthew believes that the existence of God can be proved demonstratively, and in what sense it is self-evident, cf. Gilson, *History*, p. 689.

"yet the mind raised and illuminated by a gift of understanding sees they they were possible, and thus that they were appropriate," as Augustine says (*On True Religion*) in the text[83] already cited.[84]

To 5, the answer is clear. Singulars cannot be demonstrated, and do not have necessary reason, and neither demonstration nor reason pertains to them, that it would be necessary for them to be. Nevertheless, according to Augustine, they can well be understood to have been possible, and thus appropriate, as we have said in the principal solution.[85] Otherwise, it can be said that singulars as singulars cannot be demonstrated, and there is no knowledge of them,[86] but as they come under some universal reason they can be demonstrated. Christ, although he is in a way singular, is also universally the principle of human redemption. Thus some universal reason can be found in regard to singular objects of belief by virtue of which they can be proved by reason.

To 6, the answer is clear. Contingent things cannot have for us necessary reason, nor be proved by reason. Nevertheless, we can prove that they were not impossible, and thus were appropriate. Or it must be said that contingent things considered in themselves and as contingent cannot be proved demonstratively; but contingent things related to the divine wisdom, justice, or mercy participate in the reason of the necessary things, and thus they can certainly be proved by reason.

To 7, it must be said that principles are not proved or demonstrated by demonstration *propter quid*, by the cause, because to do so would be to go on *in infinitum*; but by demonstration *quia*, by the effect. Or if they are not proved by an *ostensive* demonstration, then by demonstration *leading to the impossible*. Or else it could be said that there is no comparison between the principles of this science and those of other sciences. The principles of the other sciences ought to be presupposed as self-evident, since they are discovered by human reason and human reason advances from things which are certain to it. The principles of this science, however, should be presupposed as believed, and revealed by God, because faith goes beyond human reason and

---

[83] *Auctoritas*; cf. *supra*, p. 328, n. 13.

[84] *Supra*, p. 414.

[85] *Supra*, pp. 413 f.

[86] On the way in which, according to Matthew, the human intellect does know singulars, see Q. 4 *de cog.*, resp.; *Quaest. disp.*, I, 304. This was an important point in Augustinian-Aristotelian controversy (cf. the view of Aquinas, *Sum. theol.*, Ia, q. 86, a. 1, resp.).

is the principle of merit.[87] Nevertheless, when a gift of under-standing has been added, they come to be understood. First, then, they are presupposed by faith, and afterward understood by a gift of understanding.

To 8, the answer is clear. As we have already said, divine truths are not proved through created things by demonstration *propter quid*, or by an ostensive demonstration showing the mode of their existence, but by demonstration *quia*. Likewise, there is no demonstration to prove that miracles are going to happen, before they happen, or that they happened necessarily, after they have occurred; but that they were not impossible, and hence appropriate.

To 9, it must be said that objects of faith present great difficulty as to their reason, but they become easy by the habit of faith. It is the nature of this habit to make the difficult easy. The argument continues: "Things which have reason present no difficulty." I say that the difficulty always remains, in so far as the things are still believed. Perhaps it is more difficult to assent to these things on account of authority than on account of reason; or if on account of both, yet more on account of authority. Thus the argument altogether prefers authority to reason. To this statement that things which have reason present no difficulty, I say that in the case of things which have reason which is ostensive and by the cause, both showing the truth of the matter with reference to its principle[88] and showing its mode,[89] the statement is true. Demonstrations of objects of belief, however, are not of this kind, as we have seen in the principal solution.

[87] The *principia* of the science of theology, according to Aquinas, are obtained from revelation (*Sum. theol.*, Ia, q. 1, a. 6, ad 2); the *principia fidei* are the authorities of Holy Scripture (IIa–IIae, q. 1, a. 5, ad 2). Articles of faith are related to the doctrine of faith as self-evident principles are to the doctrine of natural reason (IIa–IIae, q. 1, a. 7, resp.), and whatever is based upon them is as surely proved in the eyes of the faithful as con-clusions from self-evident principles are in the eyes of everyone (IIa–IIae, q. 1, a. 5, ad 2). But whereas evidence from proper principles makes things apparent, evidence from divine authority does not make things apparent in themselves (IIa–IIae, q. 4, a. 2, ad 5), and, except in matters of revelation, argument from authorities is "infirmissimus" (Ia, q. 1, a. 2, ad 2). On this subject, see M. D. Chenu, "La Théologie comme science au XIIIᵉ siècle," *Arch. d'hist. doct. et litt. du moyen âge*, 1927, pp. 32–71.

On faith as the principle of merit, cf. Gregory the Great, *In evang.*, II, 26:1 (*PL*, 76, 1197); Aquinas, *Sum. theol.*, IIa–IIae, q. 2, a. 9; Bonaventure, III *Sent.*, d. 23, a. 1, q. 1 (*Opera omnia*, III, 472).

[88] *Propter quid.*   [89] *Quomodo.*

To 10, it must be said that the major premise is false. Not everything proved by reason lies under reason's judgment. To the proof of the minor premise (stated on the authority of Augustine), it must be said that a thing can be judged in two ways[90]: that it is thus, or that it ought to be thus; either judgments by the cause of the thing and by one's own illumination, in which case it is true that judgment is only of inferior things; or else judgments by the effect and by the illumination of the thing judged, and in this case it is not true. The matter under discussion is of the latter kind, as we have explained above.

To 11, it must be said that the Damascene does not wish, nor intend, to exclude serious inquiry, but inquisitive searching. In regard to his statement, "nothing beyond," I say that we are not seeking anything beyond what has been handed down to us by the Scriptures, but we are inquiring into those very things, first known to us by faith, that we may understand them by reason, as Anselm teaches in the text[91] from Book I of *Why God Became Man*, quoted above.[92]

To 12, it must be said that things which are in fact beliefs, which are strictly speaking articles of faith, altogether transcend our intellect, and therefore it is appropriate for it "to be made captive in the obedience of Christ," as the apostle[93] says. Nevertheless, as it attains by the habit and illumination of faith to the things which are to be believed, so it attains by the habit or gift of understanding to the things which are to be proved and seen by reason. The argument goes on to say that "no accident transcends or goes beyond its subject." Augustine in the same place[94] points out that an accident's transcendance of its subject can be understood in two ways: *by bestowal of form,*[95]

---

[90] Cf. Bonaventure, I *Sent.*, d. 3, pt. 1, q. 1, ad 4 (*Opera omnia*, I, 69).
[91] *Auctoritas.*   [92] *Supra*, p. 413.
[93] II Cor. 10:5.   [94] I.e., *De trin.*, IX, 4:5 (*PL*, 42, 963).
[95] *Per informationem—per operationem.* (The terms are Matthew's, but the argument is essentially that of Augustine in the passage to which he refers.) The *informatio* (or *formatio*, which is equivalent) of an object, refers to the bestowal of form in terms of color, shape, quantity, etc., and an accident does not go beyond its subject in this way. Every subject, however, has a form, and a certain *operatio*, or action, in accordance with this form (cf. Aquinas, *Cont. gent.*, III, 84, 5: "*Propria operatio rei consequitur naturam ipsius*"), and in this way an accident may have an influence beyond its subject. These two terms sometimes have widely different meanings in Aristotelian and Augustinian usages: in the Aristotelian theory of abstraction, for instance, they are (in one sense of *operatio intellectus*) equated (cf. Aquinas, III *Sent.*, d. 23, q. 2, a. 2, sol. 1), while in Augustine, as M. D. Chenu remarks (*Intro.* . . . , p. 117, n. 1), "'formatio' *est l'expression typique de la doctrine de l'illumination divine.*"

and it is true that it does not transcend its subject in this way; or *by its operation,* and in this way it does transcend it. An accident existing on this surface here influences sight existing over there; still the accident which exists here in the one subject cannot actually be in the other subject. Augustine makes this point: "The shape or color which belongs to this particular body cannot be in any other body." But it must be noted that when we say that faith or reason attain to God, either as object of belief or as object of understanding, we do not mean that these habits do this by themselves without their subject, but that the intellect which cannot of itself attain to this is raised thereto by these habits, and is there because of them.

To 13, it must be said that no objects of belief are contrary to reason or involve contradiction. In regard to the objection concerning the sacrament of the altar, I say that for an accident to be without its subject is not *contrary to reason,* but *above reason,* and hence no contradiction is involved. That "the being of an accident is to inhere," is not to be understood to mean that its being is its inherence, or that inherence itself is being, but that the nature of an accident is such that it may inhere, and it has a capacity for inherence. Definitions are not always of act, but sometimes of capacity. For instance, man is defined as "a rational animal, mortal,"[96] not because he is always actually reasoning (if this were the case he would not always be rational) but because he always has the capacity and his nature is suited for reasoning. I claim that the proposition stated is of this kind.

To 14, it must be said that the conclusion of the argument is correct. It is not proper to faith, in the nature of faith, that beliefs should be understood by reason. If this were the case nothing would be believed unless it were understood. Neither is it proper to knowledge as such, that things which are known should be believed by faith (as we are speaking here of faith and belief); for if this were true there would be no knowledge without faith, which is false.

To 15, it can likewise be answered that its conclusion is true. Just as what is hoped, while it is hoped and in so far as it is hoped, is not obtained, so what is believed, while it is believed and in so far as it is believed, is not known. Another possible answer is by the negation of the minor premise of the argument. What is hoped, while it is hoped, is obtained, although not fully possessed; likewise, what is believed, while it is believed, is not

---

[96] Cf. Augustine, *De trin.,* VII, 4:7 (*PL,* 42, 939); *Serm.* 358:3 (*PL,* 39, 1588); Bonaventure, I *Sent.,* d. 25, a. 1, q. 2, ad 1 (*Opera omnia,* I, 439).

fully known, since it is not seen by that clear vision which there will be "face to face," as the apostle[97] says. This argument can be answered in a third way. The cases are not similar, because faith is more comprehensive than hope. While hope refers only to future things, obtaining is of present things, and hence what is hoped, while it is hoped, is not obtained; but faith is of things future, present, and past, and hence it is not opposed to knowledge in the way in which hope or expectation is opposed to obtaining. We have more to say on this subject below.

To 16, it can again be said that its conclusion is true, that as certitude ultimately excludes ignorance, so obscurity and enigma exclude perfect knowledge, or exclude knowledge in this respect, this I grant, that what is believed is neither perfectly known nor completely unknown. Or it must be said that obscurity does not exclude knowledge as certitude does ignorance, because it is not opposed to it in the same way. Certitude is opposed to ignorance, but doubt, and not obscurity, is opposed to certitude; doubt, and not obscurity, excludes knowledge. But obscurity excludes clear knowledge or cognition. Hence the argument is not valid.

An answer must be made to the opposing arguments which do not well nor rightly conclude.

To 4, it must be said that it is impossible to come to knowledge of the Trinity without the illumination of faith. The philosophers who came to this knowledge did not do so by themselves or by their own power, but because they were contemporaries of the prophets to whom it was revealed, and perhaps learned it from them and left it in their writings.[98] Or, it must be said that it is not inconsistent that some of them should have been illuminated by some light of faith in regard to one article of faith and not in regard to another. This is clearly the

[97] I Cor. 13:12.

[98] A brief account of the history of this and other arguments on this point in Jewish and Christian apologetics may be found in H. A. Wolfson, *Philo* (Harvard University Press, Cambridge, Mass., 1947), Vol. I, pp. 160 ff. This was one of the arguments adopted by Justin Martyr, Tatian, Clement of Alexandria, Eusebius, and others. Augustine espoused it in his work *On Christian Doctrine* (*De doct. christ.*, II, 28:43, *PL*, 34, 56), but later abandoned it on grounds of historical improbability (*De civ. dei*, VIII, 11, 12, *CSEL*, 40, 1, 371–373; *Retract.*, II, 30, *CSEL*, 36, 136–137). In the light of his refutation, it is curious that the argument persisted in the Middle Ages and later. E. Gilson, quoting P. Lagrange's opinion (*Saint Justin*, p. 132), that "literary history knows no other example of such an enormous hoax," comments that "it was probably less a hoax than a self-delusion" (*History*, p. 557).

case with heretics, who err in one matter and think rightly in another.[99] Or, thirdly, it must be said, as we have already said (and as Richard[1] says), that even if the Trinity of Persons considered in and of itself can be proved by reason, still reason cannot grasp how this Trinity of Persons can be reconciled with complete unity of substance. It may be, therefore, that those philosophers posited the Trinity in such a way that they did not also posit with it unity of substance, as right faith holds.

To 6, it must be said that the minor premise of the argument is false. Necessary reason and the clearness of the matter are not the only means of coming to certain knowledge. There is also revelation or divine inspiration, another testimony or authority in which we must believe. This means is not lacking; for while no one can have faith of himself, since it is the gift of God,[2] yet no one who would receive it lacks it. God, "who will have all men to be saved and to come to the knowledge of the truth,"[3] is always ready to grant it, and bestows the illumination of faith, unless there is an impediment on the part of the recipient.

To 7, it must be said that the demons know that these men are punished for the sin of unbelief. They also know what they should have believed and did not believe. This does not mean, however, that they understand these things by reason. There is a difference between knowing what should be believed, and believing it, and understanding the belief by reason. For example: Suppose someone knows that grammar is the science of correct speech and writing, and therefore wishes to learn it. This does not mean that he knows grammar. When I say, "A certain boy knows that grammar is the science, etc.," and, "A demon knows what should be believed," "grammar" and "what should be believed" are asserted *materially*; but when I say "to believe this," or "to understand the belief," this is asserted *formally*.[4] Here is another example: A certain heretic sees that another heretic is punished and burned on grounds of

---

[99] This argument parallels that of Bonaventure, I *Sent.*, d. 3, pt. 1, q. 4, resp. (*Opera omnia*, I, 76); cf. the view of Aquinas: ". . . a heretic with regard to one article of faith has no faith in the other articles, but only a kind of opinion in accordance with his own will" (*Sum. theol.*, IIa–IIae, q. 5, a. 3, resp.).

[1] *Supra*, pp. 417 f.   [2] Cf. Eph. 2:8.   [3] I Tim. 2:4.

[4] *Formaliter*, contrasted with *materialiter*, refers to the kind of intelligibility constituted by grasping the formal object, in abstraction; "*la clef de la méthode aristotélicienne*" (M. D. Chenu, *Intro.* . . . , p. 99).

heresy, because he did not believe what the Church believed. He knows, therefore, what he should have believed, and that he is punished because he did not believe it. This does not mean, however, that this heretic himself believes, or understands by reason the things which are believed.

To 8, it must be said that without doubt knowledge of the Trinity is necessary to salvation. But it pertains to the nobility of the rational creature that he is destined for something so difficult to understand that it exceeds the limits and the ability of nature. Nevertheless, the higher nature is not deficient, since he both gave it the capacity (in that he formed rational nature "after his image"[5]) and added to complement it the habit of faith and the illumination of understanding, by which it can attain to that belief and understanding.[6]

To 9, it must be said that this is not a matter of greater and lesser. To love God for himself and above all things is also above the power and capability of the understanding. Or it must be said that the conclusion is true, if it is considered equally applicable in both cases. Just as it can be proved by reason that God is to be loved for himself and above all things, so it can be proved that God is to be believed to be three and one, since the truth states this; but just as God cannot be loved for himself and above all things by natural affection, so natural reason cannot prove that he is three and one.

To 10, it must be said that the conclusion is true. As what is not believed cannot be known, so what is believed must be known. But it must be pointed out (following Augustine, *Retractations*, Book I[7]) that "to know" is understood in two ways: in one way, to know is to comprehend something by certain reason; the other way is either to perceive by bodily sense or to believe on suitable testimony. It is also possible to answer against the form of the argument, because it commits a fallacy

---

[5] Gen. 1:27.

[6] The argument of this paragraph is based on Matthew's view of the degrees of conformity to God (Q. 2 *de cog.*, resp., *Quaest. disp.*, I, 255). Man's intellectual operations, as image (*imago*), are dependent upon divine illumination, but such operations must not be described as supernatural or miraculous (cf. *ibid.*, ad 2). They are natural in the sense that the very nature (*ratio*) of the image requires that it receive divine illumination to perform its *proper* function; this is in accord with the nature of the creature. (Cf. the position of Aquinas: "Because man's nature is dependent upon a higher nature, natural knowledge is not sufficient for its perfection, and some supernatural knowledge is necessary"; *Sum. theol.*, IIa–IIae, q. 2, a. 3, ad 1).

[7] *Retract.*, I, 13:5 (*CSEL*, 36, 68).

of the consequent, by the affirmation of the consequent[8]: What is not believed is not known: what is believed is known. Believing is more inclusive than knowing, if knowing is understood in its strict sense, and thus believing is included in the understanding of what it is to know. Therefore, when it is argued that what is not believed is not known, the process is good; but when it is further said that therefore what is believed is known, the affirmation is drawn from the more inclusive to the less inclusive, and hence there is a fallacy of the consequent in the inference. It is as if one said, "What is not animal is not man, therefore what is animal is man." And thus the argument is not valid, but fails according to the consequent.

[8] Cf. Aristotle, *De soph. elench.*, I, 4 (166[b]25); Bonaventure, III *Sent.*, d. 11, dub. 4., *cum nota* 5 (*Opera omnia*, III, 259).

John Duns Scotus: Commentary on the Sentences

THE TEXT

BOOK I

DISTINCTION 2, PART 1, QUESTION 2

WHETHER THE EXISTENCE OF ANY INFINITE BEING, SUCH AS THE EXISTENCE OF GOD, IS KNOWN PER SE

I

IT APPEARS THAT IT IS:

1. Damascene says, in Book One, chapter 1: "The knowledge of God's existence is implanted in all by nature."[1] But that, the knowledge of which is implanted in all, is known per se,[2] just as it is evident in *Metaphysics* II[3] that the first principles, which are as it were doors, are known per se; therefore, etc.

2. Moreover, the existence of that than which a greater cannot be thought is known per se. Now according to Anselm, in the *Proslogion*, chapter 5, God is like this; therefore, etc. Also, this is not anything finite; therefore, it is infinite. The major premise is proved, because the opposite of the predicate is incompatible with the subject. For if such a being does not exist, it is not that than which a greater cannot be thought, since, if it existed in reality, it would be greater than if it did not exist in reality, but only in the intellect.

3. Again, the existence of truth is known per se. But God is truth; therefore God's existence is known per se. The major premise is proved because it follows from its opposite, for if there were no truth, it would then be true that there was no truth; therefore, there is truth.[4]

4. Again, propositions which derive relative necessity from terms which have relative being[5]—namely, from the fact that they are in the intellect—are known per se, as in the case of

---

[1] Cf. John Damascene, *De fide orthod.*, I, 9 (*PG*, 94, 790).
[2] I.e., directly rather than by inference from other data.
[3] Cf. Aristotle, *Metaph.*, i. 1 (993b4–5).
[4] Cf. Augustine, *Soliloq.*, II, 2:2; 15:28 (*PL*, 32, 886; 988).
[5] *Entitatem.*

first principles,[6] which are known per se on account of terms which have being in the intellect. Therefore, that which derives its necessity from absolutely necessary terms, such as the statement that "God exists," will much more be known per se. The minor premise is evident, because the necessity and knowability of first principles depends, not on the existence of their terms in reality, but on the connection of the extremes[7] only as it is found in the intellect which conceives.

On the contrary:

That which is known per se cannot be denied by anyone's mind.[8] But "The fool hath said in his heart, There is no God,"[9] etc.

II

Because, according to the philosopher in *Metaphysics* II, "it is absurd at once to seek knowledge and the mode of knowing,"[10] I shall start by answering the second question, which investigates the way in which we know the proposition, "God exists.[11] And in order to solve the problem, I first indicate the nature of a proposition that is known per se and make the following statement.

When it is said that a proposition is known per se, the phrase per se does not exclude any cause whatever, since the terms of the proposition are not excluded; after all, no proposition is known if the knowledge of its terms is excluded. A proposition known per se, therefore, does not exclude the knowledge of the terms, since we know first principles in so far as we know their terms.[12] But any cause and reason is excluded if it is per se outside the terms of the proposition which is known per se. A proposition, then, is said to be known per se, when its truth is evident because of nothing else outside its own terms, which belong to it.[13]

---

[6] I.e., those self-evident principles which, according to the Aristotelian epistemology, are fundamental to all knowledge.

[7] This refers to the function of the "middle term" in connecting the extremes of the syllogism.

[8] Cf. Aristotle, *Metaph.*, III, 3 (1005ᵇ29–32).

[9] Ps. 13:1; 52:1 (P.B.V., 14:1; 53:1).

[10] Aristotle, *Metaph.*, i, 3 (995ᵃ13–14).

[11] The first question is: "Whether among beings there is anything infinite, actually existing."

[12] Cf. Aristotle, *Anal. post.*, I, 3 (72ᵇ23–25).

[13] Cf. Henry of Ghent, *Sum. quaest. ordin.*, a. 22, q. 2, *corp.* (ed. Paris, 1520, I, f. 130 R.L.).

Furthermore, what are these proper terms from which it must be evident? I say that, as far as this question is concerned, the definition is one term and the thing defined another, whether terms are taken to mean significant words or the concepts signified.

I prove this from *Posteriora* I, because the quiddity[14] or definition of one extreme is the middle term in demonstration.[15] Therefore, the other premise differs from the conclusion only as that which is defined differs from the definition, and yet the premise is a principle known per se, while the conclusion is not known per se, but is demonstrated. As far, then, as the nature of a proposition known per se is concerned, the concept of the definition is different from what is defined, since if the concept of definition and defined were the same, there would be a begging of the question in the most fundamental demonstration;[16] also, in this case there would only be two terms, and this is false.

This point is proved, secondly, by Aristotle, *Physics* I, when he says that names bear the same relation to the definition as the whole to the parts—in other words, that a confused name is known before the definition.[17] Now the name indicates confusedly what the definition indicates distinctly, because the definition analyzes into particulars.[18] Therefore, the concept of a quiddity, as it is indicated confusedly by a name, is naturally known before its concept as it is indicated distinctly by a definition, and thus it is another concept and another extreme. To go on from this: since a proposition is known per se when its truth is evident from its proper terms, and the concept of the quiddity as distinctly indicated by a definition and the concept of the quiddity as confusedly indicated by the name are different terms, it follows that a proposition will not be known per se by means of a quiddity confusedly considered, when it is not known unless the same quiddity is distinctly conceived by a definition.

This conclusion can also be proved by the fact that otherwise any other proposition whatever, which is necessary and per se in the first mode[19]—for instance, the statement that "man is an animal," and a "body," as to substance—would be known per

---

14 *Quod quid est.*
15 Cf. Aristotle, *Anal. post.*, I, 6 (75ª35–37); II, 10 (94ª11–14).
16 Cf. Aristotle, *Topica*, VIII, 13 (162ᵇ34–163ª1).
17 Note the significance attributed to definition in the elucidation of concepts.
18 Cf. Aristotle, *Phys.*, I, 1 (184ª26–184ᵇ3).
19 Cf. Aristotle, *Anal. post.*, I, 4 (73ª34–37).

se, for if the nature of each extreme is attributed by means of the distinctly conceived natures of the extremes, it is quite obvious that one extreme includes the other. Likewise, any proposition which the metaphysician could know per se by means of the definitions of the extremes, would be known per se in the special sciences, and this is not true, since the geometer does not make use of any principles as if they were known per se, save those whose truth is evident from the terms confusedly conceived, for instance, by conceiving a line confusedly. It is evident, however, that a line is length without breadth,[20] without as yet conceiving distinctly to what genus a line belongs, as the metaphysician considers it. Moreover, the geometer does not possess propositions, known per se, like other propositions which the metaphysician could conceive—for example, the statement that a line is so great, and so forth.

The point is evident, in the third place, because the demonstration of anything predicated of a defined thing is compatible with the fact that this predicate is known per se as far as the definition is concerned.

Every proposition, therefore (and only such a proposition), is known per se, when the evident truth of the conclusion proceeds, or can naturally proceed, from its terms conceived in the sense which they possess as its terms.

It is evident from this that a proposition known per se and one knowable per se are not to be distinguished, since they are the same thing. For a proposition is not said to be known per se because it is known per se by some intellect—for in that case, if no intellect knew it in actuality, no proposition would be known per se; rather, a proposition is said to be known per se because, in so far as it lies in the nature of the terms, it is natural for the truth contained in the terms to be evident in any intellect whatever which conceives the terms. If, however, any intellect does not conceive the terms, and so does not conceive the proposition, the latter as far as lies in itself is not less known per se, and thus we speak of what is known per se.

It is also evident from this that there is no distinction concerning what is known per se, in itself and to nature and to us, since whatever is in itself known per se, even though it is not actually known to any intellect, is still evidently true as far as the terms are concerned, and is known if the terms are conceived.

Nor does the distinction hold, according to which some

[20] Cf. Euclid, *Elem.*, I, def. 2 (ed. Heiberg, Leipzig, 1883, I, 3).

propositions are known per se in the first order, some in the
second, since any propositions that are known per se when their
own terms are conceived in the sense which they have as their
terms, possess evident truth in their order.

On the basis of all this, I reply to the question by saying that
a proposition is known per se if it conjoins these extremes,
being[21] and the divine essence as the latter is, or if you like,
God and the being proper to him, in the way in which God sees
that essence and being under the most proper aspect in which
this being is in God—a way in which being and essence are
now understood, not by us, but by God himself and the
blessed. For this proposition has evident truth for the intellect
on the ground of its own terms, since it is not per se in the
second mode,[22] as if the predicate were outside the nature of the
subject, but it is per se in the first mode and immediately
evident from its terms, since that into which all propositions
which state something about God, however conceived, are
resolved, is the most immediate proposition. The statement,
then, that "God exists," or "This essence exists," is known per
se, because it is natural for these extremes to make the conclusion evident to anyone who perfectly apprehends the extremes
of the proposition, since being befits nothing more than it does
this essence. So, then, understanding by the name of God
anything which we do not know or conceive perfectly, like this
divine essence, in this way it is known per se that "God exists."

But if anyone asks whether being is contained in any concept
which we conceive of God, so that a proposition in which being
is predicated of such a concept is known per se—predicated, for
instance, of a proposition whose extremes can be conceived by
us, as when some concept spoken of God, but not common to
him and to the creature, such as necessary existence or infinite
being[23] or highest good, can be in our intellect, and we can
predicate being of such a concept in the mode in which it is
conceived by us—I say that no such proposition is known per
se, for three reasons:

First, because any such proposition is a conclusion which is
demonstrable and *propter quid*.[24] My proof is this: whatever

---

21 *Esse.*   22 Cf. Aristotle, *Anal. post.*, I, 4 (73ª37–73ᵇ5).   23 *Ens.*

24 Cf. R. Garrigou-Lagrange, *God: His Existence and His Nature* (Herder,
St. Louis, 1939), I, 62: "This *propter quid*, this *raison d'être*, that would
make intelligible the laws, which, after all, are but general facts"; this in
contrast with "sciences of the *quia*, which . . . state the fact without being
able to explain it."

pertains to anything in the first place and immediately can be demonstrated *propter quid* from anything that is in it through that to which it first belongs, as through a middle term. For example, if a triangle first and foremost has three angles, equal to two right angles, it can be demonstrated from anything contained in the triangle that it has three angles, by demonstration *propter quid* through the middle term which is the triangle—namely, that any figure would have three, etc., of any species of triangle that it has three, although not in the first instance.[25] Now being belongs first to this essence as this divine essence is seen by the blessed. Therefore, anything in this essence which can be conceived by us—whether it be as it were higher or as it were a passion—can be demonstrated to exist by demonstration *propter quid*, through this essence as through a middle term, just as through the proposition, "A triangle has three angles," it is demonstrated that any figure has three. Consequently, it is not known per se from the terms, since in that case it would not be demonstrated *propter quid*.

The second reason is this: A proposition that is known per se is known per se to any intellect, once the terms are known. But this proposition, "An infinite being exists," is not evident to our intellect from the terms. I prove this by the fact that we do not conceive the terms before we believe it or know it by demonstration, and in that precondition it is not evident to us, for we do not hold it with certitude from the terms, save by faith or by demonstration.

Thirdly, nothing is known per se of a concept which is not absolutely simple, unless it is known per se that the parts of that concept are united, but no concept which we have of God that is proper to him and does not pertain to the creature is absolutely simple, or at least none that we distinctly perceive to be proper to God is absolutely simple.[26] Nothing, then, is known per se of such a concept, unless it is known per se that the parts of that concept are united, but this is not known per se, since the union of those parts is demonstrated by two reasons.

The major is apparent from the philosopher, *Metaphysics* V, in the chapter "On the False,"[27] because a reason which is false in itself is false with respect to everything; no reason, therefore, is true of anything, unless it is true in itself. Therefore, if we are to know that anything is true of any reason, or that it is

25 Cf. Aristotle, *Anal. post.*, I, 24 (85^{b}23–27; 86^{a}14–30).
26 Cf. Scotus, *Op. Oxon.*, I, d. 3, p. 1, qq. 1, 2; d. 8, p. 1, q. 3.
27 Cf. Aristotle, *Metaph.*, IV, 29 (1024^{b}31–32).

true of anything, we must know that it is true in itself; but a reason is not true in itself unless the parts of that reason are united. And just as it is necessary to know, with respect to quidditative predications,[28] that the parts of the nature can be quidditatively united, for example, that one contains the other formally, so, with respect to the truth of a proposition that affirms being, it is necessary to know that the parts of the nature of subject or predicate are actually united. For example, just as the statement, "An irrational man is an animal," is not known per se, speaking of quidditative predication, because the subject includes falsehood in itself, that is, a proposition including contradictories in itself, so the statement, "A man is white," is not known per se, if it is not known per se that "man" and "white" are joined per se in act. For if they are not conjoined in actual existence, it is true that "Nothing is a white man," and consequently the converse is true, namely, "No man is white"; the contradictory, therefore—"A man is white"—is false.

The minor is proved thus. Whatever concept we conceive, either of the good or of the true, if it is not contracted by any thing[29] so that it is not an absolutely simple concept, it is not a concept proper to God. Now I call a concept absolutely simple, when it cannot be resolved into other simple concepts, any one of which can be distinctly known by a simple act.

From this last reason,[30] the anwer is obvious if it is argued that "this is known per se, it is necessary for it to exist"—the argument being that the opposite of the predicate is incompatible with the subject, for if it does not exist, it is not "necessary for it to exist"—or that "this also is known per se, God exists." According to every explanation which the Damascene puts forward in chapter 9, the term "God" is derived from actual operation, namely, from upholding or burning or seeing;[31] according to every acceptation, therefore, "God exists" is the same as "One who operates in act exists," since as before the opposite of the predicate is incompatible with the subject.

Thus I reply to these arguments in another way, that neither of those propositions—"It is necessary for it to exist," or "One

---

[28] I.e., abstracting from actual existence, and having to do with the consistency of essences.
[29] I.e., limited by an essence.
[30] I.e., the argument above.
[31] Cf. John Damascene, *op cit.*, I, 9 (*PG*, 94, 835–838).

who operates in act exists"—is known per se since it is not known per se that the parts which are in the subject are actually united. If it is said that "the opposite of the predicate is incompatible with the subject," I say that it does not follow from this that a proposition is known per se unless the incompatibility is evident, and it is also evident that both extremes have an absolutely simple concept, or that the concepts of the parts are absolutely united.

III

As for the main argument taken from the Damascene, this can be explained with reference to cognitive power given to us by nature, by which we can known from creatures that God exists, at least in general terms—he adds there how God is known from creatures[32]—or with reference to the knowledge of God under aspects common to him and to the creature, which we know are more perfectly and eminently in God than in others. But it is evident that he is not speaking of actual and distinct knowledge of God, from what he says there: "No one knows him except in so far as he himself gives revelation."[33]

To the second argument, I say that Anselm does not state that this proposition is known per se. This is evident, because it cannot be inferred from his deduction that this proposition is true, save by two syllogisms at least. The first will be this: "An existent[34] is greater than any nonexistent; nothing is greater than the highest; therefore the highest is not nonexistent" (from indirect propositions in the second mood of the second figure[35]). The other syllogism is this: "What is not a non-existent is an existent; the highest is not nonexistent; therefore, etc." But the force of this reasoning will be discussed in the sixth argument of the following question, when I deal with the demonstration of infinity.[36]

To the proof of the major—I say that the major is false when it is taken to mean, "It is known per se that this exists," but that the major is true, yet not known per se—when this is proved by the fact that "the opposite of the predicate is incompatible with the subject," I reply that it is not evident

---

[32] Cf. *ibid.*, I, 3 (col. 795–798).
[33] Cf. *ibid.* (col. 790).
[34] *Ens.*
[35] On the figures and moods of the syllogism, cf. J. Maritain, *Introduction to Logic* (Sheed and Ward, London, 1937), 185 ff.
[36] Cf. Scotus, *Ordin.*, II., 208 f.

per se that the opposite of the predicate is incompatible with the subject, nor is it evident per se that the subject has an absolutely simple concept, or that its parts are united in effect; but both these are required if a proposition is to be known per se.

To the third argument, I reply that it does not follow from the statement, "It is known per se that truth in general exists," that "God exists"; rather, this is a fallacy of the consequent;[37] otherwise, the major can be denied. When it is argued that, "If there is no truth, it is true that there is no truth," the consequence does not hold, because truth is taken either for the basis of truth in the thing, or for truth in the intellectual act of composition and division,[38] but if there is no truth, it is not true that there is no truth, either by the truth of the thing, since there is no thing, or by truth in the intellect which combines and divides, since there is no intellect. Nevertheless, it follows correctly that "if there is no truth, it is not true that there is any truth," but it does not follow further that "it is true that there is not any truth"; this is a fallacy of the consequent, from the negative which has two causes of truth to the affirmative which is one of them.

To the last argument, I reply that propositions are not said to be known per se because the extremes have a greater necessity in themselves, or a greater necessity in the thing outside the intellect, but because the extremes, as extremes of such a proposition, make it plain that the conclusion is in conformity with the natures and conditions of the terms—and this whatever sort of being the terms have, whether in the thing or in the intellect; for the evidence of this conformity is evidence of truth in the proposition, and this is for the proposition to be known per se. But now the proposition, "Every whole is greater than its part," or something like it, naturally derives such evidence from the terms, in any intellect conceiving the terms, since it is evident from the terms that this conclusion is in conformity with the condition and natures of the terms, whatever kind of being the terms have. Thus, although the necessity of the terms is less, it does not follow that the evidence of the propositions is less.

[37] Cf. Aristotle, *De sophist. elench.*, I, 5 (167ᵇ1–13).
[38] I.e., in the judgment rather than the term or concept.

William Ockham: An Excerpt from Eight Questions on the Power of the Pope

THE TEXT

QUESTION II: THE ORIGIN OF THE SUPREME CIVIL POWER

CHAPTER I

IN THE SECOND PLACE, THE QUESTION IS RAISED whether the supreme lay power derives the character strictly proper to it[1] immediately from God. On this question there are two contrary opinions. According to one, the supreme lay power does not derive the power strictly proper to it immediately from God, because it derives it from God through the mediation of papal power. For the pope possesses the fullness of power in temporal and spiritual matters alike, and therefore no one possesses any power save from him. The things alleged above [in Question I, Chapter II] can be put forward in support of this opinion, and other reasons can also be offered. For it seems to some that, even though the pope did not have the fullness of power of this sort in temporal matters, it should still be said that the imperium[2] comes from him. From this it can be concluded that the supreme lay power —namely, the imperial power—derives the power proper to it from the pope, and not immediately from God, since it derives the power proper to it from him from whom it receives the imperium.

It remains to be proved, then, that the imperium comes from the pope, and this can be demonstrated in many ways. For the imperium comes from him to whom the keys of heavenly and earthly imperium were given; but the keys of heavenly and earthly imperium were given to Peter,[3] and consequently to

---

[1] *Proprietatem sibi proprie propriam*; this formula underlines the distinctive character of the status or power referred to (cf. *Opera politica*, I, 74).
[2] There is no common English equivalent for this term, whose shades of meaning include "empire," "imperial authority," "dominion," etc.
[3] Cf. Matt. 16:19.

his successors (distinction twenty-two, chapter one[4]), and therefore imperium comes from the pope. To state the point more fully, imperium comes from him who, by the ordinance of God (in whose power imperium most perfectly lies), is the first head and supreme judge of all mortals. Now by God's ordinance the pope, and not the emperor, is the first head and the judge of all mortals; the imperium, therefore, comes from the pope. Again, the imperium is derived from him who can depose the emperor; but the pope can depose the emperor (XV, question six, chapter *Alius,*[5]) and therefore the imperium comes from the pope. Again, the imperium comes from him who can transfer the imperium from one nation to another; but the pope can do this (Extra, *de electione, Venerabilem,*[6]) and therefore the imperium is derived from the pope. Again, the imperium comes from him by whom the emperor, once elected, is examined, anointed,[7] consecrated, and crowned. Now the emperor is examined, anointed, consecrated, and crowned by the pope (Extra, *de electione, Venerabilem*); therefore, the imperium comes from the pope. Again, the imperium comes from him to whom the emperor takes an oath like a vassal; but the emperor executes an oath of fidelity and subjection to the pope, like a vassal of the latter (distinction sixty-three, *Tibi Domine,*[8]) and therefore the imperium comes from the pope. Again, the imperium comes from him who holds both swords,[9] that is, the material and the spiritual. Now the pope possesses both swords, and therefore the imperium is derived from the pope. This seems to be Innocent IV's meaning when in a certain decretal he asserts that "the two swords of both administrations are held

---

[4] Gratian, *Decretum,* p. 1, d. 22, c. 1 (*Corpus iur. canon.,* ed. Friedberg, I, 73).

[5] *Ibid.,* p. 2, causa 15, q. 6, c. 3 (Friedberg, I, 756).

[6] *Decretal. Greg. IX,* lib. 1, tit. 6, c. 34 (Friedberg, II, 80). The Latin tags refer to "title" and "chapter" respectively.

[7] Despite the absence of MS. evidence (at least according to Sikes's critical apparatus), I have read *inungitur* rather than *iniungitur.* The sequence, "anointed, consecrated, crowned," appears in at least two other places in this work (*ed. cit.,* I, 157; 166); moreover, the argument as developed (cf. pp. 91 f.) is obviously based on the traditional coronation ritual, and refers explicitly and exclusively to these three acts. Cf. also q. 5, c. 1 (p. 157). The only significant reference to something as "enjoined" is in a quite different context (p. 98). (I am indebted to the Rev. Dr. J. J. Ryan, of the Pontifical Institute of Mediaeval Studies, for his guidance on this point.)

[8] Gratian, *Decretum,* p. 1, d. 63, c. 33 (Friedberg, I, 246).

[9] Cf. Luke 22:38.

concealed in the bosom of the faithful Church"[10]; for this reason, if anyone is not within that Church, he possesses neither. "Thus," he goes on, "both rights are believed to belong to Peter, since the Lord did not say to him, with reference to the material sword, 'Cast away,' but rather, 'Put up again thy sword into thy scabbard,'[11] meaning, 'Do not employ it by thyself.'" Here he significantly expresses the name of the second, because this power of the material sword is implicit with the Church, but is made explicit by the emperor who receives it.

Again, the imperium is derived from him to whom the emperor stands in the relation of a son to his father, of a disciple to his master, of lead to gold, of the moon to the sun.[12] Now the emperor stands in these relations to the pope (distinction ninety-six, *Si imperator*, and chapter *Quis dubitet*, and chapter *Duo sunt*[13]; Extra, *de maioritate et obedientia, Solitae*[14]); the imperium, therefore, comes from the pope. Again, the imperium is derived from him to whom the emperor is obliged to bow his head; but the emperor is bound to bow his head to the pope (distinction sixty-three, *Valentinianus*; distinction ninety-six, *Numquam*,[15]) and therefore the imperium comes from the pope. Again, the imperium comes from him by whom, on his own authority and not by the ordinance of the emperor or of some other man, it ought to be ruled during a vacancy; but the pope does this when the imperium is vacant, and therefore the imperium is derived from the pope.

[Chapters II, III have to do with different forms of the papal theory, Chapters IV to VI with different arguments for the imperial position.]

CHAPTER VII

Now that the above opinions have been considered,[16] a reply should be made in accordance with them to the arguments

---

10 Cf. E. A. Winkelmann, *Acta imperii inedita saeculi XIII et XIV* (Innsbruck, 1880–1885), II, 698; Augustine, *C. Faust.*, XXII, 77 (*PL*, 42, 450).

11 Matt. 26:52 and John 18:11, conflated.

12 Cf. Bartholomew of Lucca, *Determinatio compendiosa de iurisdictione imperii* (Hanover, 1909), 8.

13 Gratian, *Decretum*, p. 1, d. 96, c. 11; c. 9 (Friedberg, I, 340).

14 *Decretal. Greg. IX*, lib. 1, tit. 33, c. 6 (Friedberg, II, 196).

15 Gratian, *Decretum*, p. 1, d. 63, c. 3; d. 96, c. 12 (Friedberg, I, 235; 341). The bowing of the head here seems to be merely a symbol for submission to authority.

16 I.e., the "imperialist" arguments.

alleged on the other side, and first to the points put forward above (in Chapter I) against the view last stated. In answer to these, it is said that the imperium does not come from the pope, since after Christ's advent the imperium was derived from the same person as before; but before Christ's advent the imperium was not derived from the pope (as was alleged above), and therefore it has never afterward come from the pope.

But in reply to the first argument to the contrary, to the effect that, according to Pope Nicholas, Christ gave or committed to blessed Peter the rights of heavenly and earthly imperium together, it is said that Pope Nicholas' words are really to be expounded against the interpretation which at first glance appears to be proper, lest they seem to savor of heresy. The same holds for certain other things said by the same pope in the same chapter—for instance, when he says, "He alone established and founded and erected that Church," namely, the Roman, "on the rock of the faith just springing up," and when he says, "The Roman Church instituted all primates, whether the supreme dignity of any patriarch or the primacies of metropolitan sees, or the chairs of episcopates, or, for that matter, the dignity of churches of any order."[17] Unless these words are somewhat discreetly interpreted, they seem to be contrary to the divine Scriptures and the writings of the holy Fathers, because Christ did not found the Roman Church upon the rock of the faith just springing up, since the Roman Church was not founded at the beginning of the faith, nor did it found all the other Churches. For many churches were founded before the Roman Church, and many were raised up to ecclesiastical dignities even before the foundation of the Roman Church, for before the Roman Church existed blessed Matthias was elected to the dignity of apostleship (Acts, ch. 1[18]). Seven deacons also were chosen by the apostles before the Roman Church began (Acts, ch. 8[19]); also, before the Roman Church existed they "had peace throughout all Judea, and Galilee, and Samaria" (Acts, ch. 9[20]). Before the Roman Church existed blessed Paul and Barnabas were raised to the apostolic dignity by God's command (Acts, ch. 13[21]); before the Roman Church had the power of appointing prelates, Paul and

---

[17] Gratian, *Decretum*, p. 1, d. 22, c. 1 (Friedberg, 1, 73). The text is really derived from Peter Damiani, *Disceptatio synodalis* (*MGH, Libelli de lite*, I, 78).
[18] Cf. Acts 1:15–26.   [19] Cf. Acts 6:1–6.
[20] Cf. Acts 9:31.   [21] Cf. Acts 13:1–3.

Barnabas appointed presbyters throughout the several churches (Acts, ch. 14[22]). Before the Roman Church had any authority, the apostles and elders[23] held a general council (Acts, ch. 15[24]); also, before the Roman Church had the power of instituting prelates, blessed Paul said to the elders[25] whom he had called from Ephesus (as we are told in Acts, ch. 20[26]): "Take heed to yourselves, and to the whole flock, wherein the Holy Ghost hath placed you bishops, to rule the church of God." Before the Roman Church held the primacy, the churches of Antioch were so multiplied that the disciples of Christ were first called Christians there (Acts, ch. 11[27]); for this reason also blessed Peter had his see there before Rome (XXIV, question one, chapter *Rogamus*[28]), and thus he instituted churches and ecclesiastical dignities in the Antiochene church before he did so in the Roman. It is necessary, then, to attach a sound interpretation to the words of Pope Nicholas given above, lest they openly contradict the divine Scriptures. And, likewise, his other statements that follow, concerning the rights of heavenly and earthly imperium alike committed to blessed Peter, must be soundly expounded, lest they seem to savor of manifest heresy. For if they are construed as they sound at first hearing, two errors follow from them.

According to the first error, heavenly imperium comes from the pope, because Pope Nicholas says that Christ committed the rights of heavenly as well as earthly imperium to Peter. But it is certain that heavenly imperium does not come from the pope, particularly in the way in which some say, on account of that authoritative statement of Pope Nicholas, that earthly imperium is derived from the pope—namely, so that he who possesses the earthly imperium holds it as a fief from the pope—since it would be heretical to say that anyone held the heavenly imperium from the pope as a fief. Nor does the heavenly imperium come from the pope as its lord, as they claim that the earthly imperium comes from the pope as its lord, since the pope is merely in some sense the key bearer of the heavenly imperium, and in no sense its lord.

The second error which follows from Nicholas' words,

---

[22] Cf. Acts 14:22.
[23] *Seniores.*
[24] Cf. Acts 15:6 ff.
[25] *Maioribus natu.*
[26] Cf. Acts 20:17, 28.
[27] Cf. Acts 11:26.
[28] Gratian, *Decretum*, p. 2, causa 24, q. 1, c. 15 (Friedberg, I, 970). The Roman rite has a liturgical commemoration of the *cathedra* of St. Peter at Antioch (Feb. 22).

understood as certain people understand them, is to the effect that all kingdoms are derived from the pope. It is recognized that this principle works to the disadvantage of all kings who do not pay homage to the pope for their kingdoms. For the king of France seems to err dangerously in faith when he makes no acknowledgment of a superior in temporal affairs (Extra, *Qui filii sint legitimi, Per venerabilem*[29]).

These[30] say, then, that the aforesaid words of Nicholas are to be interpreted in another way than their sound suggests. Thus they say that, just as according to Gregory, in the homily for the Common of virgins[31], the "kingdom of heaven" must sometimes be understood to refer to the Church Militant, so also the "heavenly imperium" can be understood to refer to the spiritually good in the Church Militant. Therefore, the spiritually evil in the Church can also be designated by the term, "earthly imperium," and the aforesaid words of Nicholas should be interpreted as meaning that Christ committed to blessed Peter some power over the good and over the evil in the Church. Or else, some say that by the "heavenly imperium" Pope Nicholas understands the "spirituals,"[32] whose "conversation is in heaven,"[33] and by the "earthly imperium" the "seculars," wrapped up in earthly business, and that he means that the pope has power over both.

Or else it is said that Christ committed to Peter the rights of heavenly imperium, in so far as in spiritual things he has power over wayfarers predestined to the heavenly imperium, and that he also committed to him the rights of earthly imperium, in so far as he made him superior in spiritual things to the earthly emperor, whom on occasion he can even coerce. Yet just as no one holds the heavenly imperium from the pope in fief, so also no one holds the earthly imperium in fief from him.

[Chapters VIII to XV continue the detailed reply to the assertions made in Chapter I. Chapter XVI provides a reply from the papal standpoint to the objection raised in the first paragraph of Chapter VII.]

---

[29] *Decretal. Greg. IX*, lib. 4, tit. 17, c. 13 (Friedberg, II, 714 ff.).
[30] I.e., the critics of the "papalist" view.
[31] Cf. Gregory the Great, *Homil. in evang.*, XII, 1 (*PL*, 76, 1119). Patristic passages are included in the lections of the Night Office of the Breviary ("Matins"); hence Ockham's method of citation.
[32] Ockham's language here calls to mind his polemic in defense of the Franciscan "spirituals"; cf. P. Böhner, *The Tractatus de Successivis*, 6–9.
[33] Phil. 3:20.

INDEXES

GENERAL INDEX

Abailard, Peter, 18n, 80n, 99n, 219, 222, 224 f., 227, 234 f., 281n, 295n, 299n, 303n, 311n, 328n, 332n, 335n, 336n, 337n, 338n, 341n, 342n, 357n; theological method, 223; on Anselm of Laon, 223n; Christology of, 230 f., 288; on the atonement, 280 ff.; on the sacraments, 285 ff.; ethics of, 232, 289 ff.; on the law, 276 ff., 284 ff.; on sin, 291 ff.; on original sin, 58, 292; on justification, 278 ff., 284 ff.

Abel, 184, 358

Abbot, George, archbishop, 374n

Abraham, 195, 280, 285, 294, 341 ff.

Acolytes, 349

Adam, 106, 130 f., 152 f., 166, 168, 183, 184 ff., 192 ff., 198 f., 269, 272 f., 282, 292, 310 ff., 333, 342, 353, 403

Adam of St. Victor, 18n, 226, 235

Agag, 252

Albert the Great, 58 f., 227, 365 f.

Alexander III, Pope, 223, 334n

Alexander of Hales, 367

Ambrose, 104n, 106n, 109n, 195n, 381; Christology, 337; eucharistic doctrine, 48; and Theodosius the Great, 254

Ambrosiaster, 80n, 85n, 106n, 109n, 118n, 267n, 268n, 269n, 270n, 272n

Ancilla theologiae, philosophy as, 30, 48

Andrew of St. Victor, 226

Angels, 90, 106, 125 ff., 157, 182

Anglicanism, 231, 232n

Anselm of Canterbury, 13, 18n, 19, 24, 28, 31, 62 ff., 77n, 89n, 98n, 100n, 102n, 149n, 166n, 176n, 219, 224 f., 230 f., 242n, 280n, 303n,

304n, 308n, 326n, 327n, 329n, 365, 372, 386n, 422, 428, 435; on faith and reason, 47 ff., 73, 75, 97 ff., 101 ff., 183, 226, 413; as philosopher, 49 ff.; as theologian, 53 f.; on divine illumination, 52, 83 f., 368n, 382; on God's existence, 49 ff., 69 ff., 94 ff., 435; on the atonement, 54 ff., 100 ff.; on original sin, 58 f., 184 ff., 229 f.; Marian piety, 59 ff., 201 ff.; as ecclesiastical reformer, 48, 61, 208 ff., 211 f., 221; on education, 213 ff.

Anselm of Laon, 18n, 98n, 223 f., 234, 268n, 355n; on original sin, 58, 261 f.; and the *Glossa,* 223 f., 234, 267 ff., 355n; school of, on original sin, 263 ff.

Antioch, 441

Aosta, 62

Apostles, 129, 345, 350

Aquinas, Thomas, 13, 27n, 32, 77n, 80n, 149n, 155n, 219, 228, 231 f., 242n, 267n, 316n, 319n, 327n, 329n, 353n, 360n, 363, 398n, 407n, 420n, 422n; on faith and knowledge, 410n, 419n; on theology, 421n; on heresy, 425n; on the supernatural, 426n; relation to Aristotle and Augustine, 29 f., 365 f., 369 ff; Thomism, 228, 370, 372

Arabs, Arabian. See Islam

Aristotle, 30, 47, 175n, 219, 228, 247n, 257, 259, 290, 295, 382 f., 384, 386n, 388 ff., 391n, 392n, 396 f., 399n, 400 f., 404 f., 406n, 407n, 408 f., 410 f., 419n, 420n, 427n, 428 ff., 432n, 433n, 436n; role in medieval thought, 27ff., 363 ff., 370 ff.

Arts, liberal, 26, 226

"Athanasian Creed." See *Quicumque vult*
Athenians, 255 f.
Atonement. See Redemption
Attila, 249
Atto of Vercelli, 267n, 272n, 275n
Auctoritates, 103, 132, 222, 328, 379, 420 f.
Augustine of Hippo, 35, 37, 73n, 77n, 80n, 81n, 88n, 93n, 101n, 104n, 106n, 107n, 108n, 109n, 115n, 117n, 121n, 124n, 125n, 126n, 127n, 128n, 130n, 134n, 150n, 151n, 154n, 159n, 165n, 166n, 182n, 185n, 195n, 219, 252, 257n, 296n, 299n, 300n, 302n, 303n, 306n, 307n, 308n, 309n, 310n, 311n, 312n, 313n, 314n, 315n, 316n, 317n, 318n, 320n, 338n, 339, 343n, 359n, 363, 382n, 383, 384n, 385, 386n, 391, 393, 395, 397, 405 f., 418, 419n, 420, 422 f., 426, 428n, 439n; role in medieval thought, 29 ff., 58 f., 225 f., 229 f., 365, 366 ff.; on Platonic philosophy, 392; on Greek philosophy and the Bible, 424n; on faith and reason, 402 ff., 407 ff., 410 ff.; on reason, lower and higher, 316n; on divine illumination, 52, 368, 379 ff., 387 f., 400 f.; on natural law, 232; on the Mosaic law, 276 f., 339, 341; on ecclesiastical discipline, 239; on original sin, 58 f., 85n, 158n, 263 ff., 352, 354; Christology, 336 f.; sacraments, 347; eucharistic theology, 48
Aureolus, Peter, 373
Averroes, 364, 392n; Averroism, 29 f., 364 ff., 370
Avicebron, 364n
Avicenna, 364n
Azo, 250n

Babylon, 299
Bacon, Roger, 367
Balaam, 329
Balbus, Caecilius, 257n, 259n
Baptism, 188, 202, 238n, 263, 285 ff., 341 ff., 348, 352 ff., 357 f.; and confirmation, 231, 346 f.; for the dead, 270; fate of unbaptized children, 294, 344
Barbarossa, Frederick, 223
Barnabas, 440 f.
Bartholomew of Bologna, 371
Bartholomew of Lucca, 439n
Beatitude, 90 ff., 100, 112, 118, 142 f., 145 ff., 298, 332 f., 390 f.
Bec, 18, 62, 69n, 102n, 121
Becket, Thomas, 222 f.
Bede, 341, 344, 406n

Benedict, Benedictines, 35, 149n, 213n
Bérenger of Tours, 40, 47 f., 231
Bernard of Chartres, 21n, 248n
Bernard of Clairvaux, 35, 50, 60, 253n
Bethsaida, 296
Bible, 50, 97, 132, 181, 183, 244, 271, 329, 393, 440; medieval exegesis of, 40, 47, 229, 321 f.; role in medieval theology, 98n, 227; chapter and verse divisions, 228 f.; "according to the Scriptures," 267
Boethius, 27n, 73n, 88n, 143n, 159n, 175n, 334n, 385n, 395n
Bonaventure, 18n, 227, 316n, 363, 375 f., 382n, 385n, 387n, 393n, 394n, 400n, 404n, 406n, 407n, 408n, 410n, 414n, 418n, 421n, 422n, 423n, 425n, 427n; Augustinianism of, 29, 31, 367 ff.; doctrine of illumination, 379 ff.; of original sin, 59
Boniface VIII, Pope, 25, 35
Book of Common Prayer, 251n, 360n
Boso, 102n
Bossuet, J. B., 17
Bradwardine, Thomas, archbishop, 373, 374n
Bruno (Pseudo-) the Carthusian, 268n, 271n, 273n, 274n
Bruno of Segni, 48
Burchard of Worms, 221
Burgundio of Pisa, 227
Burgundy, 62, 209
Byzantium, 364

Caen, 62
Caesar, Julius, 257
Cain, 358
Cajetan (Thomas de Vio Caietanus), 19
Calixtus II, Pope, 209
Calvin, John, 17 f., 374
Canon law, canonists, 20, 25, 36, 220 ff., 232 f.
Canterbury, 62, 209
Capreolus, John, 228n
Cassiodorus, 253n, 267n
Celibacy, 178, 240 f.
Chalcedon, Council of, 151n
Character, sacramental, 347n
Charity, 91 f., 239, 273, 278, 330 f.
Chartres, 18, 26, 222, 233
Chaucer, Geoffrey, 373n
Chorazin, 296
Christology. See Incarnation
Chrysippus, 250, 257
Church, 220 f., 253, 439 ff.; Western, 23 ff.; local, 212n
Cicero, 248n, 259n
Circumcision, 263, 276, 285, 341 ff.

Claudian, 260
Clement of Alexandria, 30n, 424n
Cleopatra, 257
Codex iuris canonici, 222n
Codrus, 255 f.
Colet, John, 80n
Conciliarism, 22
Concupiscence, 58 f., 188, 229 f., 300, 311, 317 f., 319 f., 343, 345, 352 ff.
Confirmation, 231, 344 ff., 360n
Constantine I, Emperor, 253
Conversatio, 149n
Cornelius, 285, 295 f.
Corpus iuris canonici, 222n, 233
Corpus iuris civilis, 250n, 251n, 254n
Counter-Reformation, 374
Cranmer, Thomas, archbishop, 209n
Creation, 20, 31 f., 54, 131, 145, 168, 203, 232, 261; *ex nihilo*, 75 f., 137; purpose of, 148 ff.; days of, 127; creationism, 261n
Crispin, Gilbert, 55n, 106n

Damiani, Peter, 30n, 48, 440n
Dante, 37
"Dark Ages," 22 f., 220 f.
David, 192, 195, 252, 254, 264, 286
Deacons, 349 ff.
Decii, 257
Demosthenes, 250
Denys the Carthusian, 80n
Descartes, René, 18, 53
Deuteronomy, 258
Devil, 104 ff., 126, 128, 135, 140, 155, 182, 292, 302 ff., 310; "devil's rights," 107 ff., 181, 280 ff., 303, 305
Dialectic, dialecticians, 26, 28, 48, 98 f., 224 f.
Diognetus, Epistle to, 104n
Dionysius the Elder, 259
Dionysius (Pseudo-) the Areopagite, 256n, 388, 396
Discipline, ecclesiastical, 239 ff.
Discretion, years of, 263
Dives, 280
Dominicans, 24, 35, 370
Doorkeepers, 349
Dorians, 255 f.
Dualism, 262n
Durandus of Saint-Pourçain, 373

Eadmer, 60, 61n, 62n, 63, 100n; on Anselm's ecclesiastical policy, 211 f.; on Anselm's character, 213 ff.
Education, medieval, 25 ff., 39, 220, 363; of schoolboys, 213 ff.
"Enlightenment," 224

Episcopacy, episcopate, 24n, 212n, 231 f., 350 f.
Eternity, divine, 82, 85 ff.; eternal life, 54
Ethics, 232
Euclid, 431n
Eusebius of Caesarea, 424n
Eustachius of Arras, 370
Evil, 190 f.
Exorcists, 349
Ezekiel, 322 f.

Faith, 100, 102, 137 f., 168n, 238n, 278, 301; faith and reason, Anselm's view of, 49, 53 f., 97 ff.; Richard of St. Victor's view, 324 ff.; the thirteenth century Augustinians, 365, 369; Matthew of Aquasparta, 402 ff.; Ockham, 373
Fall, 59, 71 f., 104 f., 135, 140, 185 f., 194, 269, 300, 353
Fasting, 136, 241
Fathers of the Church, 55 f., 59, 159n, 224, 440; Biblical exegesis of, 321 f.; Greek, 363n; Latin, 23, 56, 222
Feudalism, 20, 56n
Flambard, Ralph, 210
Florilegia, 26
Forgiveness, 120 f., 143 f., 202, 281 f.
France, 209
Franciscans, 24, 35, 61, 365, 375 ff.; Augustinianism of, 29, 366 ff., 372 f.; "spirituals," 442n
Fulgentius of Ruspe, 56n, 307n, 336n

Gallicanism, 22
Gaunilo, 94 ff.
Gentiles, 129, 183, 256 f., 276, 278, 296, 312, 325
Gerard of York, archbishop, 210
Gerhard, J., 18
Gilbert of La Porrée, 27n
Giles of Rome, 370
Glossa ordinaria, 223 f., 234, 335n, 342n, 348n, 355, 356n, 357n, 382
God; existence of, 50 ff., 69, 73 ff., 88, 94 ff., 371 f., 428 ff.; nature of, 20, 31 f., 75 ff., 82 ff., 99; sovereignty of, 18n, 374; impassibility of, 77 f., 110; justice of, 78 ff., 107 ff., 122, 141 ff., 157 f., 181 f., 250 f., 277 ff., 300, 304 f., 308 f., 381; love of, 57, 77 ff., 81, 91, 104, 107, 181 f., 262, 278 f., 283 f., 304, 330 f.; Trinity, 31, 48, 51, 88 f., 93, 99, 154 f., 179, 183, 220, 222, 229, 299, 306, 327 ff., 334
Gog and Magog, 312
Gospel, 243, 267

Grace, 31, 59, 102, 149 f., 197, 203, 220, 232, 278 f., 283 f., 298, 300, 369, 387, 394 f.; time of, 302 f., 311 ff.

Gratian, 221 f., 227, 231, 233, 243n, 253n, 254n, 341n, 342n, 345n, 346n, 347n, 349n, 350n, 351n, 438 f., 440n, 441n; on divine and human law, 243 ff.

Greek philosophy, 19 f., 27 ff., 220, 363 ff., 392, 424n

Gregory I, Pope, 35, 98n, 109n, 125n, 132n, 166n, 253n, 256n, 294, 307n, 381, 388, 396, 402, 407n, 421n, 442; on the atonement, 56n; on baptism and circumcision, 342; on Ezekiel's vision, 322

Gregory VII, Pope, 24, 35, 209n, 221; Gregorian reform, 48, 61, 221

Gregory IX, Pope, *Decretals* of, 438 f., 442n

Gregory of Rimini, 373

Guibert of Nogent, 223n

Ham, 254

Haymo of Auxerre, 268n, 269n

Haymo of Halberstadt, 268n

Heaven, 90 ff., 106, 127 ff., 133 f., 141, 298 f., 301 f., 332 f.

Hegel, G. W. F., 53

Hell, 107, 148, 198, 203, 301 f., 305

Hellenism, 19 f., 363, 366

Heloise, 224, 235

Henry I, King, 61, 208, 210 ff.

Henry II, King, 223

Henry of Ghent, 371, 429n

Herbert of Thetford, bishop, 210n

Herluin, 62

Hervaeus of Bourg-Dieu, 267n, 268n, 269n, 270n, 272n, 273n, 274n, 275n

Hilary of Poitiers, 56n, 109n, 337

Hildebrand. See Gregory VII

Hispana, 221

Hooker, Richard, 17 f.

Hosea, 267, 275

Hugh of Lyons, archbishop, 70, 221n

Hugh of St. Cher, 80n

Hugh of St. Victor, 18n, 222, 225 ff., 230n, 235 f., 285n, 310n, 326n, 338n, 340, 345n, 346n, 347n, 349n; on the atonement, 230 f., 303 ff., 307 ff.; on the sacraments, 310 ff.; on marriage, 313 ff.; on justice, 300, 308 f.; on judgment, 306 f.; on faith and reason, 402 f., 406 f., 419

Hugh (Pseudo-) of St. Victor, 274n

Huns, 249

Ignatius of Antioch, 130n

Ignorance, defect of fallen nature, 162, 185 f., 300, 395; and moral responsibility, 291 ff., 355; not attributable to Christ, 114, 162 f.

Illumination, 52, 83 f., 368 f., 379 ff.

Image of God, 73, 146 f., 315, 394 f., 426

Immortality, 130, 147 f., 158 f., 309

Imperium, 437 ff.; imperialism, 22

Incarnation, 99, 100 ff., 104, 110, 118, 151 ff., 162 f., 166 f., 174, 176, 179, 193, 202 ff., 220, 222, 230, 288, 304 f., 307, 311, 334 ff.

Innocent III, Pope, 25, 37

Innocent IV, Pope, 438 f.

Inquisition, 36

Intellect, active, 389; potential, 389

Intention, moral, 289 ff., 355 ff.

Investitures, 61n, 208, 210 ff., 221

Irenaeus, 104n, 108n, 148n

Isaac Stella, 382

Isidore of Seville, 221, 232, 243 ff., 248n, 328n, 351n

Islam, 26 ff., 364; Islamic philosophy, 28, 42, 220, 364 ff.

Ivo of Chartres, 18n, 221 f., 227, 233, 341n, 342n, 345n, 346n, 347n; as systematic canonist, 238; on ecclesiastical discipline, 239 ff.; on clerical celibacy, 240 f.

Januarius, 346

Jeremiah, 285

Jerome, 98n, 232n, 257n, 340; Christology, 336; on penance, 348; on the general resurrection, 274

Jerusalem, heavenly, 298 f.

Jesuits, 232n

Jews, 112, 129, 183, 256 f., 292 f., 325; and the Mosaic law, 276 ff., 284 f., 287, 312; and circumcision, 342 f.; doctrine of resurrection, 274; medieval Jewish philosophy, 42, 364

Job, 192, 272

John, apostle and evangelist, 291, 408

John the Baptist, 177, 285, 348

John of Damascus, 227, 230, 405, 422, 428, 434 f.

John of La Rochelle, 80n, 367

John of Salisbury, 18n, 21n, 222 f., 223n, 233 f., 248n, 259n; on philosophy, 247, 257; on law, 248 ff., 258 ff.; on tyranny, 248; on princes and the Church, 253 ff.

John Scotus Erigena, 127n, 382n, 388n

John, King, 37, 228

Judgment, divine, 306 f.

Justice, divine, 78 ff., 107 ff., 122, 141 ff., 157 f., 181 f., 250 f., 277 ff., 300, 304 f., 308 f., 381; angelic, 131; human, 119 f., 187 f., 191, 319 f., 384; original, 58 f., 185 f., 197, 199 f., 230; in Christ, 113, 160
Justification, 18n, 80n, 205, 278 ff., 308, 312
Justin Martyr, 104n, 424n
Justinian, Emperor, 250, 251n
Justinus, 255 f.

Kant, Immanuel, 18
Kilwardby, Robert, archbishop, 375

Laicism, 22
Lanfranc, archbishop, 48, 62, 80n, 221, 270n, 274
Langton, Stephen, archbishop, 18n, 209n, 228 f., 353n, 355n; on original sin, 58, 230, 352 ff.; on conditions of morality, 232, 355 ff.; as Biblical scholar, 229; as poet, 229, 359 f.
Laon, school of, 18, 223 f., 230n, 234, 261n, 355n
Lateran Council, Fourth, 231
Latin literature, classical, 23, 220, 222
Law, 188, 223, 243 ff., 248, 250 ff., 254; natural, 243 ff., 278, 295, 302, 311 f., 344; divine, 258 f.; Mosaic, 276 f., 302, 311 f., 339, 344; civil, 245; of nations, 245; military, 245; public, 245; Roman, 245 f.; canon, 25, 36, 220 ff., 233
Lazarus, 280
Lectio divina, 229
Lectors, 349
Legates, papal, 209n
Leibniz, G. W., 18, 53
Leo I, Pope, 107n, 108n, 109n, 110n, 151n, 154n, 165n, 168n, 174n
Leo IX, Pope, 24
Lictors, 252
Logic, 26 ff., 32, 363; logica nova, 28, 47; logica vetus, 27, 48
Lombard, Peter, 18n, 27, 58, 80n, 222 f., 226 ff., 236, 267n, 268n, 269n, 270n, 271n, 272n, 274n, 275n, 285n, 334n, 341n, 355n; Christology, 230 f., 334 ff.; sacraments, 231, 338 ff.; of the old law, 341 ff.; of the new law, 344 f.; marriage, 345; confirmation, 345 ff.; and baptism, 346 f.; penance, 231, 348; sacred orders, 231 f., 349 ff.
Lombardy, 62
Lupus of Troyes, 249n
Luther, Martin, 17 f., 80n, 228, 353n, 374
Lycurgus, 256

Magic, 238n
Maimonides, 364n
Manegold of Lautenbach, 48
Marcella, 274
Marriage, 178, 188, 238n, 241, 313 ff., 344 f.
Marston, Roger, 371
Mary, Virgin, 152 ff., 166, 169 ff., 174, 193 ff., 201 ff., 281, 333, 403; second Eve, 104; immaculate conception, 60, 67, 166n, 281n, 372; assumption, 60; medieval devotion, 59 ff., 67
Mary Magdalene, 279, 281
Mass, 114, 238n, 344; medieval eucharistic controversy, 47 f., 231; transubstantiation, 231, 406, 423
Matthew of Aquasparta, 18n, 316n, 367 ff., 376, 404n, 408n, 415n, 419n, 420n, 422n, 426n; on illumination, 369, 426; on faith and reason, 402 ff.
Matthias, 440
Medicine, physical, 239 f.; spiritual, 240
Melchizedek, 255
Metaphysics, 27 ff., 30 ff., 53, 225, 371
Microcosm, 248
Middle Ages, 21 f., 33, 219, 374
Miracles, 325
Missale Romanum, 90n, 105n, 166n, 359n
Monasticism, 20, 35, 149n, 213 ff., 254
Mortality, penalty for sin, 71, 147 f., 158 ff., 192 f., 294, 300
Moses, 188, 194, 199, 311
Mysticism, 36, 50

Natalicia of saints, 130
Naturalism, 19 f., 29, 363 ff.
Neo-Orthodoxy, 51
Neoplatonism, 28 f., 366 f.
Neo-Scholasticism, 51
Nestorianism, 230
Nicaea, First Council of, 253
Nicene Creed, 204n
Nicholas I, Pope, 254, 440 ff.
Nicholas of Lyra, 80n, 234, 335n
Nihilism, Christological, 230, 334
Nineveh, 294
Noah, 254
Nominalism, 18n, 42, 48, 99, 373 f.
Normandy, 211 f.

Ockham, William, 19, 227, 372 ff., 377 f., 442n; nominalism, 373 f.; voluntarism, 54; 373 f.; place in Franciscan tradition, 373; Pelagian tendencies, 373 f.; antipapal polemic, 374, 437 ff.
Odo of Tournai (or, of Cambrai), 58

Omnipotence, divine, 76 f., 91, 106 f., 111, 113, 172 ff.
Ontological argument, 18n, 52 f., 69 f., 74 f., 94 ff., 428, 435
Orders, holy, 231 f., 344, 347, 349 ff.; minor, 231, 349 ff.
Origen, 106n, 382
Orléans, 26
Otto of Freising, 310n
Oxford, 18, 367

Papacy, 23 ff., 36 f., 61, 238n, 374; eleventh century reforms, 48, 61, 208 ff., 221; papalism, 22, 232, 437 ff.
Papinian, 250
Paradise, 130, 135, 140, 301 f., 310, 312
Paris, 18, 26, 222, 227 f., 367
Paschal II, Pope, 61, 208 ff.
Paschasius Radvertus, 48
Paul, apostle, 98, 109, 113, 165, 188, 192, 194, 199, 241, 254, 261, 268, 270, 274 f., 276 ff., 280, 282, 284, 287, 290 ff., 295, 339, 374, 399, 405, 411, 418, 440 f.; preaching at Athens, 256 f.; Pauline Epistles, 220n; *Glossa* on, 224; Peter Lombard's commentary, 227
Paulinus of Nola, 254n
Pearson, John, 19
Pecham, John, archbishop, 368, 370, 375
Pelagius, 267n; Pelagianism, 158n, 264, 373 f.
Penance, 37, 231, 239, 319 f., 344, 348
Penitence. See Penance
Peter, apostle, 267, 295, 441 f.
Peter of Poitiers, 228
Petrus Cantor, 228
Petrus Comestor, 228
Philip the Fair, King, 37
Philo, 30n, 424n
Philosophy, 27 ff., 32, 41 ff.; Anselmian, 49 ff.; thirteenth century, 363 ff.; *philosophi*, 159n, 257, 259, 295, 410
Phinehas, 188
Pius IX, Pope, 60
Plato, 259, 369n, 381, 392, 407n; Platonism, 42, 392, 408
Plautus, 171n
Polycarp, 130n
Porphyry, 27n, 408
Praepositinus, 228
Presbyterianism, 232
Pride, 300
Priesthood, 253 f., 345 f., 349 ff.
Primasius (Pseudo-), 267n, 274n
Princes, 248 ff.
Protestantism, 22, 24 f., 58
Psalter, 224

Ptolemy of Lucca. See Bartholomew of Lucca
Punishment, 122 ff., 126, 292 ff., 300
Purgatory, 301 f.
Puritans, 232n

Quaestiones, 26, 98n, 223, 229
Quicumque vult, 110n, 292, 327 f.
Quintilian, 259n
Quirites, 245 f.

Rabanas Maurus, 268n, 272n, 275n, 346 f.
Radulphus of Laon, 223n, 268n
Ratio. See Reason
Ratramnus, 48
Reason, 103, 110, 118, 138, 183; and faith, 49, 53 f., 97 ff., 132, 324 ff., 365, 369, 373, 402 ff.; and law, 244, 374; rationalism, 48, 54, 231; *ratio superior, inferior*, 316, 385, 394; *rationes aeternae*, 379 ff., 412n, 414n; *rationes seminales*, 368
Redemption, 20, 31, 232, 256 f.; Anselm on, 55 ff., 66, 100 ff., 231; Abailard on, 231, 280 ff.; Hugh of St. Victor on, 307 ff.
Reformation, 19, 231, 374
Regino of Prüm, 221
Regio dissimilitudinis, 320
Renaissance, twelfth century, 219 f., 363
Renaissance, fifteenth century, 19, 26, 374
Resurrection, 147 f., 257, 267 ff.
Richard of Mediavilla. See Richard of Middleton
Richard of Middleton, 371
Richard of St. Victor, 18n, 21n, 225 f., 235 f., 256n, 321n, 322n; in faith and reason, 226, 324 ff., 411 ff., 417 f., 425; on the Trinity, 229, 327 ff., 417 f.; on Biblical exegesis, 226, 321 ff.; on the Christian warfare, 319 f.
Robert, Count, 211
Robert of Chester, bishop, 210n
Robert of Melun, 27n, 58, 99n
Roman Church, 23 ff., 221, 231, 440 f.; culture, 23, 25, 220; law, 43, 222, 245 f., 250, 251n, 254n
Roscellinus, 47f.
Rufinus, 253n.
Rupert of Deutz, 223n

Sacraments, 31, 231 f., 238, 287, 292, 295, 301, 310 f., 312 f., 338 ff., 349 f.; of the old law, 341 ff.; of the new law, 344 f.; validity, 221; *sacramentum*, 326n, 338n

Sacra pagina, 98
Sadducees, 274
St. Victor, school of, 18, 223, 225 f., 235 f., 365. See Adam, Andrew, Hugh, Richard, Walter of St. Victor
Samaria, 293
Samuel, 254
Sancti, 159n, 265, 387
Sapientia, 29, 316n, 392, 407n
Satisfaction, 56 ff., 118 f., 124, 134 ff., 145, 150 f., 161, 194, 198, 303
Saul, 254
Scholasticism, 17 ff., 24, 30 ff., 40 f.
Schools, medieval, 18, 25 f., 39
Science, 21, 27, 32
Scientia, 29, 316n, 392, 407n
Scotus, John Duns, 18n, 30, 77n, 227, 232, 371 f., 376 f., 433n, 435n; on God's existence, 371 f., 428 ff.; on illumination, 371; on faith and reason, 371 f.; on the immaculate conception, 60, 372; voluntarism, 29, 371 f.
Seneca, 73n
Sententiae, 26, 222n, 223
Septuagint, 360n
Sequences, 226n
Sicily, 364n
Sidon, 296
Siger of Brabant, 29, 365
Sin, 31, 118 f., 138 f., 190 ff., 220, 277 ff., 287, 291 ff., 300; original, 54, 58 f., 67, 131, 166, 175 f., 184 ff., 192 ff., 229 f., 261 f., 263 ff., 341 ff., 352 ff.; satisfaction for, 134 ff., 303 ff.
Socrates, 290, 391
Sodom, 293
Soto, Dominic, 228
Spartans, 256, 260
Spinoza, B., 18
Stephen, 291 ff., 350
Stoicism, 252
Strabo, Walafrid, 223n
Suarez, Francis, 19
Subdeacons, 349
Summa sententiarum, 227, 338n, 339n, 340, 341n, 342n, 343n, 344n, 345n, 348n

Summae, 223
Swords, two, 253n, 438 f.

Tatian, 424n
Terence, 171n
Tertullian, 104n, 124n, 154n, 267n
Theobald, archbishop, 222
Theodoret, 271n
Theodosius I, Emperor, 254, 260
Theology, 53 f., 98n, 220, 229, 368
Timothy, 98
Toledo, 364n
Traducianism, 261n
Traini, Francesco, 366n
Transubstantiation. See Mass
Trinity. See God, Trinity
Turretinus, F., 18
Tyranny, 248
Tyre, 296

Unction, extreme, 344
Universals, problem of, 31, 373
Universities, medieval, 18, 26 f., 39, 363
Urban II, Pope, 155, 208, 211
Uriah, 252

Vegetius, 249n
Venantius Fortunatus, 105n
Via antiqua, 372; *moderna*, 372
Vienne, 209
Voluntarism, 29, 54, 368, 371 f., 373 f.
Vows, 241 f.
Vulgate, 229, 279n, 360n

Walter of Bruges, 371
Walter of St. Victor, 225n
Warelwast, William, 208n
Wibald of Stavelot, 223n
William II, King, 61 f., 208
William of Auvergne, 367
William of Champeaux, 223, 226
William of Moerbeke, 364n
Worms, Concordat of, 61, 221

York, 209n

Zacchaeus, 358

MODERN AUTHORS

Abelson, P., 26n
Aguirre, J. S. de, 66
d'Albi, J., 376
Allers, R., 64
Amann, E., 209n, 233, 378
Amoros, L., 368n
Anawati, M. M., 42
Antweiler, A., 65 f.
d'Arcy, M. C., 369n
Arquillière, H. X., 30n, 37, 253n
Artz, F. B., 33
Aubry, P., 235
Aulén, G., 55, 66

Baeumker, F., 65
Bainvel, J., 64
Balic, C., 376 f.
Baltbasar, N., 65
Baroni, A., 375 f.
Barry, M. I., 259n
Barth, K., 50 f., 65
Baudry, L., 378
Baumgartner, M., 367n
Belmond, S., 415n
Bennett, R. F., 35
Berger, S., 229n
Bettoni, E., 375, 377
Betzendörfer, W., 40
Biese, A., 37
Bindley, T. H., 151n
Binns, L. E., 37
Birch, T. B., 378
Bishop, E., 67
Bissen, J. M., 376
Blakeney, E. H., 252n
Blic, J. de, 58n
Bliemetzrieder, F. P., 234
Bloch, M. L. B., 20n
Boase, T. S. R., 38
Boehmer, H., 67
Boer, T. J. de, 42
Böhner, P., 372n, 374n, 377 f., 442n
Boissonnade, P., 34
Bonke, E., 373n
Bourke, V. J., 366n
Bouyer, L., 374n
Bréhier, E., 42
Bright, W., 220n
Brooke, Z. N., 24n, 34, 37, 67f.
Brunet, A., 220n, 232
Bryce, J., 34
Buescher, G. N., 378
Bukofzer, M. F., 38
Burridge, A. W., 67

Butler, C., 35, 149n
Buttimer, C. H., 235

Callus, D. A., 367n
Calvetti, C., 374n
Cappuyns, M., 53n, 65
Carlyle, A. J., 43
Carlyle, R. W., 43
Carré, M. H., 42
Carton, R., 367n
Cayré, F., 39
Ceriani, G., 64
Chatelain, E., 39
Chenu, M. D., 18n, 159n, 328n, 363n,
    366, 375, 419n, 421n, 422n, 425n
Church, R. W., 64
Cichetti, A., 65
Cicognani, A. G., 233
Cimitier, F., 37
Claeys-Bouuaert, F., 212n
Clayton, J., 64
Clerval, A., 233
Cochrane, C. N., 23n
Congar, M. J., 26n, 27n
Copleston, F. C., 42, 364n, 370n, 373n
Cottiaux, J., 235
Coulton, G. G., 34 ff.
Cousin, V., 234, 237
Crombie, A. C., 367n
Crump, C. G., 33
Cullmann, O., 24n
Curtis, S. J., 42
Curtius, E. R., 33

Daniels, A., 65
Dargan, E. P., 37
Davis, H. W. C., 34, 61n, 64, 68, 209n
Dawson, C., 22n, 33, 363n
Deane, S. N., 63
Deanesly, M., 26n, 34
Deferrari, R. J., 235, 259n, 379n, 384n,
    400n
Dekkers, E., 267n
Delhaye, P., 26n, 235
Demers, G. E., 412n
Demimuid, M., 233
Dempf, A., 37
Denifle, H., 39, 80n, 235
Destrez, J., 366n
Deutsch, S. M., 235
Dix, G., 130n, 231n
Domet de Vorges, E., 64
Doolan, A., 370n
Douie, D. L., 375
Dreves, G. M., 234

Dufourcq, A., 224n
Duhem, P., 43
Dumas, A., 209n
Dumeige, G., 236
Dunning, W. A., 43

Ebert, A., 38
Ebner, J., 236
Ehrle, F., 375
Emden, A. B., 18n, 39
Espenberger, J. N., 67, 236
Ethier, A. E., 236
Evans, A. P., 33
Evans, J., 35, 38

Fairweather, E. R., 24n
Farrar, C. P., 33
Federhofer, F., 378
Feine, H. E., 37
Filliatre, C., 65
Fischer, J., 65
Fliche, A., 24n, 34, 209n
Flick, A. C., 36
Foley, G. C., 66
Forest, A., 39, 41
Foreville, R., 209n
Foucault, A., 233
Fournier, P., 36, 233
Frascolla, G., 235
Friedberg, E. A., 233, 237
Fritz, G., 236
Funke, B., 66

Gaar, A., 267n
Gamer, H. M., 37, 56n
Gandillac, M. de, 39
Ganshof, F. L., 20n
Gardeil, A., 407n
Gardet, L., 42
Garrigou-Lagrange, R., 432n
Gaselee, S., 38
Gaudel, A., 67
Gauthier, L., 42
Gavin, F., 35
Geiselmann, J., 48
Gerberon, G., 63
Geyer, B., 40 f., 234
Ghellinck, J. de, 25n, 30n, 98n, 221,
    222n, 225, 227, 232 ff., 236, 328n,
    334n, 338n
Giacon, G., 378
Gierke, O., 43
Gilson, E., 13, 18n, 19n, 22n, 24n, 27n,
    28n, 29n, 30n, 31n, 32n, 40 f., 47n,
    48n, 51 f., 53n, 54n, 65, 88n, 235,
    248n, 320n, 349n, 364n, 365n, 366n,
    367n, 368n, 370n, 371n, 372n, 373n,
    375 ff., 388n, 405n, 413n, 415n, 419n,
    424n

Glorieux, P., 27n, 41, 274n, 373n, 406n
Goichon, M. A., 364n
Gordon, G., 21n
Grabmann, M., 26n, 27n, 39, 42, 47n,
    233, 370n, 376
Grassi-Bertazzi, G., 236
Guelluy, R., 373n, 378
Guizard, L., 233
Gumpel, P., 344n
Gwynn, A., 373n

Halecki, O., 21n
Haller, J., 36
Harnack, A., 40
Harris, C. R. S., 377
Haskins, C. H., 22n, 26n, 39, 43, 220n
Hauck, A., 36
Hauréau, B., 42, 235
Hawkins, D. J. B., 42
Headlam, A. C., 85n
Heinrichs, L., 66
Heitz, T., 40, 418n
Hislop, I., 376
Hocedez, E., 370n, 371n
Hochstetter, F., 378
Holmes, U. T., 220n
Horten, M., 42
Hove, A. Van, 233
Huber, R. M., 35
Hügel, F. von, 77n
Hughes, A., 226n
Hughes, P., 36
Hughson, S. C., 149n
Hunt, W., 37, 208n
Husik, I., 42

Imle, F., 376

Jackson, F. J. Foakes, 34
Jacob, E. F., 33
Jacquin, A., 54n, 66
Jalland, T. G., 24n, 36
James, M. R., 256n
Jarrett, B., 43
Jarry, E., 34
Johnson, E. N., 34
Jolivet, R., 369n
Jones, R. T., 67
Jugie, M., 67, 166n
Julian, J., 332n

Kaiser, E., 235
Kaup, J., 376
Kemmer, A., 64
Kent, W. H., 64
Kidd, B. J., 61n
Klein, J., 377
Kleinz, J., 236
Klibansky, R., 42

Knowles, M. D., 35
Kögel, J., 236
Kors, J. B., 67
Koyré, A., 52n, 64 f.
Kraus, J., 40 f.
Krause, J., 376
Kuttner, S., 233

Lacombe, G., 236
Lagarde, A., 36
Lagarde, G. de, 22n, 374n
Lagrange, M. J., 85n, 424n
Landgraf, A. M., 27n, 39, 41, 49n, 100n, 228n, 229n, 234, 236, 267n, 268n
Landry, B., 377
Lang, A., 373n
Lang, P. H., 38
Latourette, K. S., 34, 36
Lazzarini, R., 376
Lea, H. C., 36
Le Bachelet, X., 67, 166n
Le Bras, G., 36
Lecler, P., 253n
Leclercq, J., 60, 67, 233
Lefèvre, G., 234
Lenglart, M., 236
Lethaby, W. R., 38
Levasti, A., 64
Lewis, E., 378
Liebeschütz, H., 233 f.
Lietzmann, H., 85n
Ligeard, H., 235
Little, A. G., 35
Lloyd, R. B., 235
Lohmeyer, E., 65
Longpré, E., 376 f.
Losacco, M., 65
Lottin, O., 42, 59n, 67, 234, 237, 261n, 265n, 355n
Luchaire, A., 37
Lutz, E., 367n, 376
Luyckx, B. A., 376
Lynch, L. E., 367n

McCallum, J. R., 234
McCann, J., 35, 149n
Macdonald, A. J., 48n
McGiffert, A. C., 40
McIntyre, J., 56n, 66
McKeon, R., 43, 63, 375 ff.
McLaughlin, M. M., 38
McNeal, E. H., 34
McNeill, J. T., 21n, 37, 56n, 64
Maas, B., 64
Maccarone, M., 37
Maitland, F. W., 43
Maitre, L., 25n, 39
Mâle, E., 38

Mandonnet, P., 29n, 35, 228n, 365n, 366n
Manitius, M., 37 f.
Manoir, H. du, 67
Marias, J., 65
Maritain, J., 374n, 435n
Martin, G., 378
Martin, R. M., 67
Martin, V., 22n, 34
Martindale, C. C., 67
Masnovo, A., 367n
Maurer, A. A., 365n
Maycock, A. L., 36
Mellone, S. H., 40, 57n
Michalski, K., 42
Michel, A., 59n, 67
Micklem, N., 377
Mierow, C. C., 310n
Migne, J. P., 41, 381n
Mignon, A., 235
Minges, P., 377
Mirbt, C., 61n
Misset, E., 235
Molsdorf, W., 38
Monro, C. H., 251n
Moody, E. A., 378
Morey, C. R., 38
Mortimer, R. C., 36
Mozley, J. K., 77n
Muckle, J. T., 13, 234, 367n

Nash, P. W., 370n
Nemmers, E. E., 375
Nettleship, H., 245n
Nitze, W. A., 37, 220n
Nygren, A., 330n

O'Sullivan, J. F., 34
Orton, H., 37
Ostlender, H., 64, 234
Ostler, H., 236
Ottaviano, C., 66, 235 f.
Otten, B. J., 39

Paetow, L. J., 33
Paré, G., 220n, 232
Paulus, J., 371n
Pegis, A. C., 63, 367n, 368n
Pelster, F., 26n
Perino, R., 66
Phelan, G. B., 14, 367n
Picavet, F., 42, 48n
Pickman, E. M., 23n
Pirenne, H., 34
Pohle, J., 231n
Poole, R. L., 232 f.
Porta, J., 66
Portalié, E., 235
Pourrat, P., 35, 231n, 347n

Powicke, F. M., 18n, 34, 39, 236
Preger, W., 36
Prestige, G. L., 60
Preuss, A., 231n
Previté-Orton, C. W., 34
Prout, E. S., 63

Quadri, G., 42

Raby, F. J. E., 38
Rashdall, H., 18n, 26n, 39
Rémusat, C. de, 64, 234
Renwick, W. L., 37
Richter, E., 233
Rigg, J. M., 64
Rivière, J., 28n, 37, 55n, 66, 235
Roche, E., 377
Rohmer, J., 43
Rosenmöller, B., 376
Ross, J. B., 38
Ross, W. D., 27n, 247n
Rousseau, P., 64
Rousset, J., 209n
Rule, M., 63 f., 68, 70n
Runze, G., 53n, 65
Rush, A. C., 130n

Sägmüller, J. B., 37
Salman, D. H., 367n
Sanctis, F. de, 37
Sanday, W., 85n
Sandys, J. E., 38, 245n
Sanford, E. M., 220n
Schaarschmidt, C., 234
Schiller, J., 235
Schmitt, F. S., 63 f., 66, 68, 103n
Schmitz, R., 68
Schnürer, G., 36
Schubert, H. von, 36 f.
Schulte, J. F. von, 36, 233
Schupp, J., 236
Schwane, J., 40
Seeberg, R., 39 f., 377
Sestili, G., 376
Seyffert, O., 245n
Sharp, D. E., 375
Shircel, C. L., 377
Sikes, J. G., 224n, 234, 284n, 377
Sinclair, T. A., 37
Smalley, B., 40, 226n, 229n, 236 f.
Smeets, E., 376
Smith, A. L., 37
Smith, W., 252n
Somerville, J. W., 233
Southern, R. W., 20n, 25n, 26n, 33, 55n
Spedalieri, F., 66

Spicq, C., 26n, 40, 223 f.
Springer, J. L., 65
Steenberghen, F. Van, 29n, 39, 365n, 369n
Stegmüller, F., 27n
Stephens, W. R. W., 37, 64, 68
Stephenson, C., 20n, 34
Stöckl, A., 65
Stolz, A., 50, 64 ff.
Symonds, H. E., 24n

Taylor, H. O., 33
Teetaert, A., 375
Tellenbach, G., 35
Thatcher, O. J., 34
Théry, G., 364n
Thompson, A. H., 30n
Thompson, J. W., 33 f.
Tixeront, J., 158n
Torney, S. C., 378
Tout, T. F., 37
Tremblay, P., 220n, 232

Ueberweg, F., 41
Ullmann, W., 22n, 36, 222n

Vacandard, E., 36, 235
Vajda, G., 42
Vanni Rovighi, S., 65
Vellico, A. M., 377
Vernet, F., 236
Verweyen, J. M., 40
Vignaux, P., 42, 374n, 378
Vinogradoff, P., 43
Vossler, K., 37

Waddell, H., 38, 235
Wadding, L., 376
Walz, A., 366n
Waterton, E., 68
Webb, C. C. J., 233 f., 237, 248n
Weisweiler, H., 236
Welch, A. C., 64
Werner, K., 42
Whitney, J. P., 24n
Williams, G. H., 68
Williams, W. W., 35
Wilmart, A., 35, 68
Winckelmann, E. A., 439n
Wolfson, H. A., 18n, 30n, 424n
Wood, E. G., 220n
Wright, F. A., 37
Wulf, M. de, 18n, 41 f., 404n

Zahn, J., 36
Zuidema, S. U., 378

BIBLICAL REFERENCES

Genesis
1:1 410
1:27 . . . . .73, 426
1:27 f. 315
2:17 192
2:18–25 313
4:1–7 358
9:6 415
9:22 ff. 254
15:6 285
17:10 342
17:14 344
18:27 207
19:1 ff. 293
22:1 ff. 294
27:38 80

Exodus
3:14 88
20:5 186
20:17 215

Leviticus
16:15 339

Numbers
19:11 339
22:22–35 329
25:7 ff. 188

Deuteronomy
5:15 320
6:4 410
17:14–20 258
17:16 260
32:8 . . . . .132, 133
32:27 249

Joshua
5:2 342
8:31 188

I Samuel (I Kings, V)
15:26 to 16:13 254
15:32 f. 252

II Samuel (II Kings, V)
1:21 251
11:1 ff. 252, 286
16:7 f. 252

I Kings (III Kings, V)
13:24 294

I Chronicles
22:8 252

Ezra (I Esdras, V)
7:21 188

Job
2:4 260
3:24 72
14:4 192
19:27 272
29:16 359

Psalms
2:4 322
2:8 257
6:3 (6:4, V) 72
9:4 (9:5, V) 305
13:1 (12:1, V) 72
13:3 (12:4, V) 72, 86
14:1 (13:1, V) . . .73, 429
14:3 (13:2, V) 416
17:2 (16:2, V) 251
17:16 (16:15, V) 90
18:28 (17:29, V) 201
19:8 (18:9, V) 97
23:2 (22:2, V) 343
23:4 (22:4, V) 251
25:6 (24:7, V) 85
25:9 (24:10, V) . .81, 239
27:1 (26:1, V) 201
27:9 (26:8, V) . . .70, 85, 329
27:10 (26:9, V) 85
36:7 (35:7 f., V) 144
36:8 (35:9, V) 90
36:9 (35:10, V) 382
36:10 (35:11, V) 119
37:40 (36:39, V) 90
38:4 (37:5, V) 72
38:8 (37:9, V) 72
43:3 (42:3, V) . . .83, 359
45:3 (44:3, V) 103
47:2 (46:3, V) 258
51:5 (50:7, V) . . .85, 140, 166, 192, 264
51:10 (50:12, V) 360
51:11 (50:13, V) 71
52:3 (51:5, V) 247
53:1 (52:1, V) . . .73, 429
53:3 (52:3, V) 416
63:2 (62:2, V) 93
68:35 (67:36, V) 151
69:16 (68:16, V) 72
73:25 (72:26, V) 206
76:11 f. (75:12 f., V) .258
78:26 (77:25, V) 71
78:40 (77:39, V) 109

Psalms—continued
79:9 (78:9, V) 72
80:3, 7 (79:4, 8, V) . . .72
85:10 (84:11, V) 319
89:50 (88:53, V) 207
90:2 (89:2, V) 87
101:1 (100:1, V) 239
110:7 (109:7, V) 113
112:9 (111:9, V) 87
116:3 (114:3, V) 72
119:46 (118:46, V) . .247
119:73 (118:73, V) . .382
119:99 (118:99, V) . . .97
119:100 (118:100, V) . 98
119:142 (118:142, V).250
122:9 (121:9, V) 72
123:2 (122:2, V) 270
127:2 (126:2, V) 71
137:3 f. (136:3 f., V) .298
145:17 (144:17, V) . . .81

Ecclesiastes
4:12 255

Song of Solomon
2:5 206
5:6 206
6:13 (6:12, V) 86
8:6 255

Isaiah
7:9 . . . . .73, 324, 411
9:6 . . . . .93, 304
10:5–15 249
11:2 360
25:4 359
30:1 202
44:3 f. 360
53:7 . . . . .117, 174

Jeremiah
8:11 319
14:19 62
30:17 360
46:16 252

Lamentations
3:25 204

Ezekiel
1:5 323
1:6 323
1:7 323
13:19 239
18:22 137
18:27 . . . . .137, 287

Ezekiel—*continued*
33:16..............137
38:2...............312
39:1...............312
39:6...............312

Daniel
12:4...............322

Hosea
6:2 (6:3, V).......267
13:14..............275

Jonah
4:1 ff..............294

Wisdom of Solomon
5:15 (5:16, V).......90
9:15...............185
11:15..............415
12:15..............294
13:5...............411

Ecclesiasticus
3:21 (3:22, V).....102
10:13 (10:15, V)....300
18:1...............128
35:11..............125

Baruch
3:37 (3:38, V)......161

Matthew
3:2................348
3:17...............111
4:17...............348
5:3................247
5:8............391, 412
5:9.................91
5:27 f.............357
5:39...............215
5:44..........215, 293
6:6.................70
6:12.........120, 135
6:22...............290
7:6................349
7:12.........137, 243
8:19...............296
8:21 f.............296
9:2................282
10:8...............102
11:21..............296
11:25...............97
11:28..............359
12:35..............355
12:49..............205
13:43...............90
16:19..............437
19:12..............240
19:21..............240

Matthew—*continued*
20:1–16............272
20:15..............282
21:9.........249, 284
22:30...............90
22:37...............92
25:6...............274
25:21........91, 92, 93
25:23..............91
26:39.........111, 114
26:42.........111, 114
26:52..............253

Mark
10:5–9.............313
10:6–9.............265
11:9...............284
12:18–25...........274
12:42..............358
16:20..............325

Luke
1:28..........203, 204
1:35...............196
1:42..........202, 203
1:52...............248
2:9–14.............271
2:14...............305
2:52...............114
6:45...............355
6:48...............181
7:47.........279, 281
9:62...............241
10:22..............113
10:30..............338
10:42...............89
11:27..............207
12:49..............284
16:25..............280
18:13 f............285
19:1–10............358
19:42–44...........319
20:36..............106
22:38.........253, 438
23:34.........291, 293

John
1:1–5.............408
1:3................204
1:9................396
1:13...............274
3:5................344
3:5 f..............264
3:18...............295
4:42...............205
5:27 f.............306
5:28 f.............275
5:30...............307
5:36 f.............271

John—*continued*
6:38.........111, 114
6:44...............116
6:70 (6:71, V)......133
7:16...............114
7:22...............342
8:15...............307
8:32...............247
8:34...............109
8:44...............182
8:55...............156
9:3................293
10:17 f........117, 159
10:18..............175
10:34 f.............91
13:1...............207
14:2...............272
14:3...............91
14:6...............310
14:12..............257
14:17..............248
14:23 ff...........359
14:26..............381
14:31..111, 113, 115, 116
15:13.........278, 284
15:26..............248
16:2...............290
16:13..............248
16:15.........113, 180
16:24..........92, 93
18:10..............253
18:11....111, 113, 115, 116, 117

The Acts
1:15–26............440
1:26...............349
5:15...............257
6:1–6..............440
6:5................350
7:60...............291
9:31...............440
10:1 f.............296
10:31..............285
10:35..............129
11:26..............441
13:1–3.............440
14:22..............441
14:23..............350
15:6 ff............441
15:9...............97
15:10..............339
17:27..............399
17:28..............84
20:17, 28..........441

Romans
1:4................335
1:14...............255

Romans—*continued*

1:17	80
1:19	399
1:20	411
1:21	98, 300
1:25	93
2:13–25	276
3:2	276
3:19	276 f.
3:20	277, 339
3:21	277 f.
3:22 f.	278
3:24 f.	279
3:26	279
3:27	284
4:3	285
4:10	342
4:11	341
5:1 ff.	55
5:5 f.	284
5:8	107, 194, 284
5:10	282
5:12	85, 104, 166, 193, 292, 300
5:14	194, 199, 339
5:19	104, 193
5:20	194
7:6	247
7:13	277
7:22	188
7:23	188
7:25	188
8:1	188
8:10	192
8:13	97
8:17	91
8:20 f.	247
8:21	284
8:29	111, 206, 307
8:32	111, 114, 115, 116, 279
8:35	278
8:38	278
8:38 f.	91
9:22 f.	240
10:2	290
10:14	295
12:5	248
12:12	215
12:19	120
13:1	121, 249, 269
13:2	249

I Corinthians

1:23	257
2:8	165
2:9	90, 92
2:14	97
2:15	97

I Corinthians—*continued*

3:2	215
3:9	239
6:11	264
7:1 f.	241
7:14	263
7:27	241
7:28	241
9:22	215
11:3	270
13:12	391, 393, 395, 399, 415, 418, 424
13:13	330
14:38	295
15:2	267
15:4	267
15:5	267
15:8	268
15:9	268
15:10	268
15:11	268
15:14	268
15:15	268
15:17	269
15:21	269
15:22	269
15:23	269
15:24	269
15:25	269
15:26	270
15:27	270
15:28	270, 298
15:29	270
15:31	270
15:32	271
15:33	271
15:34	271
15:35	271
15:36	272
15:38	272
15:39	272
15:40	272
15:41	272
15:42	159, 273
15:44	90, 273
15:45	273
15:46	273
15:47	273
15:50	274
15:51	274
15:52	274
15:54	275
15:55	275

II Corinthians

3:17	247
4:4	155
5:21	292
7:4	359

II Corinthians—*continued*

8:9	310
9:7	125
10:5	239, 405, 422

Galatians

2:16	339
3:7	133
3:13	292
4:4 f.	307
4:5	206
4:26	298
5:1	310
5:6	137
5:16 ff.	359
5:17	188, 319
5:19	274
5:21	241

Ephesians

1:5	206
2:3	194, 199, 336
2:4	144
2:8	425
4:9	271
4:22	348
4:24	348
4:31 to 5:2	55
5:3	189
5:22–33	314
6:10–17	311

Philippians

2:6	204
2:8	207
2:8 f.	111, 113, 115, 116
3:20	442
4:7	319

Colossians

1:15	155
2:14	109

I Thessalonians

4:15	274

I Timothy

1:5	415
1:18	98
1:19	98
2:4	425
3:2	350
3:16	271
6:1	310
6:16	71, 78, 84, 387

Titus

3:5	202, 360

Hebrews
2:9–18 55
2:10–18 307
2:10 261
2:11 205
4:9 298
4:15 161
4:14 to 5:10 55
5:8 . . . .111, 113, 115, 116
7:1–3 255
7:7 254
9:13 339
10:10 55
10:19–22 55
11:1 402
11:6 411

Hebrews—continued
12:6 249
13:4 241

James
1:17 . . . . .116, 359

I Peter
2:14 249
2:24 292
3:7 315
3:15 101
4:11 87

II Peter
3:13 130

I John
1:5 . . . . .83, 359
1:6 248
3:1 f. 91
3:2 83
3:21 291
4:6 248
4:8 273
4:14 205
4:19 279
5:5 ff. 271

Revelation
20:7 312
21:1 130
21:4 332

Anselm to Ockham.